The Other Tongue

English in the Global Context

Braj B. Kachru, Series Editor

Members of the Advisory Board

Ayọ Bamgboṣe (Ibadan)
Charles A. Ferguson (Stanford)
Andrew B. Gonzalez (Manila)
Michael A. K. Halliday (Sydney)
Larry E. Smith (Honolulu)
S. N. Sridhar (Stony Brook)
Edwin Thumboo (Singapore)

The Other Tongue

English across Cultures
Second Edition

EDITED BY

Braj B. Kachru

UNIVERSITY OF ILLINOIS PRESS
Urbana and Chicago

Library of Congress Cataloging-in-Publication Data

The Other tongue : English across cultures / edited by Braj B. Kachru.
— 2nd ed.
    p.   cm. — (English in the global context)
Includes index.
ISBN 0-252-01869-9. — ISBN 0-252-06200-0 (pbk.)
    1. English language—Social aspects—Foreign countries.
2. Intercultural communication.   3. Language, Universal.
I. Kachru, Braj B.   II. Series.
PE2751.083   1992
420'.9—dc20   91-19287
                                                                                    CIP

"English as an International Language: Directions in the 1990s," by Peter
    Strevens, first appeared in *English Teaching Forum*, October 1987.

"Bridging the Paradigm Gap: Second-Language Acquisition Theory and
Indigenized Varieties of English," by Kamal K. Sridhar and S. N. Sridhar,
first appeared in *World Englishes* 5.1 (1986): 3–14. Reprinted by permission.

"Testing English as a World Language: Issues in Assessing Non-Native
Proficiency," by Peter H. Lowenberg, first appeared in *The Georgetown
University Round Table on Languages and Linguistics 1989: Language Teaching,
Testing, and Technology*, ed. James E. Alatis (Georgetown University Press,
                    1989). Reprinted by permission of the publisher.

"Spread of English and Issues of Intelligibility," by Larry E. Smith, and an
earlier version of "The Literary Dimension of the Spread of English," by
Edwin Thumboo, first appeared in *The Georgetown University Round Table
on Languages and Linguistics 1987: Language Spread and Language Policy*, ed.
Peter H. Lowenberg (Georgetown University Press, 1988). Reprinted by
                    permission of the publisher.

"My Language, Your Culture: Whose Communicative Competence?" by
Cecil L. Nelson first appeared, in an earlier version, in *World Englishes* 4.2
                    (1985): 243-50. Reprinted by permission.

Digitally reprinted from the second paperback printing

To the memory of
Peter Derek Strevens
August 31, 1922–November 2, 1989

Contents

Foreword to the Second Edition

Eleven years after the seminal conference on cross-cultural communication, held at the University of Illinois at Urbana-Champaign, and eight years after the publication of this book's first edition, it has become clear that the topic as a whole and this collection in particular were both timely and forward looking. Braj B. Kachru rightly judged that the explosive spread of English among those for whom it is not the "mother tongue" but "the other tongue" had created a need for a particular kind of enlightenment. A volume was needed that would introduce specialists in English—and, indeed, the educated public everywhere—to three sets of issues: first, to the remarkable sociolinguistic and geolinguistic changes that have been and still are occurring; second, to the existence of a fast-developing interdisciplinary domain that has subsequently come to be called "English as an International Language" (EIL); and third, to the growing solidity and sophistication of the intellectual studies, both descriptive and explanatory in nature, generated under the EIL rubric.

The opportunity of a second edition has enabled the editor to make changes that reflect intensive developments during the past decade. These improvements make this new edition a basic work of reference. The revised introduction provides a topical overview of events that have changed the language called English from the unplanned, heedless usage of a commercial and military colonizing power into a linguistic instrument employed for myriad uses by hundreds of millions of people. For them it is not the mother tongue; more important, their uses for English far transcend the constricting bounds of colonial domination.

This new edition of *The Other Tongue* is, as Marlowe put it in another context, "the outward sign of inward fires." The years since its first edition have favored the establishment at the University of Illinois of a Division of English as an International Language.

In short, many of the expectations outlined by Charles Ferguson in the foreword to the first edition have come to fruition, and this volume has contributed notably to that process. It is an honor to provide this new foreword, and a double honor to do so at the moment of joining the Division of English as an International Language as a George A. Miller Visiting Professor.

—Peter Strevens
Wolfson College, Cambridge University,
and the University of Illinois, August 1989

Foreword to the First Edition

The papers collected in this volume are important for the world of language scholarship—and the "real world" that lies outside it—in at least three ways. They deal with one of the most significant linguistic phenomena of our time, the incredible spread of English as a global language. They deal directly with one of the most debated current foci of linguistic research, the nature and extent of variation in natural languages. And they deal with an important topic long neglected by linguists, the structure and use of non-native varieties. Let me say a few words about each of these, in reverse order.

Non-Native Varieties of Language

Linguists, perhaps especially American linguists, have long given a special place to the "native speaker" as the only truly valid and reliable source of language data, whether those data are the elicited texts of the descriptivist or the intuitions the theorist works with. Yet much of the world's verbal communication takes place by means of languages that are not the users' "mother tongue," but their second, third, or nth language, acquired one way or another and used when appropriate. Some languages, for example, spread widely as lingua francas between speakers of different languages or serve as languages of special functions in communities of non-native speakers; this kind of language use merits the attention of linguists as much as do the more traditional objects of their research. In fact, the whole mystique of native speaker and mother tongue should probably be quietly dropped from the linguists' set of professional myths about language.

First, it is often hard to draw the boundary. Of what linguistic significance is X's native-speaking competence in language A if he has not used it since childhood and is much more at home in his later-acquired language B? Why is there something special about Y's knowledge of the local language if her parents have chosen to speak with her largely in another language so she can "get ahead"? Or what of child bilingualism, or a talented writer's use of his national language instead of his mother tongue?

Second, universal explanatory principles or a general theory of language should account for all linguistic behavior. Variation in structure as between L_1 and L_2 seems just as interesting a subject as dialect or register variation in a completely monolingual community. The phenomena of language acquisition, language convergence over time, and language shift are at the very heart of linguistics, offering valuable evidence on the learnability of natural languages by humans and the nature of linguistic change.

In describing a particular language or language variety, it is necessary to identify its users and to locate its place in the verbal repertoires of the speech communities in which it is used. Without this identification many aspects of the grammar will be mysterious, and those mysteries may range from details of phonology to features of discourse. Most of the papers in this volume make serious efforts at the necessary identifications. They are highly suggestive of possible directions for more sophisticated and linguistically significant social and individual identifications of repertoire and use.

Linguistic Variation

Recognizing that linguistics has made its greatest advances, both in theory and in the practice of writing grammars, when it takes cases of relatively homogeneous or normalized or idealized languages as its objects of description, modern linguists are increasingly tackling heterogeneous bodies of data and the variation in language structure and use which is one of the prime characteristics of human language. They are doing so in part because of inadequacies in existing theories and grammars, but probably more so because of fascination with the phenomena, the linguistically significant generalizations they find, and the new understandings they may reach of the processes of dialect differentiation and language change and the more general social and cognitive aspects of human behavior.

Variation-oriented research in linguistics, however, has been limited to a very few types. Social dialect variation, creole continua, and bilingual code-switching account for the bulk of the current research. The two kinds of variation most prominent in the worldwide development of giant speech "communities" are hardly touched. I refer, in the first place, to the standardization process by which divergent regional dialects are gradually overwhelmed by supradialectal norms, and the resulting standards develop regionally colored variation related in complex ways to the earlier dialect variation. In the second place, I refer to the spread of languages as lingua francas, or as added components within existing repertoires, or as complete replacements for other languages; in all these cases the spreading language shows variation related in complex ways to the earlier language competences of the new users.

It is one of the outstanding merits of this book that these two phenomena are acknowledged and that these kinds of variation are described and discussed. At this stage of research, the papers cannot go very far toward constructing theories or models of variation, but they certainly suggest possible lines of theory development. A sociolinguistic theory accounting for the phenomena of standardization and language spread would make a tremendous contribution toward human self-understanding and thoughts about possible futures for the inhabitants of the planet.

Spread of English

The spread of one language in relation to others is a phenomenon which presumably goes as far back in human history as the existence of a multiplicity of languages. Certainly it is documented as far back as written records go; e.g., in the second millennium B.C., Akkadian replaced Sumerian but the speech community retained the latter in certain learned uses. Also, it is a familiar phenomenon for one language to serve as a lingua franca or language of special functions (religious, commercial) over a large area of many languages: Sanskrit, Greek, Latin, Arabic, and French are examples at various periods and in different parts of the world. But there has never before been a single language which spread for such purposes over *most* of the world, as English has done in this century. The importance of this fact is often overlooked in discussions of the characteristic features of this age. The spread of English is as significant in its way as is the modern use of computers. When the amount of information needing to be processed came to exceed human capabilities, the computer appeared on the scene, transforming the processes of planning and calculation. When the need for global communication came to exceed the limits set by language barriers, the spread of English accelerated, transforming existing patterns of international communication.

We cannot know what the future will bring. At some point the spread of English may be halted, and some other language may spread to take its place. Or newly emerging patterns of communication may eliminate the need for such a single global language. But for the present the spread of English continues, with no sign of diminishing (although its use may contract in certain areas), and two trends are gaining strength. English is less and less regarded as a European language, and its development is less and less determined by the usage of its native speakers.

For some time after its transplantation by settlement and colonial administration, English was still centered on England. However, by the end of the nineteenth century North American English assumed an importance challenging the dominance of the original center. In the second half of the twentieth century England is only one of many centers of innovation and norm creation, and some authors are claiming English as an African language and as an Asian language. The predominant view, that English is a European language, is steadily being eroded and seems likely to disappear.

In some sense, the native speakers of a language may be said to "own" it or to "control" it; i.e., to determine its future structure and use by their own usage and their beliefs about the language. There are, however, cases where the control of the future passes to non-native speakers. This has most often been discussed in terms of a standard variety that is based on one region or sector of the population and then begins to take on a life of its own, diverging from its source dialect. The same phenomenon can happen with the language as a whole. In Eastern Africa there are native speakers of Swahili, descendants of native speakers of Swahili, who resent the standard variety taught in schools that is increasingly spoken by others as a second language and by new native speakers not descended from the original, native-speaking community. The linguistic influence mostly works from school standard onto other varieties, though, and some of the traditional native speakers find themselves adopting features of pronunciation, verb morphology, and syntax from the standard. The "control" of the language has passed to other people. This process is just beginning in English. Because there is no single non-native standard, the outcome will be different from the Swahili example, but the passing of control is increasingly evident.

English is widely used on the European continent as an international language. Frequently conferences are conducted in English (and their proceedings published in English) when only a few of the participants are native speakers. At such conferences the English spoken often shows features at variance with the English of England but shared by the other speakers. Continental meanings of *eventual* and *actual*, continental uses of tenses, calques on French formulas of conference procedure, various details of pronunciation, and dozens of other features mark the English as an emerging continental norm. Native speakers of English attending the conference may find themselves using some of these features as the verbal interaction takes place. It is this adaptation that I cite as an example of the trend.

For now, this trend is very limited. Native speakers in many situations around the world may have confidence that they "know" the language better than others, but the differences among native speakers from different areas and the growing importance of non-native norms will increasingly affect this confidence. Whatever the outcome, *The Other Tongue* will contribute to our understanding of these processes and will deepen our appreciation of the different kinds of Englishes in the world and the rich variety of communication and self-expression that takes place in them.

Braj B. Kachru deserves our admiration for the way he has stayed for two decades with these important questions of the spread of English, its linguistic variation, and its non-native varieties. He and his fellow contributors deserve our gratitude for this new volume of studies which pushes the field of English across cultures far ahead and should stimulate the thinking of linguists, specialists in English language and literature, developmental planners, and futurists.

—Charles A. Ferguson
Stanford University, 1981

Preface to the Second Edition

This second edition of *The Other Tongue* is published in the same spirit in which a decade ago the first edition was published: the spirit of introducing new perspectives, challenges, and questions in a multifaceted field of study and research with serious cross-cultural implications. Internationally the profession received *The Other Tongue* essentially in a spirit of excitement; the result was a stimulating debate that has still not abated. This book thus provided a springboard for looking at World Englishes and creativity in English within a refreshingly different sociolinguistic framework. One might even say that *The Other Tongue* is one of the handful of books that contributed to a new paradigm for the understanding and study of World Englishes.

This second edition is in many ways different from the 1982 edition and, I believe, addresses the questions and challenges of the '90s more adequately. The main differences are as follows. This edition is divided into six parts, as opposed to the five parts. Nine chapters are omitted, and eight new ones have been substituted; four contributors to the 1982 edition (Cecil Nelson, Peter Strevens, S. N. Sridhar, and Kamal K. Sridhar) have offered new chapters, and this new edition contains four chapters by contributors whose work was not included earlier (Yamuna Kachru, Larry E. Smith, Peter Lowenberg, and Edwin Thumboo). Part VI, "World Englishes in the Classroom: Rationale and Resources," consisting of a sole chapter, has been added. The introduction has been rewritten to reflect these changes. The index is much more extensive—therefore, I hope, more user friendly. And most chapters retained from the 1982 edition have updated references.

The past decade has been exciting for researchers in and teachers of World Englishes. Two scholarly journals and a magazine are specifically devoted to this area, *World Englishes* (Oxford), *English World-Wide* (Amsterdam), and *English Today* (Cambridge). Over a dozen books have followed the first edition of *The Other Tongue,* and courses with a new orientation on this topic are taught at various universities. It is gratifying to feel that *The Other Tongue* helped initiate this reorientation and contributed toward stimulating interest in this research area. By now an exciting interdisciplinary field has been established in which scholars from all major English-speaking countries are active participants.

I am grateful to several young researchers who, in their dissertations and research papers, provided theoretical and methodological insights and valuable cross-cultural data from different varieties of English. These scholars include Maurice Chishimba (Lusaka), Margie Berns (Lafayette, Indiana), Pornpimol Chutisilp (Bangkok), Jean D'souza (Singapore), Nkonko Kamwangamalu (Kinshasa), Benjamin Magura (Harare), Cecil Nelson (Terre Haute, Indiana), Peter H. Lowenberg (San Jose, Calif.), and Tamara Valentine (Chapel Hill, N.C.).

The first edition of *The Other Tongue* was internationally reviewed in numerous journals. The reviewers' comments have been of immense value in preparation of this second edition, which also benefited considerably from the suggestions of Yamuna Kachru, Larry E. Smith, S. N. Sridhar, and Kamal K. Sridhar.

I am pleased that this edition of *The Other Tongue* is appearing in the series English in the Global Context, published by the University of Illinois Press. In planning the volume, the counsel and unfailing positive attitude of Ann Lowry, senior editor at the Press, have been of immense value.

This volume is dedicated to the memory of a dear friend, colleague, and scholar. Peter Derek Strevens unexpectedly passed away in Tokyo on November 2, 1989. I first met Peter in 1959 when I was a graduate student at the University of Edinburgh, where he was on the faculty. For the ensuing three decades, we were constantly in touch concerning various projects of mutual interest. He was invited to the University of Illinois several times. In the fall of 1989 he joined our University as a George A. Miller Visiting Professor; plans were made for his continued stay as a professor in the Division of English as an International Language for three years. His sudden death was a great shock to his colleagues and students, and to his many friends across disciplines. Peter possessed abundant energy, intellectual keenness, and great skill as a teacher. One was envious of this unusual gift of bringing people together, which he did with great charm and sensitivity.

He was a "gentleman" in the most positive sense of the term. For a scholar the ultimate judges are, of course, his peers and students; all of Peter's peers and students in the U.S.A., in Europe, and in Africa and Asia held him in great esteem for his scholarly and human qualities, and for his repeated emphasis on the social concerns of his chosen field.

It is also appropriate that this volume be dedicated to him for more specific reasons. He was closely connected with the conference that resulted in the first edition of *The Other Tongue*. He was enthusiastic about the second edition of this volume, as is evident from the foreword. This is one of the last pieces he wrote before his death.

—Braj B. Kachru
University of Illinois
at Urbana-Champaign, 1991

Preface to the First Edition

This collection of articles, like every book, has its own genesis. It is both the culmination of a collective effort in shared research interests, and a step toward my long-standing personal goal of understanding English across cultures. *The Other Tongue: English across Cultures* is, in essence, the outcome of a cross-cultural and cross-linguistic conference held at the University of Illinois at Urbana-Champaign in 1978. It was just a coincidence that during that year the status of English as an international and intranational language was explicitly dealt with in two conferences held only three months apart. The East-West Learning Institute of the East-West Center, Honolulu, Hawaii, organized a conference in April (1–15). A selection of papers presented at that conference has been edited by its organizer, Larry E. Smith, under the title *English for Cross-Cultural Communication* (London: Macmillan, 1981). I organized the second conference, "English in Non-Native Contexts" (June 30–July 2), in conjunction with the Linguistic Institute of the Linguistic Society of America; it was hosted by the University of Illinois at Urbana-Champaign. At that conference twenty-five invited presentations dealt with English in over a dozen countries, including Ghana, India, Kenya, the Philippines, Sri Lanka, Taiwan, the United States, the United Kingdom, the West Indies, and Zaire.

A number of papers included here (to be exact, 60 percent) are substantially revised versions of papers presented at the Urbana-Champaign conference. The rest were specifically commissioned from scholars who were not present at that conference. This volume, then, is not the proceedings of the conference in a literal sense; rather, the conference provided a theme and a focus for *The Other Tongue*. In more than one sense, the conference broke the traditional pattern of such deliberations: no inconvenient question was swept under the rug. The professionals, both linguists and literary scholars, and native and non-native users of English, had frank and stimulating discussions. The issues related to English were discussed in divergent linguistic and cultural contexts, and useful generalizations were made using ample empirical data. The English-using community in various continents was for the first time viewed in its totality. A number of cross-cultural perspectives were brought to bear upon our understanding of English in a global context, of language variation, of language acquisition, and of the bilinguals'—or multilinguals'—use of English. The implications of such research on language studies in general and with particular reference to English have been lucidly discussed by Charles A. Ferguson in his foreword to this volume. In this sense, then, *The Other Tongue* is issue oriented, and not merely an anthology of case studies of English as a world language. It is true that such an anthology is overdue, but that is not the primary goal of this volume.

It was not just an accident that this conference was hosted by the University of Illinois at Urbana-Champaign. During the last two decades the University of Illinois has taken a leadership role in the study and research on English in non-native contexts through faculty research, in graduate courses, and at various conferences. The Division of Applied Linguistics of the University considers non-native English to be one of its major research areas.

I hope this volume reflects the importance of the theme, the freshness of approach, and the pragmatic view of English in the world context which were hallmarks of the conference. A new perspective on English across cultures understandably entails differences in emphasis and variations in approach to the topic. That such a perspective is needed was amply demonstrated in the presentations, and in the congenial and frank interactions in the cross-cultural setting of the conference. What transpired in discussion periods and in various social events was equally important. All that could not be captured in this volume.

This volume should serve as the first step toward our understanding of the complex issues involved in the formal and functional characteristics of the Englishes around the world. One thing is certain: there are no simple answers, no easy solutions, and no methodological remedies which apply to all users of English across cultures. No one group can carry this linguistic burden; it must be shared by the users of this international language, whether they are its native or non-native speakers.

The conference and this volume are the result of the enthusiasm, cooperation, support, and patience of many agencies, organizations, and individuals. My gratitude is particularly due to the Ford Foundation, New York, for their initial grant for the conference and to Foundation Program officers Elinor G. Barber and Melvin J. Fox for their counsel and interest. (Fox has since retired from the Foundation after making a substantial contribution to language-related research internationally, and specifically in Africa.) George K. Brinegar, Director, Office of International Programs and Studies, University of Illinois, and Carl W. Deal, Chairperson, Publications Committee of the same office, deserve thanks for including this volume in the series. The Research Board of the Graduate College of the University of Illinois supported various projects which directly or indirectly contributed toward our understanding of English across cultures. I am indebted to Charles A. Ferguson for his foreword to the volume; to James E. Alatis, Henry Kahane, Peter Strevens, Rudolph C. Troike, G. Richard Tucker, and Ladislav Zgusta for their advice and support in planning the conference; to Josephine Wilcock for her assistance in organizational matters and beyond; to Farida Cassimjee and Tamara M. Valentine for helping in library research and in preparing the final version of the manuscript; and to Ann Lowry, senior editor at the University of Illinois Press, for her technical skill, expert editorial advice, and cooperation above and beyond the call of duty.

—Braj B. Kachru
*University of Illinois
at Urbana-Champaign, 1981*

Braj B. Kachru

Introduction: The Other Side of English and the 1990s

The other side of English is concerned with English as the "other tongue," or as an additional language. "Other tongue" is not an innocent term; actually it is a multifaceted concept with a long history and different manifestations in various regions of the world. The vision of an other tongue evokes memories of language being used as a powerful—sometimes ruthless—instrument for religious and cultural subjugation and for colonization. There are elevated (standard) varieties, and not so elevated (pidgin) varieties for local commerce, international trade, and even political maneuvering. In the past the other tongues (as imposed or non-imposed languages) have been associated with majestic empires (e.g., Arabic, Chinese, Greek, Latin, Persian, Sanskrit). In our own time Dutch, English, French, Japanese, Spanish, and Portuguese have been used, in varying degrees, as the tongues of colonizers. A language has often been used as a tool for unifying a nation, for establishing political boundaries, and for creating dissent. How a language may be used (for non-communicative ends) in a particular national context is difficult to predict. But the powerful ruler, the wily colonizer, the commercial exploiter, and the religious zealot are not the only ones who envision their language being recognized—or imposed on people—as the other tongue (see Kachru 1986a).

The association of worldly power or religious sanctity with the spread of other tongues tells only part of the story. There have always been linguistic romanticists, representing various disciplines, who have seen the limitations of a culture-bound natural language as a universal language. In their view—and rightly so—a natural language always possesses cultural and linguistic affinities. Those who use it as their first language thus have certain advantages.

Why not use an artificial or constructed language as an international language? It would function as an extralinguistic tool, ideally speaking, with no cultural or linguistic connotations; consequently, no ethnocentricism would arise. As yet, no such perfect proposal has come forward, for most constructed languages show the cultural or linguistic influences of one or more natural languages.[1] The proposals for such constructed languages have come from concerned universalists of various orientations—for example, Esperanto (1887) from a Polish physician named Ludwig Zamenhof; Volapük (1880) from a German bishop named Johann Martin Schleyer; Ido (1907) from the French logician Louis de Beaufront; Interlingua (Latino sine Flexione, 1903) from an Italian mathematician named Guiseppe Peano; and Novial (1928) from the Danish linguist Otto Jespersen. Such attempts still continue, one of the latest being Lincos, "a language for cosmic intercourse" (Freudenthal 1960). Most have met with no success. The partial acceptance of Esperanto was also short lived, though the enthusiasm of its adherents has not yet abated. All such attempts are now considered linguistic esoterica, mere symbols of the desire of universalist thinkers for a code of communication that would cut across cultures.

There was, however, one visionary. John Adams (1735–1826), the second president of the United States, was not a linguistic romanticist, but he made a prediction about the universal role of English that eventually came true. Languages, like human beings, seem to have their ups and downs; yet some human beings can visualize the future of a language and even work toward realizing it. Adams—perhaps to the amazement of his contemporaries—foresaw the destiny of English when he said, "English will be the most respectable language in the world and the most universally read and spoken in the next century, if not before the close of this one" (*Life and Works IX*; see Mathews 1931). This prophecy was made on September 23, 1780.

The Other Tongue is concerned with the unfolding of this vision across the world, and with the spread of a language which, in John Adams's words, was "destined to be in the next and succeeding centuries more generally the language of the world than Latin was in the last or French is in the present age" (quoted in Mathews 1931: 42).

The spread of English across cultures has two sides. One represents those who use English as their first language, and the other represents those who use it as an additional language. A significant proportion of the world's population uses English as its *other* tongue (a second or foreign language). Such use varies, from broken English to almost native or ambilingual competence. It is this side of English that has actually elevated it to the status of an international (or universal) language. We still know very little about the form and function of the varieties that have developed as other tongues; the discussion on such varieties is still restricted to the realms of pedagogy, or to methods for teaching English as a second language. Even in books of "readings" meant for such consumers, very little, if anything, is said about the formal and functional characteristics of institutionalized World Englishes. In a typical study (Croft 1980) meant "to enlarge teachers' perspectives—to give them a broader view of the field they work in" (xiii), there is no attempt to present the English language in the global context, and to examine implications for teaching and teacher training. This is also true of books meant to assess "the state of the language," such as *The State of the Language* (1980) edited by Leonard Michaels and Christopher Ricks, and its 1990 edition by the same title, edited by Christopher Ricks and Leonard Michaels. The 1990 edition, the jacket tells us, provides "new observations, objections, angers, bemusements, hilarities, perplexities, revelations, prognostications, and warnings for the 1990s." The part on "Englishes" (pp. 3–94) does not discuss the World Englishes other than British and American. Sidney Greenbaum peripherally touches on the topic in "Whose English?" (pp. 15–23). Both editions are the result of projects initiated by the English-Speaking Union, San Francisco, and the publication of the 1990 volume is "supported by a generous grant from the George Frederick Jewett Foundation." It is still not generally realized that the other-tongue Englishes have several interesting aspects that go beyond the realms of pedagogy.[2] These varieties have their own sociological, linguistic, and literary manifestations. The global consequences (good or bad) of English as the other tongue, and certainly the perspective of those who use it as the other tongue, have hardly been presented. The side of the native speaker has been concentrated upon to the point where it has acquired a questionable status in terms of *norm, description,* and *prescription* (see Ferguson's foreword to this volume and ch. 3).

How realistic and appropriate is such attitude for our understanding of English in a world context? The demographic distribution of the two sides of English tells its own story. Chapter 3 gives us some idea about such distribution (see also Fishman et al. 1977, esp. chs. 1, 2, and 3; Kachru 1981b; Crystal 1985). If the spread of English continues at the current pace, by the year 2000 its non-native speakers

3

will significantly outnumber its native speakers. Indeed, according to some scholars that has already happened (Crystal 1985). This will mark the day when the visionaries' wish for a "universal language" comes true. But others are alarmed even with the present international profile of English.[3] The spread of English has been viewed both as a unique phenomenon of our times and as an unprecedented form of linguistic and cultural colonization (see Kachru 1986a).

Our knowledge about the motivations and attitudes favoring the spread of English is still very restricted. Fragmentary case studies have focused only on selected aspects, and very few of them possess insightful historical and contemporary dimensions. It is, however, certain that the colonist's arm has not always been instrumental in the spread of English. Let us look at some other reasons for the language's spread.

English is often learned because of its literary heritage, because of the status it may confer on the reader or speaker, because of the doors it opens in technology, science, trade, and diplomacy. Consider the well-known case of an institutionalized variety, Indian English. In India, less than fifty years after John Adams's prophecy, Raja Rammohun Roy (1772–1833) wrote a historic plea to Lord Amherst. In December 1823, trying to overcome his silence, he "humbly" says,

> The present Rulers of India, coming from a distance of many thousand miles to govern a people whose language, literature, manners, customs, and ideas are almost entirely new and strange to them, cannot easily become so intimately acquainted with their real circumstances as the natives of the country are themselves. We should therefore be guilty ourselves, and afford our rulers just ground of complaint at our apathy, did we omit on occasions of importance like the present to supply them with such accurate information as might enable them to devise and adopt measures calculated to be beneficial to the country, and thus second by our knowledge and experience, their declared benevolent intentions for its improvement.
>
> . . . When this Seminary of learning [Sanskrit School in Calcutta] was proposed, we understand that the Government of England had ordered a considerable sum of money to be annually devoted to the instruction of its Indian subjects. We were filled with sanguine hopes that this sum would be laid out in employing European gentlemen of talents and education to instruct the natives of India in mathematics, natural philosophy, chemistry, anatomy, and other useful sciences, which the natives of Europe have carried to a degree of perfection that has raised them above the inhabitants of other parts of the world. . . .
>
> We now find that the Government are establishing a Sanskrit school

under Hindoo Pundits to impart such knowledge as is clearly current in India. . . .

Roy then gives some arguments against spending money on Sanskrit studies: "If it had been intended to keep the British nation in ignorance of real knowledge the Baconian philosophy would not have been allowed to displace the system of the schoolmen, which was the best calculated to keep the country in darkness, if such had been the policy of the British legislature" (see Sharp 1920: I, 99–101).

Less well known are the cases of linguistically insulated areas. In Japan, even though English continues to be a performance variety, it has penetrated deep into the Japanese language and culture. In its localized form, English has acquired a stable status in the communicative strategies of Japanese people (see ch. 10). Japan also provides a historical footnote that is important for our understanding of English in a world context. Almost a century ago there was a proposal to abandon Japanese and "adopt instead some better, richer, stronger language, such as English or French" (Miller 1977: 41). (Note here the attitudinally significant modifiers *better, richer,* and *stronger.*) The first such proposal came from Mori Arinori (1847–99), and a later one came from Shiga Naoya (1883–1972). In his proposal Mori says:

> Without the aid of Chinese, our language has never been taught or used for any purpose of communication. This shows its poverty. The march of civilization in Japan has already reached the heart of the nation—the English language following it suppresses the use of both Chinese and Japanese. The commercial power of the English-speaking race which now rules the world drives our people into some knowledge of their commercial ways and habits. The absolute necessity of mastering the English language is thus forced upon us. It is a requisite of our independence in the community of nations. Under the circumstances, our meager language, which can never be of any use outside of our islands, is doomed to yield to the domination of the English tongue, especially when the power of steam and electricity shall have pervaded the land. Our intelligent race, eager in the pursuit of knowledge, cannot depend upon a weak and uncertain medium of communication in its endeavor to grasp the principle truths from the precious treasury of Western Science and art and religion. The laws of state can never be preserved in the language of Japan. All reasons suggest its disuse. [Mori 1873: I, vi; quoted in Hall 1973: 189]

These thoughts came from a country that was not under the colonial influence of an English-speaking power, as was, for example, India.

In the statements of Rammohun Roy and Mori we find John Adams's prediction actually being realized. While Adams's time schedule was a little off the mark, he was correct in claiming that English would become the language of the world, "because increasing population in America, and their universal connection and correspondence with all nations will . . . force their language into general use" (Mathews 1931: 42).

The impetus and support for such diffusion no doubt came from the extended period of colonization.[4] Because the sun never set on the British Empire, the English language was naturally basking. Once English was adopted in a region, whether for science, technology, literature, prestige, elitism, or "modernization," it went through various reincarnations that were partly linguistic and partly cultural. The reincarnations were essentially caused by the new bilingual (or multilingual) settings, and by the new contexts in which English had to function. Such reincarnations are well established in the regions where it has been used as an intranational language, in addition to serving international purposes (see Kachru and Quirk 1981). These non-native uses of English raise many issues in, for example, the teaching of English, curriculum design, methodology (Tickoo 1990), and literary creativity (Kachru 1988a and 1986b: 157–73), all of which have in the past been viewed mainly from the native speaker's perspective. The linguistic, literary, sociolinguistic, and educational issues are interrelated; if each is seen in isolation, the totality is lost (see ch. 3).

The Other Tongue is the first attempt to integrate and address provocative issues relevant to a deeper understanding of the forms and functions of English within different sociolinguistic and cross-cultural contexts. The questions one might ask about this bilingual (or multilingual) English speech community are not necessarily the same questions one might ask about users whose first language is English, or who are essentially monolingual. For example, what were the historical reasons for initiating bilingualism in English in various parts of Asia or Africa? What factors motivated the retention of English after the end of the colonial period? What is the sociolinguistic profile for each variety, and how does it contribute to the development of subvarieties? What linguistic and contextual parameters resulted in the *nativization* of English on the one hand, and in the *Englishization* of the native languages on the other? What new English-based codes of communication have resulted from communicative strategies such as code-mixing and code-switching? What type of interaction is there between non-native and native users in a particular setting, and what determines the choice of an endo-normative or exo-normative "standard" for each? What are the stylistic and other characteristics of the new English literature, and in what senses are these localized? What differentiates a bilingual's use of English from a monolingual's view of language use? What is the typology of non-native varieties of English at various levels?

The following chapters seek to provide answers to such questions. The situation, however, is complex. There are institutionalized and performance varieties, and within each variety there is further variation (Kachru 1981a and 1986a; Kachru and Quirk 1981; Smith, ed. 1981; Cheshire 1991). Non-native varieties are marked by their linguistic and cultural nativization. Both native and some non-native speakers have reacted to the processes of nativization and their results. (For detailed discussion, see Part II; see also Kachru 1983 and 1991.)

Let me now turn to the six parts of *The Other Tongue* in order to show their relevance to the questions raised above.

"English in the Global Context: Directions and Issues" (Part I) includes chapters on the most vital concerns of students, teachers, and researchers interested in English across cultural and language boundaries. Chapter 1 examines the sociology of English as an additional language, highlighting the factors favoring the "stable and widespread image of English." In this context, two realities concerning English are worthy of note: the fostering of the spread of English by its non-mother-tongue users, and the contribution to its functional expansion by local political authorities (e.g., in India, Sri Lanka, Nigeria, and Kenya). Chapters 2, 3, and 4 address three issues for understanding the pragmatics of English in the global context: English as an international language and the consequences of this status; the choice of norms from a wide range of varieties and language policymakers' decisions concerning the endo-normative or exo-normative standard, especially in regions where English has been institutionalized; and the implications of the spread of English on intelligibility and various issues related to research on intelligibility. Chapters 5 and 6 relate to broad theoretical and applied issues concerning the diffusion of English. Chapter 5 evaluates current paradigms of second-language acquisition and argues that there is a "paradigm gap" between second-language acquisition theory and the institutionalized varieties of English. This chapter discusses, with illustrations, how the dominant approaches to second-language acquisition have failed to account for various underlying processes and for the pragmatic contexts of World Englishes. Chapter 6 has both theoretical and pedagogical concerns, with special focus on assessment of non-native proficiency tests. These six chapters provide a backdrop and a context for the five subsequent parts of the volume.

In "Nativization: Formal and Functional" (Part II) four case studies represent Africa, China, and Japan. These regions represent both the institutionalized varieties (e.g., Nigerian English, Kenyan English) and the performance varieties (e.g., Chinese English, Japanese English). The usefulness of the distinction between institutionalized and performance varieties becomes clearer in these chapters, and this distinction provides a framework for understanding the status, functions, and pragmatic and sociolinguistic contexts for variety-specific innovations. The frequently used terms for such innovations—error, mistake, and deviation—are double-edged swords and must be used with caution (see esp. chs. 16 and 17). In a way, the chapters in Part II also address another issue: it seems that the linguistic evidence for divisiveness is not as overwhelming as the alarmists would have us believe. The underlying sociolinguistic and linguistic motivations for lexical, syntactic, and discoursal innovations are by and large shared, resulting from the new contexts into which the English language has been transplanted. Such institutionalized innovations actually result from language pragmatics, and from the interplay of linguistic, cultural, and regional identity (see Bailey and Görlach, eds. 1982; Kachru 1982 and 1986b [1990]; D'souza 1990; Foley, ed. 1988; Cheshire, ed. 1991).

What is standard English, and what are its models and norms? This is essentially a question of attitude and *power*, and the controversy over its answer has a long history (see Greenbaum, ed. 1985 and Kachru 1985). "Contact and Change: Question of a Standard" (Part III) presents a comparative perspective for grasping the intricacies of these issues. Chapters 11 and 12 discuss the considerations that led to the rise of American English from a "colonial substandard" to a "prestige language." The British attitude was essentially a reaction to the innovations American English experienced due to contact with different varieties and dialects, and with the influence of numerous languages of waves of immigrants. True, the United States does not belong to "the other side" of English, but American English has gone through several stages that are attitudinally identical to the Englishes of the other side. (For further discussion of these differences, see Greenbaum, ed. 1985; Heath 1976, 1977; Kachru 1981b; Lowenberg 1988; Markwardt and Quirk 1964; Strevens 1972.) Chapter 13 discusses the use of a non-native language in terms of a life cycle, delineating the stages of acceptance, institutionalization, and changing positions of English in language policies.

English also excels as a language of creativity in various literary genres around the world. It is therefore not surprising that Wole Soyinka, a Nigerian, was the winner of the Nobel Prize for his literary creativity in English in 1986, or that Raja Rao, an Indian novelist, was awarded the Neustadt International Prize for Literature in 1988. Scores of others have also gained world recognition. Several literary academies and governments recognize writing in English as part of the local literary tradition, as does, for example, the National Academy of Letters (Sahitya Akademi) of India. This facet of English is introduced in "Literary Creativity in the Other Tongue" (Part IV). In many respects, this use of English is unprecedented; among other things, it reveals the writers' emotional attachment to a language that traditionally has not been part of their cultural and literary contexts. It also shows the roots of English across cultures. It is true that several such English literatures have become controversial, as in India, Nigeria, and the Philippines. Their recognition has been slow in coming, and native speakers of English have shown cynicism or condescension toward them. But that controversy, and those attitudes, are unrelated to my main point.

The creative processes displayed in non-native English literatures have generally been ignored in linguistic studies, to the detriment of studies on stylistics, contrastive discourse, language acculturation, and bilingual creativity (Kachru 1986b: 159–73). This neglect shows the dichotomy and the often adversarial relationship that has existed between linguists and literary critics. Chapters 14 and 15 introduce the reader to the literary implications of the spread of English. Chapter 14 provides an overview of the underlying issues, from the viewpoint of a literary scholar and a creative writer in English, and Chapter 15 discusses the specific stylistic experimentation of two Indian English writers, Mulk Raj Anand and R. K. Narayan, and the geographically hard to place V. S. Naipaul. Such English literatures open a window, offering distinctly different views on non-Western cultures and their literary, cultural, and historical canons. They actually expand the canon of English (Kachru 1988a).

"Discoursal Strategies: Text in Context" (Part V) includes three chapters that focus on aspects of the discourse strategies used in World Englishes. Chapter 16 shows how what is "deviation" for one user of English provides "meaning" to another user. English is used in non-Western cultures consistent with local literary norms of creativity and for maintaining local patterns of life. When English is adapted to other cultures—to non-Western and non-English contexts—it is understandably *decontextualized* from its *Englishness* (or, for that matter, its *Americanness*). It acquires new identities. In the interactional networks of its new users, English provides an additional, redefined communicative code. A deviation for one beholder is an appropriate *communicative act* for another language user. We see this clearly in code-

9

mixing, code-switching (see Bhatia and Ritchie, eds. 1989), or in typical uses of language in, for example, obituaries, personal and official correspondence, matrimonial advertisements, and, of course, in the non-native English literatures. While the typical communicative acts may be shared by all the members of the English speech community, the strategies to organize language to fulfill these communicative purposes are not necessarily shared. These are specific to each *speech fellowship* of English and are organized in localized (culture-bound) stylistic conventions for various text types. English acquires a new identity, a local habitat, and a name. Such a phenomenon is not unprecedented. The same thing happened long ago to Sanskrit in India, or to Persian. In the not so distant past, we again witnessed this phenomenon with French in francophone areas of the world, and with Spanish in the New World. But the extent and degree of the spread of English, and its realizations in various cultures, are certainly unequaled. The questions these situations raise are discussed further in Chapters 17 and 18. My language, your culture: Whose communicative competence? This question and many related theoretical issues have yet to be fully addressed. The three chapters in Part V of *The Other Tongue* only scratch the surface. (For further discussion, see Kachru 1988b; Lowenberg, ed. 1988; Quirk and Widdowson, eds. 1985; Smith, ed. 1981 and 1987; Garcia and Otheguy, eds. 1989.)

"World Englishes in the Classroom: Rationale and Resources" (Part VI) attempts to provide arguments for introducing the concept "World Englishes" in the classroom. It discusses various theoretical and applied arguments for recognizing and teaching World Englishes as an interdisciplinary area and for raising consciousness and initiating awareness about this multifaceted phenomenon. This chapter also includes a select bibliography of resources for understanding (and teaching) various aspects of World Englishes. The list of resources is divided into the following sections: bibliographies, general surveys, issue-oriented studies, English literatures, discourse strategies and nativization, and journals.

In this second edition, *The Other Tongue* again provides a new perspective and a challenge for reevaluating the research agenda for scholars. On the one hand, the acquisition of English across cultures has broad promise and is not restricted to a language specialist. It is a symbol of an urge to extend oneself and one's roles beyond the confines of one's culture and language. English continues to be accepted in this role, ever since and despite the depressing colonial experience (see Bailey and Görlach, eds. 1982; McCrum, Cran, and MacNeil 1986; Cheshire 1991). The language has no claims to intrinsic superiority;

rather, its preeminent role developed due to extralinguistic factors. The importance is in what the medium conveys about technology, science, law, and (in the case of English) literature. English has now, as a consequence of its status, been associated with universalism, liberalism, secularism, and internationalism. In this sense, then, English is a symbol of the concept that Indians have aptly expressed as *vasudhaiva kuṭumbakaṃ* (the whole Universe is a family). True, not everyone may agree with this perception, but that there is such a positive reaction toward English cannot be denied (see Kachru 1986a; Kachru and Smith, eds. 1986; Crowley 1989).

The spread of English, and its adoption across cultures and languages, should be reassuring for societies that believe bilingualism (or multilingualism) is an aberration. In reality, acquiring and maintaining another language has historically been a *normal* human activity, and monolingualism is not an ideal state. It is through other tongues that other cultures can be appreciated and perhaps understood. The Indian pragmatist Mohandas K. Gandhi (1864–1948) said it so well: "I do not want my house to be walled in on all sides and my windows to be stuffed. I want cultures of all lands to be blown about my house as freely as possible. But I refuse to be blown off my feet anyway" (John, n.d.: epigraph).

I hope this second edition of *The Other Tongue* has raised additional meaningful questions that were not raised in its first edition. I also hope it has provided some answers and new perspectives. Asking significant questions is not easy; providing insightful answers is extremely difficult. It becomes more difficult if the topic cuts across world cultures and languages. If the second edition of *The Other Tongue* has partially accomplished its goal—as I believe the first edition did—that is a significant step in the right direction. Through such steps, challenging and provocative questions will continue to be asked. Through such probing, we shall grow to understand the role of the other tongues in general, and English across cultures in particular.

The other side of English continues to be important in other ways as well. It offers a laboratory for the study of exciting data from various perspectives, a testing ground for theories, and an ample field—in Asia, Africa, and the West—for interdisciplinary research. It therefore continues to be a challenging field for theoretical linguistics, for various branches of applied linguistics, and for other language-related interdisciplinary areas of research and study. The need, then, is to continue to ask right questions in the right spirit in the 1900s. That is precisely the goal of this new edition of *The Other Tongue*.

11

NOTES

1. For a detailed history and description of such proposals, see, e.g., Guerard 1922 and Jacob 1947.

2. The attitude exhibited in such approaches is generally as shown in Prator 1968. See a response to it in Kachru 1976; see also Preston 1981, Quirk 1988 and 1990, and response to them in Kachru 1991.

3. The acceptance of English as the other tongue in the post-colonial period is not, of course, unqualified and universal. Vocal groups in each English-using country resist the continued use and dominance of English. See, e.g., for South Asia, Kachru 1982 and 1986b.

4. For a detailed discussion and case studies, see, e.g., Brosnahan 1963; Calvet 1974; Fishman et al. 1977; Spencer 1971.

5. For selected references on African writing in English, see ch. 7; for India, chs. 15 and 16. See also Aggarwal 1982, Kachru 1983, and Narasimhaiah, ed. 1976. For Malaysia, Singapore, and Sri Lanka, see, e.g., Bloom 1986, Fernando 1972, Thumboo 1976, and Kandiah 1981. In their anthologies Fernando and Thumboo provide excellent introductions with specimens of writing. See also Jones 1965; King 1974, 1980; Viereck, Schneider, and Görlach 1984; Dissanayake 1990.

REFERENCES

Aggarwal, Narindar K. 1982. *English in South Asia: a bibliographical survey of resources.* Gurgaon and New Delhi: Indian Documentation Service.

Bailey, Richard, and Manfred Görlach, eds. 1982. *English as a world language.* Ann Arbor: University of Michigan Press.

Bhatia, Tej K., and William Ritchie, eds. 1989. *Code-mixing: English across languages.* Special issue of *World Englishes* 8(3).

Bloom, David. 1986. The English language in Singapore: a critical survey. Pp. 337–458 in *Singapore studies: critical surveys of the humanities and social sciences,* ed. Basant K. Kapur. Singapore: Singapore University Press.

Brosnahan, L. F. 1963. Some historical cases of language imposition. In *Languages in Africa,* ed. J. F. Spencer. Cambridge: Cambridge University Press.

Calvet, Louis-Jean. 1974. *Linguistique et colonialisme: petit traité de glottophagie.* Série Bibliothèque Scientifique. Paris: Payot.

Cheshire, Jenny, ed. 1991. *English around the world: sociolinguistic perspectives.* Cambridge: Cambridge University Press.

Croft, Kenneth, ed. 1980. *Readings on English as a second language.* 2nd ed. Cambridge: Winthrop.

Crowley, Tony. 1989. *Standard English and politics of language.* Urbana: University of Illinois Press.

Crystal, David. 1985. How many millions? The statistics of English today. *English Today* 1: 7–9.

Dissanayake, Wimal. 1990. Identity and creativity: English writing in Asia and the Pacific. Special issue of *World Englishes* 9(2).

D'souza, Jean. 1990. English—one or many? An experimental study. *World Englishes* 9(3): 371–82.

Fernando, Lloyd, ed. 1972. *New drama one.* Kuala Lumpur: Oxford University Press.

Fishman, Joshua A., R. L. Cooper, and A. W. Conrad. 1977. *The spread of English: the sociology of English as an additional language.* Rowley, Mass.: Newbury House.

Foley, Joseph, ed. 1988. *New Englishes: the case of Singapore.* Singapore: Singapore University Press.

Freudenthal, Hans. 1960. *Lincos: design of a language for cosmic intercourse.* Amsterdam: North-Holland.

Garcia, Ofelia, and R. Otheguy, eds. 1989. *English across cultures, cultures across English.* New York: Mouton de Gruyter.

Greenbaum, Sidney, ed. 1985. *The English language today.* Oxford: Pergamon Press.

Guerard, Albert L. 1922. *A short history of international language movement.* London: T. Fisher Unwin.

Hall, Ivan Parker. 1973. *Mori Arinori.* Cambridge: Harvard University Press.

Heath, Shirley Brice. 1976. A national language academy? Debate in the new nation. *International Journal of the Sociology of Language* 11: 9–43.

———. 1977. Language politics in the United States. In *Georgetown University Round Table on language and linguistics,* ed. M. Saville-Troike. Washington, D.C.: Georgetown University Press.

Jacob, Henry. 1947. *A planned auxiliary language.* London: Dennis Dobson.

John, K. K. n.d. *The only solution to India's language problem.* Madras: Published by the author.

Jones, Joseph. 1965. *Terranglia: the case for English as world language.* New York: Twayne.

Kachru, Braj B. 1976. Models of English for the third world: white man's linguistic burden or language pragmatics? *TESOL Quarterly* 10: 221–39.

———. 1981a. The pragmatics of non-native varieties of English. Pp. 15–39 in Smith, ed. 1981.

———. 1981b. American English and other Englishes. Pp. 21–43 in *Language in the USA,* ed. Charles A. Ferguson and Shirley B. Heath. New York: Cambridge University Press.

———. 1982. South Asian English. Pp. 353–83 in Bailey and Görlach, eds. 1982.

———. 1983. *The Indianization of English: the English language in India.* New Delhi: Oxford University Press.

———. 1985. Standards, codification, and sociolinguistic realism: the English language in the outer circle. Pp. 11–30 in Quirk and Widdowson, eds. 1985.

———. 1986a. The power and politics of English. *World Englishes* 5(2–3): 121–40.

13

————. 1986b. *The alchemy of English: the spread, functions and models of non-native Englishes.* Oxford: Pergamon Press. Reprinted 1990, Urbana: University of Illinois Press.

————. 1988a. Toward expanding the English canon: Raja Rao's 1938 credo for creativity. *World Literature Today* 62(4): 582–86.

————. 1988b. The spread of English and sacred linguistic cows. In Lowenberg, ed. 1988: 207–28.

————. 1991. Liberation linguistics and the Quirk concern. *English Today* 25, 7(1): 3–13.

————, and L. Smith, eds. 1986. *The power of English: cross-cultural dimensions in literature and media.* Special issue of *World Englishes* 5(2–3).

————, and Randolph Quirk. 1981. Introduction. In L. Smith, ed. 1981.

Kandiah, Thiru. 1981. Lankan English schizoglossia. *English World-Wide: A Journal of Varieties of English* 2.1: 63–81.

King, Bruce. 1974. *Literatures of the world in English.* London: Routledge and Kegan Paul.

————. 1980. *The new English literatures: cultural nationalism in a changing world.* New York: St. Martin's Press.

Lowenberg, Peter H., ed. 1988. *Language spread and language policy: issues, implications and case studies.* Washington, D.C.: Georgetown University Press.

Markwardt, Albert H., and Randolph Quirk. 1964. *A common language: British and American English.* London: British Broadcasting Corporation.

Mathews, M. M. 1931. *The beginnings of American English: essays and comments.* Chicago: University of Chicago Press.

McCrum, Robert, William Cran, and Robert MacNeil. 1986. *The story of English.* New York: Viking.

Michaels, Leonard, and Christopher Ricks. 1980. *The state of the language.* Berkeley: University of California Press.

Miller, Roy A. 1977. *The Japanese language in contemporary Japan.* Washington, D.C.: American Enterprise Institute for Public Policy Research.

Mori, Arinori. 1873. *Education in Japan: a series of letters addressed by prominent Americans to Arinori Mori.* New York: Appleton.

Narasimhaiah, C. D., ed. 1976. *Commonwealth literature: a handbook of select reading lists.* Madras: Oxford University Press.

Prator, Clifford. 1968. The British heresy in TESL. Pp. 459–76 in *Language problems in developing nations.* Ed. J. A. Fishman, C. A. Ferguson, and J. Das Gupta. New York: John Wiley.

Preston, Dennis R. 1981. The ethnography of TESOL. *TESOL Quarterly* 15(2): 105–16.

Quirk, Randolph. 1988. The question of standards in the international use of English. In Lowenberg, ed. 1988: 229–41.

————. 1990. Language varieties and standard language. *English Today* 21 (January): 3–10.

————, and Henry Widdowson, eds. 1985. *English in the world: teaching and learning the language and literatures.* London, Cambridge and New York: Cambridge University Press.

Sharp, Henry, ed. 1920–22. *Selections from educational records.* Calcutta: Bureau of Education, Government of India.

Smith, Larry E., ed. 1981. *English for cross-cultural communication.* London: Macmillan.

———. 1987. *Discourse across cultures: strategies in world Englishes.* London: Prentice-Hall.

Spencer, John. 1971. Colonial language policies and their legacies. In *Current trends in linguistics,* ed. T. A. Sebeok. Vol. VII: Linguistics in Sub-Saharan Africa. The Hague: Mouton.

Strevens, Peter. 1972. *British and American English.* London: Collier-Macmillan.

Thumboo, Edwin. 1976. *The second tongue: an anthology of poetry from Malaysia and Singapore.* Singapore: Heinemann Educational Books.

Tickoo, Makhan L. 1990. Towards an alternative curriculum for acquisition-poor environments. Pp. 403–18 in *Learning, keeping and using language,* ed. M. A. K. Halliday, John Gibbons, and Howard Nicholas. Amsterdam and Philadelphia: John Benjamins.

Viereck, Wolfgang, E. W. Schneider, and Manfred Görlach, 1984. *A bibliography of writings on varieties of English, 1965–1983.* Amsterdam: John Benjamins.

PART I

English in the Global Context: Directions and Issues

1

Joshua A. Fishman

Sociology of English as an Additional Language

The ongoing nativization of non-native Englishes in various parts of the world proceeds within the penumbra of a rather stable and widespread image of English. This image is itself both influenced by and, in turn, contributory to an international sociolinguistic balance of power that characterizes the latter part of the twentieth century. This balance of power rests solidly on three realities: (1) not only is English increasingly associated with technological modernity and power, but this association is now being fostered by non-English mother-tongue interests; (2) English is both functionally fostered and regulated by local political authorities; and (3) indigenous "preferred languages" are complementarily fostered and regulated by these same authorities.

Not only is English still spreading, but it is even being spread by non-English mother-tongue interests.

The world has previously witnessed the spread of languages of empire, the diffusion of lingua francas, and the growth of international languages. In most respects, therefore, the continued spread of English for international and intranational purposes is not novel in the annals of world history—or, if it is novel, it is so primarily in a quantitative sense, in terms of scale, rate, and degree, rather than in any qualitative sense or in terms of kind. If there is something qualitatively new under the sun in conjunction with the spread of English in the non-English mother-tongue world, it is merely that the spread has reached such an order of magnitude that it is now significantly fostered by the *non-*English mother-tongue world, rather than being predominantly dependent on resources, efforts, or personnel of the English mother-tongue world (Conrad and Fishman 1977). Whether we monitor the veritable army of English-speaking econo-technical specialists, advisors, and representatives, or whether we examine the diffusion of English publications, films, radio and television programs, literacy programs and educational opportunities, it is becoming increasingly clear that non-English mother-tongue countries are significantly active in each of these connections. Nor is their involvement merely that of Third World recipients of Western largesse. True, Third World nations *are* themselves fostering massive efforts via and on behalf of English. On the other hand, however, equally massive programs via English are being conducted by the Soviet Union, the Arab world, and mainland China—world powers that have their own well-developed standard languages and that normally oppose various political, philosophical, and economic goals of the English mother-tongue world.

Whereas the international and intranational roles of French also continue to be fostered (as do, to a lesser degree, such roles for Spanish, Russian, German, Portuguese, etc.) such efforts are conducted exclusively by current francophone (hispanoparlante, etc.) nations or by countries under French (Spanish, etc.) cultural, political, or economic domination (Gordon 1978). Similarly, English is massively employed, particularly in higher-level governmental, technological, and educational pursuits, by countries under former (or current) Anglo-American domination (Fishman, Cooper, and Rosenbaum 1977). However, English today has surpassed the charmed circle of Anglo-American econopolitical control, and is being fostered both by its opponents and by "third parties." English has become a major medium of indigenous elites ("native foreigners"), of tourism ("foreign foreigners"), of popular media, of technical publications, of the metaphor of mastery, of teenage slang, and even of language-planning models and anti-models all over the world. While the omnipresence of English also adds to the opposition to English, it obviously fosters the growth of indigenous non-native varieties (Smith 1981; Kachru and Quirk 1981). Finally, never before has any one language been so simultaneously sought after and regulated, so that it would "grow" yet "stay in its place" (i.e., be used only in functions for which it was authoritatively desired). Thus, if the *continued spread and growth of English* is one aspect of the current international sociolinguistic balance of power, another such aspect is the recurring need to control, regulate, or tame that spread.

English is being regulated via both status and corpus planning.
The growth of English-speaking "false foreigners" in various parts of the non-English mother-tongue world (e.g., West Africa, East Africa,

India, Puerto Rico) is an indication that a non-native variety of English may succeed not only in stabilizing itself cross-generationally (i.e., in nativizing itself), but also in becoming a mother tongue in certain speech networks. The latter phenomenon is much more worrisome than the former to local authorities, but taken together and added to the continued growth of English in many parts of the world (growth in listening to English, in understanding English, in speaking English, in reading English, and even in writing English) it is no surprise that these authorities have frequently decided to do something about it. A common *status-planning* goal has recently been implemented by the Philippines: English as a medium of education has been restricted to mathematics and natural sciences (the "ethnically less encumbered" subjects), whereas the bulk of the curriculum (particularly history, civics, and vocational education; i.e., the "ethnically more encumbered subjects") has been reserved for Pilipino as a medium of instruction (Fishman 1977a). This policy is in line with the relinguification and re-ethnification (Pilipinization and Philippinization) goals of the local authorities, who recognize, at the same time, that English reigns supreme in the econo-technical area. "A little bit of English for almost everyone" is considered a good thing, as is a lot of English for a select few, provided the language can be confined to its allotted domains (Cooper, Fishman, Lown, Schaier, and Seckbach 1977). Similar steps to make sure that English does not intrude upon the domains of local ideology, literature, history, and citizenship have multiplied in Tanzania, Taiwan, India, France, and Puerto Rico, and can be expected, quietly but increasingly, elsewhere as well.

Thus, in addition to the distinction of having spread further and having been indigenized more frequently than any previous lingua franca, English also has the distinction of being more frequently subjected to language-planning efforts (Fishman 1977b). Even in the corpus-planning field, "academies" and other agencies responsible for attaining language modernization plus safeguarding language authenticity ("purity," "distinctiveness," "originality," etc.) constantly point to English as the most common source of unwelcome interferences/ influences (Allony-Fainberg 1977). Whether in France or in French Canada, whether in Hebrew or in Yiddish, whether in Spain or in Spanish America, whether in Hindi, Indonesian, or Swahili—in every area and language the impact of English must be watched and regulated. At times this influence is disguised as "internationalisms," "Europeanisms," or "Westernisms," but in actuality it is more likely to be Englishisms than anything else (Ronen, Seckbach, and Cooper 1977). The academies are frequently successful in combatting Englishisms in the standard written language, but in the informal spoken language they often confront well-entrenched Englishisms that have become part and parcel of popular culture and that are essentially impossible to extirpate, even among loyalists and purists (Allony-Fainberg 1974). Nevertheless, the epic struggles of officially and centrally conducted language-planning authorities since the end of World War II have all had to face up to English, and by and large they have succeeded with respect to the written language, insofar as political circumstances have permitted. Regardless of what may have happened to the British Empire, the sun never sets on the English language; yet, little languages have learned to stand their ground with respect to English, and to carve out domains into which English has little or no entree (Rubin, Jernudd, Das Gupta, Fishman, and Ferguson 1977).

More and more local languages are being accorded special protection.
Writing in the early 1940s, Karl Deutsch reviewed the slow growth in the number of standard/literary languages in Europe: from sixteen in 1800, to thirty in 1900, to fifty-three in 1940 (Deutsch 1942). However, the growth of standard/literary languages has not stopped at the boundaries of Europe; indeed, since the end of World War II this growth has accelerated at a rate more rapid than anyone would have predicted. The number of literary languages today is easily in the neighborhood of two hundred and is still growing. On the one hand, this explosion of literary languages is due to the fact that there are more polities in the world today than at any previous time since the universalization of literacy (Fishman 1972). On the other hand, the forces of intranational cultural democracy are also receiving more recognition (or more permissive treatment) from central authorities than before (Fishman 1976). Bilingual education and even the socio-linguistic enterprise itself have contributed to (and benefited from) both of these processes, and the end is not yet in sight. There are potentially hundreds of additional ethnolinguistic collectivities seeking some recognized, protected, and elevated (i.e., literacy/power related) status for one or another of their vernacular tongues.

Thus, the Philippines, mentioned above as a prime example of a nation "regulating" English in the pursuit of a new (Pilipino/Philippine) integrative identity, has permitted local languages to become *media* of instruction during the earlier elementary grades, as well as *subjects* of instruction in all subsequent grades. A three-language policy is thus envisaged, much as it is in India. Such policies promise to become increasingly common for minority nationalities/regional ethnicities in various parts of the globe: the "national language," an even wider language of communication (very often English), and a preferred "narrower" language all find protected niches for themselves in the local educational/cultural/commercial/vocational economy.

Obviously, multilingualism is not a new phenomenon. What *is* at least somewhat new is the fact that more and more of the world's multilingualism is being governmentally recognized, sponsored, planned, and protected. This is indeed an unusual situation insofar as the spread of English is concerned, and it constitutes the third force in the international sociolinguistic balance of power. English is spreading, but its spread is being controlled and counterbalanced by the sponsored, protected spread of national and subnational languages. As a result, more and more of those who learn English do so in the context of other languages that have their own perquisites and potentials. This necessarily influences the image of English in many parts of the non-English mother-tongue world, as well as in the English mother-tongue world itself.

The Image of English: Mirror, Mirror on the Wall

Throughout the non-English mother-tongue world, English is recurringly associated with practical and powerful pursuits (Cooper and Seckbach 1977). This becomes evident when the image of English is compared, on the one hand, with the image of French and, on the other hand, with that of local integrative languages that have been fairly recently standardized. Relative to the latter, English is viewed as *less* suitable for military operations (local soldiers do not know that much English yet), for lying, joking, cursing, or bargaining (spontaneous emotion and animation are not yet expressed via English), and for unmediated prayer. On the other hand, English is recurringly viewed as *more* suitable than local integrative languages for science, international diplomacy, industry/commerce, high oratory, and pop songs (Cooper and Fishman 1977; see also Garcia and Otheguy, eds. 1989).

The image of English vis-à-vis French is even more revealing, in that the former has risen and the latter has fallen in the international balance of power. In the Third World (excluding former anglophone and francophone colonies) French is considered *more suitable* than English for only one function: opera. It is considered *the equal of English* for reading good novels or poetry and for personal prayer (the local integrative language being widely viewed as superior to both English and French in this connection). But outside the realm of aesthetics, the Ugly Duckling reigns supreme. French is widely viewed as more beautiful, musical, pleasant, rhythmic, refined, intimate, pure, soothing, graceful, tender, and lovely, but English is viewed as richer, more precise, more logical, more sophisticated, and more competence related. English is less loved but more used; French is more loved but less used. Nature abhors a vacuum: as the functional load of a formerly prestigious variety declines, affect rushes in to take up the slack. The non-francophone world has "nothing but love" for French, and in the cruel real world that is a sign of a weakness. The displacement of Irish is suffused with love. The replacement of Yiddish is accompanied by panegyrics as to its intimacy and authenticity. English gets along without love, without sighs, without tears, and almost without affect of any kind (Fishman 1977c). In a world where econo-technical superiority is what really counts, the heightened aesthetic-affective image of French smacks of weakness, innocence, and triviality.

The local integrative languages are recurringly viewed as more useful than French, although less useful "in the highest circles" than English. On the other hand, these languages, recipients of planned public protection, are recurringly viewed as less beautiful than French but more beautiful than English. There was a time not so long ago—indeed, less than a century has elapsed since then—when languages were viewed as having "made the grade" when they could boast of great poetry. Nowadays the market for poetry is down, and the absence or availability of computer programming manuals tells us whether or not a language will be "taken seriously" by its own and nearby speech communities. Given such sociolinguistic values and goals, is it any wonder that local integrative languages are viewed as Prince Charmings in overalls? They combine a modicum of affect with a modicum of practicality. But the real "powerhouse" is still English. It doesn't have to worry about being loved because, loved or not, it works. It makes the world go round, and few indeed can afford to "knock it."

Nor is the non-English mother-tongue world unique in its no-nonsense view of English. Much of the English mother-tongue world is itself quite unemotional about English, viewing it as a medium pure and simple rather than as either a symbol or a message. Most English mother-tongue countries are recent centers of mass immigration. High proportions of their populations (even among their academicians) reveal no more than a single generation of association with English. This shallowness of association with "Mother English" is, in turn, related to Anglophonie's permissiveness toward non-native Englishes all over the world, each of which likewise has little affect associated with it. The constellation sketched above seems stable enough at the moment, but the lesson of History is quite clear, even if its pace is not predictable.

If a powerful shift in *Zeitgeist* has eroded the image and functions of French (and it did so, to some extent, even within the very borders of Francophonie), then what would a massive shift in the balance of econo-technical power do to the preeminence of English? Third-party inertia would continue to reinforce English for decades or longer, but ultimately a shift would take place. If and when such a shift occurs, there may be few who will shed a tear. The world has no tears left. At any rate, crying takes time and, as all the world has learned from American English, "time is money."

REFERENCES

Allony-Fainberg, Yaffa. 1974. Official Hebrew terms for parts of the car: a study of knowledge, usage and attitudes. Pp. 493–518 in J. A. Fishman, ed. 1974.

——. 1977. The influence of English on formal terminology in Hebrew. Pp. 223–28 in J. A. Fishman, R. L. Cooper, A. W. Conrad et al. 1977.

Conrad, Andrew W., and Joshua A. Fishman. 1977. English as a world language: the evidence. Pp. 3–76 in J. A. Fishman, R. L. Cooper, A. W. Conrad et al. 1977.

Cooper, Robert L., and Joshua A. Fishman. 1977. A study of language attitudes. Pp. 239–76 in J. A. Fishman, R. L. Cooper, A. W. Conrad et al. 1977.

——, and Fern Seckbach. 1977. Economic incentives for learning a language of wider communication. Pp. 212–22 in J. A. Fishman, R. L. Cooper, A. W. Conrad et al. 1977.

——, Joshua A. Fishman, Linda Lown, Barbara Schaier, and Fern Seckbach. 1977. Pp. 197–211 in J. A. Fishman, R. L. Cooper, A. W. Conrad et al. 1977.

Deutsch, Karl W. 1942. The trend of European nationalism: the language aspect. *American Political Science Review* 36: 533–41.

Fishman, Joshua A. 1972. *Language and nationalism.* Rowley, Mass.: Newbury House.

——. 1976. *Bilingual education: an international sociological perspective.* Rowley, Mass.: Newbury House.

——. 1977a. English in the context of international societal bilingualism. Pp. 329–36 in J. A. Fishman, R. L. Cooper, A. W. Conrad et al. 1977.

——. 1977b. The spread of English as a new perspective for the study of "language maintenance and language shift." Pp. 108–35 in J. A. Fishman, R. L. Cooper, A. W. Conrad et al. 1977.

——. 1977c. Knowing, using, and liking English as an additional language. Pp. 302–27 in J. A. Fishman, R. L. Cooper, A. W. Conrad et al. 1977.

——, et al. 1968. *Readings in the sociology of language.* The Hague: Mouton.

——, ed. 1974. *Advances in language planning.* The Hague: Mouton.

——, R. L. Cooper, A. W. Conrad et al. 1977. *The spread of English.* Rowley, Mass.: Newbury House.

————, Robert L. Cooper, and Yehudi Rosenbaum. 1977. English around the world. Pp. 77–107 in J. A. Fishman, R. L. Cooper, A. W. Conrad et al. 1977.

Garcia, Ofelia, and R. Otheguy, eds. 1989. *English across cultures, cultures across English*. New York: Mouton de Gruyter.

Gordon, David C. 1978. *The French language and national identity*. The Hague: Mouton.

Kachru, Braj B., and Quirk, Randolph. 1981. "Introduction." In Smith 1981.

Ronen, Miriam, Fern Seckbach, and Robert L. Cooper. 1977. Foreign loanwords in Hebrew newspapers. Pp. 229–38 in J. A. Fishman, R. L. Cooper, A. W. Conrad et al. 1977.

Rubin, Joan, B. Jernudd, J. Das Gupta, J. A. Fishman, and C. A. Ferguson, eds. 1977. *Language planning process*. The Hague: Mouton.

Smith, Larry. 1981. *English for cross-cultural communication*. London: Macmillan.

2

Peter Strevens

English as an International Language: Directions in the 1990s

As the number of users of English worldwide surges toward a probable two billion (Crystal 1985), but those for whom it is the mother tongue fall to a fifth or less of this total, as the functions and uses of English by native speaker and non-native speaker alike become ever more numerous and unrelated to the nationality of the speaker (or writer), so a number of consequences have started to become apparent. Some of these relate simply to the need for an awareness of the facts about English today and about the speed at which changes are taking place. Some relate to issues of standards and norms within English, to educational goals and to criteria for evaluating success in learning and teaching. Some relate to profound perceptions of identity and to major differences in such perceptions between native speakers of English and non-native speakers, as when the unthinking, or ignorant, or insensitive native speaker reacts condescendingly or arrogantly to the variety of English used by a non-native user and thereby perpetuates or arouses ethnic mistrust. And some of the consequences of the vast spread of English relate to the global "industry" of teaching and learning English, which in its highest forms represents the peak—the state of the art—of what can now be achieved in the deliberate learning and teaching of languages.

World English and Englishes Today

Beginning at a general level, it is commonly accepted that the label "English" can be applied to many forms of the language which are identifiably different from each other: "American English," "British

English," "Indian English," "West African English," "Singapore English," "Australian English," etc. H. L. Mencken (1919) wrote a book entitled *The American Language*, seeking to remove the label "English" as part of his polemic campaign against what he saw as snobbery and arrogance directed by the British against the language—and, by extension, against the values, institutions, and achievements—of the Americans. Today the trend in referring to different forms and varieties is to accept differentiation within English and even to employ a new plural, "Englishes," as in the title of the new journal, *World Englishes*, expressly founded to document and discuss these phenomena, coedited for Pergamon by two of the leading academics in this field, Braj B. Kachru of the University of Illinois at Urbana-Champaign and Larry E. Smith of the East-West Center, Hawaii.[1]

What of the statistics? The number of people for whom English is the mother tongue (or "native language," or "primary language," or L_1: see below) is widely agreed to be around 350 million. This figure is based mainly on the population and school statistics of countries such as the United States, Canada, Britain, Australia, New Zealand, etc., with allowances made for the growing numbers of immigrants for whom English is not the mother tongue; together with figures for "expatriate" communities of native speakers of English in various countries. Until recently, the comparable figure of non-native speakers of English has been roughly estimated at about 700 to 750 million. That figure has been arrived at by reference to such factors as the readership of English-language newspapers in countries where English is not a major mother tongue. Now David Crystal (1985) has called for a broader view of who should be counted as "English users," to include all those who do actually use it, even on a limited scale. Crystal's estimate is between 1 billion (1000 million) and 2 billion. His argument is persuasive: I shall take as a working figure the mid-point of 1.5 billion English users.

By far the most important aspect of these figures of native speakers (NS) and non-native speakers (NNS)[2] is the ratio between them. It creates a massive paradox and has profound psychological consequences. For the figures tell us that while English is used by more people than any other language on Earth, its mother-tongue speakers make up only a quarter or a fifth of the total. Further, these immense numbers are only possible because there exist in several parts of the world—in South Asia, in parts of Africa, in the Far East, even in Europe—communities of English users in which the native speakers are heavily outnumbered by non-native speakers. One's language is a central element in one's personal, national, and ethnic identity: it is not easy for the NS to come to terms with the variations that occur in NNS use of what the NS feels to be "one's own language."

Another important aspect of the statistics is the speed with which the NNS have increased. At a guess, perhaps 1 billion of the 1.5 billion NNS English users have learned or picked up the English they use in the past twenty years. That rate of change has great implications for the English language teaching profession in many countries, to which we shall return later.

The Origins of Present-Day English

Why should it be English that has come to occupy this unique position? English is, after all, a young language compared with Chinese, or Greek, or Japanese, or Sanskrit. Nor is it convincing simply to reply that English was the language used for exploration, trade, conquest, and dominion from the sixteenth century onward: so also was Portuguese, and Spanish, and Arabic, yet they do not have dominant NNS populations. There is of course an element of historical luck about it: the explorations of Captain Cook and Captain Vancouver, the establishment of trading posts in Africa and the Orient, the colonial and penal settlements in North America and Australasia, the profit-dominated grip on India, the infamous triangular slaves-for-molasses-for-manufactured-goods traffic between Britain, West Africa, and the Caribbean, the early stages of the Industrial Revolution—all these and others since were happenings dominated by people who spoke English. But one can also view the development of the English language as having passed through several stages, since 1600, which cumulatively yet inevitably led to the present state of affairs.

It all began on a tiny scale. English first came into existence in roughly the form in which we know it today around 1350, when the influence of 300 years of Norman French occupation had been assimilated onto a basis of Germanic dialects, with some additions from the Norse of the Scandinavian invaders. For 250 years, until 1600, English was spoken only in England, probably not even by all the 7 million inhabitants. But then between 1600 and 1750 were sown the seeds of today's global spread of English, as explorers, merchant adventurers, buccaneers, traders, settlers, soldiers, and administrators went out from Britain to begin settlements and colonies overseas. And it is necessary to realize that before about 1750 all these settlers regarded themselves as English speakers from Britain who happened to be living overseas.

Yet after about 1750 and until ca. 1900, three major changes took place. First, the populations of the overseas NS English-speaking settlements greatly increased in size and became states with governments—albeit colonial governments—and with a growing sense of separate identity, which soon extended to the flavor of the English they used. Second, in the United States first of all but later in Australia and elsewhere, the colonies began to take their independence from Britain, which greatly reinforced the degree of linguistic difference: Noah Webster, for example, urged Americans to take pride in the fact of their English reflecting the dynamic new life of the United States. And third, as the possessions stabilized and prospered, so quite large numbers of people, being non-native speakers of English, had to learn to use the language in order to survive, or to find employment with the governing class. These NNS learners were of two kinds: indigenous people (e.g., in India, Hindus and Moslems; in the United States, settlers of other European origins such as Dutch, Spanish, and French, and freed slaves) and immigrants. Learning English (though not, generally speaking, being taught English) now became a major activity.

After 1900, and until about 1950, a fourth stage in the creation of today's global English took place, at an increasing pace, when the colonies began to build schools and to offer education, in English, to a small but growing fraction of the indigenous population, while in the United States, Canada, and Australia the provision began of English language classes for immigrants.

English in the Modern World: New Uses and Functions

The most recent stage, which is still going on, began around 1945 and contains two distinct strands: first, nearly all the remaining colonies of Britain became independent states, and at once the role and function of English changed from being an instrument of subservience to other, quite different ends, such as a "window on the world of science and technology," or as the only language not rejected by one section of the population or another. This has been a period, in such former British states—and also in many of the equivalent countries in the former possessions of France and Holland, and in the formerly U.S.-related territories of the Philippines, Puerto Rico, and Samoa—for the immense explosion of English teaching, both for adults and, even more, for children of school age.

The second strand of the current stage in the development of English concerns the emergence of a number of activities, movements, and subjects that are carried out predominantly (though not exclusively) in English across the world. One of the earliest examples was the international agreement to adopt English for air-traffic control; another, which began with the establishment of the United Nations, was the use of English in the numerous bodies providing international aid and administration. As the telecommunications revolution got under way, English became dominant in the international media, radio and TV, magazines and newspapers. The international pop-music industry relies on English; so, too, do space science and computing technology.[3] The importance of this strand within the recent development of English has been not just the vast numbers of people who now need or want English for these activities, but the fact that using English suddenly has nothing to do with one's nationality or with the historical facts of the spread of English-speaking colonies. The Peruvian air pilot, from a country relatively untouched by past British (or American) expansionism, nevertheless needs English for his job; the Polish doctor, spending two years working for the World Health Organization in tropical countries, also needs English; pop-music cults generate mania— using English words—in the Soviet Union as well as in Hong Kong or Germany or the United States.

The importance of seeing the spread of English in the historical perspective of stages such as those outlined above is twofold. It situates, as it were, the major different populations of NS and NNS users of English and illuminates their reasons for coming into existence; and it distinguishes these well-known "ethnocentered" uses of English, where it is whole nations and communities in which English has an established role even if only as a recognized "foreign language" in the school system, from the quite different and recent development of "non-ethnocentered" uses, where the nationality of the individual and linguistic history of his country are equally irrelevant, and what determines the use of English is his or her job, hobby, or field of study.

One further observation about English needs to be made before leaving the facts of world English. The accident of historical events has largely determined where English is used, for ethnocentered purposes, at least. But one characteristic of the language made the process easier and has contributed to the tearaway increase in the non-ethnocentered uses. English is inherently a borrowing and an Anglicizing language. Ever since its earliest beginnings it has been part of the nature of the English language to incorporate ideas, concepts, and expressions from other societies and to make them part of English. And this facility for Anglicization—there were 56 pages of rules for word formation in English in the great Quirk et al. *Grammar of Contemporary English*—was matched by an often avid desire by English users, NS and NNS alike, to borrow and neologize. There is a marked contrast here with the official view concerning French, which holds that the purity of the language would be debased by an "open door" policy on borrowings. It is an interesting speculation whether the contrasting attitudes have contributed to the different history of English and of French in this respect in the past fifty years.

Describing the size and geographical spread of English, noting the distinction between ethnocentered and non-ethnocentered uses of English, and among the ethnocentered users of English distinguishing between NS and NNS—this sets the scene but does not exhaust the range of distinctions that operate and have to be recognized within English. In particular, we need to be aware of (a) the two main branches of English, British English (BE) and American English (AE); (b) the nature of local forms of English (LFE); and (c) the notions of English as a foreign language (EFL) and English as a second language (ESL).

British English and American English: The Two Branches of the Family

It will be obvious that English existed until the early eighteenth century only as a native-speaker variety, and only in the form used in England—then later in Britain as a whole. But already by the time of the American War of Independence a form of English was current in America that was identifiably, almost proudly, American and not British. This was the beginning of the process by which types of English have proliferated. The British-American differentiation is of particular consequence, since every subsequent form of English has affinities with one of the main branches, BE or AE, rather than the other. In practice this means that English in Canada, Puerto Rico, the Philippines, and American Samoa is recognizably related to American English; all other NS and NNS varieties are recognizably related to British English, in this derivational and linguistic sense.[4]

Linguistically speaking, British and American English are far more similar than they are different. While BE and AE each possesses its own range of local dialectal variants, educated usage is by and large sufficiently similar for easy intercommunication. At the level of grammar, there are remarkably few differences of consequence, though there are a number of trivial differences of the type of: BE *in hospital*—AE *in the hospital;* BE *the book will be published on Friday*—AE *the book will be published Friday;* AE *I already had my breakfast*—BE *I've already had my breakfast;* AE *Do you have your passport with you? Yes, I do*—BE *Have you got your passport with you? Yes, I have;* and so forth. At the lexical level there are a great many possible variations, it is true; however, as far as native speakers of BE and AE are concerned, it is very rare and transitory for differences of vocabulary to interrupt the flow of meaning.

At the level of pronunciation, the systems (of vowels, consonants, stress, rhythm) are similar, but the "coloring," as it were, of the sounds

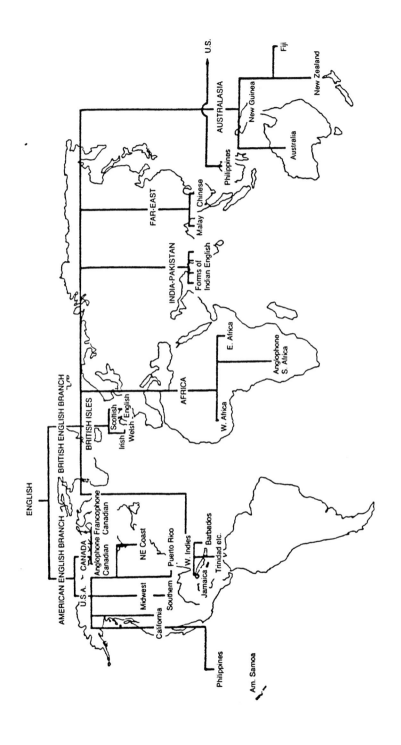

is different, and there are a number of defining features to each. Thus American English pronunciations have an "*r*-colored vowel" in words like *bird, peer, park,* etc., where many BE accents have no indication of any *r*-sound; intervocalic *t*-sounds in AE are barely voiceless at all, so that (to a BE speaker) AE *writer, waiting, matter* sound identical to *rider, wading, madder;* the stress on many two-syllable words is different, e.g., AE *CIGarette,* BE *cigarETTE,* AE *ADdress,* BE *adDRESS;* and patterns of intonation have several detailed points of difference.

In essence, BE and AE are more similar, or more different, according to whether one wishes to stress similarities or differences not just of linguistic features but of the whole way of life which each reflects and is a part of.

Local Forms of English

I referred at the outset to the existence of many Englishes: Indian English, Australian English, West African English, and so forth. Now we can see that wherever there is an English-using community, sufficiently large and sufficiently stable as a community, there may arise a localized form of English (LFE), identifiable and definable through its distinctive mixture of features of grammar, lexis, pronunciation, discourse, and style. The existence of a label like "Singapore English," "East African English," etc., is evidence that a localized form has emerged and is used in that community.

Thus LFE provides a single term to refer to the great proliferation of English in the world today. LFEs vary greatly and in numerous ways. Some are complex, with many subdivisions: "Indian English" is the name commonly applied without distinction to a great many subdivisions of the LFE of English in India. India is a non-native-speaker community, but its vast social and geographical scale ensures that the LFE consists of one version among railway officials in Mysore, another version among teachers of English in secondary schools in Bombay, yet another among civil servants in Delhi, and so forth. "Philippine English" also displays a considerable range of internal variations. "Sierra Leone English" has fewer variations, but the special history of Sierra Leone as a community originally created as a homeland back in Africa for former slaves from America and the Caribbean, and the existence of Krio, a partly English creole language unique to the capital city of Freetown, means that while Indian English and Sierra Leone English are both LFEs, their detailed anatomies, so to speak, are very different.

LFEs change with time: for example, Singapore English and Malaysian English are now more different from each other than was the case twenty years ago, because of the different history of the status and teaching of English since the two countries became separated. And new LFEs can emerge: there is growing evidence of an "Educated European English," used by business people, professional administrators from France, Germany, Holland, Italy, etc., to communicate together, and in which they recognize each other as Europeans by performing in English with common features, but each with his/her own accent. And of course there are a great many countries where no LFE recognizably exists, and others where it could be said that an LFE is beginning to emerge within a particular subgroup—for example, among Japanese scientists and business managers.

NS-NNS, Mother Tongue, Foreign Language, Second Language

In the discussion of English as an international language confusion is sometimes caused through not adequately distinguishing the four different perspectives among which the discussion fluctuates. These are: (1) *the English language* and the populations who use it; (2) *the individual* and the language or languages he/she is able to use; (3) *the status of English* within a given country; and (4) *the learning and teaching of English.*

Each of these perspectives requires a different set of terms. For the first perspective, that of the language itself and the users of it, we have already adopted the distinction between native-speaker populations and non-native-speaker populations. For the other perspectives different terms are needed.

The individual human being, viewed as a user of language, typically acquires during infancy and childhood command of the language in use around him/her during this period of development. Usually this primary language is the language used by the child's mother, which is why the conversational label *mother tongue* is often used—but of course less usually the child may not be brought up by its mother, or the mother may deliberately employ a language different from her own "mother tongue," or in a significant number of upbringings the child may simultaneously acquire more than one language and become known as *bilingual*. Having acquired one or more languages in infancy, a human being may (or may not) later gain some command— nearly always less in scope and certainty than command of the "mother tongue"—of one or more other languages. This may occur through the incidental circumstances of life—travel, emigration, marriage into a different language community—or through the operation of educational policy, whether as the conscripted recipient of obligatory language teaching at school or as the volunteer seeker after language instruction for the instrumental reasons of job or study, or for the integrative reasons of cooperation with people of another language community.

There are strong reasons for believing that the role and function within the psyche of the individual human being that is fulfilled by the "mother tongue" is different in kind from that of any subsequent language, and that while in principle any human being can gain a degree of practical command of any other language, the task of doing so is inherently different in certain ways from the acquisition of the mother tongue.[5] Hence the need, when speaking in the perspective of the individual, for terms that unambiguously distinguish between languages having these two different roles: primary language (L_1) and secondary language (L_2).[6] So in our earlier discussion of NS and NNS users of English, "native speakers" are those for whom English is the primary language; "non-native speakers" are those for whom English is a secondary language.

However, turning to the perspective of the status of English, in an English-using community where English is a secondary language for most or all of the users, its status will be one of two possible types: it will be either a *foreign language* or a *second language*. English is a *foreign language* within a community when it has no special standing but is simply "just another language"; whereas English is a *second* language when it has special standing, such as being acceptable in the courts of law, being the medium of instruction in major sectors of the educational system, being used in regional or national administration, being commonly used on radio or television, and where there are major newspapers published in English. The term *second language* can apply equally with languages other than English: French is a second language in Côte d'Ivoire and in Lebanon, for example.[7]

Bringing together some of these terms, one would say that among the NNS populations of English users some live in EFL countries and some in ESL countries, though for all these users of English it is a secondary language. To give some further examples, English is EFL in Korea, ESL in Nigeria; EFL in Brazil, ESL in Hong Kong; EFL in China, ESL in the Philippines; EFL in France, ESL in Cyprus; EFL in Sweden, ESL in Gibraltar; EFL in Indonesia, ESL in Fiji; and so forth.

Why does the FL/SL distinction matter? Is it more than simply whether there has been an earlier historical connection with Britain (or France)? The answer is that it makes a very considerable difference, when it comes to the teaching and learning of English, whether the environment is FL or SL: it affects the extent of the learner's prior familiarity with English, it affects the learner's expectations of success, and it affects both the average level of attainment reached by most learners (higher overall in ESL than in EFL countries) and the ultimate norms or goals for success which learners and teachers set themselves (aspiring to L_1–like in EFL countries, aspiring rather to an NNS target in ESL countries). This consideration leads us to a further crucial segment of the study of English as an international language: the question of norms and standards.

Attitudes, Norms, and Standards

Before discussing standards and models of English for use in teaching EFL/ESL we must face a central issue. The great majority of the world's English users, being non-native users, speak and write varieties different in detail from NS varieties. But many native speakers— perhaps the majority, even among teachers of English—overtly or unconsciously despise these varieties; these NS attitudes are in turn perceived by the non-native speaker as being arrogant, imperialist, and insulting. Thus, speaking from his own experience, Kachru (1982) says, "to have one's English labeled *Indian* was an ego-cracking linguistic insult." And elsewhere (1986), "the inevitable nativization of English by the black and brown sahibs (as the English-knowing natives were called) did not go unnoticed by the colonizers and provided a storehouse of hilarious linguistic anecdotes to be related in the 'white-only' clubs. . . .The second language user never seemed to win in this see-saw of attitudes. If he gained 'native-like' competence he was suspect; if he did not gain it he was an object of linguistic ridicule."

A precisely similar conflict of attitudes occurs whenever a native speaker criticizes or rejects non-native varieties of English. The basic reason for these native speakers' attitudes is ignorance—a total lack of awareness of the existence of flourishing, effective, functional, sometimes elegant and literary non-native varieties of English. Most NS, including teachers of EFL/ESL, have not experienced NNS varieties of English in the circumstances of their origins, e.g., in India, Singapore, West Africa, etc., or even read much about them. Consequently, they wrongly equate variations from NS norms with classroom errors and mistakes, or regard NNS varieties as some kind of interlanguage[8] on the path to NS English. In fact, most NNS varieties of English embrace a range of forms and styles pidgin-like at one extreme and NS-like at the other. The NNS user is likely to switch effortlessly from one to another as the need arises. For instance, Bamgboṣe (in Ch. 8 of this volume) describes four identifiable varieties of Nigerian English.

In fact, there is a complex world of NNS English that most native speakers are not aware of. The English language presents challenges and problems in non-native contexts, and these are being met with at least the intelligence and subtlety of the native speaker. Kachru (in Ch. 3 of this volume), for example, offers a typology of non-native Englishes: "One might . . . consider [the varieties of English] in *acquisitional* terms, in *sociocultural* terms, in *motivational* terms, and in *functional* terms.

More recently, the same author has referred to "three concentric circles of world Englishes" (in Quirk and Widdowson 1985: 12-13):

> The spread of English may be viewed in terms of three concentric circles representing the types of spread, the patterns of acquisition and the functional domains in which English is used across cultures and languages. I have tentatively labeled these: the *inner* circle, the *outer* circle (or *extended* circle), and the *expanding* circle. In terms of the users, the inner circle refers to the traditional bases of English—the regions where it is the primary language. . . .
>
> Numerically, the outer circle forms a large speech community with great diversity and distinct characteristics. The major features of this circle are that (a) English is only one of two or more codes in the linguistic repertoire of such bilinguals or multilinguals, and (b) English has acquired an important status in the language policies of most of such multilingual nations. . . .
>
> The third circle, termed the expanding circle, brings to English yet another dimension. Understanding the function of English in this circle requires a recognition of the fact that English is an international language, and that it has already won the race in this respect with linguistic rivals such as French, Russian and Esperanto, to name just two natural languages and one artificial language. The geographical regions characterized as the expanding circle do not necessarily have a history of colonization by the users of the inner circle. . . . This circle is currently expanding rapidly and has resulted in numerous performance (or EFL) varieties of English.

The history and experience of the United States and Britain have been significantly different in regard to the emergence of non-native varieties. As Britain's large number of colonies approached political independence, so there emerged the same kind of nascent pride in their own identity reflected in their language that we noticed in respect of American English two hundred years ago. Already in 1960 some British teachers of EFL in Africa were beginning to believe that it was no longer appropriate to expect Ghanaian and Nigerian schoolchildren to speak English like the British, and they already tacitly accepted the position stated more recently by the Singapore ambassador to the

United Nations: "I should hope that when I am speaking abroad my countrymen will have no problem recognizing that I am a Singaporean."

The U.S. experience in teaching English has been, by contrast, dominated by the need to teach it within the United States to great numbers of immigrants, for whom the need to assimilate to (American) native-speaker usage was more important than the need to develop an independent identity in their English. In the 1960s the more tolerant position described earlier was labeled "the British heresy" (Prator 1968), and it remains substantially true that American EFL/ESL teachers are less aware of the great diversity of English and tend more often to assume that an NS model is appropriate for all circumstances. That position has been cogently criticized in Kachru (1986).

Is There a Global Norm or "Standard" for English?

Outside the context of teaching, the norms of English are, in practice, set in relation to the NS or NNS usages outlined above: that is to say, each community sets its own goals and targets, usually without conscious decision, since there is no Academy or other authority for English which determines the norm. (For a detailed discussion, see Ch. 3.)

At the same time, there exists an unspoken mechanism, operated through the global industry of English teaching, which has the effect of preserving the unity of English in spite of its great diversity. For throughout the world, regardless of whether the norm is native-speaker or non-native-speaker variety, irrespective of whether English is a foreign or a second language, two components of English are taught and learned without variation: these are its *grammar* and its *core vocabulary.* There may be embellishments in the way of local vocabulary and expressions,[9] and there will certainly be great differences of pronunciation, but the grammar and vocabulary of English are taught and learned virtually without variation around the world.

We can be more explicit: among virtually all the myriad local dialectal variations of English worldwide, there is a "twinning" of lexico-grammar and phonology: it is unknown for the grammar and vocabulary of, say, Oklahoma rural speech to be spoken with the accent of Cape Cod; or for the accent of Birmingham, England (or for that matter, Birmingham, Alabama), to clothe the grammar and the local vocabulary of San Francisco or Singapore. Accents and lexico-grammars belong together and do not switch; also they are strictly local in their currency. *Except for one single example.* There is just one set of grammatical patterns and core vocabulary which has two absolutely crucial characteristics. First, it is accepted everywhere throughout the English-using world, not just in one single locality. And second, it has no "twinned" accent: it is spoken with any and every accent in the world. This is the grammar and vocabulary of educated usage, and it is the educational model used throughout the world.[10]

Herein lies the principal reason why the EFL/ESL teacher does not teach purely local patterns of grammar: for example, the pronoun system of English in parts of northeast England contains the same form *us* for the subject, object, and the possessive:

Us had best take us coats: happen it will rain.
(We had better take our coats: it might rain.)

The avoidance of this grammatical pattern and of the lexical item *happen* is not because the forms are "wrong," nor because they are inferior or substandard, but because they are used and accepted only in that geographical area and among that community: they would be unacceptable elsewhere. But local pronunciations, by contrast, do not cause more than passing unfamiliarity.

As long as teachers of English continue to teach the lexico-grammar of "educated/educational English," the unity of the language will transcend its immense diversity.

It is in this context that one should consider the pedagogical problem which, for the non-native speaker, learner, or teacher of English, often seems the most difficult. Which English should I learn, or teach? In particular, should I learn (or teach) American rather than British English, or vice versa? The answer given to the learner must be in two parts: first, learn educated/educational English; second, if you have a choice of an American or a British model, choose the one that will be most useful. Do not waste time agonizing over which is "better": both are equally good, and indeed it could even be that in your circumstances it is a localized form of English that will be the most appropriate. The answer given to the teacher must also be in two parts. First, teach the kind of English you use; do not try and teach British English if you speak American English, or vice versa. Second, teach as well—i.e., with as much professionalism—as you can.

Learning and Teaching English as an International Language

Consideration of norms and standards has inevitably taken us into pedagogical questions. As far as teaching English as an international language is concerned, the decisive difference in outlook (as compared with the conventional attitudes toward TEFL and TESL) is the recognition that in the great NNS populations English will be taught mostly *by* non-native speakers of the language, *to* non-native speakers, in order to communicate mainly *with* non-native speakers. Smith (1983) says:

> It is the widespread use of English which makes it an international language. This does not mean, however, that soon everyone everywhere will be speaking English, wearing jeans and dancing to a disco beat. The spread of English is not a homogenizing factor which causes cultural differences to disappear, but the use of English offers a medium to express and explain these differences. There is no desire among members of the world community when using English to become more like native speakers in their life style. Native speakers must realize that there are many valid varieties of English and that non-native speakers need not sound or act like Americans, the British, or any other group of native speakers in order to be effective English users. English is being used as an international language in diplomacy, international trade, and tourism. Native speakers need as much help as non-natives when using English to interact internationally. There is no room for linguistic chauvinism.

The same author (Smith 1983) summarizes many of the educational differences between ESOL (English for speakers of other languages; i.e., conventional ESL/EFL) and EIIL (English as an international auxiliary language).

In terms of approach and methodology, it is not so much that teaching English as an international language has introduced major changes. It is rather that the gradual sophistication in learning and teaching English has now added a new element: awareness of the fact that most ESL/EFL today relates to NNS populations requiring English for their internal purposes, or for dealing with other NNS populations, without the presence or intervention of native speakers.

The process of gradual sophistication has brought ESL/EFL a long way in barely forty years. From "teaching English" (undifferentiated as to the learners, and chiefly based on literature) to "English language teaching" (witness the title of one of the oldest professional publications in this field: *English Language Teaching Journal*) to the distinction, first made in British ELT, between EFL and ESL (ESL in British Commonwealth countries, EFL elsewhere), to TESOL (uniting, especially in America, teachers of all the varying groups of learners), adding ESP (English for specific purposes) in recognition of the emergence of non-ethnocentric uses of English, and now incorporating EIL (English for international purposes)—the trend is toward ever more

Table 1. Some Distinctive Features of ESOL vs. EIIL

	Scope and Depth of Language Treatment	"Official-dom" Public Function	Purpose of Learning	Student Population
ESOL: English as a Foreign Language	general English English for Special Purposes	school subject	(a) limited use as a tool for jobs (b) higher education Communication: low priority	Non-native speakers
ESOL: English as a Second Language	general English to greater depth and range than EFL English for Special Purposes	medium of instruction *lingua franca*	for international and internal interactions Communication: high priority	Non-native speakers
EIIL: English as an Intranational Language	general English English for Special Purposes	may be medium of instruction *lingua franca*	for internal interaction Communication: high priority	Non-native speakers
EIIL: English as an International Language	general English English for Special Purposes	international business ads sports news diplomacy travel entertainment	for international interactions Communication: high priority	Native and non-native speakers

subtle differentiations of the learners, their purposes, their speech communities.

Over the same period there has also been an extension to the range of "resource countries" providing the intellectual and material

Language Model	Performance Target	Language Interactors	Cultural Emphasis
educated native speaker	performance level of educated native speaker	$(L_2 \leftrightarrow L_1)$	culture of native speakers
educated native speaker or educated speaker of local variety of English	performance level of educated native speaker or educated speaker of local variety of English	$(L_2 \leftrightarrow L_1)$ intranational $(L_2 \leftrightarrow L_2)$	culture of (a) native speakers (b) local country- men
educated native speaker or educated speaker of local variety of English	performance level of educated speaker of local variety of English	intrana- tional $(L_2 \leftrightarrow L_2)$	culture of local countrymen
any educated English speaker (native speaker, local, or regional)	mutual intelligibility and appropriate language for situation	$(L_2 \leftrightarrow L_1)$ international $(L_2 \leftrightarrow L_2)$ international $(L_1 \leftrightarrow L_1)$	culture of specified countries

bases of EFL/ESL and supplying teachers for work in NNS countries. Originally Britain and the United States were the obvious and sole resource countries. Now increasingly Canada, Australia, and New Zealand contribute in the same way; India has supplied teachers of

English to China; Belgian teachers teach English in Morocco; while in the Arabian Gulf States a great many teachers of English are from Pakistan, or were educated in Palestine when it was a British English ESL country.

Two further dimensions of change need to be mentioned: (1) the great advance in effective learning of English through informed teaching. In its highest forms, EFL now produces some of the most rapid and effective of any language teaching. (2) Linked with this is a great increase in professionalism in teaching and in teacher preparation. These two kinds of improvement have been encouraged and made possible by the economic strength flowing from the vast demand for English. It is interesting to notice that these improvements have had a distinctively different flavor on the two sides of the Atlantic: the American intellectual basis for teacher preparation, mainly for ESL, has remained closer to theoretical linguistics; the British equivalents, chiefly for EFL, derive from applied linguistics and lean heavily on the development of a very rich classroom methodology. In both cases there has been a recent swing toward more learner-centered learning and teaching, which itself is only made possible by an increased professionalism among teachers, as they are more and more aware of English on the international plane, not simply in the confines of their own classrooms.

Conclusion

The changes with which this chapter started, namely the spread of English to its present level of perhaps 1.5 billion users and the proliferation of large numbers of different Englishes, are the same changes that have energized current developments in teaching methodology and in the professionalism of teacher preparation. And they still continue apace today. However adequately this article deals with the complexities of English as an international language, there is no doubt that in a further twenty years there will be other major chapters to add to the story.

NOTES

1. Although it does not use the plural "Englishes" in its title, another new magazine, *English Today*, takes the global existence of English as its basis and treats in more popular forms, somewhat after the style of *The Economist* or *Scientific American*, issues such as those at the heart of this chapter.

2. Crystal refers to "English users": I am equating them here with the

commoner term "English speakers." *Speaker* is, in practice, a vague term relating to speaking and to writing, indiscriminately.

3. Of course, other languages than English are employed in relation to each of these trends and activities. There is pop music in French; in rural Québec some air-traffic control is in French; French is an official language of the Council of Europe and of the European Community (the "Common Market"). Similarly, there are great areas of use for Spanish, for German, for Russian, and so forth. Nevertheless, the position of English is in practice a privileged one, and it is in a sense the superordinate language of these activities.

4. A test of this is the frequent identification of British visitors to Hawaii, by residents of Hawaii, as being Australian. They recognize the speech as "non-American" (and hence never assume that the visitors are Canadian, however "British" in other respects some Canadians may seem), but since Australian and New Zealand visitors are the British who are most frequently encountered, Hawaiian residents usually plump for "You must be Australian."

5. This is not to deny that some of the mental processes and learning mechanisms employed by the infant are used also in learning additional languages. However, there is a unique emotional and psychological role played by the very first language encountered by the infant during its early formative years. All other languages are learned by a mind that already has language: the "mother tongue" changes the young mind by the very fact of its acquisition.

6. Note that the cultural and linguistic history of an individual may eventually, in rather rare conditions, lead to a language originally learned as a secondary language becoming for all practical purposes another, or even a replacement, primary language. For this to occur the degree of command of the secondary language has to become comparable to that of the primary language; or command of the primary language may be gradually lost through attrition and lack of opportunity to use or experience it.

7. It is necessary to take precautions against confusion when using the word "second" in relation to language. The principal terms are *primary* and *secondary* language (of the individual), conveniently shortened to L_1 and L_2. It is best to avoid expressions like *second foreign language* (e.g., in school). Even the usage *second language acquisition* (SLA) is unfortunate. *Secondary language acquisition,* or *acquisition of a secondary language* (ASL) would have been terminologically preferable.

8. Among the unfortunate consequences of the popularity of *interlanguage* studies among EFL/ESL teachers (important though interlanguage may be as a concept in psycholinguistics) have been the unquestioned assumptions that (1) all deviations from an adult norm are deviations from a single NS norm, and (2) all interlanguages, or all individuals and groups, are points on a path toward a single, universal native-speaker norm. Interlanguage theory was originally developed in the context of the psychological conditions of the individual: social conditions and processes were of a minor relevance. But latterly *interlanguage* has been used almost synonymously with "social dialect,"

and assumptions have been created that fail to take account of the ways in which language is used in society.

9. Craig 1982, building on the work of Le Page, lists ten classes of additions to British English usage that categorize Caribbean English, including:

—Words which have become obsolete in England.

—Words used in a sense which has become obsolete in England.

—Borrowings from dialect, non-standard English.

—Words adapted to a new sense [in the Caribbean].

—Words whose pronunciation has been changed so radically that they must be regarded as [Caribbeanisms].

—Words which may serve a greater number of grammatical functions than in England—e.g., as transitive verbs used only intransitively in England.

—Words that have an African origin.

—Phrases which are relexifications or calques of African forms of expression.

10. It is customary, in British applied linguistics, to use the term *dialect* to refer to grammar-plus-vocabulary, and *accent* to refer to pronunciation. The educated/educational lexico-grammar described in this paragraph is then known as *Standard English* dialect.

REFERENCES

Bamgboṣe, Ayọ. 1982. Standard Nigerian English: issues of identification. In this volume.

Craig, Dennis R. 1982. Toward a description of Caribbean English. In Kachru 1982.

Crystal, David. 1985. How many millions? The statistics of English today. *English Today* 1:1.

Ferguson, Charles A., and Shirley Brice Heath, eds. 1981. *Language in the USA.* Cambridge and New York: Cambridge University Press.

Fishman, J., C. Ferguson, and J. Das Gupta, eds. 1968. *Language problems of developing nations.* New York: Wiley.

Kachru, Braj B. 1981. The pragmatics of non-native varieties of English. In Smith 1981.

———, ed. 1982. *The other tongue: English across cultures.* Urbana: University of Illinois Press.

———. 1986. *The alchemy of English: the spread, models and functions of non-native Englishes.* Oxford: Pergamon. Reprinted 1990, Urbana: University of Illinois Press.

Mencken, H. L. 1919. *The American language.* New York: Knopf.

Prator, Clifford H. 1968. The British heresy in TESL. In Fishman et al. 1968.

Quirk, Randolph, Sidney Greenbaum, Geoffrey Leech, and Jan Svartvik. 1972. *Grammar of contemporary English.* London: Longman.

Quirk, Randolph, and H. G. Widdowson, eds. 1985. *English in the world: teaching and learning the language and literatures.* Cambridge: Cambridge University Press.

Smith, Larry E., ed. 1981. *English for cross-cultural communication.* London: Macmillan.

————, ed. 1983. *Readings in English as an international language.* Oxford: Pergamon.

Strevens, Peter. 1980. *Teaching English as an international language.* Oxford: Pergamon.

————. 1982a. *What is Standard English?* Singapore: RELC.

————. 1982b. World English and the world's Englishes; or, whose language is it, anyway? *Journal of the Royal Society of Arts* (June): 418–31.

————. 1985. Standards and the standard language. *English Today* 1(2): 5–8.

3

Braj B. Kachru

Models for Non-Native Englishes

In discussing the concept "model," a distinction has to be made between the use of this term in theory construction—for example, a *model* for linguistic description (see, e.g., Revzin 1966)—and its use in pedagogical literature, where *model* is sometimes interrelated with *method* (see, e.g., Brooks 1960; Christophersen 1973; Cochran 1954; Finnocchiaro 1964; Gauntlett 1957; Halliday et al. 1964; Lado 1964; and Stevick 1957).[1] In pedagogical literature the term "model" is used in two senses: first, in the sense of acceptability, generally by the native speakers of a language; second, in the sense of fulfilling codified prerequisites according to a given "standard" or "norm" at various linguistic levels. In this sense, then, we may say that a model provides a *proficiency scale*. This *scale* may be used to ascertain if a learner has attained proficiency according to a given norm. The term "norm" is again used in two senses: in one sense it entails prescriptivism, and in another it entails conformity with the usage of the majority of native speakers, defined statistically. (For a detailed discussion, see Lara 1976.)

Motivations for a Model

The question of a model for English has acquired immense pedagogical importance, mainly for two reasons. First, non-native varieties of English have emerged in areas such as South Asia (Kachru 1969 and later), Southeast Asia (Crewe 1977; Richards and Tay 1981), Africa (Spencer 1971a), the Philippines (Llamzon 1969), and the West Indies (Craig 1982; Haynes 1982). Second, in those areas where English is a native language, as in North America and Scotland, this question of model has often been raised with reference to bidialectism.

The identification of specific "non-standard" dialects leads to questions: Which dialect should be taught for what function? And what should be the role of bidialectism in the school system? These and related questions are being debated in educational and linguistic circles (see, e.g., Bailey 1970; Bernstein 1964; Burling 1970; Ellis 1967; Labov 1966, 1969; Riley 1978; Shuy 1971; Sledd 1969; Stewart 1970; and Wolfram 1970). Educators and linguists are also concerned about maintaining national and international intelligibility in various varieties of English. (See, e.g., Christophersen 1960; Kachru 1976a; and Prator 1968. For a "state of the art" understanding of this important subject, see Tickoo, ed. 1991, esp. Section 3.)

We may discuss "model" either as a general concept, or as a language-specific concept. In language-specific terms, for example, as in the case of English, one has to discuss it in the context of sociocultural, educational, and political motivations for the spread of English. The term "spread" is used here to refer to "an increase, over time, in the proportion of a communications network that adopts a given language variety for given communicative function" (Cooper 1979: 23).

The question of a "model" is then also related to the question of language spread. In the case of the spread of English, one might ask, Does English have an organized agency which undertakes the job of providing direction toward a *standardized* model and toward controlling *language change*—as is the case, for example, with French? Such attempts to control innovations or deviations from a "standard" in English through an Academy were not taken very seriously in Britain or in North America. The first such proposals by Jonathan Swift in Britain (around 1712) and by John Adams (in 1821; see Heath 1977) in America were not received with enthusiasm. One must then ask: In spite of the nonexistence of an organized Academy, what factors have determined linguistic "etiquette" in English, and what models of acquisition have been suggested?

The documented models of English have no authority of codification from a government or a body of scholars as is the case, for example, with Spanish (see Bolinger 1975: 569) or French. The sanctity of models of English stems more from social and attitudinal factors than from reasons of authority. These models, more widely violated than followed, stand more for elitism than for authority—and in that sense they have a disadvantage. The native models of English were documented partly for pragmatic and pedagogical reasons. There was a demand from the non-native learners of English for materials on learning and teaching pronunciation, for standards of usage and correctness, and for linguistic "table manners" for identifying with native speakers.

Some native speakers also wanted "authoritative" or normative codes for "proper" linguistic behavior. Of course, there have always been linguistic entrepreneurs who have catered to such demands from consumers. In 1589 Puttenham recommended that the model should be the "usual speech of the court, and that of London and the shires lying about London within 60 miles and not much above." Cooper (1687) went a step further and provided such a book for "gentlemen, ladies, merchants, tradesmen, schools and strangers," with the enticing title *The English Teacher, or, The Discovery of the Art of Teaching and Learning the English Tongue.*

This non-authoritarian elitist prescriptivism is also found in several manuals and books on usage. A typical title, following this tradition, is *The Grammarian, or, The Writer and Speaker's Assistant; comprising shall and will made easy to foreigners, with instances of their misuse on the part of the natives of England.* This book by J. Beattie appeared in 1838. The often-quoted work on *Modern English Usage* by Fowler (1926) also belongs to this tradition. (See also, e.g., Alford 1869; Baker 1770; also relevant to this discussion are Hill 1954; Leonard 1929; Whitten and Whitaker 1939.)

In English when one talks of a model, the reference is usually to two well-documented models, namely Received Pronunciation (RP) and General American (GA). Non-native speakers of English often aim at a close approximation of these models, even at the risk of sounding affected. The works of Daniel Jones and John S. Kenyon encouraged such attempts. What Jones's *Outline of English Phonetics* (1918) or *English Pronouncing Dictionary* (1956) did for RP, Kenyon's *American Pronunciation* (1924) did for GA in a restricted sense.

What type of "standard" do these pronunciation norms provide? RP as a model is about a hundred years old and is closely associated with the English public schools. Abercrombie, in his excellent paper, considers it unique "because the public schools are themselves unique" (1951: 12). Because it is acquired unconsciously, says Abercrombie, "there is no question of deliberately teaching it." The status of RP is based on social judgment and has no official authority. The advent of broadcasting played an important role in making RP widely known; it was therefore identified with the British Broadcasting Corporation (BBC) and also termed "BBC English" (see Gimson 1970: 83; Ward 1929: chs. 1, 2). In the changed British context, Abercrombie makes three points. First, the concept of a standard pronunciation such as

RP is "a bad rather than a good thing. It is an anachronism in present-day democratic society" (1951: 14). Second, it provides an "accent-bar" which does not reflect the social reality of England. "The accent-bar is a little like colour-bar—to many people, on the right side of the bar, it appears eminently reasonable" (1951: 15). Finally, RP does not necessarily represent "educated English," for while "those who talk RP can justly consider themselves educated, they are outnumbered these days by the undoubtedly educated people who do not talk RP" (1951: 15).

The term "General American" refers to the variety of English spoken by about 90 million people in the central and western United States and in most of Canada. (See Krapp 1919; Kenyon 1924: vii, 14.) In describing GA, Kenyon was not presenting a model in the same sense in which Jones had earlier presented his. Rather, Kenyon suggests linguistic tolerance toward various American varieties of English. He is conscious of the harm done by the elitist, prescriptivist manuals for pronunciation and therefore is concerned that "we accept rules of pronunciation as authoritative without inquiry into either the validity of the rules or the fitness of their authors to promulgate them" (1924: 3). The cause for such easy "judgment" or quick "advice" on matters connected with pronunciation is that people are "influenced by certain types of teaching in the schools, by the undiscriminating use of textbooks on grammar and rhetoric, by unintelligent use of the dictionary, by manuals of 'correct English,' each with its favorite (and different) shibboleth" (1924: 3).

Kenyon's distaste for linguistic homogeneity is clear when he says, "Probably no intelligent person actually expects cultivated people in the South, the East, and the West to pronounce alike. Yet much criticism, or politely silent contempt, of the pronunciations of cultivated people in other localities than our own is common" (1924: 5). In his view the remedy for this intolerance is the study of phonetics. A student of phonetics "soon learns not only to refrain from criticizing pronunciations that differ from his own, but to expect them and listen for them with respectful, intelligent interest."

Now, despite the arbitrariness of the above two models, one usually is asked the questions: What is a standard (or model) for English?[2] And what model should be accepted? The first question is easy, and Ward (1929: 1) has given the answer in crisp words: "No one can adequately define it, because such a thing does not exist." And, in the case of English, as Strevens (1981) says, " 'standard' here does *not* imply 'imposed,' nor yet 'of the majority.' One interesting aspect of Standard English is that in every English-using community those who habitually use *only* standard English are in a minority."

Model and the Norm

It has generally been claimed (see, e.g., Bloomfield 1933: 56) that being bilingual entails having "native-like" proficiency in a language. A rigid application of this rather elusive yardstick is evident in the fast-increasing literature and growing number of texts for the teaching of English as L_2. It is more evident in the structural method which followed the tenets of structural linguistics in America. Consider for example the following, which is typical of such an attitude (see Lado 1964: 89):

> Authentic models: Teachers can now provide authentic pronunciation models easily for their students by means of a tape recorder or a phonograph. Visitors and professional speakers can be recorded for the benefit of students, thus bringing to the class a variety of good native speakers even when the teacher does not happen to be a native speaker of the target language.

In purely pedagogical methods, with no underlying serious theoretical framework, such as the structural method developed at the Institute of Education, London,[3] the same ideal goal for pronunciation was propounded.

One cannot disagree that the criterion of "native-like" control is appropriate for *most* language-learning situations. But then, one must pause and reconsider whether such a goal for performance can be applied to the case of English in *all* situations. The case of English is unique because of its global *spread* in various linguistically and culturally pluralistic societies; its differing *roles* in language planning in each English-using country; and the special historical factors involved in the introduction and diffusion of English in each English-speaking country. Therefore it is rather difficult to define the "norm" for various speakers of Englishes.

Origin of Non-Native Models

The origin of non-native models therefore must be related to what is termed "the context of situation"—the historical context, and the educational setting. Furthermore, it should be emphasized that the question of a "model" for English did not originally arise with reference to a model for "non-native" users of English. This issue has a rather interesting history, essentially with reference to the transplanted *native* varieties of English. The attitude of American English users provides a fascinating and illuminating controversy on this topic, which eventually turned into a national debate (see Heath 1977; Kahane and Kahane 1977).[4] This national debate provides a good case study of the relationship of political emancipation to language, and identification of language with nationalism. The controversy of the *American* identity of the English language has received more attention and therefore is better known, for which credit must be given to Mencken (1919). But in Britain itself there is the case of Scottish identity, and on a far-off continent, Australia, murmurs for such identity have been heard in an occasional publication (see, e.g., Kaldor 1991).

In the case of *non-native* varieties, the situation is much different. There has never been a Mencken, or a Webster. The local identity for English was never related to political emancipation or national pride. On the contrary, the general idea was that, with the end of the Raj, the English language would be replaced by a native language or languages. The demand was not for an identity with English, but for abolition of English; not for nativization of English, but for its replacement. In recent years, however, the concept has been primarily discussed with reference to non-native Englishes. What do we understand by that term? The distinction between *native* and *non-native* varieties of English (Kachru 1981; Kachru and Quirk 1981) is crucial for understanding the formal and functional characteristics of English.

In the international context, it is more realistic to consider a spectrum of Englishes which vary widely, ranging from standard native varieties to standard non-native varieties (see Kachru 1976a, 1981, 1982; Quirk et al. 1972: 13–32). The situation of English is historically and linguistically interesting and complex for several reasons. First, the number of non-native speakers of English is already significant; if the current trend continues, there will soon be considerably more non-native than native speakers of English.[5]

The spread of English is unique in another respect. Because the language is used in geographically, linguistically, and culturally diverse areas, its use cuts across political boundaries (Fishman et al. 1977; Smith 1981). The large range of varieties of English cannot be discussed from any one point of view. There are several, mutually *non*-exclusive ways to discuss their form and function. One might, for example, consider them in *acquisitional* terms, in *sociocultural* terms, in *motivational* terms, and in *functional* terms. These may further be divided as follows:

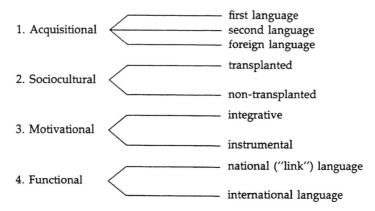

1. Acquisitional
— first language
— second language
— foreign language

2. Sociocultural
— transplanted
— non-transplanted

3. Motivational
— integrative
— instrumental

4. Functional
— national ("link") language
— international language

A further distinction is necessary between English as a second language and English as a *foreign* language. (See Christophersen 1973: 30–31; Quirk et al. 1972: 32–4.) The second language varieties of English are essentially institutionalized varieties, as in, for example, South Asia and West Africa. The foreign language varieties are primarily performance varieties, as in Iran, Japan, etc. This distinction is also important with reference to the role and functions of English in the educational, administrative, and sociocultural context of a country in which English is used as a non-native language. The distinction between a transplanted variety (e.g., American English, Indian English) and a non-transplanted variety is important for the understanding of the acculturation and "nativization" of the transplanted varieties. (For specific case studies see, e.g., Abdulaziz 1978; Bokamba 1982; Craig 1982; Haynes 1982; Kachru 1981, 1982; Kandiah 1978; Richards and Tay 1981; Wong 1981; and Zuengler 1982.)

In the literature, two types of motivations have been suggested for second language acquisition: integrative and instrumental. The distinction is essentially based on what function the L_2 learner envisions for the acquired language. If the learner's motivation is integrative, then the desire is "to identify with the members of the other linguistic cultural group and be willing to take on very subtle aspects of their language *or even their style of speech*" (Prator 1968: 474; his italics). On the other hand, the instrumental approach has been defined as basically "utilitarian"; a language is acquired as a linguistic tool, not as an instrument for cultural integration. Terms such as *library* language, *auxiliary* language, *link* language, or language for *special* purposes (LSP) are essentially utilitarian concepts, in which language is seen as a "restricted" code for a specific goal. In such contexts, acquiring a second culture is not the main motivation for learning the language. (See also Christophersen 1973.)

If we look at the global spectrum of English as a *non-native* language, we can clearly divide, as stated earlier, the non-native uses of English into two broad categories, namely, the performance varieties and the institutionalized varieties. This distinction is extremely useful and is directly related to the question of a model.

The Performance Varieties

Performance varieties include essentially those varieties which are used as *foreign* languages. Identificational modifiers, such as *Japanese* English or *Iranian* English, are indicative of geographical or national performance characteristics. These do not indicate an institutionalized status. The performance varieties of English have a highly restricted functional range in specific contexts; for example, those of tourism, commerce, and other international transactions.

Institutionalized Varieties

It is the institutionalized varieties which have some ontological status. The main characteristics of such varieties are that (a) they have an extended range of uses in the sociolinguistic context of a nation; (b) they have an extended register and style range; (c) a process of *nativization* of the registers and styles has taken place, both in formal and in contextual terms; and (d) a body of nativized English literature has developed which has formal and contextual characteristics which mark it *localized.* On the other hand, such a body of writing is considered a part of the larger body of writing labeled English literature.

An institutionalized variety always starts as a performance variety, with various characteristics slowly giving it a different status. The main characteristics of an institutionalized variety seem to be (a) the length of time in use; (b) the extension of use; (c) the emotional attachment of L_2 users with the variety; (d) functional importance; and (e) sociolinguistic status. In the development of non-native models two processes seem to work simultaneously: the *attitudinal* process, and the *linguistic* process.

A non-native model may be treated as a competitive model for teaching English as L_2 if it fulfills certain conditions. In attitudinal terms, a majority of L_2 speakers should identify themselves with the modifying label which marks the non-nativeness of a model: for example, *Indian* English speakers, *Lankan* English speakers, *Ghanaian* English speakers. A person may be a user of *Indian* English in his linguistic behavior but may not consider it the "norm" for his linguistic

55

performance. There is thus a confusion between linguistic norm and linguistic behavior.

In linguistic terms, a viable model should describe the formal characteristics of a *generally acceptable* variety. If English is used in a culturally and linguistically pluralistic context, the norm for the model should cut across linguistic and cultural boundaries. It is natural that in such a variety a part of the lexicon will have been nativized in two ways. On the one hand, native items will be used in localized registers and styles to contextualize the language. On the other hand, English lexical items may have acquired extended or restricted semantic markers. This process then extends to other levels of language, as has been shown in several studies. (See, e.g., Kachru 1981, 1983, 1986)

Development of Non-Native Models

The term "development" is used here not in the Darwinian sense, but in an essentially historical sense. I shall attempt to discuss it with reference to changing attitudes toward a model, in terms of a scale of acceptance. A variety may exist, but unless it is *recognized* and *accepted* as a model it does not acquire a status. A large majority of the non-native speakers of institutionalized varieties of English use a local variety of English, but when told so, they are hesitant to accept the fact.

The non-native institutionalized varieties of English seem to pass through several phases which are not mutually exclusive. At the initial stage there is a *non-recognition* of the local variety, and conscious identification with the native speakers. In South Asian terms, it may be called the *brown sahib* attitude. A "brown sahib" is more English than the Englishman; he identifies with the "white sahib" in manners, speech, and attitude, and feels that his brown or black color is a burden. At this stage an "imitation model" is elitist, powerful, and perhaps politically advantageous, since it identifies a person with the rulers. This is also the stage when English is associated with the colonizer, and therefore may be a symbol of anti-nationalism.

The second stage is related to extensive diffusion of bilingualism in English, which slowly leads to the development of varieties *within* a variety. The tendency then is to claim that the *other* person is using the *Indianized, Ghanaianized,* or *Lankanized* English. The local model is still low on the attitudinal scale, though it may be widely used in various functions. South Asia provides an excellent example of this attitude. In India, for example, the norm for English was unrealistic and (worse) unavailable—the British variety. In actual performance, typical *Indian* English was used. But to have one's English labeled *Indian* was an ego-cracking linguistic insult.

The third stage starts when the non-native variety is slowly accepted as the norm, and the division between the linguistic norm and behavior is reduced. The final stage seems to be that of *recognition*. This recognition may manifest itself in two ways; first in attitudinal terms, when one does not necessarily show a division between linguistic norm and linguistic behavior. This indicates linguistic realism and attitudinal identification with the variety. Only during the last twenty years or so do we find this attitude developing among the users of non-native varieties of English. Second, the teaching materials are *contextualized* in the native sociocultural milieu. One then begins to recognize the national uses (and importance) of English, and to consider its international uses only marginal.

The literature provides enough evidence that the institutionalized varieties of English have passed through one or more of these stages in Africa, South Asia, Southeast Asia, or the Philippines. I shall not elaborate on this point here.

Functional Uses of Non-Native Englishes

I have earlier used the term "context of situation" without explaining it in the context of the English L_2 situation. There is a relationship between the *context of situation*, the sociolinguistic profile, and the pedagogical model. Before claiming universality for a model, one must understand that what is linguistic medicine for one geographical area may prove linguistic poison for another area.

A sociolinguistic profile should consider the type of information suggested in Catford (1959: 141–42) and in Ferguson (1966: 309–15). The linguistically relevant information is as important as are the political, geographical, and economic factors. In addition, the attitudinal reactions toward an *external* or an *internal* model cannot be neglected. I shall return to that point in the two following sections.

The sociolinguistic context might show a cline (a graded series) both in terms of *proficiency* in English and in its *functional* uses. The English-using community must be seen in a new framework, in which a linguistic activity is under analysis within a specific sociocultural context. Within the framework of *user* and *uses* one has to take into consideration cline of participants, cline of roles, and cline of intelligibility.

Without the perspective of this relationship it is difficult for native speakers of English to understand the uses of non-native Englishes.

This type of approach has been used and recommended in several studies. (See especially Candlin 1981; Kachru 1965, 1966, 1981, 1982, 1983; Richards and Tay 1981.)

The institutionalized varieties of non-native English may be arranged along a lectal continuum. This continuum is not necessarily *developmental* but may be functional. All subvarieties within a variety (for example, basilects, mesolects, and acrolects) have functional values and may stand as clues to code diversity as well as to code development. These are, however, not mutually exclusive.

Let me now briefly elaborate on the functional aspects of a cline. One can claim that, for example, in South Asia, English is used in four functions: the *instrumental*, the *regulative*, the *interpersonal*, and the *imaginative/innovative*.[6] In each function we have a cline in performance which varies from what may be termed an "educated" or "standard" variety to a pidginized or "broken" variety. The varieties *within* a variety also seem to perform their functions, as they do in any native variety of English. (For details see Brook 1973; Kachru 1981, esp. subsection on "The Cline of Varieties"; and Quirk et al. 1972: 13–32.)

A discussion on the non-native uses of English in "un-English" contexts will entail presenting several sociolinguistic profiles relevant to a number of institutionalized varieties of English. Since I have not set that as my goal here, I will merely provide a general view of the possible functional range of non-native varieties of English.

In the case of some varieties, the English language is used in all four functions mentioned earlier. The *instrumental function* is performed by English as a medium of learning at various stages in the educational system of the country. The *regulative function* entails use of English in those contexts in which language is used to regulate conduct; for example, the legal system and administration. The *interpersonal function* is performed in two senses: first, as a *link* language between speakers of various (often mutually unintelligible) languages and dialects in linguistically and culturally pluralistic societies; and second, by providing a code which symbolizes modernization and elitism (see Sridhar 1989). The *imaginative/innovative function* refers to the use of English in various literary *genres*. In this function, the non-native users of English have shown great creativity in using the English language in "un-English" contexts. This aspect of non-native Englishes has unfortunately not attracted much attention from linguists, but has now been taken seriously by literary scholars.[7] (See Kachru 1982.)

The Range and Depth of Functional Uses

The functional uses of the non-native varieties extend in two senses. The term "range" means the extension of English into various cultural, social, educational, and commercial contexts. The wider the range, the greater the variety of uses. By "depth" we mean the penetration of English-knowing bilingualism to various societal levels. One has to consider, for example, whether bilingualism in English is restricted to the urban upper and middle classes, or whether it has penetrated to other societal levels, too. What are the implications of these functions, and their range and depth, for a model?

The degrees of *nativization* of a variety of English are related to two factors: the range and depth of the functions of English in a non-native context, and the period for which the society has been exposed to bilingualism in English. The greater the number of functions and the longer the period, the more nativized is the variety. The nativization has two manifestations, cultural and linguistic, with "cultural" here referring to the acculturation of English. The result is that, both culturally and formally, the English language comes closer to the sociocultural context of what may be termed the *adopted* "context of situation." This new, changed "context of situation" contributes to the deviations from what originally might have been a linguistic "norm" or "model."

Attitude of Native and Non-Native Users toward Non-Native Varieties

In view of the unique developments and functions of the institutionalized non-native varieties of English, one might ask: What has been the attitude of native speakers and native users of English toward such non-native Englishes? The native speakers' attitude toward the development and the nativization of institutionalized varieties has traditionally not been one of acceptance or ontological recognition. Because of the linguistic manifestation of the nativization, these varieties have been considered *deficient* models of language acquisition. This attitude has not been restricted to speech performance, but extends to lexical and collocational items which are determined by the *new* sociocultural context in which the English language is used in Africa or Asia. It seems that the contextual *dislocation* (or transplantation) of English has not been recognized as a valid reason for "deviations" and innovations. Thus, the parameters for making judgments on the formal and functional uses of English continue to be culturally and linguistically ethnocentric, though the pragmatic context for such Englishes is "un-English" and "non-native" (see Kachru 1981, 1986). A decade ago, I mentioned with some elation (Kachru 1969) that with World War II a new attitude of "linguistic tolerance" had developed, which was reflected in proclamations such as "hands off pidgins" (Hall 1955) and "status for colonial Englishes." Now, a decade later, this statement warrants a postscript with reference to colonial Englishes. One has to qualify the earlier statement and say that this attitude was restricted to two circles. First, a body of literary scholars slowly started to recognize and accept the commonwealth literature in English written by non-native users of the language as a noteworthy linguistic and literary activity. Britain was somewhat earlier in this recognition. Second, a few British linguists, notably Firth (1957: 97), Halliday et al. (1964), Strevens (1977: 140), and Quirk et al. (1972: 26), accept the linguistic and functional distinctiveness of the institutionalized non-native varieties. It seems that even in America the linguistic fringe has been rather slow in providing such recognition and looking at these varieties in a pragmatic perspective. (For a detailed discussion, see Kachru 1976a, 1981, 1982, 1983. For Quirk's recent views, see his papers in Tickoo 1991.)

The non-native speakers themselves have not yet been able to accept what may be termed the "ecological validity" of their *nativized* or *local* Englishes. One would have expected such acceptance, given the acculturation and linguistic nativization of the new varieties. On the other hand, the *non*-native models of English (such as RP or GA) are not accepted without reservations. There is thus a case of linguistic schizophrenia, the underlying causes of which have yet to be studied. Consider, for example, the following tables. (For details, see Kachru 1976a.)

Table 1. Indian Graduate Students' Attitude toward Various Models of English and Ranking of Models According to Preference

Model	Preference		
	I	II	III
American English	5.17	13.19	21.08
British English	67.60	9.65	1.08
Indian English	22.72	17.82	10.74
I don't care		5.03	
"Good" English		1.08	

Table 2. Faculty Preference for Models of English for Instruction

Model	Preference		
	I	II	III
American English	3.07	14.35	25.64
British English	66.66	13.33	1.53
Indian English	26.66	25.64	11.79
I don't know		5.12	

Table 3. Graduate Students' Self-Labeling of the Variety of Their English

Identity marker	%
American English	2.58
British English	29.11
Indian English	55.64
"Mixture" of all three	2.99
I don't know	8.97
"Good" English	.27

What does such an attitude imply? In Ghana, for example, *educated* Ghanaian English is acceptable; but as Sey (1973: 1) warns us, it does not entail competence in speaking RP since in Ghana "the type that strives too obviously to approximate to RP is frowned upon as distasteful and pedantic." In Nigeria the situation is not different from Ghana or India (see Kachru 1976a). Bamgbose (1971: 41) emphasizes that "the aim is not to produce speakers of British Received Pronunciation (even if this were feasible!) . . . Many Nigerians will consider as affected or even snobbish any Nigerians who speak like a native speaker of English." In another English-using country, the Philippines, the model for "Standard Filipino English" is *"the type of English which educated Filipinos speak and which is acceptable in educated Filipino circles"* (Llamzon 1969: 15). There seems to be some agreement that an *external* model does not suit the linguistic and sociolinguistic ecology of Africa, the Philippines, or South Asia.

Deviation, Mistake, and the Norm

I have used the term "deviation" in this study and earlier (Kachru 1965: 396–98) with reference to the linguistic and contextual *nativeness* in the non-native varieties of English. This term needs further elucidation since it is crucial to our understanding of the question of the model. The inevitable questions concerning the linguistic and contextual deviation are: What is the distinction between a "deviation" and a "mistake"? And, how much deviation from the norm is acceptable pedagogically, linguistically, and (above all) with reference to intelligibility?

We shall make a distinction between the terms "mistake" and "deviation" on linguistic and contextual levels. A "mistake" may be unacceptable by a native speaker since it does not belong to the linguistic "norm" of the English language; it cannot be justified with reference to the sociocultural context of a non-native variety; and it is not the result of the productive processes used in an institutionalized non-native variety of English. On the other hand, a "deviation" has the following characteristics: it is different from the norm in the sense that it is the result of the new "un-English" linguistic and cultural setting in which the English language is used; it is the result of a productive process which marks the typical variety-specific features; and it is systemic within a variety, and not idiosyncratic. There is thus an explanation for each deviation within the context of situation. It can be shown that a large number of deviations "deviate" only with reference to an idealized norm. A number of "deviations" labeled as "mistakes" are present in native varieties of English but are not accepted when used by a non-native speaker.

In earlier studies on the non-native Englishes by educators, specialists in the teaching of English, and native speakers in general, the deviations in such varieties of English have been treated essentially as "deficiencies" in foreign language learning (e.g., Goffin 1934, Passé 1947, and Smith-Pearse 1934 for South Asian English; Hocking 1974 for African English). It seems to me that a crucial distinction is warranted between a deficient variety and a different variety. Deficiency refers to acquisitional and/or performance deficiency within the context in which English functions as L_2. On the other hand, a different model refers to the *identificational* features which mark an educated variety of language distinct from another educated variety. The exponents of "difference" may be at one or more linguistic levels. The following examples from South Asian English illustrate identificational features.

1. *Phonetics/Phonology*
   (a) *Series substitution* involves substitution of the retroflex consonant series for the English alveolar series.
   (b) *Systemic membership substitution* involves the substitution of members in a system with members of another class; for example, the use of stops in place of fricative θ and $\eth$, or substitution of "clear l" for "dark l."

(c) *Rhythmic interference* entails the use of syllable-timed rhythm in place of the stress-timed rhythm of English (see Nelson 1982).

2. *Grammar*

I shall list some characteristics discussed earlier in Kachru (1965, 1969, 1983). A discussion on African varieties of English is available in Bokamba (1982), Bamgboṣe (1982), Sey (1973), and Zuengler (1982).

(a) There is tendency to use complex sentences.
(b) Selection restrictions are "violated" in *be* + *ing* constructions (e.g., use of *hear* and *see* in *I am hearing, I am seeing*).
(c) A "deviant" pattern appears in the use of articles.
(d) Reduplication is common (e.g., *small small things, hot hot tea*).
(e) Interrogatives are formed without changing the position of subject and auxiliary items (e.g., *What you would like to eat?*)

3. *Lexis*

The productive processes used in lexis have been discussed, for example, in Sey (1973), Kachru (1965, 1975, 1983) and Llamzon (1969). The term "lexis" includes here what may be termed non-native collocations (Kachru 1965: 403–5). Consider, for example, *turmeric ceremony, dung-wash, caste mark, police wala,* and *lathi charge* from Indian English, *chewing-sponge, cover-shoulder, knocking fee, dunno drums,* and *bodom head* from Ghanaian English.

4. *Cohesiveness*

Discussion of phonology, grammar, and lexis presents only one part of the total picture of the difference between "deficient" and "different" in a non-native variety. It is equally important to account for the following:

(a) the cohesive characteristics of the text which mark it distinct, for example, in terms of its Nigerianness, Kenyanness, or Indianness (see Chs. 16, 17, 18 of this volume);
(b) the lexical and grammatical features which mark the register type and the style type;
(c) the features which separate the literary genres of one non-native variety from another non-native variety (see Chs. 14, 15 of this volume).

The focus is then on setting up a relationship between the communication domains or contexts and their formal manifestations.

A non-native variety is "deviant" not only in having specific phonetic, lexical, or grammatical characteristics, but it is also "deviant" as a communicative unit, if we compare it with other native or non-native communicative units. It is therefore necessary to establish what Firth terms a "renewal of connection" (see Firth 1956: 99 and 1957: 175) between the "interpretive context" ("the context of situation"), which gives the text a meaning, and its formal characteristics. The "differences" in each institutionalized non-native variety may thus be viewed in a larger context, which incorporates the "context of situation," and not purely from the view of language deficiency. (See figure.)

If one adopts a functional view of the institutionalized varieties, it might help to abandon earlier views about two very important questions concerning intelligibility and the applicability of a mono-model approach to all the non-native varieties of English. I shall now discuss these briefly.

Model vs. Intelligibility

In the prescriptive literature on second language acquisition, the concepts "norm" or "model" seem to play a pivotal role, primarily with regard to the non-native speaker's being "intelligible" to native speakers of English. The concept of "intelligibility" is the least re-searched and least understood in linguistic or pedagogical literature (see Kachru 1981; Nelson 1982). The difficulty is that intelligibility seems to have a number of variables, and when used with reference to English it becomes more elusive. Therefore we must use the term in a specific sense. The questions one has to ask are: What is meant

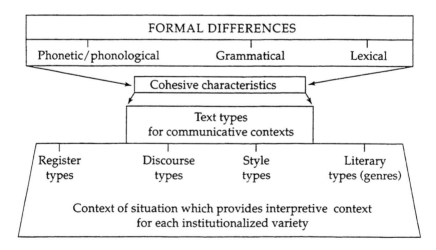

by intelligibility with reference to each linguistic level? Who is the judge for determining intelligibility in various varieties of English — the users of the varieties themselves, or the idealized native speakers? What parameters should be used to distinguish intelligibility between those varieties of English which are essentially regional or national (e.g., Indian English), and those varieties within a variety which have exclusively *international* functions? What role does a native speaker of English (and what type of native speaker) play concerning the judgment about the non-native varieties? What is the relationship between intelligibility of formal (linguistic) exponents and the contextual exponents?

"Intelligibility" has been interpreted in a rather narrow sense in earlier studies. Such studies have focused primarily on decoding a phonetic/phonological signal at the lexical level. Earlier studies, especially those of Catford (1950) and Voegelin and Harris (1951), mentioned the importance of "situation" and "effectiveness" in intelligibility. Nelson (1982) attempts to provide the parameters of intelligibility for non-native Englishes.

The intelligibility of the institutionalized non-native varieties of English forms a cline. Some speakers are more intelligible than are others, the variables being education, role, region, etc. The situation in the non-native varieties is not different from that in Britain or the U.S.A. The situation in Britain has been succinctly presented by Ward:

> It is obvious that in a country the size of the British Isles, any one speaker should be capable of understanding any other when he is talking English. At the present moment, such is not the case: a Cockney speaker would not be understood by a dialect speaker of Edinburgh or Leeds or Truro, and dialect speakers of much nearer districts than these would have difficulty in understanding each other.

In a well-known cone-shaped diagram (see Ward 1929: 5) Daniel Jones has graphically represented the situation: "as we near the apex, the divergencies which still exist have become so small as to be noticed only by a finely trained ear" (Ward 1929: 6). Ward also rightly presents the argument of "convenience or expediency" (1929: 7), observing that "the regional dialect may suffice for those people who have no need to move from their own districts."

The case seems to be identical to that of non-native varieties of English. Intelligibility then has to be defined in regional, national, and international terms. (For further discussion, see Ch. 4.)

Monomodel vs. Polymodel Approach

In view of the special characteristics of the English speech community in various parts of the world, the pragmatic question is: Is it possible to suggest a monomodel approach, as opposed to a polymodel approach (Kachru 1977)? A monomodel approach presupposes that there is a homogeneous English L$_2$ speech community, and that the functional roles assigned to English in each area are more or less identical. More important, it assumes that the goals for the study of English in various parts of the world are more or less similar. Such a position presupposes that the "context of situation" for the use of English in all the English-speaking areas is identical. It has already been demonstrated that such is not the case (see, e.g., Kachru 1976a, 1981; Richards 1972; Strevens 1977).

The assumptions underlying a *polymodel* approach are diametrically opposed to the *monomodel* approach. A polymodel approach is based upon pragmatism and functional realism. It presupposes three types of variability in teaching English for cross-cultural communications; namely, variability related to *acquisition*, variability related to *function*, and variability related to the *context of situation*. We may then have to recognize a *cline* in terms of the formal characteristics of an L$_2$ variety of English; *functional* diversity in each English-speaking area; and diversity in *proficiency*.

The concept of "cline of bilingualism" (Kachru 1965: 393–96) may, therefore, be recognized as fundamental for the discussion of a model for English. The cline applies not only to the proficiency at the phonetic/phonological levels; it must also be interpreted in a broader sense, including the overall sociolinguistic context.

Conclusion

And now, in conclusion, let us face reality. The truth is that the non-native Englishes—institutionalized or non-institutionalized—are linguistic orphans in search of their parents. Several native and non-native users of English do not understand that they are adding insult to injury by calling these varieties "deficient Englishes." The development of such varieties is not unique to English; in a lesser degree Hindi, Persian, French, and Spanish have also developed such transplanted varieties.

The problem is that even when the non-native models of English are linguistically identifiable, geographically definable, and functionally valuable, they are still not necessarily attitudinally acceptable. There is an "accent bar" which continues to segregate the non-native users. The acceptance of a model depends on its users: the users must demonstrate a solidarity, identity, and loyalty toward a language variety. In the past, the Americans demonstrated it (though not unanimously), and the result is a vigorous and dynamic *American* English. But then, when it comes to recognizing and accepting the varieties within American English, or accepting other non-native Englishes, Americans have shown reluctance, condescension, or indifference. The users of non-native varieties also seem to pass through linguistic schizophrenia, unable to decide whether to accept a mythical non-native model or to recognize the local functional model instead.

I must also mention the unique international position of English, which is certainly unparalleled in the history of the world. For the first time a natural language has attained the status of an international (universal) language, essentially for cross-cultural communication. Whatever the reasons for the earlier spread of English, we should now consider it a positive development in the twentieth-century world context. We should realize that this new role of English puts a burden on those who use it as their *first* language, as well as on those who use it as their *second* language. This responsibility demands what may be termed "attitudinal readjustment." I have elsewhere discussed "the seven attitudinal sins" (Kachru 1976a: 223–29) which the native speakers are committing in their attitude toward the non-native varieties; a classic case is presented in Prator (1968). (See also Tickoo, ed. 1991.)

The non-native users' attitudinal readjustment toward English entails the following acts, among others. First, non-native users must now dissociate English from the colonial past, and not treat it as a colonizer's linguistic tool.

Second, they must avoid regarding English as an evil influence which necessarily leads to Westernization. In South Asia and Africa the role of English in developing nationalism and mobilizing the intelligentsia at large for struggles toward freedom cannot be over-emphasized. Although it is true that such use of English has resulted in a linguistic elitism, that has also been true in the past of Sanskrit and Persian, and recently of Hindi.

Third, non-native users should accept the large body of English literature written by local creative writers as part of the native literary tradition. Indian English literature, West African English literature, and Philippine English literature not only have pan-national reading publics, but have also become part of a larger body of world writing in English. These literatures not only interpret the national traditions and aspirations to readers across linguistically and culturally pluralistic areas; in addition, they have an international reading public. (See, e.g., for Indian English literature, Kachru 1976b: 168–73, 1978a, 1978b, 1983; Lal 1969: i–cliv; for other literatures in English see Bailey and Görlach 1982.)

Fourth, it is important to distinguish between the national and the international uses of English. It is primarily the national uses of the institutionalized varieties which contribute toward the nativization of these varieties.

Fifth, non-native users ought to develop an identity with the local model of English without feeling that it is a "deficient" model. The local (non-native) models of English are functionally as much a part of the linguistic repertoire of people as are the native (non-Western) languages. After all, in Asia or Africa it is not unusual to find that the number of users of English exceeds the number of speakers of several of what the Indian constitution terms "scheduled languages" (or nationally recognized languages). In India, the number of English-using bilinguals is about 5 percent of the total population; the numbers of speakers of six scheduled languages are close to or even much less than this figure, i.e., Assamese (1.63%), Kannada (3.96%), Kashmiri (0.45%), Malayalam (4%), Oriya (3.62%), and Punjabi (3%).

The international profile of the functions of English is encouraging: we may at last have a universal language as an offshoot of the colonial period. In this context, two questions may be asked. First, is there a coordinating agency which has a realistic view of the international and national functions of English? Second, do the non-native users of English feel that any significant theoretical and methodological leadership is being provided by those British or U.S. agencies which are involved in the teaching or diffusion of English? The answers to these questions, while not discussed in this chapter, are closely related to our concern for studying English in the world context.

NOTES

1. I am grateful to several agencies for their support of my research on this and related topics on non-native varieties of English, specifically to the Research Board of the Graduate College and the Center for International Comparative Studies, both of the University of Illinois at Urbana-Champaign. This is a revision of a paper presented at a conference on "Progress in Language Planning," Language Research Center, William Paterson College, April 30–May 1, 1979.

2. I should mention that other models, such as Scottish (English) or Australian, have been suggested in the literature. But the main viable models in the past have been RP and GA.

3. The term "structural" in this method is not related to structural linguistics as understood in North America or in Britain. What I have said about the Institute of Education, London University, is no longer applicable. The position changed in the 1960s.

4. Also see Jones (1965) for a survey of the "triumph" of English and "a history of ideas concerning the English tongue—its nature, use, and improvement—during the period 1476–1660."

5. See Gage and Ohannessian 1977. For recent figures, see Crystal 1985.

6. My view of these four terms is somewhat different from that of Basil Bernstein (1964), who originally used these terms. The functional model proposed in Halliday (1973) extends the model to nine language functions: *instrumental, regulatory, interactional, personal, heuristic, imaginative, representative* or *informative, ludic,* and *ritual.*

7. This fast-growing body of writing provides impressive evidence for linguistic and contextual nativization of the English language. The result is the development of English literatures with areal modifiers, such as *West African* English literature, *Indian* English literature, *Caribbean* English literature, and so on. These modifiers convey not only the geographical variation, but also the cultural and sociolinguistic attitudes. These literatures are one manifestation of the national literatures in multilingual and multicultural non-Western English-using nations. In India, for example, one can claim that there are only three languages in which pan-Indian literature is produced with an *all-India* reading public: English, Sanskrit, and Hindi (Kachru 1981). For a detailed bibliography on commonwealth literature in English, specifically in Africa, India, and the West Indies, see Narasimhaiah 1976.

REFERENCES

Abdulaziz-Mikilifi, M. H. 1978. Influence of English on Swahili: a case study of language development. Paper presented at the Conference on English in Non-Native Contexts, University of Illinois, Urbana.

Abercrombie, D. 1951. R.P. and local accent. *The Listener,* 6 September 1951. Reprinted in Abercrombie, D., *Studies in phonetics and linguistics.* London: Oxford University Press.

Alatis, J., ed. 1969. *Georgetown monograph on language and linguistics.* Washington, D.C.: Georgetown University Press.

———, ed. 1978. International dimensions of bilingual education. *Georgetown University roundtable on languages and linguistics.* Washington, D.C.: Georgetown University Press.

———, and G. R. Tucker, eds. 1979. Language in public life. Georgetown University roundtable on languages and linguistics, 1979. Washington, D.C.: Georgetown University Press.

Alford, H. 1869. *A plea for the Queen's English*. London: Strahan.

Avis, W. S. 1967. *A dictionary of Canadianisms on historical principles*. Toronto: W. J. Gage.

Bailey, B. L. 1970. Some arguments against the use of dialect readers in the teaching of initial reading. *Florida FL Reporter* Spring/Fall 3: 47.

Bailey, R. W., and M. Görlach. 1982. *English as a world language*. Ann Arbor: University of Michigan Press.

Baker, R. 1770. Reflections on the English language. 2nd ed. (1779) entitled 'Remarks on . . .' London: Bell.

Bamgboṣe, A. 1971. The English language in Nigeria. In Spencer 1971a.

———. 1982. Standard Nigerian English: issues of identification. In this volume.

Bazell, C. E., et al., eds. 1966. *In memory of J. R. Firth*. London: Longmans.

Beattie, J. 1838. The grammarian; or, the writer and speaker's assistant; comprising shall and will made easy to foreigners, with instances of their misuse on the part of the natives of England. London.

Bernstein, B. 1964. Elaborated and restricted codes: their social origins and some consequences. *American Anthropologist* 66: 55–69.

Bloomfield, L. 1933. *Language*. New York: Holt, Rinehart and Winston.

Bokamba, E. 1982. The Africanization of English. In this volume.

Bolinger, D. 1975. *Aspects of language*. New York: Harcourt Brace Jovanovich.

Bright, W., ed. 1966. *Sociolinguistics: proceedings of the UCLA sociolinguistics conference, 1964*. The Hague: Mouton.

Brook, G. L. 1973. *Varieties of English*. London: Macmillan.

Brooks, N. 1960. *Language and language learning: theory and practice*. New York: Harcourt, Brace and World.

Burling, R. 1970. Colloquial and standard written English: some implications for teaching literacy to non-standard speakers. *Florida FL Reporter* Spring/Fall: 9–15, 47.

Candlin, C. 1981. Discoursal patterning and the equalising of interpretive opportunity. In Smith 1981.

Catford, J. C. 1950. Intelligibility. *English Language Teaching* 1: 7–15.

———. 1959. The teaching of English as a foreign language. In *The teaching of English*, ed. R. Quirk and A. H. Smith. London: Martin, Secker and Warburg. Reprinted London: Oxford University Press, 1964.

Christophersen, P. 1960. Toward a standard of international English. *English Language Teaching* 14: 127–38.

———. 1973. *Second-language learning: myth and reality*. Harmondsworth: Penguin.

Cochran, A. 1954. *Modern methods of teaching English as a foreign language: a guide to modern material with particular reference to the Far East*. Washington, D.C.: Educational Services.

Cooper, R. L. 1979. Language planning, language spread, and language change. In *Language in public life*, ed. J. Alatis and G. R. Tucker. Washington, D.C.: Georgetown University Press.

Craig, D. 1982. Toward a description of Caribbean English. In Kachru, ed. 1982a.

Crewe, W., ed. 1977. *The English language in Singapore.* Singapore: Eastern Universities Press.

Ellis, D. S. 1967. Speech and social status in America. *Social Forces* 45: 431–37.

Ferguson, C. A. 1966. National sociolinguistic profile formulas. In *Sociolinguistics: proceedings of the UCLA sociolinguistic conference, 1964.* The Hague: Mouton.

Finnocchiaro, M. 1964. *English as a second language from theory to practice.* New York: Regents.

Firth, J. R. 1956. Descriptive linguistics and the study of English. In Palmer 1968.

———. 1957. A synopsis of linguistic theory, 1930–55. In Palmer 1968.

Fishman, R., R. L. Cooper, and A. W. Conrad. 1977. *The spread of English.* Rowley, Mass.: Newbury House.

Fowler, H. W. 1926. *A dictionary of modern English usage.* London: Oxford University Press.

Gage, W. W., and S. Ohannessian. 1977. ESOL enrollments throughout the world. *Linguistic Reporter* November. Reprinted in *English Teaching Forum* July 1977.

Gauntlett, J. O. 1957. *Teaching English as a foreign language.* London: Macmillan.

Gimson, A. C. 1962. *An introduction to the pronunciation of English.* London: Edward Arnold.

Goffin, R. C. 1934. *Some notes on Indian English.* S.P.E. Tract No. 41. Oxford.

Hall, R. A. 1955. *Hands off pidgin English!* Sydney: Pacific.

Halliday, M. A. K. 1973. *Explorations in the functions of language.* London: Edward Arnold.

———, A. McIntosh, and P. Strevens. 1964. The linguistic sciences and language teaching. London: Longmans.

Haynes, L. 1982. Caribbean English: form and function. In Kachru, ed. 1982a.

Heath, S. B. 1977. A national language academy? Debate in the nation. *Linguistics: An International Review* 189: 9–43.

Hill, A. A. 1954. Prescriptivism and linguistics in language teaching. *College English* 15 (April): 395–99. Reprinted in H. Allen, ed., *Readings in applied English linguistics.* New York: Appleton-Century, 1958.

Hocking, B. D. W. 1974. *All what I was taught and other mistakes: a handbook of common errors in English.* Nairobi: Oxford University Press.

Jones, D. 1918. *An outline of English phonetics.* Rev. ed., 1956. Cambridge: Heffer.

———. 1956. *Everyman's English pronouncing dictionary.* London: Dent.

Jones, R. F. 1965. *The triumph of the English language.* Stanford: Stanford University Press.

Kachru, B. B. 1965. The Indianness in Indian English. *Word* 21: 391–410.

———. 1966. Indian English: a study in contextualization. *In memory of J. R.*

Firth, ed. C. E. Bazell, J. C. Catford, M. A. K. Halliday, and R. H. Robins. London: Longman.

———. 1969. English in South Asia. In *Current trends in linguistics, V*, ed. T. Sebeok. The Hague: Mouton.

———. 1973. Toward a lexicon of Indian English. In *Issues in linguistics: papers in honor of Henry and Renée Kahane*, ed. B. B. Kachru, R. B. Lees, Y. Malkiel, A. Pietrangeli, and S. Saporta. Urbana: University of Illinois Press.

———. 1975. Lexical innovations in South Asian English. *International Journal of the Sociology of Language* 4: 55–94.

———. 1976a. Models of English for the third world: white man's linguistic burden or language pragmatics? *TESOL Quarterly* 10(2): 221–39.

———. 1976b. Indian English: a sociolinguistic profile of a transplanted language. In *Dimensions of bilingualism: theory and case studies*. Special issue of *Studies in Language Learning*. Urbana: Unit for Foreign Language Study and Research, University of Illinois.

———. 1977. The new Englishes and old models. *English Language Forum* July 15(3): 29–35.

———. 1978a. Toward structuring code-mixing: an Indian perspective. In *Aspects of sociolinguistics in South Asia*. Special issue of *International Journal of the Sociology of Language* 16: 27–46.

———. 1978b. Toward structuring code-mixing: an Indian perspective. In *International dimensions of bilingual education*, ed. J. Alatis. Washington, D.C.: Georgetown University Press.

———. 1979. The Englishization of Hindi: language rivalry and language change. In *Linguistic method: essays in honor of Herbert Penzl*, ed. I. Rauch and G. Carr. The Hague: Mouton.

———. 1981. The pragmatics of non-native varieties of English. In Smith 1981.

———, ed. 1982a. *The other tongue: English across cultures*. Urbana: University of Illinois Press.

———. 1982b. South Asian English. In Bailey and Görlach 1982.

———. 1983. *The Indianization of English: the English Language in India*. New Delhi: Oxford University Press.

———. 1986. *The alchemy of English*. Oxford: Pergamon. Reprinted 1990, Urbana: University of Illinois Press.

———, and R. Quirk. 1981. Introduction. In Smith 1981.

Kahane, H., and R. Kahane. 1977. Virtues and vices in the American language: a history of attitudes. *TESOL Quarterly* 11(2): 185–202.

Kaldor, S. 1991. Standard Australian English as a second language and as a second dialect. Pp. 68–85 in Tickoo 1991.

Kandiah, T. 1978. Disinherited Englishes: the case of Lankan English. *Navasilu* 3(1979/81): 75–89 and 4: 92–113.

Kenyon, J. S. 1924. *American pronunciation*. Ann Arbor: George Wahr.

———, and T. A. Knott. 1953. *A pronouncing dictionary of American English*. Springfield, Mass.: Merriam.

Krapp, G. P. 1919. *Pronunciation of standard English in America.* New York: Oxford University Press.

Labov, W. 1966. Some sources of reading problems for Negro speakers of non-standard English. In *New directions in elementary English,* ed. A. Frazier. Urbana, Ill.: National Council of Teachers of English.

——. 1969. Contraction, deletion, and inherent variability of the English copula. *Language* 45(4): 715–62.

Lado, R. 1964. *Language teaching: a scientific approach.* New York: McGraw-Hill.

Lal, P. 1969. *Modern Indian poetry in English: an anthology and a credo.* Calcutta: Writers Workshop.

Lara, L. F. 1976. *El concepto de norma en linguistica.* Mexico, D.F.: El Colegio de Mexico.

Leonard, S. A. 1929. The doctrine of correctness in English usage, 1700–1800. Madison: University of Wisconsin Studies in Language and Literature No. 25.

Llamzon, T. A. 1969. *Standard Filipino English.* Manila: Anteneo University Press.

Mencken, H. L. 1919. *The American language.* New York: Alfred A. Knopf.

Narasimhaiah, C. D. 1976. *Commonwealth literature: a handbook of select reading lists.* Delhi: Oxford University Press.

Nelson, C. L. 1982. Intelligibility and non-native varieties of English. In Kachru, ed. 1982a.

Palmer, F. R., ed. 1968. *Selected papers of J. R. Firth, 1952–59.* London: Longman.

Passé, H. A. 1947. The English language in Ceylon. Ph.D. dissertation, University of London.

Pickering, J. 1816. A vocabulary or collection of words and phrases which have been supposed to be peculiar to the United States of America. In *The beginnings of American English: essays and comments.* Chicago: University of Chicago Press, 1931.

Platt, J. T. 1975. The Singapore English speech continuum and basilect 'singlish' as a 'creoloid.' *Anthropological Linguistics* 17: 7.

——. 1976. The sub-varieties of Singapore English: their sociolectal and functional status. In W. Crewe 1977.

Prator, C. H. 1968. The British heresy in TESL. In *Language problems of developing nations,* ed. J. A. Fishman, C. A. Gerguson, and J. Das Gupta. New York: John Wiley and Sons.

Puttenham, G. 1589. *Arte of English poesie.* London.

Quirk, R., S. Greenbaum, and J. Svartvik. 1972. *A grammar of contemporary English.* London: Longman.

Revzin, I. I. 1966. *Models of language.* London: Methuen. Originally published in Russian, 1962.

Richards, Jack C. 1972. Social factors, interlanguage and language learning. *Language Learning* 22(2): 159–88.

——, and M. W. J. Tay. 1981. Norm and variability in language use. In Smith 1981.

Riley, R. D. 1978. Should we teach urban black students standard English? *Lektos: Interdisciplinary Working Papers in Language Sciences* 3(1): 93–119.

Sey, K. A. 1973. *Ghanaian English: an exploratory survey.* London: Macmillan.

Shuy, R. W. 1971. Social dialects and second language learning: a case of territorial overlap. *TESOL Newsletter* September-December.

Sledd, J. 1969. Bidialectism: the linguistics of white supremacy. *English Journal* 58: 1307–15, 1329.

Smith, L., ed. 1981. *English for cross-cultural communication.* London: Macmillan.

Smith-Pearse, T. L. N. 1934. *English errors in Indian schools.* Bombay: Oxford University Press.

Spencer, J., ed. 1963. *Language in Africa.* London: Cambridge University Press.

———. 1971a. *The English language in West Africa.* London: Longman.

———. 1971b. Colonial language policies and their legacies. In *Current trends in linguistics,* VII, ed. T. Sebeok. The Hague: Mouton.

Sridhar, K. 1989. *English in Indian bilingualism.* New Delhi: Manohar.

Stevick, E. W. 1957. *Helping people learn English: a manual for teachers of English as a second language.* New York: Abingdon Press.

Stewart, W. 1970. Current issues in the use of Negro dialect in the beginning reading texts. *Florida FL Reporter* 3–6.

Strevens, P. 1977. *New orientations in the teaching of English.* London: Oxford University Press.

———. 1981. Forms of English: an analysis of the variables. In Smith 1981.

Tickoo, M. L., ed. 1991. *Language and standards: issues, attitudes, case studies.* Singapore: SEAMEO Regional Language Centre.

Voegelin, C., and Z. Harris. 1951. Determining intelligibility among dialects. *Proceedings of the American Philological Society* 95(3): 322–29.

Ward, I. C. 1929. *The phonetics of English.* Cambridge: Heffer.

Whitten, W., and F. Whitaker. 1939. *Good and bad English.* London: Newnes.

Wolfram, W. 1970. Sociolinguistic implications for educational sequencing. In *Teaching standard English in the inner city,* ed. R. Fasold and R. Shuy. Washington, D.C.: Center for Applied Linguistics.

Wong, I. F. H. 1981. English in Malaysia. In Smith 1981.

Zuengler, J. E. 1982. Kenyan English. In Kachru, ed. 1982a.

4

Larry E. Smith

Spread of English and Issues of Intelligibility

In recorded history there has never been a language to match the present global spread and use of English (Strevens 1982, Quirk and Widdowson 1985, Kachru 1986, Smith 1983). Crystal (1985) has estimated that as many as 2 billion people have some ability in English. Whether we accept Crystal's figure or not, it is certain that, whatever the total number, non-native users of English outnumber the native users.

With such spread of the language, a frequently voiced concern is the possibility that speakers of different varieties of English will soon become unintelligible to one another. My response to such a statement is that for at least the last two hundred years there have been English-speaking people in some parts of the world who have not been intelligible to other English-speaking people in other parts of the world. It is a natural phenomenon when any language becomes so widespread. It is not something that is "going to happen" but something that has happened already and will continue to occur. I take the position that it is unnecessary for every user of English to be intelligible to every other user of English. Our speech/writing in English needs to be intelligible only to those with whom we wish to communicate in English. For example, there may be many people in India who use English frequently among themselves and who are not intelligible to English-speaking Filipinos who also frequently use English among themselves; members of these two groups may not, as yet, have felt the need (or had the opportunity) to communicate with one another. These Indians and Filipinos may use English to communicate only with fellow countrymen and have little or no difficulty in doing so. If that is so, neither group needs to be concerned about its international intelligibility. Of course, there are many Indians and many Filipinos who use English to interact internationally, and they are the ones who must be concerned about mutual intelligibility.

Perhaps the concern about intelligibility can be rephrased in the following way: In international situations where people wish to communicate with one another in English, how intelligible are speakers of different national varieties? With the global spread of English, is the problem of understanding across cultures likely to increase in frequency?

Elsewhere (Smith and Nelson 1985) I have argued that native speakers are not the sole judges of what is intelligible, nor are they always more intelligible than non-native speakers. I have taken the position that the greater the familiarity a speaker (native or non-native) has with a variety of English, the more likely it is that s/he will understand, and be understood by, members of that speech community. I have suggested that understanding is not speaker- or listener-centered but is interactional between speaker and listener, and that understanding should be divided into three categories:

(1) intelligibility: word/utterance recognition;
(2) comprehensibility: word/utterance meaning (locutionary force);
(3) interpretability: meaning behind word/utterance (illocutionary force).

These three categories could be thought of as degrees of understanding on a continuum, with intelligibility being lowest and interpretability being highest.

This chapter reports on a pilot study designed to help determine: (1) what differences, if any, there are in the intelligibility, comprehensibility, and interpretability of selected taped material of nine national varieties; (2) how familiarity of topic and familiarity of national variety influence the listener's understanding of these varieties; and (3) if the language proficiency of the speaker and/or listener influences the intelligibility, comprehensibility, and interpretability of these varieties.

For this study, the nine national varieties, represented on tape, were spoken by educated speakers (at the graduate level at the University of Hawaii) from China, India, Indonesia, Japan, Papua New Guinea, the Philippines, Taiwan, the United Kingdom, and the United States. The tests of intelligibility, comprehensibility, and interpretability based on these recordings were administered to three different groups of native and non-native educated users of English.

Subjects

To test assumptions concerning the effects of proficiency in English and familiarity with topic and speech variety on understanding (intelligibility, comprehensibility, and interpretability), I wanted both native and non-native educated English users as subjects. I wanted these subjects to range in their proficiency in English and in their familiarity with the content of the selections, as well as familiarity with the national variety of English being used by the speakers. The three groups were: (1) non-native speakers (NNS), (2) native speakers (NS), and (3) mixed (NS and NNS).

Group 1: Non-native Speakers

This group was made up of ten non-native English speakers from Japan whose English proficiency ranged from scores of 375 to 600 on the TOEFL test; four of these were students in the Hawaii English Language Program (HELP) at the University of Hawaii and six were students at the Japan-America Institute of Management Science (JAIMS) in Honolulu. Subjects in this group were familiar with the Japanese variety of English, as well as the content of the Japanese speaker's presentation of "Forms of Address" (i.e., how Japanese address non-Japanese in English at international meetings). Since they had studied English for at least ten years and were students in the United States, they were also somewhat familiar with the American and British varieties of English and with the content of the U.S. and British speakers' presentations on "Forms of Address" (i.e., how British and Americans address outsiders in English at international meetings). However, these subjects were not familiar with any of the other speech varieties or with the topic of forms of address used in the other countries.

Group 2: Native Speakers

This group was made up of ten native speakers of American English who were undergraduate students at the University of Hawaii. All were quite familiar with the American English used by the American speaker on the tape, as well as the content of her presentation. They were not totally familiar with any other of the speech varieties on the tapes but had had greater exposure to the Japanese and Filipino varieties than to any of the others. They knew little or nothing about forms of address in any country other than the United States.

Group 3: Mixed

This group was composed of one native and eight non-native speakers, one each from Burma, China, Indonesia, Japan, Korea, the Philippines, Thailand, and the United States. Each of these people was fully fluent in English (better than 600 on the TOEFL test). As East-West Center graduate students, they had all become familiar with several different national varieties of English. They were also familiar to some extent with the forms of address used in different countries because of their interactions at the East-West Center with people from many parts of the world.

All three groups were balanced for age, sex, and educational background. The subjects with the lower TOEFL scores were highly intelligent and well educated, but they had not had much experience interacting in English.

Test Materials

In order to have educated English speakers of the nine national varieties interacting with one another, I used graduate and postgraduate students at the University of Hawaii who were fluent in English. The speakers were asked to explain to an interactor who was of another national variety the forms of address used by the speaker's countrymen when they used English to address outsiders. The respondent was, in each case, a person whom the speaker did not know and who knew little about, but was interested in, the speaker's country. The respondent was instructed, in the speaker's presence, to listen to the speaker, interrupt with questions of clarification when necessary, and give evidence of understanding the speaker by paraphrasing the important points the speaker made. The speaker was instructed to make sure the respondent understood how people in his/her country would address an outsider in English, for example, at international meetings both inside and outside his/her country. Both were told that the recording session was to be informal but real. That is, they were to speak to each other as peers in an informal situation; they were not to pretend that they were other people or that the setting was another place. They were to recognize and accept the fact that they were two people in a recording studio at the East-West Center in Honolulu. Once the speaker was satisfied that the respondent understood what the speaker had said about the topic, the conversation should stop. The interactors were told that they could make notes but that neither was to read directly from the notes. The sessions were totally unrehearsed and lasted from 20 to 40 minutes. The tapes of these sessions were edited down to ten minutes of conversation which could be used as material for the comprehensibility and interpretability tests. For the intelligibility test, the subjects heard a part of the preedited conversation, not chosen as part of the ten-minute selection. This was done so that the subjects would not hear any part of the conversation twice. In addition to the conversations with speakers of the nine national varieties mentioned above, one tape involving a speaker from Burma and a respondent from Thailand was also made to use in a demonstration of the testing procedure for all three subject groups.

Although no formal attempt was made to evaluate the difficulty level of the interactions, all were judged to be approximately equal in that (1) both speaker and respondent were fully proficient in English and believed themselves to be educated speakers of their national variety of English, (2) each person spoke clearly, and (3) the number of embedded sentences and the speed of delivery were approximately the same for all interactions. Of course, the setting and topic were always the same and technical jargon was never used. In each case, if the speaker was male the respondent was female, and vice versa, so that on each tape both sexes were represented.

Three types of test questions were developed. The cloze procedure was used to test intelligibility (word/utterance recognition). Multiple choice questions were written to test comprehensibility (word/utterance meaning). Subjects were asked to paraphrase a small portion of the conversation they had heard in order to test their level of interpretability (meaning behind word/utterance). The test questions and directions were recorded by the same speaker.

Procedure

I began each testing session by saying to each of the three subject groups that I was doing a study on the degrees of understanding of different national varieties of English and that I appreciated the subjects' willingness to cooperate. I said that the results of the tests would have no effect on their academic work but that I was sure they would do their best. I then told them we would have a trial test, and that they could ask any question about the procedure during this sample test. Each subject group then listened to the tape about forms of address in Burma and filled out the sample test items for the cloze procedure (intelligibility), multiple choice (comprehensibility), and paraphrasing (interpretability). During this time I encouraged the subjects to ask any questions, and I answered them. After the sample test I asked them to fill out the more subjective questionnaire (see Appendix) and allowed them to ask questions about it. On that form they were asked to state such things as (1) how easy/difficult it was for them to understand the speaker and respondent; (2) how much of the total conversation they had understood; (3) the nationalities of the speaker and the respondent; and (4) the English proficiency level of the speaker and the respondent.

For each of the five paired recordings, each subject group first listened to the ten-minute conversation, with the respondent asking questions and paraphrasing the important points. At the end of each conversation the subjects were given a test which consisted of (1) a cloze procedure of a passage with ten blanks (one at every seventh word) to be filled in as they listened, phrase by phrase, to a part of the original, longer conversation that they had not heard before; (2) three multiple-choice questions based on the ten-minute conversation that they had heard; and (3) three phrases taken from the ten-minute interaction which were to be paraphrased according to the meaning of the phrases in the conversation. This system was followed for each of the five paired recordings. (That is, (1) the subjects heard a tape about a country; (2) the subjects were tested on that country; (3) the subjects heard the next tape about another country; (4) the subjects were tested on that country. This continued until all five paired recordings had been heard and tested.) The order of the five pairs of taped conversations was different for each subject group to insure that any practice effect was balanced across varieties.

I administered all of the tests to the three subject groups on separate days within a two-month period (October/November 1986). Identical playback equipment was used for each group, always in quiet surroundings. The tests were all graded by the same individual within a few days after they were completed and given to me for analysis.

Results and Discussion

Listed in Tables 1, 2, and 3 are the tabulated results of the three parts of the test for each of the three groups. The speakers (with respondents in parentheses) that the subjects heard are listed in alphabetical order by country on the left side. In each case, the percentage listed is the percentage of subjects in that group which answered 60 percent or more of the test items correctly. For example, from Table 1 we learn that, when listening to the speaker from the United Kingdom interacting with her respondent from Papua New Guinea, 70 percent of the nonnative subjects got 60 percent or more of the intelligibility test items correct, whereas 100 percent of the native speaker subjects and 100 percent of the mixed subjects got 60 percent or more of the intelligibility items correct.

When we examine the results as tabulated in Tables 1, 2, and 3, it is evident that all three subject groups did best on the test of intelligibility. All of the native subjects, all of the mixed subjects, and 92 percent of the non-native subjects got 60 percent or more of the intelligibility test items correct. It appears that all of the interactions were highly intelligible to the three subject groups, but that the most intelligible were those with the speakers from Japan (respondent from

Table 1. Intelligibility: 60% and above

Test material	Subjects			
Speaker (respondent)	NNS: 10, all from Japan	NS: 10, all from U.S.	Mixed: 9 (1 NS and 8 NNS, each from a different country)	Average %
China (Taiwan)	90	100	100	97
India (Philippines)	100	100	100	100
Japan (China)	100	100	100	100
United Kingdom (Papua New Guinea)	70	100	100	90
United States (Indonesia)	100	100	100	100
Average	92	100	100	

Table 2. Comprehensibility: 60% and above

Test material	Subjects			
Speaker	NNS (10)	NS (10)	Mixed (9)	Average %
China (Taiwan)	40	80	60	60
India (Philippines)	40	90	60	63
Japan (China)	80	80	70	77
United Kingdom (Papua New Guinea)	90	100	100	97
United States (Indonesia)	60	60	60	60
Average	62	82	70	

Table 3. Interpretability: 60% and above

Test material	Subjects			
Speaker	NNS (10)	NS (10)	Mixed (9)	Average %
China (Taiwan)	40	60	89	63
India (Philippines)	10	40	78	43
Japan (China)	40	60	89	63
United Kingdom (Papua New Guinea)	10	50	89	50
United States (Indonesia)	30	40	100	57
Average	26	50	89	

China), India (respondent from the Philippines), and the United States (respondent from Indonesia). The pair with the speaker from China and respondent from Taiwan and the pair with the speaker from the United Kingdom and respondent from Papua New Guinea were somewhat less intelligible. Language proficiency may have made a difference in the results of the intelligibility test, but being a native speaker was not a deciding factor since the mixed group—with eight non-natives and one native—performed equally well on the test.

When examining Table 2, concerning comprehensibility (word/ utterance meaning), we note that the averages for all three groups were lower. Sixty-two percent of the non-native subjects, 82 percent of the native subjects, and 70 percent of the mixed subjects got 60 percent or more of the comprehensibility test items. The speaker from the United Kingdom with the respondent from Papua New Guinea were the most comprehensible, with 90 percent of the non-native group getting 60 percent or more of the test items correct, and all of the native group and all of the mixed group doing the same. This is interesting, because this is the pair that was the least intelligible. It is also interesting that the Japanese speaker with the Chinese respondent was the second most comprehensible pair, with the pairs from India/ Philippines, U.S./Indonesia, and China/Taiwan being about equal in difficulty for comprehensibility. I had expected all of the subject groups to comprehend the tapes about forms of address in the United States, as well as the one about forms of address in the United Kingdom, more easily than the others because each of the groups had studied English for at least ten years and had learned a great deal of cultural information about both countries. In other words, they knew the topic and were somewhat familiar with each of these speech varieties. I also expected the Japanese group and the American group to comprehend more easily the tapes about forms of address in their respective countries, since they obviously knew the information upon which the test for their country was based. A possible reason why the subjects failed to do this is that, although new information was given on each tape, the general topic was the same. This may explain why familiarity with topic was not a major factor in the subjects' ability to comprehend the interactions. If the topics had been Noh theater, nuclear physics, or anything else rather than forms of address, the effects of familiarity with the topic might have been greater.

As I tabulated the subjective questionnaire about each pair of interactors, I found other information which offered another possible explanation. In both cases dealing with the American and Japanese subjects listening to a speaker from their country interacting with a respondent from another country, the responses of the subjects to the respondents may have been a factor in the somewhat surprising results. All of the native-speaker subjects (i.e., the Americans) responded that they could easily understand the American speaker, but only 30 percent said that they could easily understand the respondent, who was from Indonesia. Sixty percent of the non-native group (i.e., the Japanese) responded that they could easily understand the Japanese speaker, but 70 percent said that they had some difficulty with the respondent, who was from China. Their difficulty in understanding the respondent ("accent too heavy") may have caused them to have comprehensibility problems with the entire conversation.

Table 3 provides some insightful information. It is evident that the mixed subjects (one native and eight non-natives, each from a different country) who had the greatest familiarity with different speech varieties were best able to interpret correctly the interactions of the five pairs of interactors. Twenty-six percent of the non-native speakers, 50 percent of the native speakers, and 89 percent of the mixed subjects got 60 percent or more of the interpretability test items. The mixed subject group was better on all five pairs than were the native or non-native subject groups. This is an important finding, since I believe interpretability is at the core of communication and is more important than mere intelligibility or comprehensibility.

This part of the study offers supporting evidence that familiarity with several different English varieties makes it easier to interpret cross-cultural communication in English. No doubt this is influenced by the fact that familiarity with different speech varieties also involves an awareness of cultural differences and some knowledge of different cultures. This is not to say that proficiency in the language is unimportant; the mixed group was fully fluent in English, although not at the native-speaker level, except for one. Additional evidence that proficiency is important is the fact that the native-speaker subject group was better at interpreting all five interactions than the less proficient non-native subject group. The non-native and native subject groups found the China/Taiwan and the Japan/China pairs easiest to interpret, and all three subject groups found the India/Philippines pair the most difficult to interpret. Only the mixed group found the U.S./Indonesia pair the easiest to interpret, perhaps because they were the only ones familiar with many varieties of English. The native-speaker group and the non-native-speaker group were not familiar with the Indonesian speech variety, and this may have been a factor in their inability to interpret the U.S./Indonesia interaction correctly.

Other responses from the subjective questionnaires were also of interest. Table 4 shows the percentage of each subject group that thought they understood 60 percent or more of the conversations between the five sets of interactors. The mixed group of subjects, which was most familiar with different national varieties of English, had the most confidence in their ability to understand the conversations. Note that all of the native-speaker subject group thought they understood the U.S./Indonesia pair, and that 90 percent of the non-native subject group (i.e., the Japanese) thought that they understood the Japan/China pair. Familiarity with topic and familiarity with at least one of the speech varieties being used in a conversation apparently cause one to believe that s/he understands most of what s/he hears.

Table 5 shows the percentages of subjects making accurate guesses as to the nationalities of the pairs in the conversations. Again, the mixed subject group was best, followed by the native-speaker group and the non-native speakers. I was surprised, however, that although

Table 4. Percentage of subject groups that thought they understood 60% or more of the conversations between the five sets of interactors

Test material	Subjects		
Speaker	NNS (10)	NS (10)	Mixed (9) %
China (Taiwan)	30	100	100
India (Philippines)	10	90	100
Japan (China)	90	90	100
United Kingdom (Papua New Guinea)	30	90	100
United States (Indonesia)	40	100	100

Table 5. Percentage of subjects making accurate guesses as to the nationalities of the pairs in the conversations.

Test material	Subjects		
Speaker	NNS (10)	NS (10)	Mixed (9)
			%
China	50	100	100
(Taiwan)*	70	60	100
India	20	90	100
(Philippines)*	60	100	100
Japan	90	100	100
(China)*	80	100	100
United Kingdom	70	70	89
(Papua New Guinea)*	10	20	100
United States	90	80	100
(Indonesia)*	0	0	10

*The country of origin was actually mentioned on the tape.

five of the ten interactors on the tapes identified themselves as being nationals of a particular country, only the mixed group identified their nationalities accurately. (I was not surprised that few subjects recognized the Indonesian speaker, since they had been exposed to so few Indonesians. I believe it would have been the same for the person from Papua New Guinea if he had not identified himself.) The native-speaker group was not as able to identify correctly their fellow American as well as the non-native subject group or the mixed subject group did. The native-speaker subjects were better able to identify the nationalities of the interactors from China, Japan, India, and the Philippines than they were the speaker from the United States. The non-native subject group identified the speakers from Japan most easily and identified speakers from the United States more easily than they did speakers from the United Kingdom. I believe that the native-speaker subject group would be surprised to learn of their low percentage of accuracy and that the non-native subject group would be surprised at their high degree of accuracy. The mixed subject group did well and, except for the Indonesian respondent, seemed confident in their responses. They would perhaps be surprised that they didn't guess the British person's nationality with greater accuracy.

Responses to two other items on the questionnaire deserve reporting. The questions dealt with the subjects' perceptions of the interactors' level of education and proficiency in English. The two questions (see Appendix) were identical except that number 7 was about the presenter and number 8 was about the respondent. The question was, "Based on what you heard, it seems that the presenter/respondent is (check as many as you wish): highly educated/educated/not well educated/a native English speaker/a non-native English speaker/a speaker of Standard English/a speaker of nonstandard English."

Table 6 gives the tabulated results. The interactors were perceived by a great majority of the subjects to be educated or highly educated. A small percentage (10%) of the non-native-speaker subjects thought the speaker from India was not well educated, and an equally small percentage (10%) of the native-speaker subjects thought the respondents from Papua New Guinea and Indonesia were not well educated. Subjects in the mixed group thought all of the speakers and respondents were highly educated or educated.

All three subject groups did well in correctly identifying the interactors as native or non-native English speakers. The majority were accurate in every case except one: 60 percent of the native-speaker subjects guessed that the respondent from Papua New Guinea was a native speaker of English. In spite of this, the native-speaker group was able to label correctly more of the interactors as native or non-native than either of the other two subject groups, with the mixed group a close second.

What I find most interesting about Table 6 is the final listing, which concerns the subjects' perceptions about the interactors using Standard or non-Standard English. Most of the native-speaker subject group and the non-native-speaker subject group thought everyone used Standard English. The only exceptions were the speakers from India and Japan. Fifty percent of the non-native subject group thought the speaker from India used non-Standard English. The native-speaker subject group was equally divided about the speakers from India and Japan in that 40 percent thought they used Standard and 40 percent thought they used non-Standard. I was pleased to learn that many native and non-native speakers of English would label most educated speakers of non-native English as users of Standard English. The mixed subject group was more critical and seemed to have had a stricter criterion for Standard English. Thirty-three percent of this group thought that the speaker from the United States used non-Standard English. I had thought that many non-native speakers and most native speakers would label people who were clearly non-native users as speakers of non-Standard English. It seems clear that non-native English speakers need not be indistinguishable from native speakers in order to be judged as using Standard English. These results

Table 6. Subjects' perceptions of interactors' level of education and proficiency in English

Countries of interactors	Subjects' perceptions		
	HE/E/NWE %	NS/NNS %	SE/NSE %
NNS (10):			
China	50/50/0	20/80	50/10*
Taiwan	30/70/0	10/70*	50/20*
India	30/60/10	0/100	30/50*
Philippines	50/50/0	30/70	50/30*
Japan	40/60/0	20/70*	60/30*
China	40/60/0	10/90	80/0*
United Kingdom	40/60/0	70/20*	50/30*
Papua New Guinea	50/40/0*	40/50*	40/20*
United States	50/50/0	80/20	70/20*
Indonesia	10/90/0	40/60	50/30*
NS (S10):			
China	70/30/0	0/100	70/10*
Taiwan	40/60/0	30/70	50/20*
India	10/90/0	20/80	40/40*
Philippines	10/90/0	0/100	50/30*
Japan	10/90/0	0/100	40/40*
China	0/100/0	0/100	70/10*
United Kingdom	50/50/0	90/10	70/0*
Papua New Guinea	20/70/10	60/40	60/20*
United States	40/40/0*	100/0	80/0*
Indonesia	20/60/10*	20/80	60/30*
Mixed (9):			
China	67/33/0	0/100	78/22
Taiwan	33/67/0	0/100	22/78
India	56/44/0	33/67	67/33
Philippines	56/44/0	22/78	67/33
Japan	11/89/0	0/100	11/89
China	22/78/0	0/100	50/50
United Kingdom	56/44/0	89/11	89/11
Papua New Guinea	22/78/0	33/67	33/67
United States	44/56/0	78/22	67/33
Indonesia	11/89/0	11/89	11/89

Key: HE Highly educated   NNS Non-native speaker of English
     E   Educated   SE   Standard English
     NWE Not well educated   NSE Non-Standard English
     NS Native speaker of English *   Some subjects did not reply.

support the interpretation that it is possible for Standard English to be spoken with many different accents. I believe that this is one of the very positive results of the vast spread of English across the globe.

Conclusion

In order to determine whether the spread of English is creating greater problems of understanding across cultures, this pilot study was done with three types of subject groups (non-native, native, and mixed) involving nine different national varieties. Understanding was divided into three elements: intelligibility, comprehensibility, and interpretability. Evidence supports the position that there are major differences between intelligibility, comprehensibility, and interpretability as defined in the study. Intelligibility (word/utterance recognition) is easier than comprehensibility (word/utterance meaning) or interpretability (meaning behind word/utterance). Being able to do well with one does not ensure that one will do well with the others. Having familiarity with the information presented did not seem to affect any of the three groups, but those subjects having a greater familiarity with different varieties of English performed better on the tests of interpretability than did those who lacked such familiarity. Being familiar with topic and speech variety did affect the subjects' perceptions of how well they had understood. Language proficiency does influence intelligibility, comprehensibility, and interpretability, but it seems to be most important for comprehensibility. Native speakers (from Britain and the United States) were not found to be the most easily understood, nor were they, as subjects, found to be the best able to understand the different varieties of English. Being a native speaker does not seem to be as important as being fluent in English and familiar with several different national varieties. These results indicate that the increasing number of varieties of English need not increase the problems of understanding across cultures, if users of English develop some familiarity with them.

APPENDIX

Directions: Answer the following questions by putting a check mark ($\sqrt{}$) in
the appropriate space provided, according to how you feel about
the taped material that you have just heard.

1. Could you understand what the presenter said?

	:	:	:
easily	: with some difficulty	: with great : difficulty	: not at all

2. Could you understand what the respondent said?

	:	:	:
easily	: with some difficulty	: with great : difficulty	: not at all

3. How much of the conversation did you understand?

	:	:	:	:	:
90%>	: 75%–89%	: 61%–74%	: 50%–60%	: 34%–49%	: <33%

4. Did you have difficulty understanding the conversation?
Yes _____ No _____ If Yes, check the appropriate reasons.
(You may check as many as you wish.)
_____ I could not understand the meaning of what was said.
_____ One or both speakers spoke too quickly.
_____ The accent of the presenter was too heavy.
_____ The accent of the respondent was too heavy.
_____ Other (please write) _____
5. What is the presenter's nationality? _____
6. What is the respondent's nationality? _____
7. Based on what you heard, it seems that the presenter is (check as many
as you wish):
highly educated _____ educated _____ not well educated _____
a native English speaker _____ a non-native English speaker _____
a speaker of Standard English _____ a speaker of non-Standard
English _____
8. Based on what you heard, it seems that the respondent is (check as many
as you wish):
highly educated _____ educated _____ not well educated _____
a native English speaker _____ a non-native English speaker _____
a speaker of Standard English _____ a speaker of non-Standard
English _____

REFERENCES

Crystal, David. 1985. How many millions? The statistics of English today. *English Today* 1: 7–9.

Kachru, Braj B. 1986. *The alchemy of English: the spread, models and functions of non-native Englishes.* Oxford: Pergamon Press. Reprinted 1990, Urbana: University of Illinois Press.

Quirk, Randolph, and H. G. Widdowson, eds. 1985. *English in the world: teaching and learning the language and literatures.* Cambridge: Cambridge University Press.

Smith, Larry E., ed. 1983. *Readings in English as an international language.* Oxford: Pergamon Press.

———, and Cecil E. Nelson. 1985. International intelligibility of English: directions and resources. *World Englishes* 3: 333–42.

Strevens, Peter. 1982. World English and the world's Englishes, or, whose language is it, anyway? *Journal of the Royal Society of Arts* 5311: 418–31.

5

Kamal K. Sridhar and S. N. Sridhar

Bridging the Paradigm Gap: Second-Language Acquisition Theory and Indigenized Varieties of English

Theories of second-language acquisition (hereafter, SLA), by and large, have been developed and tested without serious reference to data from the acquisition of English in those settings where indigenized varieties of English (hereafter, IVEs) such as Indian English, Singapore English, Nigerian English and Filipino English play institutionalized roles.[1] On the other hand, most studies dealing with the description and acquisition of IVEs do not engage current theoretical concerns or employ empirical methods. This chapter attempts to analyze the reasons for this absence of dialogue and to outline a functionally oriented paradigm that could give a more insightful account of the phenomena, and thereby a more satisfactory theory of SLA.

The Neglect of IVEs: Empirical and Theoretical Reasons

Current theoretical and empirical studies of SLA contain few references to IVEs or their acquisition (see, for example, the textbooks by Brown 1980, Dulay et al. 1982, and Klein 1986, or the papers in Krashen 1981, Anderson 1983a, 1984, and Rutherford 1985, among others). And, as we shall see below, the few references to IVEs in the theoretical literature (e.g., Selinker 1974 and Nemser 1971) either derive from assumptions which can be shown to be untenable or are still programmatic (Andersen 1983b).

   This neglect of IVEs is surprising in the light of a number of facts and claims about SLA theories. First, the theories purport to be applicable to SLA in general and do not place IVEs outside their purview. Second, much SLA theorizing (and testing) has dealt with

The Other Tongue

the acquisition of English. Third, learners of IVEs are, numerically as well as in terms of the range and diversity of variables they represent, one of the most significant segments of second-language acquirers in the world today.

It may be argued that this exclusion is simply a function of the theorists' unfamiliarity with the contexts in which IVEs are acquired; and that, in any case, a theory is best stated in the most general manner possible, and it is up to other researchers to challenge its validity by bringing up counterexamples.

This argument seems reasonable, though only to a limited extent. While the field of SLA, over the last decade or so, has moved rapidly and decisively to embrace empirical methods, research on the acquisition of IVEs has remained descriptive and intuitive. A few recent studies have employed rigorous empirical methods (e.g., Apte 1980 and Walwadkar 1984), but such studies are exceptions rather than the rule. Most studies in the area analyze random examples from student speech (or, more commonly, writing) without giving a systematic account of such crucial details as the source of the data, the elicitation procedure employed, the regularity and representativeness of the phenomenon in question, etc. Although these data can serve as valuable sources of initial hypotheses, their contribution to the dominant research questions in the field of SLA, such as the role of transfer vis-à-vis overgeneralization, remains limited. There is an urgent need for detailed studies of the acquisition of IVEs using systematic data collection procedures, rigorous analytical methods, and explicit reporting conventions.

Nevertheless, the value of the data, however systematic, is relative to the insightfulness of the hypotheses they support or refute. Herein lies another major weakness of the available studies of the acquisition of IVEs. Most studies in this area are derivative: they start out with an uncritical acceptance of the theoretical axioms and hypotheses presented in the "mainstream" SLA research and do little more than *illustrate* the hypothesized learner strategies, such as transfer, overgeneralization, simplification, etc. (e.g., Wong 1983) or the operation of Slobin's "charges to language" (Richards 1982), using IVE examples. While such studies may be useful as a pedagogical tool in courses in SLA in countries where IVEs are used, they contribute little to theory construction or validation because of their empirical limitations and openness to alternative analyses. What is needed is a reevaluation of the applicability of SLA theories to the particular circumstances in which IVEs are acquired, rather than simply legitimizing IVE learners as "normal" second-language acquirers according to currently fashionable models.

The empirical limitations of the studies of the acquisition of IVEs outlined above can be only a partial explanation for the failure of SLA theory to account for IVEs. This failure stems also from a number of *theory-internal* limitations that have prevented the field from taking a broad enough perspective. For, over the last two decades, there has developed a large body of insightful, though descriptive, literature on IVEs that has not been taken into account in proposing theories of SLA. As a result, the current theoretical paradigm of SLA has turned out to be too parochial and of limited value in explaining the distinctive characteristics of SLA in the context of IVEs. We hope an analysis of these limitations will contribute toward a better understanding of the dynamics of the acquisition of IVEs, and hence toward a more general and explanatory theory of SLA.

The descriptions of IVEs (see Kachru 1982a, 1983, 1986a; Smith 1981; Platt and Weber 1980; Spencer 1971; Pride 1982; Noss 1983; Llamzon 1969; Bailey and Görlach 1982; Platt et al. 1984; Crewe 1977; Tongue 1974; Ubahakwe 1979; among others) demonstrate that the settings where IVEs are acquired and used (South Asia, Southeast Asia, West and East Africa, among others) are markedly different from those presupposed in the theoretical literature on SLA.[2] It would be instructive to contrast these as a preliminary to a discussion of how concentration on one type of setting to the exclusion of the other may lead to the theory's loss of explanatory power.

Assumptions Underlying SLA Theory and Research

SLA theory's neglect of, and consequent lack of relevance to, IVEs derives from a number of implicit and explicit assumptions about SLA that underlie the theory and much of the empirical work in the area. The first of these is the assumption that the goal of SLA is, or ought to be, to acquire native-like competence in the target language (not only in terms of pronunciation and grammatical norms but also in the range of speech acts, styles, register differentiation, etc.) and hence the success of the learner's acquisition is to be judged accordingly. Second, it is assumed that the input available to the learner is extensive and intensive enough to permit acquisition of the full range of active competence in the target language. Third, the process of SLA is studied without reference to the functions that the second language is expected to perform for the learner and in the learner's community. Fourth, the role of the learner's first language is evaluated strictly with reference to its contribution in interfering with or (less frequently) facilitating the structures of the target language, and no attention is paid to its contribution to the communicative function at hand. Fifth, it is assumed that the ideal motivation for success in second-language learning is what is called "integrative" motivation, that is, one that involves admiration for the native speakers of the language and a desire to become a member of their culture. Finally, the lion's share of research attention has gone to the acquisition of phonology and syntax at the expense of the study of the acquisition of the lexicon and, until recently, pragmatics.

Characteristics of IVE Acquisition Settings

The acquisitional environment of IVEs differs from those that have been the focus of theorizing and experimentation in SLA in a number of ways. We will discuss a few major differences, relating to: (a) the target of acquisition, (b) the input to the acquisition process, (c) the role of the acquired language in relation to the other languages in the learner's repertoire, (d) motivations of the learners, and (e) lexical and pragmatic aspects of IVE acquisition. Some of the facts stated here are quite familiar to students of IVEs, but, to our knowledge, they have not been explicitly discussed in relation to the concerns of SLA theory, nor does the "mainstream" SLA literature show sufficient awareness of them.

Target

The second-language learner in target language environments is expected to be able to use the language effectively with native speakers. Hence, the intended outcome is defined in terms of the competence of the ideal native speaker of the standard variety. This assumption is extended implicitly and explicitly to second- (including IVE) and foreign-language contexts in pedagogic theory and practice. Virtually every book and article in the field talks about "successful" acquisition, "errors," "aberrant" or "deviant" structures, etc., taking the native standard variety as the unchallenged norm.

However, the situation is different in the acquisition of IVEs. IVEs are acquired primarily for use with other speakers of IVEs (see Kachru 1976 and Shaw 1981); the native-speaker norm is irrelevant in these contexts. In fact, as Smith (1983) has pointed out, the majority of uses of English as a second language around the world today involve interactions of one non-native speaker with another, rather than the prototypical situation of a native speaker and a non-native speaker assumed in ESL textbooks. Moreover, as many studies of IVEs have pointed out (Kachru 1982b: 45; Bamgboṣe 1971: 41; Sey 1973: 1), a variety that approximates too closely to the native standard (e.g., RP) is "frowned upon" as "distasteful and pedantic," "affected or even snobbish." The native norm alienates the non-native speakers from their milieus. This is true not only of the spoken language, but also of the written. Respected IVE authors speak of the need to indigenize the language to make it a suitable vehicle for carrying the weight of their Indian or African experience (Raja Rao and Chinua Achebe, to cite two). Attitude surveys show that, although the prescriptive norms still exert their force, understandably, a sizable and growing segment of teachers and learners believes that the model of instruction should be an IVE (Kachru 1976; Smith 1981).

Input

The variety of English that is available to the learners as primary input is overwhelmingly the indigenous variety of English (Indian English, West African English, etc.) and not native varieties such as British or American English. In the overwhelming majority of cases, IVEs are learned from teachers who are non-native speakers and, perhaps, whose teachers were also non-native speakers. Most learners of IVEs never get to interact with a native-variety speaker during their acquisition period. In fact, the spoken native varieties are hardly understandable to the learners, except in slow, deliberate speech, and even then there are serious comprehension difficulties, both phonological and contextual/cultural. Second, IVEs are acquired in contexts of restricted input, although not so restricted as in cases where pidgins develop. In many rural areas the learners' only exposure to English takes place in the English class at school. Although the amount of exposure to English available to the learner of an IVE is substantially more than that available in situations where English is learned as a foreign language, it is still much less than what is available to a learner of English in, say, the United States. It is therefore misleading to refer to the IVE context as a *second* language context in the sense in which the term is used for acquisition where the target language is the native language of the majority of speakers. Third, a related point, the nature of the input is significantly different. The learner is not exposed to the full range of styles, structures, and speech acts that one normally associates with the use of a language as the primary vehicle of verbal communication in a society. The ordinary (non-Westernized) learner of English in India isn't exposed to the use of English to maintain and transact informal, everyday, affective interpersonal relationships (the mother tongue is used for these); instead, he or she is exposed to academic and bureaucratic registers and literary styles. The English that he or she hears outside of class is of little relevance to his or her interests in the early years of acquisition of English. At this stage, the learner's "intake" is effectively restricted to whatever is available in the classroom.

Role of IVEs in the Verbal Repertoire

Learners of IVEs go on to use English alongside other languages in their repertoire. As sociolinguistic surveys of the use of English by learners and professionals have shown (Parasher 1980; K. K. Sridhar 1982), English functions like the H(igh) variety in a diglossic situation with respect to the other languages in a number of domains in bi- and multilingual communities. This complementarity of functions shows that English is not called upon to serve all the functions that it may serve for a monolingual English speaker; hence it is wrong to assume that the IVE learner should exhibit the same range of competence as the learner in a "melting-pot" target language environment. The model of bilingualism appropriate to the IVE contexts is therefore an "additive" one.

In fact, there is empirical evidence to show that the functions of English not only complement but also overlap those of the local languages in a number of domains, such as friendship, correspondence, transactions, etc. (Parasher 1980; K. K. Sridhar 1982). Code-switching and code-mixing are formal manifestations of this overlap. Furthermore, there is a good deal of evidence, as pointed out by Kachru (1986a), that the user of English in these varieties presupposes a bilingual competence on the part of the receiver. The fact that IVEs are acquired in such contexts of intensive and extensive bilingualism is of central importance in developing explanatory models of their acquisition and use.

Motivation

Sociolinguistic surveys of the attitudes and motivations of IVE learners (Kachru 1976; Shaw 1981) have shown that, in these settings, "the reasons for studying English and the skills desired are overwhelmingly the ones normally labeled instrumental" (Shaw 1981: 121). The effectiveness of instrumental motivation in promoting second-language proficiency has been demonstrated by Lukmani (1972) for a group of non-Westernized women in Bombay, and by Gardner and Lambert (1972) for Filipino learners of English. As Shaw (1981: 121) correctly points out, "The generally high level of English ability observed in the [IVE settings] seems to throw doubt on the hypothesis that integrative motivation is essential for achievement in second (language) acquisition. At least the whole aspect of integrative motivation should be reexamined in terms of a desire among learners to join an indigenous group of English language speakers or a vague international one rather than a group of foreign native speakers."

Lexical and Pragmatic Aspects

Some of the most distinctive characteristics of IVEs involve innovations in the lexicon, collocational possibilities, and the ways in which speech acts such as thanking, complimenting, urging, consoling, etc., are carried out in the adapted language. Unfortunately, it is precisely these areas, which reflect the distinctive cultural experiences and conventions of the community, that SLA has had little to say about until recently (see Wolfson and Judd 1983). It is therefore not surprising that researchers in IVEs feel that SLA theories have failed them in that they provide no apparatus for characterizing the distinctiveness of, say, Nigerian English, even when the grammar may not deviate from the native standard.

Dangers of an Uncritical Application of the Current SLA Paradigm

The contrast between the assumptions of the current SLA paradigm and the features of IVE settings outlined above suggests that the concepts of the former are not readily transferable to the IVE situations. We shall demonstrate this point with reference to some of the more important concepts in SLA theory, such as *interlanguage, pidginization, creolization,* and, most important, *transfer.*

The term *interlanguage* (and others used interchangeably with it, such as *approximative systems*) has been used in the SLA literature to refer to a variety of intermediate systems between the native language and the "target language," such as the intermediate stages in the second language learners' language, immigrant varieties, institution-alized (indigenized) non-native varieties (IVEs), and different types of pidgins. For Selinker, who introduced the term in recent SLA theory, "successful" second-language learners are those "who seem to achieve native-speaker 'competence,' i.e., those who learn a second language so that their 'performance' is indistinguishable from that of native speakers" (1974: 49). According to him, "perhaps a mere 5 percent of all learners" achieve this competence; the rest—the overwhelming majority—end up with an interlanguage. This interlanguage is a product of a number of major processes, such as language transfer, transfer of training, second-language learning strategy, second-language communication strategy, overgeneralization of target language structures, and other minor ones, such as hypercorrection, spelling pronunciation, etc. The most crucial problem in SLA theory, according to Selinker, is accounting for the phenomenon of *fossilization*, i.e., "regular reappearance or reemergence in IL productive performance of linguistic structures which were thought to be eradicated" (1974: 36). Fossilizable phenomena are "linguistic items, rules, and subsystems which speakers of a particular (native language) will tend to keep in their [interlanguage] relative to a particular (target language)" (36). He goes on to note that "many of these phenomena reappear in IL performance when the learner's attention is focused upon new and difficult intellectual subject matter or when he is in a state of anxiety or other excitement, and strangely enough, sometimes when he is in a state of extreme relaxation" (36). As an example, he cites "Indian English as an IL with respect to English" which "seems to fossilize the that complement or *V that* construction for all verbs that take sentential complements" (37). Later he emphasizes that "not only can entire competences be fossilized in individual learners performing in their own interlingual situation, but also in whole groups of individuals, resulting in the emergence of a new dialect (here Indian English), where fossilized competences may be the normal situation" (38).

There are many problems with this account. First, although Selinker doesn't make this explicit, interlanguage as a phenomenon of SLA is an unstable system. Corder (1967), Nemser (1971), and many other researchers have talked about the "atypical rapidity" with which interlanguages change in the learner. The "fossilized" structures of Indian English that Selinker discusses, on the other hand, are stable characteristics of the variety, not only of the learners' languages, and have persisted across generations. Second, in Selinker's system, fossilized structures "reappear" under a special set of circumstances, e.g., conditions of anxiety, "extreme relaxation," etc. This implies that in other circumstances non-fossilized, presumably target-like, features may be used. Again, this is not representative of the majority of IVE users. For the majority of speakers of Indian English, the so-called fossilized structures are the "normal" structures, and they have no others in their competence. Further, the application of the term *interlanguage* to IVs suggests that they represent an intermediate acquisitional stage on their way toward native or native-like norms. As we have seen, the acquisitional target for IVE speakers is not the native norm but an indigenized one. Calling the IVEs interlanguages or their structural features fossilizations does violence to both the phenomena and theoretical constructs.

Equally unilluminating are some of the other concepts used in current SLA theory, such as pidginization and creolization. (For a discussion of how IVEs do not fit into the current sociolinguistic typologies see K. K. Sridhar 1985.) Despite Andersen's (1983b) admirable attempt to untangle the issues in this muddy area (cf. Andersen 1983a), one cannot help agreeing with Sankoff's observation that "we have about reached the limits of the potential usefulness of the terms 'pidginization' and 'creolization'" (Sankoff 1983: 242). For pidginization in process terms has come to be a shorthand for "component processes" of LA such as "simplification," "negative transfer," etc.— themselves agonizingly difficult to distinguish from one another— which seem to obtain in all non-primary-language acquisition. It is also misleading in that it suggests that the outcome would be a pidgin while it is not. In any case, the concept is inappropriate for IVEs for at least two reasons: (a) the restricted input that the IVE learner has access to is not so restricted as to prevent him/her from becoming a bilingual in it, and (b) the structural modifications involved in the learning and evolution of IVEs include at least as much complexification as simplification.

The concept of creolization as a model of IVE acquisition appears at first to be more appropriate than pidginization, for it seems to capture several important characteristics of IVEs. These include, to use a slightly modified version of Andersen's (1983a: 31–32) typology: the use of English forms with non-English meaning, function, and distribution; non-English meanings, forms, and distributions (at least partially) derived from the substrate languages; non-English structures (at least partially) determined by Slobin's cognitive and perceptual constraints, such as his famous "operating principles" and "charges to language," as well as from linguistic universals; and innovations already present in the input. However, this is creolization only metaphorically; for, as Bickerton (1983: 238) observes, creolization is done mainly by children. The learners have an "abnormal" language background; it gives you a first language, not a second. Once again, it is clear that there is no substitute for studying the phenomena empirically, in *sui generis* terms, and postponing pidgeonholing until we have a clearer understanding of what actually goes on in the acquisition of IVEs.

Consequences of the Neglect of IVEs in SLA Theorizing

While the attempts to fit IVEs into the current theoretical constructs of SLA have been unsuccessful and misleading, the neglect of IVEs has also been detrimental to the development of theory. As an example of this, we shall discuss the treatment of the role of transfer in the acquisition process. The constrastive analysis hypothesis has had an interesting and complicated history in SLA, so our discussion will be limited to its relevance to the understanding of indigenized varieties.

SLA theory in the 1970s dismissed the role of mother tongue in acquisition as marginal, if not irrelevant, especially in syntax, thanks to the misleading correlation between transfer and behaviorist learning theory proposed first in Dulay and Burt (1974) and repeated in Dulay et al. (1982). The negative evaluation of transfer in pedagogical circles and the preoccupation of the overwhelming majority of empirical studies of SLA with acquisition in native-variety settings also contributed to a downplay of transfer. In this climate of opinion, it became fashionable to reinterpret putative cases of transfer as outcomes of such other "respectable" acquisition strategies as overgeneralization (e.g., Jain 1974). As Kachru (1980) has shown, many alleged instances of overgeneralization can equally plausibly be shown to be consistent with a theory of transfer. Of late, even "clear" cases of transfer (such as the retention of resumptive pronouns in relative clauses by Arab and Persian learners) have come to be interpreted as due to the learners' selection of unmarked parameter settings (Hyltenstam 1984).

However, anyone familiar with the formal and pragmatic characteristics of IVEs of English cannot fail to be struck by the fact that many of these features can be related to features of the speakers' mother tongue in a fairly transparent fashion (cf. Kachru 1983; Bokamba 1982; and Platt and Weber 1980, among others). And, given that transfer is as a process perfectly consistent with a "cognitivist" (i.e., hypothesis formation and testing) theory of SLA (see S. N. Sridhar 1980), there seems to be little motivation for being apologetic about claiming IVEs to be, in good part, products of transfer. Indeed, Quirk et al. (1972) refer to IVEs as "interference varieties." We prefer the term "transfer" to "interference" because of the potential negative connotations of the latter. This is, of course, not to deny that other processes are operating to produce the structural and pragmatic characteristics of IVEs.

In fact, recent research (e.g., the papers in Gass and Selinker 1983) shows that what is at issue is not the operation of transfer as a significant process in SLA, but the conditions under which transfer operates. In this connection it is interesting to note Ervin-Tripp's observation that (more) mother-tongue influence was found in "learning conditions in which the second language was not the language of the learner's larger milieu, so that the learning contexts were aberrant both in function and frequency of structures" (1974: 121). This observation, though based on foreign language learning contexts, is applicable, *mutatis mutandis*, to IVEs as well, though Ervin-Tripp's characterization of the contexts of limited exposure as "aberrant" is disturbing. This is an example of how the preoccupation with acquisition in target language environments had led to a loss of perspective. SLA researchers seem to overlook the fact, which scholars of IVE have been stressing for quite some time (Kachru 1976; Strevens 1982), that many times more learners acquire second languages in contexts of limited exposure than in host environments. Muysken (1984) seems to be one of the few researchers in SLA to take note of this fact. He observes, "L₂ learning modeled on the speech production of L₂ speakers may well be the norm, worldwide, rather than the exception" (102).

Crucial to understanding the role of transfer in IVEs is a recognition of the roles of the language being acquired (and used) in the learner's verbal repertoire. As we have seen, English, in multilingual contexts, such as in India or Singapore, complements and overlaps with the other languages in the bilingual's repertoire, and it is used to interact with other bilinguals. As a result, the user of English expects bilingual competence in his or her interlocutors. Because of this shared bilingual repertoire, transfer of elements from the shared languages is not an obstacle to easy communication. Far from impeding intelligibility, transfer acts as the grease to make the wheels of bilingual communication turn smoothly. Given that transfer features are not idiosyncratic to learners but shared by speakers with the same substratal languages, they serve as effective simplification strategies, modes of acculturation (see Lowenberg 1986) and as markers of membership in the community of speakers of a given indigenized variety. In cases of pragmatic transfer, for example, where the semantic formulae characteristic of a speech act in the mother tongue are transferred in the performance of analogous speech acts in English, even though the native variety might employ a different set of semantic formulae (see Olshtain and Cohen 1983), transfer serves as an effective strategy of acculturation which draws upon shared cultural presuppositions. Thus, transfer in an indigenized variety does not have the same negative value—in terms of either potential interference with intelligibility or attitudinal devaluation—that it has in the context of acquisition of a native variety in a monolingual setting. In other words, the functions of transfer in second-language contexts are not in principle different from those in language contact situations in general. In studies of language contact, it is expected and accepted that borrowed items undergo change due to acculturation and linguistic assimilation (Weinreich

1953). Similarly, given that all the languages of the learner's repertoire are actively used in second-language contexts, it is to be expected that the languages interact with one another's formal features. The abhorrence of transfer derives from an artificial view of bilingual language storage and processing based on two questionable assumptions: one is that the ideal bilingual keeps his or her languages separate—both in storage and in actual use (a view that derives from Weinreich 1953); the other is that the ideal bilingual is as proficient in each of his or her languages as the ideal speaker of the respective languages (cf. Bloomfield 1933). There is ample evidence that each of these assumptions is wrong. We have shown in an earlier paper that linguistic and psycholinguistic evidence argues for an interactional model of bilingual processing (Sridhar and Sridhar 1980). Grosjean (1982) has persuasively argued for a notion of bilingual competence in which the languages in the repertoire complement one another's strengths and weaknesses to produce the type of composite language competence suited to the demands on the bilingual. In addition, linguistic and sociolinguistic studies of code-mixing in communities where IVEs are used have shown that English and the local languages operate in complex syntactic relationships within single sentences (Kachru 1978; S. N. Sridhar 1978; and Poplack 1978, among others). Given that such mixing is the norm for the type of language situation that the learner is exposed to and hence the type of language that he or she will be called upon to use, it is hardly surprising that transfer should play a central part in the acquisition process. Needless to say, it is unrealistic prescriptivism to evaluate the success of second-language learning with reference to transfer-free norms in such contexts.

The dangers of ignoring the bilingual's repertoire in SLA are also illustrated by Egbe's (1979) discussion of the acquisition of English by Nigerian learners. Observing that Nigerian learners tend to use formal polite terms where informal polite expressions would be appropriate in native varieties, Egbe argues that this is not a deficiency in their English but a consequence of the availability of Nigerian pidgin English for informal uses. Similar arguments can be offered for the alleged "gaps" in the learners' competence noted in other indigenized varieties. In devising measures of acquisitional success or accuracy, it is therefore necessary to take into account the functions that the learner's language is intended to serve, rather than to assume that the learner aims at acquiring the full range of native competence in English

There are many other areas of SLA theory where putatively universal concepts and processes have been proposed without taking note of potential contradiction from IVE data. A case in point is

Kellerman's (1978) claim that items that appear to be language specific (e.g., idioms) will be less prone to transfer. No one familiar with the literature on Indian or West African English, let alone the literature *in* those IVEs (see S. N. Sridhar 1982), could entertain such a claim. Such propositions betray the narrow theoretical and empirical foundations of current SLA theories.

Yet, there are some signs that this situation might be changing. Andersen (1983b: 17) lists "indigenized language" as a distinct "setting or type of acquisition" in his typology of SLA contexts and processes, and classifies IVEs as "creoloids" following Platt (1977), rather than creoles. Muysken (1984: 101)—working independently of IVEs—advocates a perspective on SLA that corresponds to the paradigm argued for in this chapter and in the literature on IVEs (e.g., Kachru 1965 and later): "to see second language learning as becoming a member of a speech community, governed in the same way as other forms or verbal behavior by norms that obtain in that particular speech community."

Welcome aboard!

Conclusion

We have argued that there is a lack of articulation between theories of SLA and research on the acquisition and use of IVEs. On the one hand, the theories have either overextended the constructs based on acquisition in monolingual, target language settings, giving a distorted picture of IVEs, or ignored them altogether. Thus, SLA theory has been counterintuitive and limited in explanatory power with regard to a very substantial segment of the second-language learner population. Studies of IVEs, on the other hand, have remained descriptive and atheoretical, rather than based on rigorous and systematic empirical research. Thus, their distinctiveness from the prototypes assumed in SLA theories has not been convincingly demonstrated. This chapter has been an attempt to show that, despite the absence of empirical research on the acquisition of IVEs, attention to the particular situations in which they are acquired and used, and especially their roles in the communicative patterns of their multilingual societies, will contribute to a broadening of perspective and reevaluation of the universal applicability of many of the concepts employed in current SLA theory. Paradoxical as it may seem, SLA researchers seem to have neglected the fact that the goal of SLA is bilingualism. Attention to IVEs may help remind us of this useful idea and contribute to the formulation of a more widely applicable—if more complex—theory of SLA.

NOTES

1. Earlier versions of this paper were presented at the Second Language Acquisition Circle of New York and the Georgetown University Roundtable in Languages and Linguistics. We have benefited from discussions with Miriam Eisenstein, Braj B. Kachru, Peter Lowenberg, and Peter Strevens, but they are, of course, blameless for the opinions expressed here.

2. For discussion of the number of users and learners of English as a second language around the world, and in IVE settings, see Fishman et al. 1977, Gage and Ohannessian 1974, Strevens 1982, and Kachru 1986b.

REFERENCES

Andersen, R., ed. 1983a. *Pidginization and creolization as language acquisition.* Rowley, Mass.: Newbury House.
———. 1983b. Introduction: the language acquisition interpretation of pidginization and creolization. Pp. 1–56 in Andersen 1983a.
———. 1984. *Second languages: a cross-linguistic perspective.* Rowley, Mass.: Newbury House.
Apte, M. 1980. "Acquisition of English syntax by Marathi learners: an investigation." M. Litt. dissertation. Hyderabad: Central Institute of English and Foreign Languages.
Bailey, R. W., and M. Görlach, eds. 1982. *English as a world language.* Ann Arbor: University of Michigan Press.
Bamgboṣe, A. 1971. The English language in Nigeria. Pp. 35–48 in Spencer, ed. 1971.
Bickerton, D. 1983. Comments on Valdman's "Creolization and second language acquisition." Pp. 235–40 in Andersen 1983a.
Bloomfield, L. 1933. *Language.* New York: Henry Holt.
Bokamba, E. 1982. The Africanization of English. In this volume.
Brown, H. D. 1980. *Principles of language learning and teaching.* Englewood Cliffs, N.J.: Prentice-Hall.
Corder, S. P. 1967. The significance of learners' errors. *International Review of Applied Linguistics* 5(4): 161–70. Reprinted in *Error analysis: perspectives on second language acquisition.* Ed. Jack C. Richards. London: Longman, 1974. Pp. 19–27.
Crewe, W., ed. 1977. *The English language in Singapore.* Singapore: Eastern Universities Press.
Dulay, H., and M. Burt. 1974. You can't learn without goofing. Pp. 95–123 in *Error analysis: perspectives on second language acquisition.* Ed. J. C. Richards. London: Longman.
———, and S. Krashen. 1982. *Language two.* New York: Oxford University Press.
Egbe, D. I. 1979. Spoken and written English in Nigeria. Pp. 86–106 in Ubahakwe 1979.

Ervin-Tripp, S. 1974. Is second language learning like the first? *TESOL Quarterly* 8: 111–27.

Fishman, Joshua A., R. L. Cooper, and A. W. Conrad. 1977. *The spread of English: the sociology of English as an additional language.* Rowley, Mass.: Newbury House.

Gage, W. W., and S. Ohannessian. 1984. ESL enrollments throughout the world. *Linguistic Reporter* 16(9): 13–16.

Gardner, R. C., and W. E. Lambert. 1972. *Attitudes and motivations in second language learning.* Rowley, Mass.: Newbury House.

Gass, S., and L. Selinker, eds. 1983. *Language transfer in language learning.* Rowley, Mass.: Newbury House.

Gonzalez, A. 1983. When does an error become a feature of Philippine English? Pp. 150–72 in Noss 1983.

Grosjean, F. 1982. *Life with two languages: an introduction to bilingualism.* Cambridge: Harvard University Press.

Hyltenstam, K. 1984. The use of typological markedness conditions as predictors in second language acquisition: the case of pronominal copies in relative clauses. Pp. 39–58 in Andersen 1984.

Jain, M. P. 1974. Error analysis: source, cause and significance. In *Error Analysis.* Ed. J. C. Richards. London: Longman.

Kachru, Braj B. 1967. The *Indianness* in Indian English. *Word* 21: 391–410. Revised version in Kachru 1983.

———. 1976. Models of English for the Third World: white man's linguistic burden or language pragmatics? *TESOL Quarterly* 10(2): 221–39.

———. 1978. Code-mixing as a communicative strategy in India. Pp. 193–207 in *International dimensions of bilingual education.* Ed. J. E. Alatis. Washington, D.C.: Georgetown University Press.

———. 1982a. *The other tongue: English across cultures.* Urbana: University of Illinois Press.

———. 1982b. Models for non-native Englishes. In this volume.

———. 1983. *The Indianization of English: the English language in India.* Delhi: Oxford University Press.

———. 1986a. *The alchemy of English.* Oxford: Pergamon Press. Reprinted 1990, Urbana: University of Illinois Press.

———. 1986b. American English and other Englishes. In Kachru 1986a.

Kachru, Y. 1980. Transfer in overgeneralization: contrastive linguistics revisited. *TESL Studies* 3: 152–62.

Kellerman, E. 1978. Giving learners a break: native language intuitions as a source of predictions about transferability. *Working Papers on Bilingualism* 15: 59–92.

Klein, W. 1986. *Second language acquisition.* Cambridge: Cambridge University Press.

Krashen, S. 1981. *Second language acquisition and second language learning.* Oxford: Pergamon Press.

Llamzon, Teodoro A. 1969. *Standard Filipino English.* Manila: Ateneo University Press.

Lowenberg, Peter H. 1986. Sociocultural context and second language acquisition: acculturation and creativity in Malaysian English. *World Englishes* 5(1): 71–83.

Lukmani, Y. 1972. Motivation to learn and language proficiency. *Language Learning* 22: 261–73.

Muysken, P. 1984. The Spanish that Quechua speakers learn: L₂ learning as norm-governed behavior. Pp. 101–19 in Andersen 1984.

Nemser, W. 1971. Approximative systems of foreign language learners. *International Review of Applied Linguistics* 9(2): 115–23.

Noss, R. B., ed. 1983. *Varieties of English in Southeast Asia.* Anthology Series 11. Singapore: Singapore University Press.

Olshtain, E., and A. D. Cohen. 1983. Apology: a speech act set. Pp. 18–35 in *Sociolinguistics and language acquisition.* Ed. N. Wolfson and E. Judd. Rowley, Mass.: Newbury House.

Parasher, S. V. 1980. Mother-tongue English diglossia: a case study of Indian bilinguals' language use. *Anthropological Linguistics* 22: 151–68.

Platt, John. 1977. *Subvarieties of Singapore English: their sociolectal and functional status.* In Crewe, ed. 1977.

———, and Heidi Weber. 1980. *English in Singapore and Malaysia.* Kuala Lumpur: Oxford University Press.

———, and Ho Min Lian. 1984. *The new Englishes.* London: Routledge & Kegan Paul.

Poplack, S. 1978. "Sometimes I'll start a sentence in Spanish, y termino en Espanol: toward a typology of code-switching." Working paper No. 4. New York: Language Policy Task Force, Centro de Estudios Puertorriquenos, City University of New York.

Pride, J. B., ed. 1982. *New Englishes.* Rowley, Mass.: Newbury House.

Quirk, R.; S. Greenbaum, G. Leech, and J. Svartvik. 1972. *A grammar of contemporary English.* London: Longman.

Richards, Jack C. 1982. Rhetorical and communicative styles in the new varieties of English. Pp. 227–48 in Pride 1982.

Rutherford, W. E., ed. 1985. *Language universals and second language acquisition.* Amsterdam: Benjamins.

Sankoff, G. 1983. Comment on Valdman's "Creolization and second language acquisition." Pp. 241–45 in Andersen 1983a.

Selinker, L. 1974. Interlanguage. Pp. 31–54 in *Error analysis: perspectives on second language acquisition.* Ed. J. C. Richards. London: Longman.

Sey, K. A. 1973. *Ghanaian English: an exploratory survey.* London: Macmillan.

Shaw, Willard. 1981. Asian student attitudes toward English. Pp. 108–22 in *English for cross-cultural communication.* Ed. Larry E. Smith. New York: St. Martin's Press.

Slobin, D. I. 1978. Language change in childhood and history. Pp. 185–214 in *Language learning and thought.* Ed. J. Macnamara. New York: Academic Press.

Smith, Larry E., ed. 1981. *English for cross-cultural communication.* London: Macmillan.

———. 1983. *Readings in English as an international language.* Oxford: Pergamon Press.

Spencer, John. 1971. Colonial language policies and their legacies. In *Current trends in linguistics.* Ed. T. A. Sebeok. Vol. VII: Linguistics in Sub-Saharan Africa. The Hague: Mouton.

Sridhar, K. K. 1982. English in South Indian urban context. Pp. 141–53 in Kachru 1982a.

Sridhar, S. N. 1978. On the functions of code-mixing in Kannada. In *Aspects of sociolinguistics in South Asia.* Ed. B. B. Kachru and S. N. Sridhar. Special issue of *International Journal of the Sociology of Language* 16: 109–17. The Hague: Mouton.

———. 1980. Contrastive analysis, error analysis and interlanguage: three phases of one goal. Pp. 91–119 in *Readings in English as a second language.* Ed. K. Croft. Boston: Winthrop.

———. 1982. Non-native English literatures: context and relevance. Pp. 291–306 in Kachru 1982a.

———. 1985. Sociolinguistic theories and non-native varieties of English. *Lingua* 68: 85–104.

———, and Sridhar, K. K. 1980. The syntax and psycholinguistics of bilingual code-mixing. *Canadian Journal of Psychology* 34:407–16.

Strevens, P. 1982. World English and the world's English—or, whose language is it anyway? *Journal of the Royal Society of Arts* (June): 412–28.

Tongue, R. K. 1974. *The English of Singapore and Malaysia.* Singapore: Eastern University Press.

Ubahakwe, E. 1979. Adapting the role of the English language in Nigerian education. Pp. 279–92 in *Varieties and functions of English in Nigeria.* Ed. E. Ubahakwe. Ibadan: African Universities Press.

Walwadkar, R. 1984. "Error analysis: the use of overgeneralization and transfer as learning strategies in the acquisition of negation, yes/no questions and wh-questions." M. Litt. dissertation. Hyderabad: Central Institute of English and Foreign Languages.

Weinreich, U. 1953. *Languages in contact: findings and problems.* The Hague: Mouton.

Wolfson, Nessa, and Elliot Judd. 1983. *Sociolinguistics and language acquisition.* Rowley, Mass.: Newbury House.

Wong, I. F. 1983. Simplification features in the structures of colloquial English. Pp. 125–49 in Noss 1983.

6

Peter H. Lowenberg

Testing English as a World Language: Issues in Assessing Non-Native Proficiency

The past few years have been marked by considerable sophistication in the refinement of English language testing. Among their many advances, researchers and practitioners have successfully begun to incorporate a large number of learning, teaching, and contextual variables in the design and evaluation of test instruments. However, to date, relatively little attention has been focused on the variability inherent in the linguistic "norms" for English that are generally tested. In identifying these norms, most researchers in testing appear to assume implicitly that the benchmark for proficiency in English around the world should be the norms accepted and used by "native speakers" of English.

Such an assumption is no longer universally valid. In support of this claim, data are presented from the "non-native" varieties of English (Kachru 1986; Lowenberg 1986a) that have developed in countries formerly colonized by Britain or the United States where English is still used as a second, often official, language in a broad range of *intra*national domains, including government, commerce, the mass media, and education. Such former colonies include Bangladesh, Botswana, Brunei, Burma, Cameroon, Ethiopia, Fiji, Gambia, Ghana, India, Israel, Kenya, Lesotho, Liberia, Malawi, Malaysia, Malta, Mauritius, Namibia, Nauru, Nigeria, Pakistan, the Philippines, Seychelles, Sierra Leone, Singapore, South Africa, Sri Lanka, Sudan, Swaziland, Tanzania, Tonga, Uganda, Western Samoa, Zambia, and Zimbabwe (Conrad and Fishman 1977; *Encyclopædia Britannica* 1986).[1]

In these settings English is used daily by non-native speakers in the absence of native speakers, in non-Western sociocultural contexts, and in constant contact with other languages in multilingual speech communities. As a result, it often undergoes what Kachru (1986) has termed "nativization." That is, it develops new linguistic features at all linguistic levels, features that would be considered deviant if used in countries where the "native speaker" varieties of English (e.g., British or American English) predominate. However, in their non-native contexts, these linguistic innovations and modifications are so systematic that many have become de facto local norms for English usage. In fact, attitudinal research (Kachru 1976; Shaw 1981) indicates that in at least two countries with widely attested non-native varieties, India and Singapore, approximately 50 percent of college-educated English users believe nativized features should be the local norms for English usage and the models for English language teaching.

This chapter proposes an approach for beginning to identify these norms in one non-native variety: Malaysian English. A brief survey of the sociolinguistic context in which English has developed and is used in Malaysia is followed by an analysis of divergences from the norms of American English in sample texts written by Malaysians in several domains of "Standard" English. Based on Trudgill (1983) and Tay and Gupta (1983), the standard model of a variety of English — native or non-native — is here defined as the linguistic forms of that variety that are normally used in formal speaking and writing by speakers who have received the highest level of education available in that variety. Standard English is the accepted model for official, journalistic, and academic writing and for public speaking before an audience or on radio or television.

The focus in this analysis is on morphosyntactic features in Standard English because these features can be easily identified and classified for cross-varietal comparison, because they have already been well described in British and American English, because authoritative prescriptive norms for them are frequently available in such sources as school textbooks and newspaper style sheets, because proficiency in these forms is measured in most standardized tests of English proficiency, and because many of these features result from processes that are very productive in all varieties of English.[2] Analysis is of written, as opposed to spoken, texts, since regional phonological rules (such as word-final consonant cluster simplification) can often mask the realization of morphosyntactic norms, and since written language has a greater likelihood of being successfully monitored or edited, making possible a distinction between sporadic "mistakes" and systematic acquisitional "errors" (see Corder 1967 [1974]).

Where relevant, also included are examples of Standard British

English which diverge from American norms in ways similar to Malaysian English; of Standard Singapore English, used by Malaysia's southern neighbor; and of recent innovations in registers of Standard American English. Sources of data are major English-language newspapers in England, the United States, and Malaysia; scholarly texts written by British, American, and Malaysian linguists; the style sheet for the Singapore *Straits Times*, the parent publication of Malaysia's preeminent English language newspaper, the *New Straits Times*; Malaysian government publications; and ESL textbooks authorized by the Malaysian Ministry of Education.

This analysis is followed by suggestions as to how familiarity with possible nativized features in Malaysian English can be used to distinguish "varietal differences" from personal "acquisitional deficiencies" in assessing the English proficiency of Malaysian speakers of English.

Malaysian English: Past and Present

Malaysian English began to develop during the British colonization of the Malay peninsula and western Borneo from the late eighteenth through the mid-twentieth centuries. The British established schools, especially in the urban trading centers on the west coast of the Malay Peninsula, where English was first taught and then used as the medium of instruction and of other school activities. The privileged recipients of this education—children of elite families from the indigenous Malay and large South Asian and Chinese immigrant populations—came to use English increasingly in their daily affairs.[3] As a result, when the British began to withdraw from the area in the late 1950s, English had become the dominant language of the non-European elites, both as a language of power and prestige and as an interethnic link language (Le Page 1962; Platt and Weber 1980; Asmah 1985).

At the time of its independence in 1957, the Federation of Malaya retained English as one of two official languages, along with the major indigenous language, Malay, which was also selected as the sole national language. English continued to serve as the dominant language of education, government and law, and large-scale banking and commerce (Le Page 1962). The second half of the 1960s brought implementation of a policy to increase the use of Malay in the expanded nation of Malaysia. In 1969 the Ministry of Education initiated a policy whereby all English-medium schools were to become Malay-medium (Llamzon 1978; Platt and Weber 1980). By 1983 this process had been completed nationwide at the primary through tertiary levels of education (Lowenberg 1988).

One result of this language policy has been a dramatic increase in Malaysians' use of Malay, renamed *Bahasa Malaysia,* and a corresponding decrease in their use of English, particularly outside the cities (Lowenberg 1986b). This diminishing use of English, especially in the schools, has produced widespread popular concern that the general level of English proficiency among Malaysians is in decline. The English-language newspapers frequently run such headlines as "First Aid Needed for Our English" (*New Sunday Times,* 4/21/85) and "Decline and Fall of the English Language" (*New Straits Times,* 5/11/ 85).

However, such preoccupations with an overall decline in English proficiency among Malaysians overlook the fact that English is still widely used by the current Malaysian elites, who were educated in English-medium schools during the colonial or initial postcolonial periods and are still quite proficient in English.[4] Augustin (1982) reports that of 1.1 million Malaysians who completed secondary school between 1956 and 1970, almost 70 percent had an English-medium education. As a result, Augustin concludes, "the educated . . . Malaysians now in the prime of life and who play leadership roles in government and trade are fairly competent in the use of English." These English-educated elites are concentrated in the urban centers of the Malay peninsula, where approximately 25 percent of the population uses English "extensively . . . for intergroup communication" (Augustin 1982: 251–52). They still set the standards for English usage as leading journalists for the most prestigious English-language newspapers, and as writers and editors of the government-authorized English language textbooks (Lowenberg 1991). The following morphosyntactic examples of Malaysian English are taken from those sources.

Morphosyntactic Innovations in Malaysian English

The following Malaysian examples reflect the same types of divergences from Standard American English that occur in Standard British English. Examples (1) through (3), from reputable sources of Standard British English, indicate a major process by which British and American English often differ: the treatment as count nouns of mass nouns that consist of countable units.

(1) Some small initial fall-off in *attendances* is unavoidable. (*Times of London,* 10/27/86: 17; in Algeo 1988: 7)

(2) ... iceberg *lettuces* are down in price and should be selling for between 35p and 55p, depending on size. (*Daily Telegraph,* 8/9/85: 6; in Algeo 1988: 7)

(3) The teacher records a set of advertisements for *entertainments.* (Porter and Roberts 1987: 185)

All of the italicized items would be incorrect in contemporary Standard American English. However, items (4) and (5) demonstrate that this process is also productive in American English, especially when it is extended by writers whose scholarship is highly regarded, such as the noted American linguists Charles Ferguson, Shirley Brice Heath, and Jean Berko Gleason.[5]

(4) Equally certainly, twenty-five authors and two editors do not know enough to write this book, and by virtue of *knowledges* and viewpoints they may not provide as cohesive a book as a single author. (Ferguson and Heath 1981: xxxviii)

(5) Parents' eagerness to teach their 6-month-old children the prelinguistic routine "bye bye" is *one evidence* of their desire to show that their baby is on its way to being a socialized person. (Berko Geason 1988: 276)

A Malaysian linguist of equivalent stature in Southeast Asia, Asmah Haji Omar, has likewise extended this process in (6).

(6) In this context, there were variations such as (code) *switchings* between English and their own language. (Asmah 1985: 20)

Further Malaysian extensions of this process in domains of Standard English occur in (7), from the front page of the leading daily English newspaper, and in (8), from an ESL textbook published by the Ministry of Education.

(7) Complaints of threats and *intimidations* have surfaced and these could affect the security situation in the State ... (*New Straits Times,* 5/1/86: 1)

(8) *A consideration* for others is most important. (Koh and Leong 1976: 238)

Differences across varieties of Standard English also frequently develop in fixed collocations of verbs with particles and prepositions, as in (9) and (10), again from credible Standard British English sources. The italicized items here would be deviant in Standard American English.

(9) This envisaged 16 to 20 "technology schools" in big cities, each *catering for* 1000 selected pupils ... (*Times of London,* 9/ 15/86: 1; in Algeo 1988: 25)

(10) The learner will only be able to show that his "knowledge" of the text is *approximating to* that of the teacher through tests, reproduction, and answers to "higher inference" questions. (Porter and Roberts 1987: 182)

Similar constructions in Malaysian English occur in examples (11) through (14), from an Oxford University Press ESL text, a government publication, and two major English-language newspapers.[6]

(11) *Give* your book *in.* (Howe 1974: 125)

(12) . . . Mr. Pierre MacDonald said at a press conference in Kuala Lumpur on April 30 to *round up* a four-day visit, that . . . (*Malaysian Digest*, May 1987: 9, publication of Ministry of Foreign Affairs, Malaysia)

(13) That way the forms would be filled and processed within minutes, rather than have the passengers *fill up* all the details while at the checkpoint. (*The Sunday Star,* 3/31/85: 2)

(14) With three days to go before acceptance, the battle for Umno Youth Exco seats is *hotting up.* (*New Straits Times,* 6/14/80: 1)

A third type of cross-varietal morphosyntactic divergence occurs in prepositional collocations, as in (15), produced by the internationally respected British linguist John Swales.

(15) Yet we appear to have a multi-targeted arrow *to hand* that will cover the wide ground of interest we are seeking . . . (Swales 1985: 218)

Examples (16) and (17), from the style sheet of the Singapore *Straits Times,* illustrate how such differences from Standard American English occur in street locations in non-native varieties of Standard English.

(16) She lives *in 6th Avenue.* (*Straits Times Press*, 1985: 4)

(17) I live in an apartment *at Belmont Road.* (*Straits Times Press,* 1985: 177)

These Singaporean norms may be following norms of British English (cf. Schur 1987; Algeo 1988). At any rate, the same system applies in Malaysian (18), where *jalan* is the Malay equivalent of English *street.*

(18) A woman lost an envelope containing about $13,000 to a snatch thief *in Jalan Bandar Raya* today. (*New Straits Times,* 5/7/86: 4)

Differences or Deficiencies?

In this type of analysis, it is crucial to distinguish possible "innovations," which result from such extensions of productive linguistic processes as those in the preceding examples, from features that are clearly "mistakes" in any variety of Standard English, in that they do not result from these processes. An example of such a mistake in a domain of Standard American English occurs in (19).

> (19) But a U.S. district judge in New York *temporary* banned railroad machinists from honoring picket lines . . . (*Washington Post*, 3/6/89: A4)

It is likewise important to limit sources of items proposed as normative for a variety to those likely to have been written by the most highly proficient speakers of that variety. Not all English speakers who write in the domains of Standard English have attained this level of proficiency. For example, the italicized items in (20), taken from a Malaysian English-language newspaper published on the island of Borneo, appear to reveal personal deficiencies in the writer's and/or editor's acquisition of English, rather than differences across varieties of Standard English.[7]

> (20) The sources feared that delegates in Saturday's meeting *may proposed* for *a 10-cent increases*. (*Sabah Times*, 6/27/80: 16)

Even in the prestigious *New Straits Times*, advertising copy, which is not always written or carefully proofread by highly proficient English speakers, may reflect such deficiencies, as in (21).

> (21) You can choose from the different types of *floors' layouts* of our Triple Storey Shop Office . . . (Advertisement in *New Straits Times*, 57/86: 13)

Although *floors' layouts* may be analogous to British English *drugs overdose* or *departures lounge*, the use of the possessive here is not based on such a productive process.

In other cases, determination of acceptability can be more difficult. For example, the student writer on the Indiana State University student newspaper who uses *violated against* (22) three times in the same article may not be an unimpeachable reflection of Standard American English.

> (22) Morris claims his First Amendment rights were *violated against* when an ISU Safety and Security Officer demanded Morris give him his sign. (*The Indiana Statesman* [Indiana State University, Terre Haute], 2/16/89: 1)

Malaysian instances of such questionable acceptability occur in (23) and (24), taken from the "Letters to the Editor" section of the *New Straits Times* and an advertisement reproduced in an Oxford University Press ESL textbook.

(23) Never in my wildest *imaginations* did I think that you could come up with such a superbly managed show... ("People's Page," *New Straits Times*, 6/22/83: 15)

(24) Take up diets you can trust... and exercises that are *good to* you. (Magazine advertisement reprinted in Vaz 1978: 35)

All of the italicized items in (22) through (24) could result from the same productive processes that yield examples (1) through (14). However, in (22) through (24), we can surmise less about the writers' proficiencies in Standard American or Standard Malaysian English than we can in (1) through (14).[8]

Yet another problem in identifying Standard English in non-native varieties is that ESL textbooks not published by a major press or the Ministry of Education may not accurately reflect English norms. Tan (1982), the source of example (25), is such a Malaysian English textbook.

(25) One day I went to the roadside stall to buy some durians. I *took up* one and sniffed at it. (Tan 1982: 56)

Ultimately, however, even if we can control for productivity of linguistic processes underlying divergences and for the English proficiency of sources, it is impossible to determine from data as limited as these whether an item is a token of a developing varietal norm or simple a nonce innovation by an educated Malaysian English speaker. Clearly, a much broader data base, such as the Brown Corpus or the Survey of English Usage, is called for.

Implications for Assessing English Proficiency

Meanwhile, even such preliminary studies as this one can have important implications for testing non-native speakers' proficiency in English. Most obviously, such analyses suggest limits on how far it can be assumed that norms of Standard American English extend to other varieties of Standard English, native or non-native.

One practical implication of this observation concerns the international validity of certain items in the Test of English for International Communication (TOEIC), which the Educational Testing Service (ETS) has been administering since 1979. TOEIC is "designed to test the English language as it is used internationally in business, commerce, and industry"(Educational Testing Service 1987: 2). ETS points out that the TOEIC differs from the Test of English as a Foreign Language (TOEFL), which "is designed to determine how well a candidate can use English in colleges and universities in the United States" (Educational Testing Service 1986: 3). Thus, whereas the TOEFL is based on the norms of Standard American English, the TOEIC is implicitly unbiased toward any variety of Standard English.[9]

However, item (26), considered incorrect in a commercially published practice book for the TOEIC, would be acceptable in Standard Singapore or Malaysian English (see (16) through (18) above), as well as in Standard British English (cf. Schur 1987: 408; Algeo 1988: 13).

(26) He lives *in Main Street.* (Lougheed 1986: 13).

Cross-varietal differences likewise become a factor in (27), a practice problem in the official ETS bulletin for the TOEIC. The student's task here is to identify the italicized item that is ungrammatical.

(27) Please *fill out* the enclosed form *to tell* us *how* you think *about* our service. (Educational Testing Service 1987: 18)

The ungrammatical item here is *how*. However, the construction *fill out* might well also be unacceptable to a student who had learned to *fill up* a form in Malaysia, as in (13) above, or to *fill in* or *fill up* a form in Standard British English (Trudgill and Hannah 1985: 58; Schur 1987: 135).

Examples (28) and (29), similar in examinee task to (27), are items that appeared in a TOEIC test (Educational Testing Service 1980: 27–28).

(28) *His* proposal met *with a lot of resistances.*

(29) The new *equipments shipped* from Hong Kong will be *the only* items *on sale* this week.

Resistances and *equipments*, which result from the same productive process yielding (1) through (8) above, may well be acceptable to educated speakers of Malaysian or other non-native varieties of Standard English.

Another implication of the development of non-native norms concerns assessments of the English proficiency of the many foreign students enrolled in American universities who come from countries such as Malaysia, where non-native varieties have been linguistically and attitudinally identified.[10] Evaluators of these students' English proficiency can attempt to distinguish "deficiencies" in a student's general English proficiency from "differences" in the student's usage that diverge systematically from Standard American English as a result of highly productive morphosyntactic processes and might therefore be considered Standard English by highly educated English users in the student's home country.

Analysis of (30) and (31), taken from entrance examination essays written by Malaysian graduate students in linguistics at Georgetown University, illustrates how such a distinction might be made.

(30) But most of all, it helped so much when I started to *enroll into* several writing courses *in George Mason University.*

(31) I began to follow their *advices. One of my instructor in George Mason University* said that when a person learns a language he also learns the culture of the language.

All of the underscored items in (30) and (31) violate the norms of Standard American English and would most likely be considered incorrect by American university instructors. However, the constructions *enroll into* and *advices* could both result from productive processes illustrated in (1) through (14), and could thus possibly be acceptable in Standard Malaysian English. *In George Mason University,* which occurs in both (30) and (31), might likewise reflect correct prepositional usage in Standard Malaysian English, in a manner analogous to (18). In contrast, *one of my instructor* in (31) clearly does not result from any productive process in English, and is therefore most likely a mistake or an error in all varieties of Standard English. Such analyses of students' writing can help evaluators to distinguish between these students' overall deficiencies in Standard English and minor morphosyntactic adjustments that they must make in order to conform to the norms of Standard American English during their studies in the United States.

Conclusion

This chapter has argued that the tradition of limiting the norms for Standard English to those of its native speakers is no longer universally valid. It has also proposed one approach for identifying morphosyntactic norms in Standard English that applies to both the native-speaker and the non-native varieties of English.[11]

This identification of norms in non-native varieties of English is an area of linguistics in which research is still just beginning. Recently published studies have investigated nativization processes not only in morphology and syntax, but at other linguistic levels as well, including discourse (see, e.g., Kachru 1985 and Smith 1987). Accurate analysis and description of these norms present formidable challenges for researchers, both conceptually and methodologically.

Meanwhile, however, insights from limited studies such as this one can have practical applications for improving the design of proficiency tests in English as a non-native language and for analyzing non-native speakers' deviations from native-speaker norms. On a more theoretical level, such research can be useful in writing a truly comprehensive grammar of English as a world language, and should yield valuable insights on basic processes of language variation and change.

NOTES

1. Richards 1979 has estimated that the total number of users of non-native varieties of English around the world may be almost as large as the total number of native speakers. While this claim is most likely exaggerated, the number of speakers of non-native varieties is certainly quite substantial. For example, Kachru 1984 estimates that 27.4 million Indians regularly use English, giving India the third largest population of English speakers in the world after the United States and Britain.

2. For discussions of nativization processes at other linguistic levels in non-native varieties in general, and in Malaysian English in particular, see Platt, Weber, and Ho 1984, Kachru 1986, Lowenberg 1986a, 1986b, 1991, and Smith 1987.

3. The Malays, Chinese, and South Asians remain present-day Malaysia's largest ethnic groups. In 1985 the ethnic distribution of Malaysia's total estimated population of 15,676,700 was 55.8 percent Malay and 33.3 percent Chinese; of the 10.9 percent "others," the majority were South Asian (*Encyclopædia Britannica* 1986:736).

4. Le Page 1984: 118 observes that "the urban middle classes of all ethnic groups try to retain English"; even the urban middle-class Malays, who stand to benefit most from the shift to Bahasa Malaysia, "may go to some lengths to ensure that their children are bilingual [in English] too, since a good command of English is still an advertised requirement for highly paid jobs, at least in the commercial sector."

In contrast, as Abdullah Hassan (personal communication) points out, many young Malaysians with only limited proficiency in English come from rural areas where, until a recent expansion in the provision of universal education, little if any instruction in English was available. Therefore, the "deterioration" in the Malaysian population's proficiency in English may not be as severe as some observers lament.

5. It is noteworthy that (3), as well as (10), produced by two British linguists, appears in a volume that was published, and therefore tacitly accepted, by an American publisher.

6. Particularly interesting is (14), *hotting up*, which I have now read on three occasions in the *New Straits Times*.

7. The constructions *in Saturday's meeting* and *proposed for* in (20) could reflect extensions of productive processes of the types manifested in (9) through (18). See discussion of (22) through (24).

8. In addition, the writers of (22) through (24) probably do not have

sociolinguistic status as innovators equivalent to that of, for example, the authors of (4) through (6).

9. Queried by telephone, the TOEIC Program Office at Educational Testing Service stated that the norms used for TOEIC are from native-speaker varieties and do not include non-native varieties.

10. According to data compiled by the Institute for International Education (reported in Magner 1988), in the school year 1987–88, 356,190 foreign students were enrolled in U.S. junior colleges, colleges, and universities in the United States. Of this total, more than 90,700—over 25 percent—came from the countries listed above as using English as a second language with some official status and from the British colony of Hong Kong, where English is an official auxiliary language. Moreover, among the fifteen polities with the most foreign students in the United States in 1987–88, five—India (21,010), Malaysia (19,480), Hong Kong (10,650), Nigeria (8,340), and Pakistan (6,570)—have widely attested non-native varieties of English.

11. Also necessary for the identification of non-native norms in a particular variety will be judgments of the acceptability of specific innovations in that variety by that variety's most highly educated speakers.

REFERENCES

Algeo, John. 1988. British and American grammatical differences. *International Journal of Lexicography* 1(1): 1–31.

Asmah Haji Omar. 1985. Patterns of language communication in Malaysia. *Southeast Asian Journal of Social Science* 13(1): 19–28.

Augustin, John. 1982. Regional standards of English in peninsular Malaysia. Pp. 248–58 in *New Englishes*. Ed. John Pride. Rowley, Mass.: Newbury House.

Berko Gleason, Jean. 1988. Language and socialization. Pp. 269–80 in *The development of language and language researchers: essays in honor of Roger Brown*. Ed. Frank K. Kessel. Hillsdale, N.J.: Lawrence Erlbaum Associates.

Conrad, Andrew, and Joshua Fishman. 1977. English as a world language: the evidence. Pp. 3–76 in *The spread of English*. Ed. Joshua Fishman, Robert Cooper, and Andrew Conrad. Rowley, Mass.: Newbury House.

Corder, S. P. 1967. The significance of learners' errors. *International Review of Applied Linguistics* 5(4): 161–70. Reprinted in *Error analysis: perspectives on second language acquisition*. Ed. Jack C. Richards. London: Longman, 1974. Pp. 19–27.

Educational Testing Service. 1980. *Test of English for international communication*. Princeton: Educational Testing Service.

———. 1986. *Guide for TOEIC users*. Princeton: Educational Testing Service.

———. 1987. *Bulletin of information, test of English for international communication*. Princeton: Educational Testing Service.

Encyclopædia Britannica. 1986. *Britannica book of the year 1986*. Chicago: Encyclopædia Britannica, Inc.

Ferguson, Charles A., and Shirley Brice Heath. 1981. Introduction. Pp. xxv–xxxviii in *Language in the USA*. Ed. Charles A. Ferguson and Shirley Brice Heath. Cambridge: Cambridge University Press.

Howe, D. H. 1974. *New guided English. Book 1*. Kuala Lumpur: Oxford University Press. Reprinted by Penerbit Fajar Bakti Sdn. Bhd., Kuala Lumpur, 1986.

Hua Wu Yin. 1983. *Class and communalism in Malaysia*. London: Marram Books.

Kachru, Braj B. 1976. Models of English for the Third World: white man's linguistic burden or language pragmatics? *TESOL Quarterly* 10(2): 221–39.

———. 1984. World Englishes and the teaching of English to non-native speakers: context, attitudes, and concerns. *TESOL Newsletter* 18: 25–26.

———. 1986. *The alchemy of English*. Oxford: Pergamon Press. Reprinted, Urbana: University of Illinois Press, 1990.

Kachru, Yamuna. 1985. Discourse analysis, non-native Englishes and second language acquisition research. *World Englishes* 4(2): 223–332.

Koh, Judy, and Suat Chin, Leong. 1976. *Dewan's communicative English, book 4*. Kuala Lumpur: Dewan Bahasa dan Pustaka, Ministry of Education.

LePage, Robert B. 1962. Multilingualism in Malaya. In *Symposium on multilingualism, Proceedings of the second meeting of the Inter-African Committee on Linguistics*. July 16–21, 1962, Brazzaville. London: Committee for Technical Cooperation in Africa.

———. 1984. Retrospect and prognosis in Malaysia and Singapore. *International Journal of the Sociology of Language* 45: 113–26.

Llamzon, Teodoro A. 1978. English and the national languages in Malaysia, Singapore, and the Philippines: a sociolinguistic comparison. *Cross Currents* 5(1): 87–104.

Lougheed, Lin. 1986. *English, the international language*. Tokyo: Addison-Wesley.

Lowenberg, Peter H. 1986a. Non-native varieties of English: nativization, norms, and implications. *Studies in Second Language Acquisition* 8(1): 1–18.

———. 1986b. Sociocultural context and second language acquisition: acculturation and creativity in Malaysian English. *World Englishes* 5(1): 71–83.

———. 1988. Malay in Indonesia, Malaysia, and Singapore: three faces of a national language. Pp. 146–78 in *With forked tongues: what are national languages good for?* Ed. Florian Coulmas. Ann Arbor, Mich.: Karoma Publishers.

———. 1991. Variation in Malaysian English: the pragmatics of languages in contact. Pp. 364-75 in *English around the world: sociolinguistic perspectives*. Ed. Jenny Cheshire. Cambridge: Cambridge University Press.

Magner, Denise K. 1988. Students from Asia made up more than half of all foreigners at U.S. colleges last year. *Chronicle of Higher Education*, October 26, p. A39.

Platt, John, and Heidi Weber. 1980. *English in Singapore and Malaysia*. Kuala Lumpur: Oxford University Press.

―――, and Ho Min Lian. 1984. *The new Englishes*. London: Routledge & Kegan Paul.

Porter, Don, and Jon Roberts. 1987. Authentic listening activities. Pp. 177–87 in *Methodology in TESOL*. Ed. Michael H. Long and Jack C. Richards. New York: Newbury House.

Richards, Jack C. 1979. Rhetorical and communicative styles in the new varieties of English. *Language Learning* 29: 1–25.

Schur, Norman W. 1987. *British English, A to Zed*. New York: Facts on File Publications.

Shaw, Willard. 1981. Asian student attitudes toward English. Pp. 108–22 in *English for cross-cultural communication*. Ed. Larry E. Smith. New York: St. Martin's Press.

Smith, Larry E., ed. 1987. *Discourse across cultures: strategies in World Englishes*. New York: Prentice-Hall.

Straits Times Press. 1985. *Our style: the way we use words in* The Straits Times. Singapore: Straits Times Press, Ltd.

Swales, John. 1985. ESP—the heart of the matter or the end of the affair? Pp. 212–23 in *English in the world*. Ed. Randolph Quirk and Henry Widdowson. Cambridge: Cambridge University Press.

Tan Chor Whye. 1982. Sistem kursus ulangkaji S.P.M., the new communication English, subject 122. Kuala Lumpur: Pustaka Sistem Pelajaran Sdn. Bhd.

Tay, Mary W. J., and Anthea Fraser Gupta. 1983. Towards a description of Standard Singapore English. Pp. 173–89 in *Varieties of English in Southeast Asia*. Ed. Richard B. Noss. SEAMEO Regional Language Centre.

Trudgill, Peter. 1983. *Sociolinguistics*. Revised edition. Harmondsworth: Penguin Books.

―――, and Jean Hannah. 1985. *International English: a guide to varieties of Standard English*. 2d ed. London: Edward Arnold.

Vaz, Fleur. 1978. *English-communication for syllabus 122*. Kuala Lumpur: Oxford University Press.

PART II

Nativization: Formal and Functional

7

Eyamba G. Bokamba

The Africanization of English

Africa is considered today to be perhaps the most multilingual region in the world, with more languages spoken per capita than anywhere else. It is estimated that 1,000 to 1,140 languages are spoken in Africa (Voegelin and Voegelin 1964).[1] Except in a very few cases, African nations are multilingual; the typical country lacks both an indigenous nationwide language of communication and a language policy that proposes the development and implementation of such a language.[2] This situation has facilitated the penetration and entrenchment of the former colonial powers' languages (i.e., English, French, and Portuguese) as the official media of communication for administration, education, commerce, and diplomacy in African states.

As is to be expected in such a multilingual contact situation, the interaction of the three European languages with African languages has produced very interesting sociolinguistic phenomena, e.g., code-switching and code-mixing, structural changes in the European and African languages involved, and continued debates on the Africanization of education and the language of instruction.

The phenomena of code-switching and code-mixing in English have been discussed at some length in the literature (Ansre 1971; Scotton 1972; Abdulaziz 1972; Parkin 1974; Agheyisi 1977; Scotton and Ury 1977). A great deal of attention has recently been devoted to the question of language policies in African education, and there is every indication that this will continue (see, e.g., Ansre 1970, 1975; Gbedemah 1971; Foster 1971; Whiteley 1971; Spencer 1971b; Mhina 1975; Bamgboṣe 1976; Bokamba 1976, 1979; and Bokamba and Tlou 1977). Very little attention, however, has been given to the study of the influence of African languages on European languages in general, and on English in particular. The reverse situation, viz., the influence of English, French, and Portuguese on African languages, has remained almost completely neglected.

These are areas of great sociolinguistic interest that might be pursued simultaneously with promising theoretical and practical results. Such a study, however, is beyond the scope of this chapter. Here I shall focus on the varieties of English referred to collectively as *African English*. In particular, I shall discuss the influence of African languages on English, with special reference to Ghanaian, Nigerian, and the Eastern Bantu languages of Kenya and Tanzania. I shall then examine briefly the sociolinguistic implications of this phenomenon on English, and on African languages in general.

Africanisms in African English

The paucity of studies on what I shall term African English seems to suggest that there is no such distinct variety of English. Yet, when a Nigerian or a Ghanaian speaks English, no matter what his/her level of education, native speakers of English have no difficulty identifying the accent as African. While the contact between African languages and English during the colonial period was much shorter (about eighty-five years) than that between Indian languages and English, where a number of interesting varieties of English have emerged (Spencer 1971b; Kachru 1976, 1983), it is still possible to identify nascent varieties that one might call Liberian,[3] Sierra Leonean, Ghanaian, Nigerian, Kenyan, or East African English.

These Englishes share certain properties that can be identified as *Africanisms*, in that they reflect structural characteristics of African languages. Specifically, these properties can be discovered at all linguistic levels: phonological, morphological, semantic, and syntactic. For my present purposes, any English construction that reflects a structural property of an African language will be called an Africanism. My discussion will be restricted to the syntactico-semantic properties of sentences produced by educated[4] Africans, because of the lack of data from other speakers.

Consider in this regard, first, the case of syntactic constructions. Bamgboṣe (1971: 37) cites a letter from a primary school graduate which contained the following passage:

(1) With much pleasre [sic] and respect I inscribe you *this few lines* and with the hope that *it* will *meet you in good condition of health* [emphasis added].

This was the opening sentence of the letter. Bamgboṣe does not reveal the author's native language, though he may have been a Yoruba speaker. But regardless of the author's mother tongue, the sentence indicates the embedding of the syntactic properties of a West African language in the derivation of an English sentence. These properties are adjectival agreement and subject-verb agreement. Most West African languages (unlike Bantu) do not require overt agreement markers between a noun and its modifier if the latter is a quantifier or is part of an expression containing such an element, as in "this few lines," above.

Furthermore, there is no overt subject-verb agreement in most West African languages (again, unlike Bantu). The incorrect choice of the subject pronoun "it" in the second clause in (1) seems to reflect this characteristic. Note that the pronoun agrees with the adjectival phrase "this few" rather than with the noun "lines," as expected. A general syntactico-semantic property of African languages is reflected in the expression "meet you in good condition of health." Part of the problem here is due to the fact that in many African languages the verbs *find, meet,* and *encounter* are realized by a single verb which is often the equivalent of *meet* in English. The other problem is cultural: African languages characteristically inquire about or make reference to an addressee's welfare as an initial step in either face-to-face greetings or letter writing. Such a tradition does not exist in English; hence the inappropriateness of the expression in the sentence cited in (1).

The very obvious deviations from Standard (British?) English exemplified in (1) may suggest that the speaker was translating directly from his mother tongue.[5] Whether or not this was the case is not at issue here; the point is that the sentence reflects known characteristics of a group of African languages, and that these are easy to detect. In certain cases, however, the embedding of an African language structure into English is accomplished with such sophistication that it becomes difficult, if not altogether impossible, to detect it unless one is familiar with the speaker's native language. Consider the following passage cited by Kirk-Greene (1971: 132) from a published work in Nigerian English:

(2) It is now known to my poorself the hows and whys of politics. As from now I shall call group of politicians— Peoples [sic] of varied wishes that assume one name. Politics is forced out tears by intense anger. One can not remember any time both in dream and normal life that poorself stood among honourable ones, expressing in opposition terms against

a number more than one, of course, except in concerts. That
eyes, so unforseeing have forced the youths to talk with
anger, what they have tried with all politeness. . . . It is
therefore the idea to exchange ideas. The exchange of ideas
in plays and conversation about down fall or up lift of any
part of earth. This will result to total wipe off of ignorance
and plant eternal freedom of thought with unlimited progress
and wide knowledge.

According to Kirk-Greene, the author of this passage was an Igbo
speaker. While the passage is admittedly deviant in many respects, it
sounds more English than the sentence cited in (1). Furthermore, (2)
might be taken as a philosophical essay by a non-English speaker who
is not necessarily an African. But anyone who is familiar with African
languages will be able to identify many of the lexical expressions and
syntactic constructions as originating from a West African language—
in this case, Igbo. Other examples cited by Kirk-Greene from speakers
of the same language include the following:

(3) a. The effect of this attitude was compensating.
    b. I can wipe off any uncalled for time of assumptions in
       any person's mind.
    c. Today will be marked at the boards of your hearts.

These sentences, as Kirk-Greene correctly points out, are difficult to
explain syntactically and semantically. The medium is English, but the
meaning is very obscure unless one knows the language and/or culture
underlying expressions such as "uncalled for time of assumptions"
and "boards of hearts."

A number of other typical deviations in syntax have been noted
in Nigerian, Ghanaian, and Kenyan Englishes (Kirk-Greene 1971; Sey
1973; Chinebuah 1976; Angogo and Hancock 1980; Zuengler 1982).
These include: (1) omission of function words; (2) semantic extension
of certain lexical items from African languages to cover various
meanings and functions in English; (3) occurrence of certain redun-
dancies, including the pluralization of mass nouns; (4) retention of
anaphoric pronouns in non-subject relativization; (5) use of affirmative
answers to yes/no questions; (6) unusual word order in adjectival
phrases containing demonstrative or possessive pronouns; and (7)
omission of the element "more" in comparative constructions. Each
of these deviations is discussed briefly below.

Of these common characteristics, the omission of function words
such as definite and indefinite articles appears most widespread in
African English. Kirk-Greene (1971: 133), for example, has found

sentences such as (4) to be common in the Nigerian English of Hausa, Igbo, and Yoruba speakers:

(4) a. Let strong football team be organized.
    b. He won by overwhelming majority.
    c. He gave me tough time.

Similar constructions have been observed by Sey (1973: 29ff.) in what he terms Educated Ghanaian English (EGE). Examples cited by Sey include the following:

(5) a. I am going to cinema.
    b. I am going to post office.
    c. I may continue with the interview or examine few more applications.

This deviation is not restricted to the speech and writing of low-level speakers of English (e.g., those having only a secondary education). It has been observed at higher levels as well. The passage cited in (2) is one example; a second example consists of the following sentences found in the introductory page of an official document published by the Ministry of Information of Nigeria (1977: 3).

(6) a. Education in Nigeria is no more a private enterprise, but a huge Government venture that has witnessed a progressive evolution of Government's complete and dynamic intervention. . . .
    b. It is Government's wish that any existing contradictions, ambiguities, and lack of uniformity in educational practices in the different parts of the Federation should be removed. . . .

Admittedly, the omission of the definite article here is sporadic; but the fact that there is any omission at all in a document of this type is sufficient to indicate the spread of the phenomenon. From a comparative point of view, it is noteworthy that the same phenomenon is exhibited in South Asian English (Kachru 1983).

One major source of errors that lead to the production of deviant sentences like those in (4)–(6) is transference from the speaker's native languages (Kirk-Greene 1971; Sey 1973; Chinebuah 1976; Angogo and Hancock 1980). Most African languages do not have overt articles, so determination is achieved derivatively. Another source is analogy from Standard English itself, particularly from certain idiomatic expressions such as "going to hospital/church/school." It is difficult to determine with any certainty, therefore, the main source of such deviations. My inclination is to believe that interference from African languages plays a critical role.

Somewhat related to the deviation just exemplified is the influence of certain generic lexical items in African languages in conveying meanings and covering functions such as those performed by indefinite articles and/or pronouns, as well as a range of adjectives, in English. In Bantu-speaking Africa, for example, it is not uncommon to hear or read sentences like the following:

(7) a. The boy saw one person [i.e., someone].
    b. He is a real/whole person [i.e., an adult].

Such constructions appear to be, in part, translation equivalents of lexical items like the Swahili *mtu mmoja* (one person/someone) and *mtu mzima* (an adult/a fine or wholesome person). The Hausa words *wani* and *wata*, which have several meanings including "another," "a certain," and the indefinite article, have, according to Kirk-Greene (1971), a similar influence on English spoken by Hausas. He cites the following examples—

(8) a. You are a big somebody [i.e., an important person].
    b. You are a sociable somebody [i.e., sociable person].

—and points out that analogous constructions can be found in Igbo and Yoruba English.

Although structures like these have been noted in more than one Anglophone African nation, they do not appear to be as prevalent or as troublesome as the redundant pluralizations of uncountable nouns. Consider, for instance, the sentences in (9) from Nigerian English (Kirk-Greene 1971: 134) and those in (10) from Ghanaian English (Sey 1973: 26–27).

(9) a. I lost all my *furnitures* and many valuable *properties*.
    b. There were thunderous *noises* of laughter and *chats*.
    c. She walked in such *paces* that combined her college *learnings* of how to behave.

(10) a. The teachers will be given the *respects* they deserve.
     b. But in modern warfare . . . the *damages* caused are great.
     c. I was in charge of all *correspondences*.

Kirk-Greene does not indicate at what level of English proficiency sentences like (9) are produced, but he states that they are drawn from letters and published novelettes. This suggests that we are dealing with advanced speakers of English as a second language (i.e., those with post-primary education). As for the sentences in (10), Sey states that such deviations are commonly observed in the speech and writing of pre-university speakers in Ghana.

The problem illustrated in (9)–(10) is due less to the lack of a distinction between countable and mass nouns in African languages than to the semantic inconsistencies of English itself. As Sey (1973: 27) quite correctly points out,

> (11) There appears to be (a) no consistent semantic relationship between countable and uncountable uses of nouns [in English], nor (b) any clearly discernible motivation for using some normally uncountable nouns in countable functions but not others.

African languages in general do distinguish between mass and countable nouns, but the range of the former does not correspond to that of English. For example, nouns such as *fish, chicken,* and *lamb,* which are considered as either countable or uncountable in English, depending on whether they are taken as food items or as living entities, are classified as countable in most African languages. In other words, the ambiguous category found in English does not commonly occur in African languages. It is not surprising, therefore, to find words like *furniture, property, chat, pace, shade,* and *correspondence* pluralized in African English. All of these (except perhaps *noise,* which generally occurs only in the plural) are countable in most African languages.

A related deviation is the interposing of an independent subject pronoun between a subject noun and its verb. Such a phenomenon is often observed in the English speech of Bantu language speakers (e.g., Kenyans, Tanzanians, Zambians):

> (12) a. My daughter *she* is attending the University of Nairobi.
> b. The boys *they* like to play outside even if it is cold.
> c. Robert *he* is currently employed by the UNESCO.

The most probable source of this deviation is the redundancy found in the subject-verb agreement system of Bantu languages, whereby a subject prefix obligatorily occurs with a finite verb whether or not the subject noun surfaces. A number of other interesting deviations from a Bantu-speaking area are discussed in Zuengler (1982).

Another characteristic deviation noted in African English is the occurrence of resumptive anaphoric pronouns in non-subject relativization.

> (13) a. The guests whom I invited *them* have arrived.
> b. The book which I bought *it* is lost.
> c. Taking a course in a country which *her* language you did not know is a big problem.

    d. You are going to do your course [i.e., studies] in a country where you have never been *there* before.

Chinebuah (1976: 75–76) asserts that sentences like (13c-d) are widespread in West African English and specific to the Kwa and Gur subfamilies. In fact, these structures are much more widespread than Chinebuah seems to believe: relative clauses with resumptive pronouns are a typological characteristic of many African languages, including Arabic. One finds them in West African and East African English as well. This deviation can, therefore, be best explained as a transference error.

    Of the various syntactico-semantic deviations found in African English, none has perhaps caused more confusion in communication than the use of affirmative answers to negative yes/no questions. For instance, the typical responses to questions like (14a) and (15a) in African English would be (14b) and (15b), respectively, or simply *yes*:

(14) a. Hasn't the President left for Nairobi yet?
     b. Yes, the President hasn't left for Nairobi yet.

(15) a. Didn't you see anyone at the compound?
     b. Yes, I didn't see anyone at the compound.

When a full answer such as (14b) or (15b) is given, there is less confusion than when *yes* alone is used. This is evidenced in sentences like (16b) below, which is the response to comment (16a).

(16) a. I hope you won't have any difficulty with your fees next term.
     b. I hope so [i.e., I hope what you have said will indeed be true].

This phenomenon is not unique to African English: it has also been observed in South Asian English (Kachru 1983). Constructions such as (14)–(16) have parallels in many African languages and may be reasonably analyzed as instances of interference. For example, (17c) would be acceptable as a reply to the Lingala (a Bantu language) question (17a) only if the second part of the sentence is affirmative. Similarly, (17b) would be acceptable only with the parenthesized meaning, and (17d) is unacceptable.

(17) a. Boliyákí te?   Didn't you (pl.) eat?
     b. Ee. (Toliyákí te.) Yes. (We didn't eat.)
     c. *Te. (Toliyákí te.) No. (We didn't eat.)
     d. *Ee. (Toliyákí.)   Yes. (We ate.)

Kirk-Greene (1971: 133–34) cites similar examples from Hausa:

(18) a. bai zo ba?   Hasn't he come?
     b. i   Yes [i.e., what you have said is right: he has not come].
     c. a′a   No [i.e., what you have said is wrong: he has come].

In contrast, the replies corresponding to (14b), (15b), and (16b) in English would involve negation:

(19) a. No, the President hasn't left for Nairobi yet.
     b. No, I didn't see anyone at the compound.
     c. I hope not.

Generally, an affirmative answer to questions like (14a) and (15a) would be given only if the facts were contrary to what the questions implied. As can be seen from the examples in (14)–(16), the logic of negative yes/no questions in African English deviates from this pattern; however, it is consistent with the pattern found in African languages.

Word order in constructions involving possessive or demonstrative pronouns constitutes another area of difficulty. In Bantu languages, for example, adjectives generally follow the noun they modify. When a possessive and a demonstrative pronoun occur in the same noun phrase, they follow the noun, with the possessive generally preceding the demonstrative. In Hausa (a West African language), the possessive follows the noun and the demonstrative precedes it (Kirk-Greene 1971). These structural characteristics often influence the production of English sentences by primary school learners, as may be seen in the following sentences.

(20) a. I met the teacher our new.
     b. Your both children want to speak to you.
     c. That your brother, will he come?
     d. Saying Amen to those his prayers . . .

(20a,b) were produced by Bantu-speaking Africans and (20c,d) by Hausa speakers.

Another area in which African English is characteristically deviant involves comparative constructions. In English, comparatives generally require the comparison of two terms, the *standard* (in the main clause) and the *compared* (in the comparative clause), with regard to some shared property. The standard is introduced by a comparative element such as *-er* (suffixed to a class of adjectives), *more, less,* or *worse,* and is followed by the correlative element *than* in the comparative clause:

(21) a. Kenyatta was older than Nkrumah.
     b. Nkrumah was younger than Kenyatta.

    c. Monkeys are more dexterous than leopards.
    d. Leopards are less dexterous than monkeys.

In many West African and Bantu languages, however, the standard is generally introduced by a verb such as *exceed* or *surpass*, which already incorporates the notion of superiority. In constructions involving comparison of inequality, as in (21) above, no comparative elements are needed: the comparison is simply conveyed by the verb, as may be seen from the Lingala and Swahili sentences in (22) and (23).

(22) *Lingala:* (a) Lomekano lu:na *lulekákí* luye na makasi.
          test that *it-exceeded* this in difficulty
          (That test was harder/more difficult than this one.)
      (b) Ngomba ya Kilimanzaro *eleki* (ngomba) ya Kenya na molai.
          Mt. of Kilimanjaro *it-exceed* Mt. of Kenya in height
          (Mount Kilimanjaro is higher/taller than Mount Kenya.)
(23) *Swahili:* (a) Mtihani ule ulikuwa mgumu *kuliko* huu.
          test that it-was hard *exceeding* this
          (That test was harder/more difficult than this one.)
      (b) Mlima wa Kilimanjaro ni mrefu *kuliko* (mlima) wa Kenya.
          Mt. of Kilimanjaro is tall *exceeding* (Mt.) of Kenya
          (Mount Kilimanjaro is taller/higher than Mount Kenya.)

Similar constructions in many other African languages appear to influence the production of comparatives in English, as suggested by the following sentences (Chinebuah 1976).

(24) a. It is the youths who are skillful in performing tasks *than* the adults.
    b. They would have *more* powder on the hand and in their faces.

These sentences indicate that the speakers were aware of the rule for deriving comparison of inequality constructions, but that they applied it only partially. This is a common deviation found in African English.

    Let us now turn to semantic deviations. This is perhaps the most interesting and dynamic area in which African English shows its creativity, particularly with regard to the derivation of new words. Lexical items in African English may be created in four principal ways: by semantic extension, semantic shift, semantic transfer, and coinage (Kirk-Greene 1971; Sey 1973).

Semantic extension involves adding a meaning(s) to a Standard English word. Consider, for example, the meanings of the italicized words in the following sentences (Sey 1973: 95–98).

(25) a. He sent me some *amount*.
  b. People have been running (away) with my huge *amounts*.

(26) a. I had no ticket, but I got in by *arrangement*.
  b. By *arrangement* you can go to heaven.

(27) a. I know him very well. He is in fact my *bench*.
  b. He is my *benchman*.

(28) a. He *bluffs* too much.
  b. He replied, putting his hands inside his pockets and *bluffing* arrogantly, boistering eye signals of inviolable romance.
  c. The fellow is too *boisterous*—too much. The storekeeper said.

According to Sey (1973), each italicized item in these sentences maintains its Standard English meaning but has also acquired additional ones. In particular, the word *amount* in (25) means "money," with which it is used interchangeably, as well as "cash." The word *arrangement* in (26) refers to special arrangement, preferential treatment, or mutual arrangement. This word also occurs adjectivally, usually with *man* and rarely with *woman*, in expressions such as "he is an arrangement man"—that is, a person who habitually gets what he wants, not by normal means, but through his connections (Sey 1973). A similar expression in Nigerian English is "long legs," as in "he has long legs." *Bench* and *benchman* in (27) are synonyms and mean "a crony or intimate friend"; *bluff* in (28a, b) has the reading of either "to give the impression of self-importance in an amusing way" or "to dress ornately/fashionably" (Sey 1973). In (28c), *boisterous* means to "be bad tempered or quarrelsome." The words *bluff* and *arrangement* are not restricted to Ghanaian English; they occur also in Nigerian and East African English.

Closely related to this mode of derivation are semantic shifts. These involve the redefinition of the characteristic patterns of a word within the semantic field so that its central contexts become marginal, and vice versa (Sey 1973). Sometimes archaic and technical terms replace common ones in everyday speech. For example, the italicized words in (29) have as their meanings those given in parentheses, rather than the generally accepted ones:

(29) a. Even watering the Agricultural Survey Officer's garden was more dignified than what I had to do—*carrying* [on head] *blocks* [i.e., rectangular blocks of concrete for building] for the markets that were being built.

b. The most important point however is that already we are seven and a half million strong and quite a number of these cannot get jobs to do, so we should cut down on *bringing forth* [i.e., having babies].

Other examples include the use of *family* for descendants of the same ancestor, house, or lineage; *machine* for sewing machine; *minerals* for soft drinks; *play* for dance; *senior service* for upper class; *park* for football field; *serviceable* for a person (or, occasionally, an animal) that is always willing to serve.[6]

Another mode of deriving new words involves semantic transfer: the complete reassignment of the meaning of a word. For example, the expressions *to see red, steer, cut,* and *town council* in (30) have readings that are completely different from or inconsistent with those generally accepted:

(30) a. You'll *see red!* Said the angry carpenter to the frightened boy.

b. To my surprise I found him [the driver] resting on the *steer* and fell asleep.

c. As a result, he lost control of the *steer* and the car run into a nearby bush.

d. I asked her to dance, but she *cut* me.

e. They must pay the *town council* people more because they are responsible for the health of the people.

Sentence (30d) is from Kenyan English, whereas the rest are from Ghanaian English. The expression *to see red* in (30a) is a threat to harm or punish a person, while *steer* in (30b, c) means "steering wheel." The verb *cut* in a sentence like (30d) has the reading "to refuse"; it appears to be common in the speech of Swahili speakers at the pre-university level. The same expression is also reported to be common in South Asian English and might also occur in Black American English. *Town council* in West African English refers to a sanitary department, especially to lower-ranking officers (Sey 1973).

The final and most interesting mode of lexical derivation is deliberate coinage. It is in coinage that African English exhibits the rich derivational morphology that is so characteristic of African languages: new lexical items can be derived via prefixation, suffixation, combination of both, or by reduplication and compounding. These processes apply equally to nominal, verbal, adjectival, and adverbial derivations. Nominalization via prefixation and suffixation is illustrated by sentences (31a-f) and (31g), cited in Kirk-Greene (1971: 139) and Sey (1973: 80), respectively:

(31) a. Both U. and E. had pre-knowledge of one another's *wheretos* of going and *whereabouts*.
 b. There's no *rigging* it, I've got to learn French.
 c. The girls are facing a lot of *hardcap* [i.e., hardship].
 d. The ladies of the town conferred them [titles] on me after a very ripe *deservation*.
 e. [It is] his wife to whom he has given nothing *coinable* [i.e., no money].
 f. Be you assured that members are *impossibles, impregnables* of the country.
 g. The people described the *enstoolment* of X as illegal.

All of these, despite their oddity, are derived analogically according to existing English rules, although they do not occur in Standard English.

In addition to affixational derivations, one commonly finds cases of compounding:

(32) a. You have to be careful with these *been-to boys*. You can't trust them.
 b. Where in the world did you get such a *me-and-my-darling* [i.e., a small sofa or love seat]?
 c. We stopped at Awutu to buy some *bush meat* [i.e., game].
 d. He doesn't use a *chewing-stick* to clean his teeth.
 e. The *gate fee* for the cinema show is four shillings.
 f. I saw your *my dear* at the church [i.e., girlfriend/boyfriend].
 g. I have been going to the *small room* a lot, sir [i.e., toilet].
 h. I was a *tight friend* of your sister [i.e., close/intimate friend].

Examples (32c-h) are cited by Sey (1973) as Ghanaianisms, but they occur elsewhere in West African English, though perhaps less frequently (see, e.g., Bamgboṣe 1971, 1982). Other examples of compound nominals include *bone-to-flesh dance* (a close dance between a man and a woman), *push baby* (maidservant), *European appointment* (high-level white-collar position), *known faces* (acquaintances), and *white-black-man* (black intellectual who behaves as a white man). Some of these are loan translations from African languages, while others are derived analogically.

Equally interesting are derivations involving verbs, which exploit the morphology of English and African languages to their fullest extent. Some of the most interesting examples are given in Kirk-Greene (1971: 140).

(33) a. U. with his dazzling red eyes . . . *shadowed* R. much.
   b. Each and every day one was well informed to *cope up* with any eventuality.
   c. My gentleman *naked* himself [i.e., undressed].
   d. I was *coupled* at the dance [i.e., found a dancing partner].
   e. Are you *nauseating* for Nigeria yet [i.e., are you homesick]?
   f. Any persons who were interested in any of the social clubs he had mentioned or *unmentioned* . . .
   g. I opened the door and *visualized* [i.e., saw] a very familiar face.
   h. Sorry not to have been *chanced* to write before.

Other common verbs in African English include *destool, enstool, fabricate, manage with, branch, chase, to be on seat, take in, to be with,* and *to move with,* as in the examples below (Kirk-Greene 1971; Bamgboṣe 1971; Sey 1973; Bokamba 1991).

(34) a. Nana X claimed that since he had been illegally *destooled* by the old regime, and the N.L.C. brought him back to the stool, he would not give it back . . .
   b. They were *enstooled* in the stool house where they poured libation to the ancestors whom they had succeeded.
   c. All my mates there have paid their money, and if I beg them to *manage with* them . . .
   d. Do you *fabricate* [i.e., make] chairs and other types of furniture at the Carpentery School?
   e. I am going to *chase* that girl [i.e., win her affection].
   f. I am going to *branch* at my uncle's house.
   g. The minister *is not on seat.* Come back later.
   h. My wife *took in* [i.e., became pregnant] last month.
   i. The servant *is with* your knife.
   j. I don't like it when my son *moves with* bush boys.
   k. I *hear* a smell. Is something burning in the kitchen?

Sentences like these are found both in everyday speech and in published works and are not to be considered simply as slips of the tongue. Very few of them (e.g., 34a, i, k) can be explained in terms of L_1 interference; the rest are independent developments based on English rules.

While one might argue that these verbs and many others like them can be derived both from English and African sources, the formation of adverbs in African English appears to be a uniquely African phenomenon. Most African languages do not have many adverbs or adjectives, for that matter. To compensate, they exploit the process of reduplication, using either nouns or adjectives to derive adverbs:

(35) a. *Hausa:* sànnu   slow(ly)
     b.   sànnu sànnu   slowly, carefully
     c.   baĥi   black (masc.)
     d.   baĥi baĥi   blackish
(36) a. *Lingala:* noki   quick
     b.   noki noki   quickly
     c.   malémbe   slow; soft/gentle
     d.   malémbe malémbe   slowly; softly/gently
(37) a. *Swahili:* pole   meek, mild, gentle
     b.   pole pole   meekly, mildly, gently
     c.   mmoja   an individual
     d.   mmoja mmoja   individually/singly

This process leads to the production of deviant sentences like (38) in African English:

(38) a. Don't drag your feet, son! Walk *quick quick!*
     b. Life is a big challenge, you have to take it *small small.*
     c. You are eating too *fastly.* Take your time and eat *slow slow.*

where *quick quick* means "quickly," *small small* means either "slowly" or "bit by bit," and *slow slow* means "slowly." This type of reduplication cannot be interpreted as an expression of intensity, as might otherwise be the case in certain African languages; the reduplicated adjectives in these sentences function as adverbs.

Why do such syntactic and semantic deviations occur in the English varieties spoken in Africa? The discussion thus far has suggested two possible sources for these deviant constructions: L_1 or mother tongue interference, and analogical derivation based on English. It has been suggested, further, that L_1 interference may be more pervasive than analogical derivations (see also Bamgboṣe 1982).

While such an answer might adequately account for the phenomena observed here, it fails to explain why interference and analogical derivations of the type noted here occur at all. Furthermore, such an answer treats African English as an isolated phenomenon, failing to take into account the milieu in and the conditions under which English is learned and used in Anglophone Africa. The fact of the matter is that African English is simply an aspect of a more general phenomenon that has been taking place with regard to what Kachru (1976) calls "transplanted" languages. Many of the syntactic and semantic deviations presented here have been noted in other varieties of English (Kachru 1965, 1975, 1976, 1981; Bailey and Robinson 1973; Strevens 1977). Kachru (1965: 398–99), for example, discusses many of the modes of lexical derivation identified in this chapter. Kachru (1976: 156–58) presents five major syntactic deviations characteristic of Indian English. Two of these (reduplication and misuse of articles) are analogous to the ones noted with respect to African English.

The fact that such similarities cut across language and national boundaries clearly indicates that African English is not a unique phenomenon, but a common development to be expected, given the milieu in which English is taught and spoken as a foreign language in Africa. These similarities suggest, further, that certain shared factors underlie the production of these varieties of English. Such factors have been referred to in the literature under the generic terms *indigenization, contextualization,* or *nativization* (Kachru 1965, 1981; Bailey and Robinson 1973; Strevens 1977). That is, English is adapted to local or regional linguistic conditions, and thereby deviates systematically from the Standard dialect.

It should be pointed out here that the situation in which English is learned and spoken in Anglophone Africa (excluding Liberia, Zimbabwe, and South Africa) is essentially no different from that in which other European languages are used officially. Africa is traditionally divided into three linguistic zones (Anglophone, Francophone, and Lusophone) in terms of the official language adopted by each country. However, these divisions reflect more the political zones of influence of the former colonial powers (Britain, Belgium, France, and Portugal) than the objective realities of the language situation in the continent. It is estimated, for instance, that no more than 10 percent of the population of any African country speaks the official language (Alexandre 1967), except in the English-settled nations of Liberia, South Africa, and Zimbabwe. If that is correct (as it seems to be, on the basis of educational development statistics), we are dealing here with populations that are 90 percent non-conversant in English, French, or Portuguese, and whose only media of communication are African languages. It is therefore inaccurate to refer to African nations as Anglophone, Francophone, and Lusophone.

Admittedly, the number of English speakers in Africa will increase steadily as the use of English as a compulsory school subject expands. Fishman et al. (1977) have amassed impressive statistics on the spread of English in the world, showing that, among other things, English is becoming one of the most important languages in Africa with regard to mass media, international communication, and education. In education, for example, Fishman et al. (1977: 16) report that 47.1 percent of primary school students and 96.9 percent of those in secondary schools throughout Africa are enrolled in English classes. These are the highest percentages on any continent, according to the authors.

But they do not say anything about the number of speakers. This number, contrary to Mazrui's (1975) claim regarding the growth of what he terms "Afro-Saxons," will remain very small for some time to come, for several reasons. First, except in an infinitesimally small number of interracial families where English is the language of communication at home (Mazrui 1975), African speakers learn English at school and use it for very specific functions: education, official business (including office work, administration, and commerce), international diplomacy, and broadcasting. Broadcasting is also carried out in African lingua francas (e.g., Hausa, Igbo, and Yoruba in Nigeria; Akan, Ga, and Ewe in Ghana; Swahili and Kikuyu in Kenya), as is daily communication. Second and third, the mastery of English is not possible until about the third year in secondary school, and there are very few qualified teachers to effectively implement the use of English as the medium of instruction at all levels of education. Under these conditions, it is not surprising to find so many deviations from Standard English in African English.

An equally important dimension of this Africanization of English in Africa is the deliberate attempt by African writers, especially novelists, to preserve and communicate African culture in their writing. Consider in this regard the following passage from Gabriel Okara's book, *The Voice* (1970: 25).

(39) When Okolo came to know himself, he was lying on a floor, on a cold, cold floor lying. He opened his eyes to see but nothing he saw, nothing he saw, for the darkness was evil darkness and the outside night was black black night. Okolo lay still in the darkness enclosed by darkness, and he/his thoughts picked in his inside. Then his picked thoughts his eyes opened but his vision only met a rocklike darkness. The picked thoughts then drew his legs but his legs did not come. They were as heavy as a canoe full of sand. His thoughts in his inside began to fly in his inside darkness like frightened birds hither, thither, homeless. . . . Then the flying thoughts drew his hands but the hands did not belong to him, it seemed. So Okolo on the cold cold floor lay with his body

141

as soft as an over-pounded foo foo. So Okolo lay with his eyes open wide in the rocklike darkness staring, staring.

Okara is one of Nigeria's and Africa's finest poets. The above passage is often said to represent the author's conscious effort to impose the structure of Ijö (his mother tongue) on English in an attempt to preserve the African thought (Madubuike 1975). Another African writer, the renowned Nigerian novelist Chinua Achebe (1966: 20), has also experimented with the idea of integrating African language structure and thereby transmitting African thought in English:

(40) a. I want one of my sons to join these people and be my eyes there. If there is nothing in it you will come back. But if there is something there you will bring home my share. The world is like a Mask, dancing. If you want to see it well you do not stand in one place. My spirit tells me that those who do not befriend the white man today will be saying *had we known* tomorrow.

   b. I am sending you as my representative among those people — just to be on the safe side in case the new religion develops. One has to move with the times or else one is left behind. I have a hunch that those who fail to come to terms with the white man may well regret their lack of foresight.

The first passage reflects not only an Igbo cultural background, but also a linguistic style that is not uncommon in many African languages. The second passage, in contrast, lacks these characteristics and gives the impression that something is missing.

All these factors — interference from mother tongues, adaptations necessitated by the language learning and contact situation in multilingual African societies, and the deliberate attempts by Africans to preserve and transmit African cultural thought in English — conspire, as it were, to form what I have termed African English. These factors constitute the sources and *raison d'être* of this variety of English.

Implications for Language Policies in Education

The occurrence and development of African English raise a number of important questions that bear critically on the issue of language policies vis-à-vis education in Africa. Various arguments have been advanced to support the retention of English, French, and Portuguese as the languages of instruction in African education (Alexandre 1967; Foster 1971; Whiteley 1971). Because the fallacy of these arguments has already been demonstrated in Ansre (1975), Bokamba (1976), and Bokamba and Tlou (1977), the subject needs no more discussion here, except to point out a few implications of these data for current policies.

The literature on language acquisition tells us that second-language learning is a task beset from the outset by all sorts of problems (Lenneberg 1967; Dulay and Burt 1974; Jain 1974; Seliger 1978). The situation is further complicated when L_2 is learned in a non-native context. That African English should show consistent deviations from Standard English is not at all surprising; rather, it is consonant with current theories of language acquisition. But what these deviations show, in part, is that learners have not quite mastered the official language; as a result, poor academic performances on the part of the students and low outputs for the academic institutions are unavoidable. There is reason to believe that the high failure rates in African secondary school and university admission examinations are directly related to proficiency in the language of instruction (Gbedemah 1971; Apronti 1974; Bokamba 1976, 1979; Bokamba and Tlou 1977; Afolayan 1976). Given that primary education is currently *terminal* for 85 to 90 percent of the children, one wonders about the utility of English and other European languages for such children. It is clear from such statistics (UNESCO 1976) that the use of these languages as media of instruction at this level is both counterproductive and unnecessarily costly; therefore, such use cannot be viewed as efficient or conducive to national progress.

Even if one were to grant that some degree of progress is achieved, to the extent that African schools forge a small intellectual elite at exorbitantly high cost of human and financial resources, these benefits are more than offset by the fact that the entrenchment and expansion of the official languages preclude the development of African languages.[7] If African languages cannot be developed to serve as media of education and wider communication within and across national boundaries, then the emerging intelligentsias become culturally alienated from and useless to their societies. The roles of European and African languages in African education must, therefore, be carefully evaluated so that comprehensive and realistic language policies that are consonant with African developmental goals can be adopted.[8]

NOTES

1. Our knowledge of the actual number of languages (as opposed to dialects) spoken in Africa is very sketchy at this point; thus these estimates must be taken with a great deal of caution.

2. Except for the Northern African nations which have adopted Arabic as their national language, only three Sub-Saharan states have adopted indigenous national languages. These are: Amharic for Ethiopia; Somali for Somalia; and Swahili for Tanzania. Kenya declared Swahili the official language of the government in 1974, but has not yet implemented a language policy. The remaining countries have adopted the languages of their former colonizing powers.

3. I am aware that there is very little agreement on what constitutes, for example, Liberian English or Nigerian English; but to the extent that we can isolate certain features of English as characteristic of African languages, we have a variety of a sort.

4. The term "educated African" will here refer to any African who has at least completed primary school.

5. When Bamgboṣe 1971 was published, a graduate of an elementary school in Nigeria was expected to have received at least three years of training in and use of English. It is unlikely, therefore, that the student in question was consciously translating his letter word-for-word from his mother tongue.

6. Peter Trudgill (in personal communication) has informed me that *minerals* and *park* are used in the same way in British English and should, therefore, be properly called *Britishisms*.

7. One consequence of the French colonial language policy, which forbade the use of African languages in education in the colonies, is that the development and standardization of these languages were delayed by several decades. This policy contrasted with those of Britain and Belgium, whereby African languages were incorporated into the educational system as subjects and media of instruction; as a result, a number of lingua francas developed and flourished to an extent unparalleled in the former French colonies. Current African policies may have a similar effect on the further development of African languages if nothing is done to modify them.

8. See also the following recent publications: Cheshire, ed. 1991, esp. chs. 29–36; and additional references in Bokamba 1991.

REFERENCES

Abdulaziz, M. 1972. Triglossia and Swahili-English bilingualism in Tanzania. *Sociology of Language* 1: 197–213.

Achebe, C. 1966. The English language and the African writer. *Insight* 20 (Oct.-Dec.).

Afolayan, A. 1976. The six-year primary project in Nigeria. Pp. 113–34 in Bamgboṣe, ed. 1976.

Agheyisi, R. 1977. Language interlarding in the speech of Nigerians. Pp. 97–110 in Kotey and Der-Houssikian, eds. 1977.

Alexandre, P. 1967. *Langues et langage en Afrique Noire.* Paris: Payot.

Angogo, R., and Hancock, I. 1980. English in Africa: emerging standards or diverging regionalisms? *English World-Wide: A Journal of Varieties of English* 1(1): 67–96.

Ansre, G. 1970. Language policy for the promotion of national unity and understanding in West Africa. Mimeographed. Lagon: Institute of African Studies, University of Ghana.

———. 1971. The influence of English on West African languages. In Spencer, ed. 1971a.

———. 1975. Four rationalisations for maintaining the European languages in education in Africa. Paper read at the International Congress of African Studies on the Use of African Languages in Education, Kinshasa, Zaire, December, 1975.

Apronti, E. O. 1974. Sociolinguistics and the question of national language: the case of Ghana. *Studies in African Linguistics* Supplement 5: 1–20.

Bailey, R. W., and Robinson, J. L. 1973. *Varieties of present-day English.* New York: Macmillan.

Bamgboṣe, A. 1971. The English language in Nigeria. In J. Spencer, ed. 1971a.

———, ed. 1976. *Mother tongue education: the West African experience.* Paris: UNESCO.

———. 1982. Standard Nigerian English. In this volume.

Bokamba, E. G. 1976. Authenticity and the choice of a national language: the case of Zaire. *Présence Africaine* 99/100: 104–42. Also in *Studies in the Linguistic Sciences* 6(2): 23–64.

———. 1979. On the necessity of a bilingual educational policy in Sub-Saharan Africa. Paper read at the Symposium on Language Policies in African Education, University of Illinois, Urbana, July 1978.

———. 1991. West Africa. Pp. 493–508 in Cheshire 1991.

———, and Tlou, J. L. 1977. The consequences of the language policies of African states vis-à-vis education. In Kotey and Der-Houssikian, eds. 1977.

Cheshire, J., ed. 1991. *English around the world: sociolinguistic perspectives.* Cambridge: Cambridge University Press.

Chinebuah, I. K. 1976. Grammatical deviance and first language interference. *West African Journal of Modern Languages* 1: 67–78.

Dulay, H., and M. K. Burt. 1974. A new perspective on the creative construction process in child second language acquisition. *Language Learning* 24: 253–78.

Fishman, J. A., R. L. Cooper, and A. W. Conrad, eds. 1977. *The spread of English: the sociology of English as an additional language.* Rowley, Mass.: Newbury House.

Foster, P. 1971. Problems of literacy in Sub-Saharan Africa. In Sebeok, ed. 1971.

Gbedemah, F. K. 1971. Alternative language policies for education in Ghana. Ph.D. dissertation, UCLA.

Herbert, R. K., ed. 1975. *Patterns in language, culture, and society: Sub-Saharan Africa.* Special volume of Working Papers in Linguistics, no. 19. Columbus: Ohio State University.

Jain, M. P. 1974. Error analysis: source, cause and significance. In Richards, ed. 1974.

Kachru, Braj B. 1965. The *Indianness* in Indian English. *Word* 21(3): 391–410.

———. 1975. Lexical innovations in South Asian English. *International Journal of the Sociology of Language* 4: 55–74.

———. 1976. Models of English for the Third World: white man's linguistic burden or language pragmatics? *TESOL Quarterly* 10(2): 221–39.

———. 1976b. Indian English: a sociolinguistic profile of a transplanted language. In Kachru 1976c.

———. 1976c. *Dimensions of bilingualism: theory and case studies.* Special issue of *Studies in Language Learning.* Unit for Foreign Language Study and Research, University of Illinois, Urbana.

———. 1981. The pragmatics of non-native varieties of English. In Smith, ed. 1981.

———. *The Indianization of English: the English language in India.* New Delhi: Oxford University Press.

Kirk-Greene, A. 1971. The influence of West African languages on English. In Spencer, ed. 1971a.

Kotey P. F., and H. Der-Houssikian, eds. 1977. *Language and linguistic problems in Africa: proceedings of the VIIth conference on African linguistics.* Columbia, N.C.: Hornbeam Press.

Lenneberg, E. H. 1967. *Biological foundations of language.* New York: John Wiley & Sons.

Madubuike, I. 1975. African literary communications and the European languages: the case of Francophone writers of Senegal. In Herbert, ed. 1975.

Mazrui, A. 1975. *The political sociology of the English language: an African perspective.* The Hague: Mouton.

Mhina, G. A. 1975. The Tanzania experience in the use of Kiswahili in education. Paper read at the International Congress of African Studies on the Use of African Languages in Education, Kinshasa, Zaire, December, 1975.

Ministry of Information, Nigeria. 1977. *Federal Republic of Nigeria national policy on education.* Lagos: Federal Ministry of Information Printing Division.

Okara, G. 1970. *The Voice.* London: Heinemann Educational Books.

Parkin, D. J. 1974. Language switching in Nairobi. In Whiteley, ed. 1974.

Richards, J. C., ed. 1974. *Error analysis: perspectives on second language acquisition.* London: Longmans.

Ritchie, W. C., ed. 1978. *Second language acquisition research: issues and implications.* New York: Academic Press.

Scotton, M. C. 1972. *Choosing a lingua franca in an African capital.* Edmonton, Alberta: Linguistic Research, Inc.

———, and Ury, W. 1977. Bilingual strategies: the social functions of code-switching. *Linguistics: An International Review* 193: 5–20.

Sebeok, T., ed. 1971. *Current trends in linguistics, vol. 7: linguistics in Sub-Saharan Africa.* The Hague: Mouton.

Seliger, H. W. 1978. Implications of a multiple critical periods hypothesis for second language learning. In Ritchie, ed. 1978.

Sey, K. A. 1973. *Ghanaian English: an exploratory survey.* London: Macmillan.

Smith, L., ed. 1981. *English for cross-cultural communication.* London: Macmillan.

Spencer, J., ed. 1971a. *The English language in West Africa.* London: Longmans.

——. 1971b. Colonial language policies and their legacies. In Sebeok, ed. 1971.

——. 1971c. West Africa and the English language. In Spencer, ed. 1971a.

Strevens, P. 1977. *New orientations in the teaching of English.* London: Oxford University Press.

UNESCO. 1976. *Education in Africa since 1960: a statistical review.* Conference of Ministers of Education of African Member States, Lagos, January 27–February 4, 1976. Paris: UNESCO.

Voegelin, C. F., and Voegelin, F. M. 1964. *Languages of the world: African fascicle one. Anthropological Linguistics* 6(5).

Whiteley, W. H. 1971. Language policies of independent African states. In Sebeok, ed. 1971.

——, ed. 1974. *Language in Kenya.* Nairobi: Oxford University Press.

Zuengler, J. 1982. Kenyan English. In *The other tongue: English across cultures.* Ed. Braj B. Kachru. Urbana: University of Illinois Press.

8

Ayọ Bamgboṣe

Standard Nigerian English: Issues of Identification

The question whether there is a "Nigerian English" should, at this point, have become a non-issue. For one thing, it is generally known that in a language contact situation, particularly a close one where an exoglossic language becomes a second language with an official role in a country, the second language is bound to be influenced by its linguistic and cultural environment.[1] For another, the existence of several different "Englishes" is now generally accepted by linguists.[2] However, many educated Nigerians still believe there is no such thing as Nigerian English, even though their own speech and usage provide ample evidence of its existence.[3] A Nigerian expert in TEFL declared recently: "I do not believe that there is *Nigerian English* now in the linguistic, demographic, and sociological senses in which there is an American English, Australian English and British English."[4]

Some of those who deny that there is a Nigerian English may genuinely believe that the English they speak is no different from one of the native varieties of English; but I have a feeling that those who feel this way must be very few. Most of those who refuse to accept that there is a Nigerian English are genuinely worried about the implication of accepting a Nigerian variety of English as an appropriate model, particularly in language teaching. They fear that, in time, such a variety may degenerate into a different language, like pidgin English. Hence, they insist that "only the best, native-speaker, performance level should be aimed at"[5] in higher education. Closely related to this view is a tendency toward purism. The so-called deviant or non-standard forms found in Nigerian English are regarded by some as "mistakes," rather than as evidence of a distinct type of English in Nigeria.[6]

One noticeable effect of the refusal to accept the existence of a Nigerian English is the perpetuation of the myth that the English taught in Nigerian schools is just the same as, say, British English; a corollary myth is that teachers of English, even at the primary school level, are capable of teaching this model effectively. In our teaching and examinations we concentrate on drilling and testing out of existence forms of speech that even the teachers will use freely when they do not have their textbooks open before them.

Identifying Varieties of Nigerian English

Lack of acceptance of the existence of a Nigerian English has not deterred linguists from observing and describing the varieties of English used in Nigeria. Brosnahan started a trend of ranging the varieties on a scale and linking them with levels of education: "The speakers of English in Nigeria encompass all gradations from the British educated speakers of an approximation to Received Pronunciation of Southern English to the large numbers whose knowledge of English is limited to a few words of a pidgin variety" (1958: 99). Brosnahan then went on to identify four levels of Nigerian English:

Level I: Pidgin; spoken by those without any formal education.

Level II: Spoken by those who have had primary school education. Most speakers belong to this level.

Level III: Spoken by those who have had secondary school education. Marked by increased fluency, wider vocabulary, and conscious avoidance of Level I usage.

Level IV: Close to Standard English but retaining some features of Levels II and III. Spoken by those with university education.

Banjọ (1971a: 169–70) took the identification further by indicating the linguistic characteristics of the different varieties and introducing variables of international intelligibility and social acceptability. His own four varieties are as follows:

Variety 1: Marked by wholesale transfer of phonological, syntactic, and lexical features of Kwa or Niger-Congo to English. Spoken by those whose knowledge of English is very imperfect. Neither socially acceptable in Nigeria nor internationally intelligible.

149

Variety 2: Syntax close to that of Standard British English, but
with strongly marked phonological and lexical peculiarities. Spoken by up to 75 percent of those who
speak English in the country. Socially acceptable, but
with rather low international intelligibility.

Variety 3: Close to Standard British English both in syntax and
in semantics; similar in phonology, but different in
phonetic features as well as with regard to certain
lexical peculiarities. Socially acceptable and internationally intelligible. Spoken by less than 10 percent
of the population.

Variety 4: Identical with Standard British English in syntax and
semantics, and having identical phonological and
phonetic features of a British regional dialect of
English. Maximally internationally intelligible, but
socially unacceptable. Spoken by only a handful of
Nigerians born or brought up in England.

A comparison of the two schemes shows a remarkable similarity,
except at the bottom and top ends of the scale. In Banjọ's scheme,
pidgin (Brosnahan's Level I) is excluded and treated as a separate
language from English, while in Brosnahan's scheme Native English
(Banjọ's Variety 4) is not treated as a variety of Nigerian English.[7] We
are left with the following correspondences: Level II = Variety 1; Level
III = Variety 2; and Level IV = Variety 3.

Two issues arise from the varieties identified above. The first is
the question of education as a variable in identifying speakers of the
different varieties. The second is the question of which variety is the
best candidate for a standard Nigerian English.

Level of education is an attractive parameter for characterizing
level of usage; it has been used not only for Nigerian English, but
also for Ghanaian English.[8] But it is open to one main objection: there
are speakers who perform below, or above, the expected level of
competence based on their level of education. Several writers have
drawn attention to this problem.[9] In fairness to Brosnahan (1958), who
based his varieties of Nigerian English on level of education, it must
be pointed out that he was aware of the need to qualify the criterion:
he adds that "opportunity for its use [i.e., English], innate ability and
intelligence and perseverance with schemes of private study and
correspondence schools all tend to smooth out the differences left by
different opportunities of formal education" (Brosnahan 1958: 100).
What this means, in effect, is that education as a variable is to be used
flexibly. One would expect a university graduate to be a Variety 3

speaker, but if a few such graduates cannot attain that standard, they should be classified with speakers of the appropriate lower variety. Similarly, a primary school leaver who has had prolonged exposure to English or who has been able to improve himself through private study will be classified with speakers of a higher variety. Used in this way, level of education will be no more than a statement of probability. The expectation will of course be that *most* university graduates will be Variety 3 speakers, while most primary school leavers who have had no additional exposure to English will be Variety 1 or 2 speakers.

There is remarkable unanimity about the variety of English that can be called "Educated Nigerian English." It is that variety which is closest to Native English, being "same"with it in syntax and phonology, "similar" in semantics, but "different" in lexis and phonetics. Criper (1971) has identified for Ghanaian English a subtype of this variety which is identical in all respects, except that its phonology is not "same" but only "similar" to that of Native English. It is quite possible that there are Nigerian speakers of Variety 3 English who make all the phonological distinctions found in a native variety of English; but my guess is that such people must be very few in number. A recent study (Ekong 1978) has shown that a group of perfectly intelligible Variety 3 speakers of Nigerian English produces consistently only sixteen vowel contrasts out of a possible twenty-four contrasts (including diphthongs and triphthongs) in Received Pronunciation as described by Daniel Jones.[10] This situation seems more typical of the vast majority of Variety 3 speakers. When the two other variables of acceptability and international intelligibility are considered, Variety 3 or Educated Nigerian English stands out as the only plausible candidate for a standard Nigerian English.

Identifying Nigerian Usages in Nigerian English

An inevitable point of departure in describing usage in a second-language situation is a conscious or unconscious comparison with a native variety of the language concerned. This is precisely what has been done in the description of Nigerian English. Labels such as "same," "different," or "similar" must be justified in terms of observed usage in the varieties to which they are applied. Three approaches may be identified: the interference approach, the deviation approach, and the creativity approach.

The interference approach attempts to trace Nigerian usages to the influence of the Nigerian languages. This approach is certainly most relevant as far as the phonetics of Nigerian English is concerned.[11]

But as I have pointed out elsewhere, even at this level there are "features which are typical of the pronunciation of most Nigerian speakers of English" (Bamgboṣe 1971: 42) irrespective of their first-language background. Besides, a typical pronunciation may result from a factor other than interference. For example, most speakers of English from the eastern part of Nigeria pronounce the possessive "your" as [jua] or [ja], even though all the languages in that area have the sound [ɔ]. The prevalence of this pronunciation is no doubt due to its widespread use by teachers and generations of pupils who have passed through the same schools.

The interference approach is even less justifiable in lexis and syntax. Adekunle (1974) attributes all of Standard Nigerian English's Nigerian usages in lexis and syntax to interference from the mother tongue. It is quite easy to show that while some usages can be so attributed, the vast majority, at least in Educated Nigerian English, arise from the normal process of language development involving a narrowing or extension of meaning or the creation of new idioms. And most such usages cut across all first-language backgrounds. For example, when "travel" is used in the sense "to be away," as in *My father has traveled* (= My father is away), it is not a transfer of a first-language expression into English, but a modification of the meaning of the verb "to travel."

One final objection to the interference approach is that not all cases of interference can validly be considered Nigerian usages. Some clearly belong to the level of pidgin English. For instance, the absence of a gender distinction in third-person pronominal reference may result from first-language interference, e.g., *He talk say* . . . (= He/She says that . . .), but it is unlikely that this will be considered a feature of any variety of Nigerian English.[12]

The deviation approach involves a comparison of observed Nigerian usage with Native English, and the labeling of all differences as "deviant."[13] Such deviance may result from interference, or from an imperfect attempt to reproduce the target expressions. For example, *Borrow me your pen* (= Lend me your pen) is clearly a case of interference from a first language which makes no lexical distinction between "lend" and "borrow." On the other hand, the pluralization of "equipment" in *We bought the equipments* indicates a failure to grasp the distinction between countable and mass nouns.

There are two main weaknesses in the deviation approach. First, it tends to suggest that the observed usage is "imperfect" or "non-standard" English. The fact that some so-called deviations have now achieved the status of identifying markers of a standard Nigerian

English tends to be overlooked in a description that lumps all divergences together as deviant usage. Second, the deviation approach ignores the fact that certain characteristic Nigerian usages in English result from the creativity of the users.

The creativity approach tends to focus on the exploitation of the resources of Nigerian languages as well as of English to create new idioms and expressions. According to this approach, a usage which might otherwise have been classified as resulting from interference or deviation is seen as a legitimate second-language creation.[14] Thus, from the expression *She has been to Britain* a new noun, *been-to,* has been created to describe anyone who has traveled overseas, particularly to Britain.

The main advantage of the creativity approach is that it recognizes the development of Nigerian English as a type in its own right. But not all cases of usage in Nigerian English can properly be regarded as arising from creativity. Besides, certain usages motivated by creativity are, at best, substandard English. Amos Tutuola's novel, *My Life in the Bush of Ghosts,* is a good example of this. The incidents in the novel take place "in those days of unknown year" when "slave wars were causing dead luck to both young and old"; and the hero visits "Deads'-town" and sees "born and die babies" as well as "triplet ghosts and ghostesses."[15] (See also Ch. 16.)

The above discussion shows that while each approach throws some light on the nature of Nigerian English, none is by itself adequate to characterize the whole spectrum of Nigerian English. Besides, not every feature thrown up by each approach necessarily exemplifies Nigerian English. A combination of all approaches is therefore required, and a certain amount of subjective judgment regarding acceptability will be required in determining what falls within or outside the scope of Nigerian English.

One issue which constantly arises in determining a truly Nigerian usage is whether what is being held out as a local variant is not instead "incorrect" English. There are a number of reasons why this continues to be a serious issue. First, as has already been mentioned, it is inherent in a second-language situation for a comparison to be made with a native variety of the language concerned. Differences then have to be classified somehow; often opinions differ as to whether some are "errors" or correct local variants.[16] Perhaps this point is best illustrated by the following opinion: "My contention is that although one finds some differences between certain usages by some Nigerians and, for instance, British usages, most of such differences are due to mistakes of some sort; they should not be regarded as 'typically

Nigerian' especially as they have not been proved to be general" (Salami 1968: 105).

Second, arising from the tradition of "error analysis" among practitioners of TESL, which has generally involved taking school-children's or students' essays to bits and carefully noting the "errors" and "deviations," it has become difficult to draw the line between a local variant and an actual error. Some cite extremely numerous examples of usages in such essays as instances of Nigerian English, while others maintain that they are merely "mistakes and solecisms."[17]

Third, the teaching and examining of English in Nigeria tend to ensure that local variants will continue to be labeled "errors." Children are taught that to say "senior brother" is wrong; they should say "elder brother." Yet the former is used by a majority of educated Nigerian speakers of English. I recall a moderation meeting for the English paper of the West African school certificate examination. One of the idioms to be tested was "putting back the clock," which in Nigerian English is putting back *the hands* of the clock. It is interesting that only two of the persons present at this meeting knew the correct version of this idiom. One was a native speaker; the other had consulted a dictionary of English idioms in preparation for the meeting. Quite clearly, this is a case where the latter version has become an authentic Nigerian usage in English.

There can be no solution to the issue of errors until another related issue is considered. This is the question of whose usage is to be accepted as typical or standard. I have already subscribed to the view that majority usage will not necessarily determine the standard; that is why I accept Banjo's Variety 3 as the only plausible Standard Nigerian English. But Variety 3 itself contains usages which may be regarded as nonstandard.[18] The subjective element again enters: Whose usage is to be accepted? I hasten to suggest that it should not be that of the purist (who does not believe in a Nigerian English anyway), nor that of the foreign-educated elite (whose usage is, on the whole, not very different from a standard variety of English). The natural and spontaneous usage of the locally educated Nigerian user of English is a more reliable guide to the identification of typical Nigerian usage.[19]

Some Typical Features of Standard Nigerian English

In order to illustrate such features as I consider typical, I provide (below) examples based on my general observation of the use of English by Variety 3 speakers. I believe these features cut across different first-language backgrounds, and no amount of drilling or stigmatization is going to lead to their abandonment. The features are identified at the following levels: phonetics and phonology, morphology and syntax, lexis and semantics, and context.[20]

Phonetics and Phonology

Several phonetic features reflect the first language or regional background of the speakers; but there are also general phonetic features, such as the following: (1) A reduced vowel system involves various substitutions, such as [e] for [ei], [o] for [ou], [a] for [ɐ:] and [ə], and a frequent obliteration of the distinction in vowel quality between the vowels of *beat* and *bit*, *cord* and *cod*, with the former being substituted for the latter. (2) Syllable-timed instead of stress-timed rhythm is employed, with a reduced system of intonation. (3) An epenthetic vowel [u] or [i] may be introduced between a word-final syllabic consonant and the preceding consonant; e.g., in *bottle* and *button*, respectively. (4) Consistent spelling pronunciation occurs in words ending in orthographic *-mb*, *-ng*, and their derivatives; e.g., *bomb*, *climb*, *bomber*, *plumber*, *sing*, *hang*, *singer*, *hanger*. (5) Characteristic stress patterns occur, as in the following words: 'success, main'tenance, ˌrecog'nize, ˌinvesti'gate, ˌcongratu'late, ma'dam, 'circumference. (6) Contrastive stress is avoided in sentences. Instead of *"John* did it," we are likely to have "It was John who did it." (See also Atoye 1991 and Criper-Friedman 1990.)

Morphology and Syntax

These are generally the same as in Standard English, except for features such as the following: (1) Peculiar word formation may occur with plurals (e.g., *equipments*, *aircrafts*, *deadwoods*), antonyms (*indisciplined*), and adverbials (*singlehandedly*). (2) Dropping of "to" from the infinitive after certain verbs; e.g., *enable him do it*. (3) A preposition may be employed where Native English will avoid or will use a different preposition; e.g., *voice out* instead of "voice" (I am going to voice out my opinion), *discuss about* instead of "discuss" (We shall discuss about that later), *congratulate for* instead of "congratulate on" (I congratulate you for your brilliant performance). (4) A focus construction is often used, involving the subject of the sentence as focus and an anaphoric pronoun subject, e.g., *The politicians and their supporters, they don't often listen to advice.*[21] *A person who has no experience, can he be a good leader?*

Lexis and Semantics

As has often been observed, most differences between Nigerian English and other forms of English are to be found in the innovations in lexical items and idioms and their meanings. Following are some of the features concerned. (1) New lexical items may either be coined from existing lexical items or borrowed from the local languages or from pidgin, either directly or in translation. For examples of coinage, consider *barb* (to cut [hair]) from "barber," *invitee* (guest) from "invite," *head-tie* (woman's headdress), and *go-slow* (traffic jam). Loanwords and loan translations are generally drawn from different aspects of the cultural background, including food, dress, and customs for which there are quite often no exact equivalent lexical items in English; e g., *akara balls* (beancakes), *juju music* (a type of dance music), *bush meat* (game), *tie-dye cloth* (cloth into which patterns are made by tying up parts of it before dyeing), and *white-cap chiefs* (senior chiefs in Lagos whose rank is shown by the white caps they wear). (2) Some lexical items acquire new meanings; e.g., a *corner* becomes a "bend in a road," *globe* is an "electric bulb," *wet* means "to water (flowers)," and a *launcher* is someone called upon to declare open a fund-raising function. *Locate* means "to assign to a school or town" and is used when speaking of newly qualified teachers. *Land* is "to finish one's intervention or speech," *environment* is a "neighborhood," and *bluff* means "to give an air of importance." (3) Other lexical items have retained older meanings no longer current in Native English. *Dress*, "move at the end of a row so as to create room for additional persons," is a retention of the earlier meaning recorded by the *Shorter Oxford English Dictionary*: "to form in proper alignment." *Station*, "the town or city in which a person works," is a retention of the earlier meaning recorded by the same source: "the locality to which an official is appointed for the exercise of his functions." (4) Certain idioms acquire new forms or meanings. *To eat one's cake and have it* is an inversion of "to have one's cake and eat it" (Example: You can't eat your cake and have it). *As at now* replaces "as of now" (Example: As at now, there are only two men available). (5) Some totally new idioms are developed; e.g., *to take in* for "to become pregnant" (Example: She has just taken in). *Off-head*, "from memory," is similar to Standard English *offhand* (Example: I can't tell you the number off-head). *To take the light* means to make a power cut (Example: Has the National Electrical Power Authority (N.E.P.A.) taken the light again?). And *social wake-keeping* refers to feasting, drumming, and dancing after a burial (Example: There will be social wake-keeping from 10 p.m. till dawn. See also Adegbija 1989.)

Context

Even when lexical items or idioms have roughly the same meanings as in Native English, they may be used in completely different contexts.

Examples which have been given in the literature include the use of *sorry* as an expression of sympathy, for example, to someone who sneezes or stumbles, or *wonderful* as an exclamation of surprise.[22] To these may be added the use of *please* as an indication of politeness (for example, in a formal or official letter), *Dear Sir* for opening a personal letter to someone older than oneself,[23] and *my dear* for addressing practically anyone, including strangers.

One aspect of context that goes into the making of Nigerian English is the use of certain characteristic expressions in given registers. To take just the example of the language of obituaries, one knows immediately that one is dealing with Nigerian English when one sees such expressions as: "With gratitude to God for a life well spent, we regret to announce the death of our beloved father, grandfather, and great-grandfather, Chief Dr. X," where the opening phrase, together with the multiple reference to the deceased, has become a cliché; or "The wicked have done their worst," which reflects the widespread belief that most deaths result from the wicked action of some known or unknown enemies.

In spite of many educated Nigerians' reluctance to accept the above features as manifestations of Nigerian English, there is some proof that the pressure exerted by their widespread use is beginning to force such people to adopt some of the expressions in order to communicate effectively. Take, for instance, someone trying to describe a *traffic jam* and quickly correcting himself to say a *go-slow*. Recently I caught myself saying, *Let's go and wet the flowers*, even though I know that the appropriate expression is *Let's go and water the flowers*. What all this shows is that standardizing factors already exist which will tend to pull usage in the direction of more characteristically Nigerian forms. This trend will be hastened by the fact that education is now available to many more people, and that some of the best models of Nigerian English are now to be found among university graduates, including secondary school and university teachers. (For further discussion, see Kujọrẹ 1985.)

Conclusion

Discussions of particular types of English necessarily tend to concentrate on the features peculiar to each type, because of the initial preoccupation with establishing an identity for the type in question. It is unfortunate, however, that such discussions have tended to play down the similarities between the type being described and other types. As Quirk (1962: 95–96) has rightly pointed out, "the remarkable thing is the very high degree of unanimity, the small amount of divergence" between the various Englishes of the world. This basic similarity makes it possible for each type to absorb a fair number of distinctive local variants and usages.

Writing about what he calls "the British heresy in TESL," Prator (1968: 464) describes "a second-language variety of English" as "a tongue caught up in a process that tends to transform it swiftly and quite predictably into an utterly dissimilar tongue." Suffice it to say that this prediction has been borne out neither by Nigerian English nor by the other Englishes of West Africa. Mazrui (1975: 16) has also predicted that those who speak English as a native language in Africa— "the Afro-Saxons"—are bound to multiply. Even if this prediction turns out to be untrue (as seems likely), the continued use of English as a second language by a sizable proportion of Nigerians of different generations is bound to ensure the continued development of a Standard Nigerian English.

NOTES

1. Note in this connection the perceptive comment by Christophersen (1960: 131) about the difference between a foreign language and a second language, the former being used for "absorbing the culture of another nation" and the latter "as an alternative way of expressing the culture of one's own."

2. See, e.g., the reference by Quirk (1962: 95) to Standard English as an "ideal" which "cannot be perfectly realized," since we must expect different realization. In this connection, Halliday, McIntosh, and Strevens (1964: 294) specifically draw attention to the emergence of an "educated West African English" which is in the process of replacing "British English with RP" as a model.

3. One important personality, while visiting our department of linguistics, was told that the department was interested in research on Nigerian English; he commented that that was a waste of time, as there was no such thing as Nigerian English. A few minutes later he said, on being interrupted, "let me land"—the Nigerian equivalent of "let me finish."

4. This statement, made in a discussion by Professor S. H. O. Tomori, who claims an experience of "fifty years of listening to English and thirty years of teaching it," is reported in the *International Association of the Teachers of English as a Foreign Language Newsletter*, no. 54 (August 1978): 15.

5. Ibid.

6. See, e.g., Salami 1968: 104–5.

7. Criper 1971, in a classification of Ghanaian English, rules out both pidgin and Native English. This appears to be a more satisfactory solution because pidgin has become a language in its own right, and Native English cannot properly be considered a variety of Ghanaian or Nigerian English.

8. See, e.g., Criper 1971: 7 and Sey 1973: 18.

9. See Salami 1968: 102–3, Bamgboṣe 1971: 38, Banjọ 1971a.

10. In this experiment, consistent production of vowel contrast is based on elicitation from more than half of the informants with respect to each vowel. The lowest score was 51 percent for the vowel [iə] and the highest was 100 percent for [i] and [ɛ]. See Ekong 1978: 82.

11. Dunstan 1969 provides a good illustration of the interference of certain Nigerian languages in the spoken English of speakers of those languages.

12. Note that the absence of concord between the subject and the verb is also a feature of lower varieties of Nigerian English.

13. See, e.g., Adesanoye 1973, who regards as "deviations" all the features marking his different varieties of written English in Nigeria.

14. For an example of such an approach, see Obiechina 1974.

15. See Tutuọla 1954: 17, 18, 62, 63. Note "dead luck" (= bad fortune), "Deads'-town" (= City of the Dead) and "born and die babies" (= babies who are believed to die and return, usually to the same parents).

16. An example of such disagreement is Walsh 1967: 47, who says that expressions such as "all the equipments" and someone running "for his dear life" are instances of legitimate Nigerian English, while Adesanoye 1973: 45 says that these expressions "are very clearly errors."

17. Compare the attitude of Kirk-Green 1971, who leans toward acceptance of such usages as Nigerian English, with that of Salami 1968, who rejects them.

18. Banjo 1971b: 126 draws attention to the "varying quantities of what could be regarded as substandard features in the formal prose of Nigerian graduates."

19. The level of education will generally be university, although, as stated earlier, others with lower levels of education but prolonged exposure to English will also qualify as Variety 3 users of English.

20. Some features in morphology, lexis, and semantics are similar to those found in Ghanaian English; see, e.g., Sey 1973. This shows that there is a basis for talking about larger varieties such as "West African English."

21. Such sentences appear to be acceptable in Native English only if there is a demonstrative or a contrastive stress on the pronoun subject: e.g., "These politicians and their supporters, *they* are the ones who don't often listen to advice."

22. See Bamgboṣe 1971: 44 and Kirk-Green 1971: 137.

23. Quirk 1962: 217 has drawn attention to the fact that formulas for opening and closing personal or official letters are fixed: "well-educated people do not mix these formulas and they tend to think poorly of those who do." However, as Bamgboṣe 1969: 87 has pointed out, in the context of Nigerian English, one has little choice but to mix formulas (i.e., to open with "Dear Sir" and close with "Yours sincerely"), since it will be considered impolite to address an older person by his surname, and positively disrespectful, if not impudent, to use his first name.

REFERENCES

Adegbija, Efurosibina. 1989. Lexico-semantic variation in Nigerian English. *World Englishes* 8(2): 165–77.

Adekunle, M. A. 1974. The standard Nigerian English. *Journal of the Nigeria English Studies Association* 6(1): 24–37.

Adesanoye, F. 1973. A study of the varieties of written English in Nigeria. Ph.D. dissertation, University of Ibadan.

Atoye, Raphael O. 1991. Word stress in Nigerian English. *World Englishes* 10(1): 1–6.

Bamgboṣe, Ayọ. 1969. Registers of English. *Journal of the Nigeria English Studies Association* 4(1): 81–88.

———. 1971. The English language in Nigeria. In Spencer 1971: 35–48.

Banjọ, L. Ayọ. 1971a. Towards a definition of "standard Nigerian spoken English." Pp. 165–75 in *Actes du 8e Congrès de la Société Linguistique de l'Afrique Occidentale*. Abidjan: Université d'Abidjan.

———. 1971b. Standards of correctness in Nigerian English. *West African Journal of Education* 15(2): 123–27.

Brosnahan, L. F. 1958. English in southern Nigeria. *English Studies* (39): 97–110.

Christophersen, Paul. 1960. Towards a standard of international English. *English Language Teaching* 14(3): 127–38.

Criper, Lindsay. 1971. A classification of types of English in Ghana. *Journal of African Languages* 10(3): 6–17.

Criper-Friedman, Lindsay. 1990. The tone system of West African coastal English. *World Englishes* 9(1): 63–78.

Dunstan, Elizabeth, ed. 1969. *Twelve Nigerian languages (a handbook on their sound systems for teachers of English)*. London: Longmans.

Ekong, Pamela A. 1978. On describing the vowel systems of a standard variety of Nigerian spoken English. M.A. project, University of Ibadan.

Fishman, J. A., C. A. Ferguson, and J. Das Gupta, eds. 1968. *Language problems of developing nations*. New York: John Wiley and Sons.

Halliday, M. A. K., A. McIntosh, and P. Strevens. 1964. *The linguistic sciences and language teaching*. London: Longmans, Green.

Kirk-Green, A. 1971. The influence of West African languages on English. In Spencer 1971: 123–44.

Kujọrẹ, Obafemi. 1985. *English usage: some notable Nigerian variations*. Ibadan: Evans Brothers.

Mazrui, Ali A. 1975. *The political sociology of the English language*. The Hague: Mouton.

Obiechina, E. N. 1974. Varieties differentiation in English usage. *Journal of the Nigeria English Studies Association* 6(1).

Prator, C. H. 1968. The British heresy in TESL. In Fishman, Ferguson, and Das Gupta 1968: 459–76.

Quirk, Randolph. 1962. *The use of English*. London: Longmans, Green.

Salami, A. 1968. Defining "a Standard Nigerian English." *Journal of the Nigeria English Studies Association* 2(2): 99–106.

Sey, K. A. 1973. *Ghanaian English: an exploratory survey.* London: Macmillan.

Spencer, John, ed. 1971. *The English language in West Africa.* London: Longmans.

Tutuọla, Amos. 1954. *My life in the bush of ghosts.* London: Faber and Faber.

Walsh, N. G. 1967. Distinguishing types and varieties of English in Nigeria. *Journal of the Nigeria English Studies Association* no. 2, 47–55.

9

Chin-Chuan Cheng

Chinese Varieties of English

The varieties of English spoken by native Chinese around the world presumably share certain features because of common language background.[1] However, there are differences in the status of English and its function in different areas, such as the People's Republic of China, Taiwan, Hong Kong, Malaysia, Singapore, and Chinatowns in the United States. There are no detailed in-depth studies of any of these varieties, though in recent years some attention has been given to English in certain political settings—for example, in Singapore and Malaysia (Platt 1977) and in Hong Kong (Richards and Luke 1981). Here I will deal with the varieties of English in mainland China. These varieties display a cline of proficiency, beginning with pidgin (Kachru 1969), while they manifest the different sociopolitical perceptions of the West evident in different stages of Chinese history.

Today, English is the most-studied foreign language in China. In some areas English instruction starts in the third grade of elementary school, and most middle school students take English to satisfy foreign language requirements (Lehmann et al. 1975; Cheng 1975; Light 1978; Cowan et al. 1979). Adults are also interested in learning English. As Cowan et al. (1979) report, 242,000 students were enrolled in a television English course produced by the "Chinese Television University" in Beijing in 1979. The primary purpose of the study of English—or of any Western language—in the recent past has been essentially "to serve the revolution" (Lehmann et al. 1975) and is now to gain access to Western science and technology. The increased flow of Western tourists and businessmen to China has also made it crucial to use English, though in restricted contexts (Cowan et al. 1979).[2]

In spite of the number of people involved in learning English, there is no English-speaking Chinese community; nor does English serve as an interlanguage among the nation's fifty-six ethnic groups. In this sense, the functions of English are much different in China than in Africa (see Bamgboṣe 1982) and in South Asia (see Kachru 1981). While some Chinese writers—for example, Armand Su—write primarily in Esperanto, I know of no significant works of literature in English or other foreign languages by Chinese authors living in China.

English is used primarily in international communication, and written English in China appears in publications mainly for international consumption. The international function often requires a unified expression, not only in ideology, but also in language. Therefore one finds identical or very similar expressions used in various publications. This tendency toward fixed expressions is also noticeable in spoken English. To an outsider, both spoken and written varieties appear stilted.

Recently the most outstanding feature of English in China has been the prevalence of terse and politicized lexical items and phrases. These terms are unintelligible to outsiders who are not familiar with the Chinese context. Thus there appears to be a kind of English peculiar to the Chinese culture: one might call it Sinicized English. This variety has not derived its characteristics from an earlier version of English in China, nor will it necessarily remain invariant in the future. My intention here is to show that peculiarities of English in China reflect the sociopolitical situation there. In examining the history and the current situations of the Chinese varieties of English, I hope to demonstrate that when China is inward-searching, the English there acquires more Chinese elements, and when China is outward-looking, the English is more Western.

The Earliest Phase

Kachru (1981) characterizes the origin of non-native Englishes as follows: "The non-native Englishes are the legacy of the colonial period, and have mainly developed in 'unEnglish' cultural and linguistic contexts in various parts of the world, wherever the arm of the Western colonizers reached." In the case of China, the Western powers reached only a few ports, and one linguistic consequence of that limited contact was the development of pidgin varieties.

The British established their first trading post in Guangzhou (Canton) in 1664. The development of pidgin English there reflected the Chinese "Middle Kingdom" conception of the universe. The

Chinese held the British, like all "foreign devils," in low esteem, and would not stoop to learning the foreign tongue in its full form (Hall 1966). The British, on the other hand, regarded the "heathen Chinese" as beyond any possibility of learning, and so began to modify their own language for the natives' benefit. Hall (1966) shows traces of an earlier Cantonese Pidgin Portuguese in Chinese Pidgin English (see also Todd 1974), although Reinecke et al. (1975) remark that such a relationship is in dispute. Whatever the relationship, it is certain that pidgin English apparently took shape in the first quarter of the eighteenth century in Guangzhou. Beginning in 1843, when the so-called Treaty Ports were established, it spread to the southeastern coastal cities and the Changjiang (Yangtze) valley. During the last decade of the nineteenth century, as a consequence of social and political disfavor and of the preference for Standard English, it started to decline. Chinese Pidgin English is now virtually dead, with only marginal use remaining among a few Chinese speakers in the British colony of Hong Kong (Whinnom 1971).

Based on Reinecke's (1937) dissertation, "Marginal Language," Hall (1944) divides the history of Chinese Pidgin English into four phases: original, "classical," expanding, and declining. He further points out that, throughout its life, Chinese Pidgin English was mostly a means of communication between foreign masters and Chinese servants, and a medium used in retail shops catering to foreigners. During the period of expansion, however, it was used between foreigners and upper-class Chinese, as well as by servants and tradesmen.[3]

Chinese Pidgin English deviated considerably from Standard English. For example, consider the following sentence (which I have converted into standard orthography from the phonetic symbols appearing in Hall 1944: 108, 1966: 152): *Tailor, my have got one piece plenty hansom silk; my want you make one nice evening dress.* The use of *my* for *I* and *my* (the latter not shown in this example) was a result of the reduction of English morphology. In Chinese, the possessive is formed by adding a particle to the pronoun; there is no case change, such as from *I* to *my*. Because this is true in all dialects, one may safely infer that the reduction in this instance is a case of interference (or transfer) from Chinese.

Toward Westernization: English as a Tool

At the turn of the present century, the Chinese perceived a great need for modernization, which in essence meant Westernization. Learning foreign languages in their full forms was a prerequisite to acquisition of Western knowledge. At the same time, there was also a great surge of nationalism; pidgin English was occasionally disparaged as "coolie Esperanto" (Reinecke et al. 1975). Hall (1973: 79) explains the decline of pidgin as follows:

> In the case of Chinese Pidgin English a standoffish attitude characterized both sides, for the Chinese more than matched the Europeans in their sense of national superiority. If only two language groups are involved, the side that feels it suffers loss of status because it speaks pidgin may come to insist on learning the other side's full language; this happened in China after 1900.

Such an attitude necessitated that English become part of a standard post-primary curriculum. Some schools even started teaching English as early as the third grade (Zhu 1978).

In the several decades immediately preceding 1950, English was equated with British literature, as is also the case in parts of Africa and South Asia. In schools, especially at the university level, English learning meant memorizing the works of Shakespeare and other writers of the past; contemporary writings were rarely studied. Zhu (1978) mentions that English majors could write quaint and sentimental essays in imitation of Charles Lamb, but they were unable to write short articles to comment on current national and international situations. Bookish rather than colloquial English was the norm in conversations. Such a bias against contemporary English existed because the university curricula were transplanted, without much modification, from the United States and Britain. In those English-speaking countries, it was only natural to study literature in college. Chinese students, in contrast, at that time had no opportunity to learn spoken English. In some missionary schools English was the only language spoken, and the teachers were often foreigners—but their Chinese students were few in number. The Chinese situation was, again, not much different from the Indian (Kachru 1969) or the Nigerian (Bamgboṣe 1982).

In the first half of the twentieth century, China came into more frequent contact with foreign countries. Many works were translated from English and other languages into Chinese. English was known well by a comparatively small educated elite; yet the impact of English on the Chinese language was significant, especially in the written form. Wang (1955) devotes a lengthy chapter to discussion of "Westernized grammar," expounding mainly on the influence of English grammar on Chinese. An infusion of new lexical items occurred, along with modification of some aspects of Chinese syntax. The new lexical items were formed by transliteration or by compounding words with similar meanings. This Westernization brought about an increase in the number of polysyllabic words, for example *modeng* (modern), *moteer* (model), *shehui* (society), and *yuanliang* (excuse).

At the syntactic level, the influence of English on Chinese can be exemplified by the length of phrases and the use of passive verb forms. In Chinese, the modifying part comes before the modified; therefore Westernized Chinese sentences often contain long modifiers before the head noun to accommodate English subordinate clauses. In the following, sentence (a) is English, (b) is Westernized Chinese, and (c) is "normal" Chinese (Wang 1955: 282–83):

(a) People who regard literary taste simply as an accomplishment, and literature simply as a distraction, will . . .

(b) *Naxie*   ba   wenxue   xingwei   renwei

those   CO-VERB   literary   taste   regard

chunran   yizhong   caiyi,   ba

simply   a kind   accomplishment   CO-VERB

wenxue   renwei   chunran   yizhong

literature   regard   simply   a kind

xiaoqianpin   de   *renmen,*   jiang . . .

distraction   POSSESSIVE   people   will

(c) *Yigeren ruguo* ba wenxue xingwei renwei chunran yizhong caiyi, ba wenxue renwei chunran yizhong xiaoqianpin, jiang . . .

The Westernized style puts the head noun *renmen* (people) at the very end of the long modifier. The normal Chinese, however, brings out the subject *yigeren* (a person) at the very beginning and uses *ruguo* (if) to qualify it.

The passive preposition (also called co-verb) *bei* was limited to sentences expressing suffering from some action. The English passive has extended the use of *bei* beyond pejorative to positive senses: *Ta bei juwei zhuxi* (He was elected chairman), or *Ta bei kuajiangle yifan* (He was greatly praised).

Whereas Chinese underwent these changes under the influence of English, the English language in China received little modification. This was the situation when China looked outward for change in the country.

Model for Chinese English

The term "Westernization," used above with reference to Wang (1955), is actually *ouhua*, "Europeanization." For many years the West was Europe, and British English was the standard model. British English has remained more or less the standard since the 1950s, even though the United States had already attained the height of its influence politically, economically, and linguistically. Several factors contributed to the continued dominance of British English. First, Chinese education was very much under the influence of the Soviet system. English curricula were designed on the basis of those of the Soviet Union (Xiong and Cheng 1980), where British English was more or less the standard. Second, there was not much contact between China and the United States. The Cold War, McCarthyism, and the U.S. economic blockade perhaps contributed to a negative feeling toward American English. In contrast, the United Kingdom and China established diplomatic relations early. Furthermore, there have even been a few British citizens on the editorial staffs of English-language publications in Beijing. Until 1979, as Cowan et al. (1979) report, foreign English-language experts were provided primarily by the governments of Britain, Canada, and New Zealand. This earlier impact is visible even now, and can be seen in the English edition of the weekly journal *Beijing Review*. The *Beijing Review* indicates what written English is like in China today. The most apparent feature of British English is the spelling; e.g., the use of *-our* for *-or: in honour of* (May 6, 1977, p. 33); *labouring people* (April 28, 1978, p. 10); *scientific endeavour* (April 7, 1978, p. 16). Words such as *programme* also prove this point. The preference for British English is not limited to the one journal. Lehmann et al. (1975), reporting on the visit by the first U.S. linguistics delegation to China in 1974, mention that British English was obviously preferred there, simply a consequence of history and attitude.

Developing Political English According to the Chinese System

As one reads the *Beijing Review*, however, one immediately sees that the British features are overshadowed by the distinct vocabulary of the text: "The gang arbitrarily described the political line and the achievements of 1975 as a 'Right-Deviationist wind to reverse correct verdicts'" (December 29, 1978, p. 13). Sentences like this, as Brumfit (1977) points out, appear to the native English speaker as bizarre in some sense. Indeed, it is hard for the reader who does not know the cultural (especially political) background of contemporary China to comprehend such writings.

167

Several articles in this volume deal with the "nativization" of English; I will illustrate this phenomenon in the political register of Chinese English, with examples from the *Beijing Review*. The weekly journal, with the Chinese subtitle *Beijing Zhoubao* (Beijing Weekly), has been in existence for more than twenty years. It is now published in English, French, Spanish, Japanese, German, Arabic, and Portuguese editions. The English edition was formerly called *Peking Review*. Beginning on January 1, 1979, all foreign-language publications using the Latin alphabet in China adopted the Chinese *pinyin* romanization system for spelling Chinese names, instead of the customary British Wade-Giles system. *Peking* is now spelled *Beijing*, and so is the title of the journal.[4] The journal usually contains the following sections: weekly chronicle, events and trends, articles and documents (translated from Chinese), special features, "round the world," and "on the home front." The translation is usually done by native Chinese staff members, with native English speakers adding the final touches. The translations represent typical renditions of English in China.

The function of the *Beijing Review*, and of all foreign-language journals in China, is to serve the international community. In discussing the "communicative competence" question, Kachru (1981) argues eloquently for the need to separate the uses of non-native English into local, national, and international contexts. English in China fills no local or national function. While students of English may be required to study the journal and other English-language publications, they are not the intended readership.

During the Cultural Revolution (1966–76), the Chinese people were deeply involved in a series of political movements and struggles, and China was to a large extent cut off from the outside world. In fact, individuals who read foreign materials without official sanction ran the risk of being labeled as *chong yang mei wai* (worship and have blind faith in things foreign). In these years politics were in command; and, since politics were mainly based on threat, during the times of intense struggle one often had to echo what was said in the official newspapers. As the same phrases were repeated time and time again, shorter idioms were formed to substitute for them. These idioms or abbreviated terms became ubiquitous. Naturally, the English language must accommodate itself to a culture as powerful and rich as China's, and to the currents of the time. This phenomenon is essentially what Kachru (1976, 1981) identifies as language pragmatics of non-native Englishes.

The impact of Chinese cultural parameters on English is especially conspicuous in the joint communiqué issued on February 1, 1979, in

Washington, D.C., by the visiting Vice-Premier Deng Xiaoping and President Carter. One sentence declares: "They reaffirm that they are opposed to efforts by any country or group of countries to establish hegemony or domination over others, and that they are determined to make a contribution to the maintenance of international peace, security and national independence" (February 9, 1979, p. 3). Because *hegemony* was a Chinese code word for "Soviet expansionism," and the U.S. side did not want to involve itself in the Sino-Soviet feud, *or domination over others* was added to soften the tone. Indeed, during Vice-Premier Deng's visit, Western reporters were busy looking up the meaning and pronunciation of *hegemony*. At the same time, the Chinese visitors were painstakingly searching for a Chinese translation of *rodeo*.

The distinct Chinese cultural element in English is shown mostly in idioms, phrases coined during political movements, lexical connotations and semantic shifts, and the style of discourse. The editors of the *Beijing Review* may add explanatory notes for the English reader's benefit: "There is much that is new on the educational front since the overthrow of the 'gang of four' and particularly since the reform of the college enrollment system and the criticism of the 'two estimates' " (May 5, 1978, p. 6). A footnote explains the "two estimates," but "gang of four" is supposedly well known, and no further clarification is given.

The Chinese elements in English may not always require elucidation. First of all, Chinese sayings and idioms are usually not annotated:

> When one drinks water, one must not forget where it comes from; when we think of these things, how can we not show our profound gratitude to our great leader Chairman Mao and our respected and beloved Premier Chou and cherish their memory? [April 7, 1978, p. 16]
>
> But they were like "mayflies lightly plotting to topple the giant tree." [Ibid.]

The first phrase of the first example is a translation of *yin shui si yuan*, and the quote in the second example is *fu you han shu*, both idiomatic expressions in Chinese. Because these direct translations are easy to understand, no footnotes are called for.

Words such as *bad egg* (from Chinese *huai dan*) for "villain" or "bad guy," and *running dog* (from *zou gou*) for "lackey," have become standards in Chinese derogatory remarks or polemics. Terms coined in recent political movements are not readily understandable from their constituent words, but because they occur so frequently, no explanations are provided:

To make the matter worse, the gang cooked up works centering on the struggle against "capitalist-roaders" in co-ordination with their attempt to usurp Party and state leadership under the pretext of "combating the capitalist-roaders." [April 28, 1978, p. 8]

Having destroyed the gang's "iron and steel and hat factories" and condemned its crime of savagely attacking and persecuting them, our cadres are displaying renewed revolutionary spirit. [March 10, 1978, p. 12]

A *capitalist roader* (from Chinese *zou zi pai*) is someone who takes the road leading to capitalism, i.e., someone who is in favor of a capitalist social system. *Iron and steel and hat factories* (from Chinese *gangtie gongchang maozi gongchang*) are where cudgels are made to beat (to criticize), and caps are fabricated to force upon someone's head (to label); hence the phrase means "wanton attack." The phrase *right deviationist wind to reverse correct verdicts,* given earlier, is a translation of the Chinese term *youqing fan an feng,* which means the rightist trends to invalidate the gains of the Cultural Revolution. The phrases in quotes in these examples were often used without quotes previously. A regular reader would have no difficulty understanding them, although a casual reader or a novice would find them incomprehensible. In fact, even Chinese native speakers who live outside mainland China and who do not follow Chinese political events are often nonplussed by these terms.

Some phrases often appear in the same order, even though there is no apparent logical sequence:

We must grasp the three great revolutionary movements of class struggle, the struggle for production and scientific experiment at the same time . . . [April 28, 1978, p. 4].

The general task facing our people in the new period of development in socialist revolution and socialist construction is firmly to carry out the line of 11th Party Congress, steadfastly continue the revolution under the dictatorship of the proletariat, deepen the three great revolutionary movements of class struggle, the struggle for production and scientific experiment . . . [March 10, 1978, p. 13].

In the new period of socialist revolution and socialist construction in our country, the realization of the four modernizations is politically the most important thing. [September 8, 1978, p. 10]

In the original Chinese text, *san da geming yundong* (three great revolutionary movements) is usually the only wording, but the *Beijing Review* editors add the explanatory words *of class struggle, the struggle for production,* and *scientific experiment* to enumerate the three items.

The whole string thus becomes a fixed phrase. Even at the height of the Cultural Revolution a few years ago, when "continued" or "perpetual" revolution was very much the theme of the political movements, no change of word order occurred in *socialist revolution and socialist construction.* These are actually translations from Chinese phrases which have fixed word orders. Such expressions have become so frequently used that some Chinese printing houses simply mold them in one block; as the typesetter picks up the first character, he conveniently gets the whole phrase.

In terms of lexical connotations, it is well known that in different societies some words have certain social values or stigmas attached to them. For example, *capitalist* and *bourgeois* are negative, but *communist* and *propaganda* are positive in China: "At the Chinese Communist Party's National Conference on Propaganda Work in 1957, Chairman Mao made a scientific analysis of the intellectuals in our country" (July 8, 1977, p. 13). Here *propaganda* has a perfectly respectable meaning.

In terms of syntax, readers may find the *Beijing Review*'s sentences somewhat longer than usual. Indeed, nouns with short modification in Chinese often have to be translated into English with embedded sentences. Moreover, complex sentences appear more often in political documents, in both Chinese and English. My feeling is that the syntax of the *Beijing Review* is not particularly Sinicized. For many years one could find articles in the *Beijing Review* profusely quoting Chairman Mao's aphorisms; it is also common to find articles recounting situations in the times "before Liberation." Naturally, these features reflect the current way of life in China.

To recapitulate, English in the *Beijing Review* shows its distinctiveness mainly by way of lexical items. In other parts of the world, however, as Kachru (1981) clearly shows, the transfer of a non-native English speaker's native linguistic and cultural elements is not restricted to the lexicon, but appears in syntax as well (see also, e.g., Bokamba 1982, Craig 1982, and Zuengler 1982). The reason for the lack of a significant transfer of Chinese syntax in the *Beijing Review* has to do with the fact that the English writings are done by specially trained translators, and the feeling that one should not impose Chinese syntax which would confound the international reader. The lexical items as presented above are clearly culture bound. There is no doubt that some of these items or phrases can be replaced by words appropriate to British or American practice (e.g., *dramatic work* instead of *propaganda work*), but then one risks the loss of authenticity.

Four Modernizations: Moves against Sinicized English

As China diverts its energy to science and technology, massive political movements will diminish. This desire to end excessive political struggle is clearly expressed in a recent document. The Communiqué of the Third Plenary Session of the 11th Central Committee of the Communist Party of China, adopted on December 22, 1978, emphasizes that the large-scale turbulent class struggles have more or less come to an end, and that the people should direct their work and attention toward the modernization of agriculture, industry, national defense, and science and technology. As political movements diminish, the number of the politicized phrases unintelligible to the casual reader will decrease. Moreover, as a tourist industry develops, China will have to use more words familiar to Westerners.

Moves away from the politicized and stereotyped expressions are currently under way. In the *Beijing Review*, change is the rule, rather than the exception. For example, 1978 saw a reduction in the profusion of quotes from Chairman Mao; furthermore, such quotes are now printed in the regular text type font, rather than in the boldface. Such changes are not unique to the *Beijing Review*; rather, they originated in Chinese-language publications.

Ideas for change in the English language in China have come mainly from English teachers there. Some teachers have recently voiced their views against the use of Sinicized English. China is now eager to learn foreign things and ways, and English teachers are collecting foreign English-language textbooks to aid their compilation of teaching materials.

This move toward modernization is in reaction to the ways of the past decade. As I have pointed out elsewhere (Cheng 1975), social relevance is an important requirement in China's foreign language teaching. Typical content from "social practice" is exemplified in "classroom practice." An extreme interpretation of this requirement said that, if things depicted in the textbook all happened in a community unknown to the students, that text would be devoid of social reality. Hence we found the lessons in one English textbook (*English*, Volume 2, Intermediate level; Shanghai People's Publishing House, 1974) to have titles such as "Serve the People," "Carry the Struggle to Criticize Lin Piao and Confucius Through to the End," "Tachai Marches On," "Recounting the Family's Revolutionary History," etc., mainly relating to Chinese society.

The emphasis on one's own society to the exclusion of the foreign culture, as practiced a few years ago in China, is somewhat extreme.

Zhu (1978) mentions that the authorities politicized the aims of foreign language teaching, selecting for reading lists too many writings which were inappropriate to foreign norms, Sinicized, or related solely to China. In some schools only two months in the entire three years of training were spent in reading original English materials. To correct that bias, more materials written in the West have now been incorporated. For example, in issue number 104 (1980) of the monthly magazine *Yingyu Xuexi* (English Language Learning), about half of the sixty-five pages are devoted to reading materials, and the other half to articles. Among the readings, only one was a translation from Chinese and about China ("The Green Pine" by Chen Yi); the others were written by Westerners or about Western culture: "The Hero" by Edmondo d'Amicis (rewritten in English), "The Skeleton of the Future" by Hugh MacDiarmid (Christopher Murray Grieve), "A Day's Wait" (Ernest Hemingway), "Six Humorous Stories" (selected from L. A. Hill's Intermediate Comprehension Pieces), "The Million Pound Note" (unsigned), "The Rainmaker" (from Lucky Accidents in Science), and "Pipelines" (unsigned).

Some English-language teachers have also voiced their views against the fixed translations of some Chinese terms which are not intelligible to foreigners. For example, Xiong and Cheng (1980) mention that *pinnong* should be translated as "peasant of poor origin," and that *Uncle PLA man* should not be used at all. In translations appearing in officially printed materials such as the *Beijing Review*, these terms have become fixed. The Chinese word *pinnong* is officially translated as "poor peasant"; the Chinese-English dictionary compiled at the Beijing Foreign Language Institute (1978) also gives "poor peasant" as its definition. This term is in fact a social class designation. But Xiong and Cheng argue that, from a sentence *Zhege pinnong jiating fengyi zushi*, the translation "The family of this poor peasant is well fed and well clothed" does not render the meaning correctly. The translation should therefore be changed. With regard to *Uncle PLA man*, they say that foreigners simply cannot derive any sense from it.

In the area of phonology, Xiong and Cheng (1980) mention that English students in China have used IPA transcriptions in textbooks and dictionaries as guides for pronunciation, rather than listening to native speakers; thus a special kind of pronunciation and intonation has developed. Naturally, there must be a wide range of phonological differences, because of Chinese dialect background and degree of proficiency. However, these registers are not sociolinguistically outstanding, and detailed treatments of them fall outside my present scope.

As the current trend is toward modernization, it is felt that there is a need to teach and use "genuine" and "idiomatic" English (see, e.g., Wei 1978). On the other hand, it is also time to clean up old English translations which render the Chinese meanings inadequately. Wu (1979) shows many incorrect English translations of Chinese terms in the last hundred years. Zhao (1978, 1979) challenges the correctness of the official English version of Chairman Mao's poems. In the near future the Chinese variety of English will certainly move closer to that of the West.[6]

Conclusions

China regarded the people outside its boundaries as barbarians until the seventeenth century. Though for several hundred years China was ruled by the Mongols and the Manchus, no foreign languages were imposed on the Han Chinese. The introduction of English into China in the eighteenth century occurred during a time of self-complacency. The Chinese then did not know much about the outside world, so English was imposed on people with an inward-looking mentality, people who were not eager to learn other tongues. Because the language had to be modified, Chinese pidgin developed.

Then, between 1850 and 1950, Westernization movements emerged, and China began looking outward, aspiring to learn things foreign. Because the English language was a valuable tool for modernization, the Chinese began to learn it in its full form. In turn, Chinese also acquired certain English features.

In the 1960s and 1970s, China was isolated to some extent and was entangled in its own domestic affairs (the Cultural Revolution). It was again a time of inward-looking mentality, euphemistically characterized as self-reliance. Chinese elements took hold of the English language in China. In reaction to the inward-looking Cultural Revolution, the Four Modernizations movement emerged. Chinese elements are gradually giving up their hold in English.

Thus English in China largely reflects the sociopolitical situations there. The patterns of the Chinese varieties of English are clear: When China is inward-looking, the English there acquires more Chinese elements; when China is outward-searching, English there is more like the norm in the West.

NOTES

1. I thank Bruce A. Sherwood for commenting on an earlier version of this paper, and Wang Yihua for providing me with several journals from China dealing with foreign language teaching.

2. Xu 1978 lists the missions of foreign language teaching in China in the past as (1) to propagate great achievements of New China, (2) to establish contacts with people of various countries by means of foreign languages, (3) to use foreign language as a tool in the struggle with imperialist countries. He says that the newly added mission is to serve the learning of modern science and knowledge.

3. In the past, some writers used the pidgin (or a pseudo form) to create a humorous effect (Reinecke et al. 1975).

4. The *pinyin* system was established in 1958 and has been in use in schools and other areas, but the government decided to use it in foreign-language publications only recently. It was also recently adopted by the United Nations and by the U.S. Board on Geographic Names.

5. The difficulties in translating metaphors into English are discussed in Chen 1979.

6. For recent research on English in China, see Wu 1985 and Zhou and Feng 1987.

REFERENCES

Bamgboṣe, Ayọ. 1982. Standard Nigerian English: issues of identification. In this volume.

Beijing Foreign Language Institute. 1978. *A Chinese-English dictionary.* Beijing: Shangwu Yinshu Guan.

Bokamba, Eyamba G. 1982. The Africanization of English. In this volume.

Brumfit, C. J. 1977. The English language, ideology and international communication: some issues arising out of English teaching for Chinese students. *English Language Teaching Documents,* pp. 15–24. London: British Council.

Chen, Wenbo. 1979. Chengyu Yingyi shi xingxiang he yuyi de maodun (Contradictions between image and metaphor in English translation of Chinese idioms). *Waiyu Jiaoxue Yu Yanjiu* (Foreign Language Teaching and Study) 4: 44–51, 23.

Cheng, Chin-Chuan. 1975. Trends in foreign language teaching in the People's Republic of China: impressions of a visit. *Studies in Language Learning* 1(1): 153–62.

Cowan, J. Ronayn; Richard L. Light, B. Ellen Mathews, and G. Richard Tucker. 1979. English teaching in China: a recent survey. *TESOL Quarterly* 13(4): 465–82.

Craig, Dennis R. 1982. Toward a description of Caribbean English. In Kachru 1982.

Hall, Robert A., Jr. 1944. Chinese Pidgin English grammar and texts. *Journal of the American Oriental Society* 64(3): 95–113.

———. 1966. *Pidgin and creole languages.* Ithaca: Cornell University Press.

———. 1973. Pidgin languages. Pp. 91–114 in *Varieties of present-day English,* ed. Richard W. Bailey and Jay L. Robinson. New York: Macmillan.

Kachru, Braj B. 1969. English in South Asia. In *Current trends in linguistics, V,* ed. Thomas Sebeok. The Hague: Mouton.

———. 1976. Models of English for the Third World: white man's linguistic burden or language pragmatics? *TESOL Quarterly* 10(2): 221–39.

———. 1981. The pragmatics of non-native varieties of English. In Smith, ed., 1981.

———, ed. 1982. *The other tongue: English across cultures.* Urbana: University of Illinois Press.

Lehmann, Winfred P., et al. 1975. *Language and linguistics in the People's Republic of China.* Austin: University of Texas Press.

Light, Timothy. 1978. Foreign language teaching in the People's Republic of China. In *On TESOL '78: EFL policies, programs, practices,* ed. Charles Blatchford and Jacquelyn Schachter. Washington, D.C.: TESOL.

Platt, John T. 1977. A model for polyglossia and multilingualism (with special reference to Singapore and Malaysia). *Language in Society* 6: 361–78.

Reinecke, John E. 1937. Marginal language. Ph.D. dissertation, Yale University.

———; David DeCamp, Ian F. Hancock, Stanley M. Tsuzaki, and Richard E. Wood. 1975. *A bibliography of pidgin and creole languages.* Honolulu: University of Hawaii Press.

Richards, J., and Luke Kang-Kwong. 1981. English in Hong Kong: functions and status. Paper presented at the seminar on varieties of English, RELC, Singapore, April, 1981.

Shanghai Peoples Publishing House. 1974. *English: intermediate level.*

Smith, Larry E., ed. 1981. *English for cross-cultural communication.* London: Macmillan.

Todd, Loreto. 1974. *Pidgins and creoles.* London: Routledge and Kegan Paul.

Wang, Li. 1955. *Zhongguo Yufa Lilun* (Theory of Chinese grammar). Beijing: Zhonghua Shuju. (Original edition, 1944, Shanghai: Shangwu Yinshu Guan.)

Wei, Yuanshu. 1978. Qiantan waiyu jiaoyu xiandaihua (Plain talks on modernization of foreign language teaching). *Waiguo Yu* (Foreign Language) 2: 1–2.

Whinnom, Keith. 1971. Linguistic hybridization and the "special case" of pidgins and creoles. In *Pidginization and creolization of languages,* ed. Dell Hymes. London: Cambridge University Press.

Wu, Jingrong. 1979. Women zouguo de daolu (The path we have taken). *Waiyu Jiaoxue Yu Yanjiu* (Foreign Language Teaching and Study) 3: 1–6, 40.

Wu, Yi'an. 1985. Code-mixing in English-Chinese bilingual teachers of the People's Republic of China. *World Englishes* 4(3): 303-17.

Xiong, Delan, and Cheng, Musheng. 1980. Waiyu jiaoxue poqie xuyao gaige (Foreign language teaching urgently needs to be reformed). *Guangming Ribao* (Guangming Daily), April 4, 1980, p. 2.

Xu, Guozhang. 1978. Lun waiyu jiaoxue de fangzhen yu renwu (On the policy and mission of foreign language teaching). *Waiyu Jiaoxue Yu Yanjiu* (Foreign Language Teaching and Study) 2: 6–15.

Zhao, Zhentao. 1978. Jiu Mao Zhuxi shici Yingyi ben tantan yiwen zhong de jige wenti (Discussion on some problems of translation with respect to the English edition of Chairman Mao's poems). *Waiyu Jiaoxue Yu Yanjiu* (Foreign Language Teaching and Study) 1: 21–26.

———. 1979. Zai tan Mao Zhuxi shici Yingyi ben yiwen zhong de wenti (Problems of translation in the English edition of Chairman Mao's poems revisited). *Waiyu Jiaoxue Yu Yanjiu* (Foreign Language Teaching and Study) 2: 7–12, 6.

Zhou, Zipei, and Feng Wenchi. 1987. The two faces of English in China: Englishization of Chinese and nativization of English. *World Englishes* 6(2): 111-25.

Zhu, Shuyang. 1978. Luetan waiyu jiaoxue de yixie jingyan he gaijin yijian (Discussion on foreign language teaching experience and ideas for improvements). *Waiyu Jiaoxue Yu Yanjiu* (Foreign Language Teaching and Study) 2: 16–22.

Zuengler, Jane. 1982. Kenyan English. In Kachru 1982.

10

James Stanlaw

English in Japanese
Communicative Strategies

An outsider might say the English language in Japan has not developed into an institutionalized variety (Kachru 1981), as it has in South Asia or parts of Africa. Japanized English—or, as some prefer, "Japlish" (Pierce 1971)—is essentially a performance variety.[1] But to an insider, the function of English cannot be isolated from communicative strategies in Japanese society. The use of English loanwords is an integral part of one such strategy. I shall illustrate this point by focusing on the form and function of English borrowing in Japanese today. The Japanization of such borrowing exemplifies what has been termed "nativization" by linguists (Kachru and Quirk 1981) or "acculturation" by anthropologists.[2]

The extent of this borrowing, its historical roots, and the use of English in the Japanese school system will be briefly discussed below. The processes of nativization of English will be described, with examples, in the next sections, and current research will be mentioned. I will conclude with some speculations as to why English borrowings are so extensively used as a communicative strategy in Japanese.

Historical Contact

Language contact in Japan goes back at least a thousand years. Buddhism and Chinese scholars arrived in the sixth century. Numerous foreign languages have been found in Japan ever since (Umegaki 1978), even during the period of isolation (*sakoku*) from 1640 to 1853, when Dutch traders were still allowed to land at the island of Deshima in Nagasaki Bay.

According to Umegaki (1978: 32), the various cultural and linguistic contacts between Japan and the rest of the world may be summarized in the following six phases. The first phase (9th to 13th century) was the period of Buddhist impact, with an emphasis on Chinese learning and linguistic exposure to Chinese and Sanskrit. The second phase (14th to 16th century) brought Christianity through European contact, and some exposure to Portuguese. The third phase (17th to 18th century) was essentially a period of isolation, though there was contact with Dutch learning and language. The fourth phase (19th century), the period of Meiji enlightenment, saw renewed contact with Western culture and exposure to English, German, and French. The fifth phase (early 20th century) initiated the contact with contemporary Western culture; it saw the development of Taisho democracy and the rise of Japan as an important world power. The last phase (late 20th century) opened Japan to world culture and economic importance, and it has seen a more open attitude toward world languages, especially English.[3]

There have been periods of contact with the English language since Will Adams[4] was stranded near Edo in 1600. However, Commodore Perry's arrival in 1854, and the social unrest in Japan at the time, instigated a Japanese interest in learning English well enough to read Western books and to speak with these new visitors. This curiosity brought many English words into the Japanese vocabulary, and English quickly replaced Dutch as the language used to learn about the West. In his autobiography Fukuzawa, an influential Meiji-period educator and writer, stated that "As certain as day, English was to be the most useful language of the future" (1899: 98). Serious attempts to designate English the official language of Japan were made by "public figures of such great prestige that their recommendations could not help having a considerable impact," even though implementation of these proposals was impossible (Miller 1977: 41–42). One such advocate was Mori Arinori, the first minister of education, who claimed that "our meager language, which can never be of any use outside of our islands, is doomed to yield to the domination of the English tongue, especially when the power of steam and electricity shall have pervaded the land" (quoted in Sonoda 1975: 17).

As contact between Japan and the West increased, there was an influx of British and American technical advisors; likewise, Japanese students and statesmen traveled abroad. An immense fascination with Western customs and ideas facilitated the adoption of English loanwords. In 1867 the American missionary James Hepburn printed *A Japanese and English Dictionary; with an English and Japanese Index* and

179

introduced the romanization system which is still the most popular today. Many schools taught English, and it became fashionable for Japanese students to intersperse their conversations with English words (Sonoda 1975: 16).

The Taisho period (1912–26) was marked by an increase in the number of English borrowings and the fall into disuse of loanwords from other languages, most noticeably Dutch and Portuguese (Ueno 1968). While most of the English loanwords of the Meiji period had to do with Western culture, many of those of the Taisho period had to do with everyday topics: *takushī* (taxi), *rajio* (radio), *sararīman* (salaried man).

With the rise of militarism and nationalism in the 1930s and World War II, the government tried to purge Japan of all foreign influences. The commonly understood *anaunsā* (announcer) was replaced by the esoteric *hōsō-in* (literally "broadcast person"), and *rekōdo* (record) was supplanted by *onban* (literally "euphonic board").

English regained its former level of popularity and prestige immediately after World War II, and the Occupation spurred even more linguistic borrowings. Political and economic opportunities led many Japanese to learn at least some English, or an incipient pidgin called "Bamboo English" (Miller 1967: 262; Norman 1955). Another variety of postwar pidgin, termed *pangurisshu* (from *pansuke* "streetwalker," plus *ingurisshu*, "English"), was used for verbal communication "between non-Japanese-speaking foreigners and the extensive world of their local lady friends of every variety and description" (Miller 1967: 263).

Since the Occupation, the use of English has continued to grow. There are now loanword dictionaries of all sizes and descriptions, with the largest and most reliable, Arakawa's *Kadokawa gairaigo jiten* (1977), containing over 27,000 entries. Today, almost all advertising uses loanwords of English origin. For example, Horiuchi (1963: 49) found only one advertisement—for a typical Japanese food—that used no English loanwords or phrases when he examined advertisements for one month in the widely circulating *Asahi* newspaper. But perhaps the best indication of the current acceptability of loanwords appeared in Prince Mikasa's entry in the 1965 Imperial Court poetry contest. Since even traditional Chinese loanwords are usually avoided in this literary style, it was quite significant that the prince used the term *berutokonbea* (conveyer belt) in his poem. In 1976 the emperor used the phrase *hiroki damu miyu* (a view of the broad dam) in his own entry (Passin 1980: 73). As Miller (1967: 267) says, this cannot help but "teach us a profound lesson about the degree to which loanwords of every variety, especially from English, have permeated modern Japanese life."

Types of Japanese English: The "Cline of Proficiency"

Among the Englishes described in this volume, the variety spoken in Japan is unique. It is not an official language, a lingua franca, or a second language in the same sense as in the other contexts described here. It is not a remnant of colonialization[5] or the legacy of zealous missionaries, and though it is taught in the schools it has never been institutionalized[6] (as, say, in India or Nigeria) to function as the primary language of higher learning. English is required on college entrance exams, and a typical Japanese student may study it for six to ten years; still, few Japanese actually *speak* English well enough to converse with foreigners beyond a rudimentary exchange of greetings.[7] Almost every bookstore has an "English corner" offering hundreds of the latest texts, annotated novels, tapes, and learning aids. Major newspapers print extra weekly supplements for studying English, and several popular journals are devoted to the subject.[8]

There is, therefore, a *cline of proficiency* in the use of English in Japan, ranging from people fluent in both spoken and written discourse to those who know only a few vocabulary items. Though most Japanese people are not fluent in English, and the variety they use may be essentially a performance variety rather than an institutionalized variety, anyone with even cursory exposure to Japan knows that English plays an important role in their everyday lives.

Sources of English Borrowing

English loanwords can be heard in Japan in everyday conversation, on television and radio programs or announcements, and in political speeches. Newspapers,[9] popular magazines, and books all use loanwords. They may appear as section headings, such as *opinion pēji* (opinion page); in titles, like *sandē sukūru* (Sunday school); and in the main body of the text. Technical and professional journals use English loanwords for a specialized vocabulary, e.g., *sōrā fureā* (solar flares), *tenshon* (tension—of metals), *nyū refuto* (new left).

The vocabulary of sports borrows from English quite readily, though often with a slight Japanese twist on the words involved, e.g., *sekando ōbā* (over second), *sayonara hōmu ran* (a game-ending home run). Men's magazines also use numerous English loanwords, especially when dealing with sexual topics. For instance, in the weekly magazine

Purēboī (a Japanese version of the American *Playboy*) one finds such items as *būbusu* (boobs), *majikku pawā* (magic power—aphrodisiacs), and *datchi waifu* (Dutch wife—an inflatable bed partner). Many English loanwords also appear in the adult *manga*, the men's comics genre unique to Japan.

One of the most interesting and prevalent uses of English is on personal "artifacts"—T-shirts, sweaters, handbags, and other belongings. When an English word is borrowed orally into Japanese, it undergoes substantial phonological modification, even if it is a proper name. When the word is then printed in a book or newspaper, this modification is reflected in a special Japanese syllabary called *katakana*,[10] used for foreign terms. When words are borrowed on T-shirts, however, they are not modified phonologically or written in *katakana*.

English borrowings are often seen on things other than apparel. Women's purses are sometimes decorated with cartoon characters like Snoopy or Popeye, and men's bags often bear sports names or sports-related terms (*champion*, or *official team*). One common word is *cityboy*, meaning a debonair, sophisticated young man, used somewhat like the American term "playboy."[11]

English, then, is used in a variety of contexts by a variety of speakers in a variety of ways, depending on the strategy and context of communication.

Range and Context of English Borrowings

In 1931 Sanki Ichikawa predicted, "The influence of foreign languages—especially English—on Japanese is of such importance that probably not only words and expressions will continue to be borrowed in greater numbers but even the structure and grammar of the Japanese language will be considerably modified." He found that Japanese had borrowed more than 1,400 words, most of which were "quite naturalized in Japanese" (1931: 141). The following (albeit extreme) example, given by Matsumoto forty years later (1974: 5), shows extensive use of English loanwords in Japanese:

> We, that is, the Matsumoto family, live in a *manshon*, too. At this moment, I am watching *beisu-booru* on *terebi*. My wife is out shopping at a *depaato*, and later she will stop at a *suupaa* to get *pooku choppu*, *pan*, *bataa*, *jamu*, and perhaps some *sooseji* for breakfast. My daughter has gone to the *byuuchii saron* to get a *paama*. Oh, the *terehon* is ringing.
> We cannot live a day in Japan today without these loan words. Language purists lament the fact. The nationalists would wipe out all

foreign-sounding words from our vocabulary. But where will they be without *takushii, terebi, rajio, tabako, biiru, shatsu, beruto* and *meetoru*?

According to the National Language Research Institute's 1964 study of ninety different magazines published in the early 1950s, almost 10 percent of Japanese vocabulary items come from Western languages. Of these borrowed Western words, 80.8 percent come from English, which suggests that approximately 8 percent of the total Japanese vocabulary is derived from English (Higa 1973: 79).[12] Miller (1967: 249) speaks of the "total availability" of the English vocabulary for borrowing into Japanese: today, "virtually any English word in the book is fair game in writing or in public speaking."

There is also a cline of "foreignness" for English loans. Words like *rajio* (radio) and *tabako* (cigarette) seem to be regarded as completely Japanese by native speakers; in contrast, many of the latest loanwords occurring in advertising or professional journals are short lived or have limited circulation. English terms may be brought in to fill certain "lexical gaps," as in the case of *tīn'ēja* (teenager) or *haī-tīn* (high teen— a person 16 to 19 years old), instead of the Japanese term *jūdai* (meaning anyone 10 through 19). However, it is clear from the examples above that the filling of lexical gaps is only one reason for the English borrowing process. It is also clear that semantic borrowing is independent of the existence of the term in either language.[13]

Kachru (1978a) explains the "lexical sets" of borrowed items with what he terms "contextual units." In a language contact situation, especially where more than two languages are involved, the borrowing may depend on register or style. There may be a mutual expectancy or dependency between the lexical borrowing from a particular language and a specific register. For example, in Hindi, Persian loanwords may be used in legal contexts, Sanskrit ones in literary or philosophical writings, and English ones in technical or political registers. It is difficult to demonstrate such clear-cut distinctions for the use of English in Japanese. English loanwords can be used by anyone, regardless of age, sex, or education, though certain technical or scholarly terms might be limited to specialists. Some registers, such as advertising, are thought to be permeated with English (Horiuchi 1963; Quackenbush 1974). While most written and oral advertisements do use loanwords, how much this varies from other registers is still an empirical issue.

Processes of Nativization

Phonology[14]

The process of phonological assimilation of English loanwords into Japanese has been discussed extensively by both Japanese (e.g., Isshiki

1957; Kawakami 1963; Ohye 1967a, 1967b; Sonoda 1975; Umegaki 1978) and Western scholars (e.g., Gauntlett 1966; Lovins 1973; Neustupný 1978; Pierce 1971; Quackenbush 1974). Therefore, only a few illustrations will be given. No consonant clusters exist in Japanese, so vowels are inserted between two consonants in borrowed English words; e.g., *kurisumasu* (Christmas), *makudonarudo* (MacDonald's). A word may not end in a consonant except for the syllabic *n*; e.g., *resutoran* (restaurant). English /r/ or /l/ sounds are usually manifest as Japanese /r/ in the loanword; e.g. *raito* (light, right).[15] These are some of the phonetic characteristics considered typical of English words brought into Japanese.

Morphology

Japanese is a loose SOV language, highly agglutinative and marked for case. Verbs must be sentence-final, but there is optionality in the placement of agent, patient, and locative or time phrases, though usually subjects or topics come at the beginning of the sentence. Like other SOV languages, Japanese is post-positional. A typical sentence pattern might be:

sumisu— san	wa	yūbe-no-nyūsu	o	mi-mashita	ka
proper honorif. name	topic marker	noun	object	verb tense	interrog. marker
Smith		last night's news		watched	?

Mr. Smith, did you watch the news last night?

The majority of English loanwords are nouns[16] (Hinds 1974: 93; Sonoda 1975: 173), and most nouns are taken into Japanese in the singular form, even though their use may have required the plural in English—e.g., *surī-sutoraiku* (three strikes), *foa-bōru* (four balls). When an English loanword is borrowed as a noun, it is usually unchanged, and will behave syntactically and morphologically like other Japanese nouns.

terebi	o	mi—	mashita	ka
loan	case marker	verb	tense	interrog. marker
television		watched		?

Did you watch TV?

If a loanword is to be used as an adverb, it takes the particle *ni* and does not decline using *-ku*, as do adverbs derived from true Japanese adjectives.

kare	wa	songu	o	naisu—	ni	utau
3rd pers.	topic	loan	case	loan	case	verb
masc.pron.	marker		marker		marker	
he		song		nicely		sings

He sings nicely.

If an English loanword is to be used as an adjective, it is marked with the particle *na* and rarely takes the true adjective ending *-i* or its declensions.[17]

kare	wa	nau—	na	hito	desu	ne
3d pers.	topic	loan	part.	noun	copula	sent.
masc.pron.	marker					part.
he		"now"		person	is	right?

He's a real modern "with it" person, isn't he?

Sonda (1975: 190) gives several other examples of English loanword adjectives: *chāmingu-na* (charming), *romachikku-na* (romantic), *derikēto-na* (delicate), *gurotesuku-na* (grotesque), *supesharu-na* (special). Sonada also mentions that degrees of comparison are syntactically indicated in Japanese by the use of the free-form morphemes *motto* (more) and *ichiban* (most). Thus, comparative phrases involving loanwords might be something like *motto senchimentaru* (more sentimental [than]...) or *ichiban senchimentaru* (the most sentimental [among]...).

Syntax

Most loanwords which can be used as verbs take the auxiliary suffix *suru* (do), as in *appu-suru* (to improve, go up) or as in the following example:

dō desu,	tenisu—	o	shimasen	ka
idiom	loan	case	suru+	interrog.
		marker	tense	marker
What-do-you-say	tennis		to do	?

What would you think about having a game of tennis?

Other examples include *gorofu-suru* (to play golf) or *gōru-in-suru* (goal in—to fulfill, for example, the goal of getting married).[18]

Personal pronouns do exist in Japanese, but until recently they had never been used as much as in English. Names, kinship terms, or titles are used instead of *kare* (he) or *anata* (you). An increase in personal pronoun usage has been attributed to the influence of English

(Passin 1980: 14–23); still, there never seems to have been a case where a personal pronoun has been borrowed as the subject of a sentence.[19] There are a few—but very popular—phrases where the personal pronoun *mai* (my) is used to modify a noun, as in *mai kā* (my car),[20] *mai kā zoku* (those who drive their own cars), or *mai hōmu*. Passin (1980: 24–29) believes that this term highlights a new social and psychological point of view in Japan, that of the assertion of individuality. Thus the productiveness of the *mai* prefix is not surprising, and can be seen to be extended to such things as *mai pēsu* (at my own pace), *mai puraibashii* (my privacy), or *mai seihin* (my product).[21]

Vocabulary

There are several ways in which Japanese incorporates new English vocabulary items. One common method is to adopt the English loan with the required phonological modification, but with little change in its form or structure; e.g., *takushī* (taxi), *basu* (bus), *tabako* (cigarette).[22] However, several other processes involve either restricting or expanding the original meaning in English (Sonoda 1975; Hinds 1974; Ozawa 1970; Miura 1979; Matsumoto 1974; Fukao 1979; Yokoi 1978).

Truncation, or shortening, is a very popular means of using an English word. Often the meaning remains unchanged; e.g., *sūpā* (supermarket), *terebi* (television), *depāto* (department store), and *demo* (demonstration). Sonoda (1975: 198) claims that, if a borrowed word contains two morphemes, the part most likely to be dropped is the one which plays the grammatical role, and not the semantically important segment—e.g., *sararīman* (salariED man), *kōn bīfu* (cornED beef), *sukī* (skiING). If there are several syllables in a word, or if several nouns are involved, the reduction is usually made in the non-initial nouns or syllables.

Another common way of shortening is through acronyms, e.g., *ō-eru* (office lady), *pī-āru* (public relations), *ō-bī* (old boy), *dī-pī-ī* (developing, printing, and enlarging), *shī-emu* (commercial message), *dī-kē* (dining kitchen). This process seems to be shared with other non-native Englishes (see Kachru 1966). These acronyms may be totally new Japanese creations, as in *OL*, the term for the modern Japanese working girl, or *DPE*, the sign that appears in every photography store window. They may also be used as modifiers of other nouns, as in *CM songu*, a jingle used on a television or radio commercial. Abbreviations may also be taken from English, but the meanings may be somewhat altered; *PR* in Japanese only refers to advertising.

Sometimes even native Japanese words will be abbreviated in roman letters, and will be spoken of, and pronounced, in that way.

NHK (standing for *Nippon-Hōsō Kyōkai*) is the common way to refer to the national public television of Japan. Another example, *H* (pronounced *etchi*), comes from the Japanese term *hentai* (perverted) and means something dirty, or an unusual interest in sex.

Native affixes are easily applied to foreign words (Weinreich 1953: 31), and in this way many English loanwords are used in Japanese. Consider, e.g., *amerika + jin* (an American person), *shin + kanto + ha* (neo-Kantianism), *Kātā-shiki* (Carter's style), *dai-sutoraiki* (large strike), *amerika + sei* (made in America). There are also some cases where English affixes can be applied to native Japanese terms, as in *puro yakyū* (pro baseball), or *shaber + ingu* (talking). These may also be applied to loanwords as well, as in *semi + sofuto + karā* (semi-soft collar).

Sonoda (1975: 214) claims that compounding is the most productive method of expanding the borrowed English vocabulary. He believes that two-thirds of the borrowed items have been formed in this way,[23] e.g., *ero-guro-nansensu* (erotic grotesque nonsense), *ōrudo misu* (old miss—a spinster), *masu komi* (mass communications), *wan pīsu* (one-piece dress).

Blendings are special compounds where one element is an English loanword and the other a native term, e.g., *nūdo shashin* (nude picture), *meriken ko* (American powder—flour), *denki sutando* (standing desk lamp). English loanwords may also include a phrase or a fixed collocation, e.g., *ofu dei* (off day), *tēburu supīchi* (table speech—after-dinner speech), *atto hōmu* (at home), *ai rabu yū* (I love you). (See also Kachru 1982 and Zuengler 1982.)

For some concepts brought into Japan from the West, the old literal Japanese translation of the term is eventually replaced by the English loanword. *Entaku* (taxi) becomes *takushī*, *kōshaki* (elevator) becomes *erebētā*, and *higyō* (strike) becomes *sutoraiki* (Sonoda 1975: 231).

The Semantics of English Borrowing

Semantic Restriction

Sonoda (1975) and Ozawa (1970, 1976) have suggested some typologies for the semantic borrowing of English loanwords. In the first case, the meaning of the English word is restricted when it is brought into Japanese. *Rikuesuto* (request) in Japanese is used only in asking a band to play a certain song; *mishin* (machine) refers only to a sewing machine; *manshon* (mansion) is applied only to high-rise condominiums;

naitā means a night baseball game; *kappu* (cup) is a prize won in a contest; *nega* (negative) refers only to photographic processing.

Semantic Shift

A semantic shift may occur in the connotation or nuance of a borrowed English loanword, as in *madamu* (proprietress of a bar), *miruku* (condensed milk—milk for coffee), or *nēmu* (name, embroidered on a personal article). *Mōningu* is short for *mōningu-sābisu* ("morning service," a restaurant's breakfast special) or is used in special compounds like *moningu shō* (morning show).

Semantic Extension or Redefinition

Sometimes a loan will undergo a complete change in meaning from the way it is used in English.[24] *Haiyā* (hire) refers to a chauffeur-driven car; *ōrai* (all right) is shouted when helping a vehicle back up; *uetto* (wet) means sentimental or soft-hearted, while *dorai* (dry) means unsentimental or businesslike. Loanwords are also used to create new terms from nonexistent sources,[25] e.g., *bēsu-appu* (base up—an increase in the standard of living), *chīku dansu* (cheek dance—ballroom dancing), *rūmu kūrā* (room cooler—air conditioner), or *Dekansho* (Descartes, Kant, and Schopenhauer) (Hinds 1974: 94). English loanwords may occasionally be used as slang expressions, e.g., *panku* (puncture—to deliver a baby), *sukuramburu* (scramble—the flow of people crossing a busy street after the stoplight has changed), *rimokon* (remote control— a husband who goes straight home after work is *rimo-kon*-ed [Matsumoto 1974: 24]).[26]

Sociolinguistic Functions of English

There is a large body of theoretical literature on language contact dealing with the use of a language in linguistically plural contexts (Haugen 1950, 1953; Vogt 1954; Weinreich 1953). Case studies describing this behavior in actual speech situations also abound (Hymes 1964; Fishman 1968, 1972; Gumperz and Hymes 1972; Scherer and Giles 1979). However, little attention has been paid to these factors in examining the way English loanwords are used by Japanese people in speech, on artifacts, and in written sources, or to the way English loanwords are nativized by being brought into the cognitive system of Japanese speakers.[27] This section constitutes a preliminary attempt to describe some of these processes.

Among Japanese college students, there seems to be a tendency for men to use more loanwords in academic discussions than in everyday speech. In one experiment the number of English loanwords used by three male university students was noted over a period of several days. The total number of loans used in academic contexts was also tallied. "Academic context" was defined as discussion germane to their field with either majors or non-majors, discussions with classmates about classroom or department activities, or mention of department, classroom, or major topics to others not involved in, or directly discussing, their discipline. One student was in medical school; his data were collected over a fourteen-hour period. Two other students, upperclassmen in political science and economics, were observed for eight hours and five hours, respectively. Data were gathered in natural settings with the investigator present as an observer or, sometimes, a participant. No attempt was made to guide the conversation or intentionally elicit English loanwords. Data and notes were collected unobtrusively, so estimates occasionally had to be made.

All three male informants seemed to use loanwords slightly more often when speaking about academic topics; in contrast, the women informants tended to use English loanwords *less* often when talking about things related to their major.

Table 1. English Loanwords Used by Japanese College Students

		Male students			Female students	
		Medicine	Political Science	Economics	Psychology	Business
Total	hours	14	8	3	6	3
	# loans	210	192	41	114	138
Nonacademic settings	hours	10.5	2.75	1.5	4.25	2
	# loans	96	69	17	65	74
	%	46	36	41	57	54
Academic settings	hours	3.5	5.25	1.5	1.75	1
	# loans	114	123	24	49	64
	%	54	64	59	43	46

Several difficulties arise if one attempts to draw definitive conclusions from frequency counts such as these. There are the obvious methodological problems of the number of subjects, equal proportions of men and women, and various rates of speech between individuals in a conversation. Different majors may have different tendencies to use loanwords (see Ichikawa 1931).[28] The frequency of loanword usage may also depend on the speaker's knowledge of English. Finally, in the broad category of non-academic topics there may be any number of occasions when loanwords *are* used frequently. For example, loanwords pervade—and seem almost necessary for—men's discussions of baseball, tennis, golf, horse racing, and the Olympics. In these contexts two or three loanwords per sentence are not uncommon. Both younger and older female informants tend to use English loanwords when discussing topics like the latest fashions or cosmetics, or when talking about romantic intrigues (real or fictional) or speaking of marriage plans.

A more fruitful approach to these variables involves examining the dynamics of the situation. For example, Brown and Gilman (1960) have shown that language can be a measure of solidarity; so the use of English loanwords in a conversation might depend on the closeness of the relationship between the speakers. An American anthropologist in Japan can find it rather difficult to make an accurate estimate of the strength of a friendship between two individuals, especially after knowing some informants for only a few weeks or months. However, there does seem to be some pressure not to use large numbers of English loanwords at first meetings. Several informants have indicated that when people whom they do not know sprinkle their conversations with too much English, the speech may sound affected, especially if the loans are complicated or esoteric.

Brown and Levenson (1978) have noted that code-switching and the use of slang or jargon are strategies for communicating needs or desires. Such observations might be supported by the language of the Japanese *sararīman* (white-collar workers, or rising business executives) in their middle or late thirties. When describing products or making sales presentations, their speech is filled with English loanwords. These are not limited to specialized technical terms, where the Japanese equivalents might be awkward or uncommon.

Japanese people in general, and men in particular, seem to use English loanwords more than Japanese terms when speaking of romance, sex, or male or female companions. In some cases new words like *bōi furendo* (boyfriend), *gāru furendo* (girlfriend), or *gāru hanto* (girl hunting) are being used where there were no satisfactory Japanese equivalents. A new term may be coined, based on an English loanword, as in *rabu-hoteru* (a hotel that rents by the hour, afternoon, or evening and is openly used by lovers for romantic rendezvous). However, many other loanwords are borrowed from English but added to a Japanese term or otherwise given a Japanese twist. Such a case is *onna-petto* (from Japanese "woman" and English "pet"), meaning the object of someone's sexual fantasy, or *gē-bōi* (gay boy), meaning any male homosexual. Instead of the Japanese *shuin* (masturbation), which is rather clinical, Japanese young men commonly use *masutābēshiyon* or *onanī* (from "onanism"). A book may even bear the title *How to Onanī*. Less charged terms dealing with relationships are also beginning to use loans, e.g., *hazu* (husband), *waifu* (wife). When asking a girl out, a young man will most likely use the word *dēto* (date), and he will use an English loanword if he refers to a sexual topic or makes an off-color remark (e.g., *pinku mūdo* [pink mood] when referring to something with sexual overtones).

A few other situations should also be mentioned; for example, contemporary music, entertainment fields, and news broadcasting. Also, most people use slightly fewer loanwords when conversing with elders than when speaking with those their own age or younger. Certain social factors tend to imply differential loanword use, though compounding of variables makes clear conclusions difficult to draw. Teenagers tend to use more loanwords, perhaps because of certain topics of conversation—sports, cars, boyfriends and girlfriends.

The more important conclusion to be drawn from these data is that some people use more loanwords than others just as part of their individual personality or speaking style, and depending on the context. The data do not support the view that a person's sex determines the frequency of loanword use. In the study mentioned above, the ratio of loanwords used to total time investigated was 15, 24, and 13.6 for the men, and 19 and 46 for the women. The average was 20.4 per hour. The frequency of use depends on the person, style, and topic.

English in Education and the Media

The formal study of English in Japan is extensive. There are over 50,000 English teachers, though the ability of many is questionable (Reischauer 1977: 399). According to policies established by Japan's Ministry of Education, all middle school and most senior high school students should study a foreign language. Hayes (1979: 365) points out that approximately 99 percent of middle school students begin studying English in seventh grade. About 70 percent of the high school students continue studying English, as do 20 percent of those who attend college. If a middle school student (seventh through ninth grade) plans on entering a university, he must have had 525 hours of English instruction. A terminal high school student will have had 315 hours. Along with the instruction given in the public schools, there are hundreds of private English language academies of varying competence and repute, as well as many *juku* (cram schools for entering a university) which offer English language and literature as subjects. Even in the early grades, lessons on Japanized English are given. For example, Fukao (1979: 234) mentions the following items that had to be identified on a recent fifth-grade test: *aidea* (idea), *kontorasuto* (contrast), *nansensu* (nonsense), *menyū* (menu), *mania* (mania), *raibaru* (rival), *sensu* (sense), *popyurā* (popular), *rūzu* (lose), *kyatchi-furēzu* (catch phrase).

English loanwords are very popular in Japanese broadcasting, and they are not limited to advertising. For example, on daytime TV game shows, contestants are often asked to identify English loanwords. Such words are also found in program openings, closings, and in conversations on talk shows. Tokyo area television stations recently began "dual broadcasting," transmitting some programs in both Japanese and English. In homes possessing one of the newer television sets, either language can be tuned in.

All indications are that the use of English loanwords is at least as extensive in books, newspapers, and magazines as it is in everyday speech.[30] The following headlines are just a few of the ones that used loanwords in a single edition of a typical daily newspaper:[31] *gasu more—ni kai renzoku* (Gas Leak—Second Time in a Row); *hotto jamu '80, faitingu jamu—mūdo jōjō, yagai no kaihōkan mo* (Hot Jam 80, A Fighting Jam—The Best Mood, and an Open Outdoor Feeling [referring to a concert]); *gyamburu, sake, shakkin . . . kyatchā—"yakyu suki" no ura no kao* (Gambling, Drinking, Debts . . . Catcher Who "Loves Baseball" Shows Another Face).

Many of the data published in the research literature have been based on printed sources (Bailey 1962; Hirai 1978; Ozawa 1970, 1976; Sonoda 1975; Umegaki 1978). As mentioned before, certain genres,[32] such as magazines dealing with sex and the men's comic books, use an inordinate number of English loanwords. In these magazines one finds English loanwords written both in roman letters and in *katakana* syllabary (e.g., *samā* big *purezento* [summer big present] depicts a nude girl holding a pistol). The *manga* comics seem to do this with greater regularity; in this sense the *manga* might be a sort of blend between the usually *katakana*-using print medium and the roman-letter-using artifacts.

Attitudes toward English Borrowing

The reasons for the expansion in the Japanese vocabulary are of interest in both theoretical and applied settings. There are several possible reasons why English loanwords are so popular.

Bruner, Goodnow, and Austin (1956) claim that the human thinking process divides the world into "conjunctive" concrete concepts and "relational" concepts; the latter exist only with respect to each other. Higa (1975: 85) believes this may explain why seemingly unnecessary English words are borrowed into Japanese, at least for the dialect spoken in Hawaii. Presumably he means that when a word is introduced which has no exact equivalent in Japanese ("curry"), the other related words (such as "rice") also tend to be borrowed, regardless of whether Japanese equivalents already exist. However, this statement seems to oversimplify a highly complex interaction between the social situational, the symbolic, and the cognitive levels of the use of English loanwords by Japanese speakers. To follow up on this example, in Japan today two words for rice are commonly used: *gohan*, a native term, and *raisu*, a loan from English. The preference for one word over another may depend on style (Makino 1978; Sibata 1975) or on any number of other sociolinguistic variables. *Raisu* seems to be used for food of non-native origin (as in *raisu karē*), while native foods use *gohan* (as in *tori gohan* [chicken and rice], *kaki gohan* [oysters and rice], or *kuri gohan* [chestnuts and rice]). This might imply that *raisu* and *gohan* are used in two different contexts, and that they probably involve different feelings or connotations as well. There also seems to be a tendency to use the word *gohan* in traditional Japanese-style restaurants (*shokudō*), while *raisu* may be used in a *resutoran*, a large, modern Western-style restaurant. Lest one assume that *raisu* is always used with foreign dishes or occasions while *gohan* is used otherwise, the data are not consistent. Some informants claim that *raisu* should be used with homemade foods served in small local restaurants, while modern medium-sized restaurants will use *gohan*. The specific ways in which reference and situation interact are some of the most important and interesting topics for research in the Japanese-English contact situation, and they still need to be untangled.

English loanwords may also be brought into Japanese through the use of advertising.[33] This is the most common reason given by informants when they are asked why so many English words appear in Japanese. Japanese companies spend almost $5 billion a year on advertising, second only to the United States' $33 billion (Dunn and Barban 1978: 696). Of that amount, over half is spent on print media. However, the quantity of goods from Japan entering the United States is greater than the quantity of American goods exported to Japan— yet almost no Japanese loans appear in English.[34] True, different sociolinguistic mechanisms might be operating for the two countries. But as yet no one has offered any evidence that advertising is the cause (rather than a reflection) of the use of English loanwords by Japanese speakers.[35]

Though there may be elements of prestige involved in the use of loanwords, there are also pressures which act against their use. Many Japanese people believe that loanwords are overused. For example, consider the following dialogue from a beginning Japanese language text (Yoshida et al. 1973: 286):

> Kono aida, *"kuru*-na *tatchi* de *hãdo*-na *akushon* o *dairekuto*-ni *sãbisu*-suru *Naporeon Soro"* to iu eiga no senden ga arimashita. Ichi-do kiita dake de do iu imi ka wakarimasu ka?
>
> The other day I saw this ad saying, *"Napoleon Solo—direct served hard action* with a *cool* touch." How are you supposed to understand that the first time through?

The use of English loanwords has no official support. The Ministry of Education's Department of National Language, as a matter of policy, "has never published anything that contains loanwords of Western origin" (Sibata 1975: 169).

Dolgin, Kemnitzer, and Schneider (1977) claim that certain "negative" symbols (in this case, some native Japanese words) might be "displaced" by less threatening symbols (English loanwords). Evidence to substantiate this claim can be seen in the high frequency of loanwords used when sexual topics are discussed. Some informants also claim that *tibi*[36] (tuberculosis) is preferable to the native Japanese term *kekkakubyo*.[37] (See Annamalai [1978] and Kachru [1978a, 1983] for discussions of the Indian situation.)

Individual speakers use English loanwords in highly creative and personal ways, as this example indicates (Sibata 1975: 170):

> In the script I found the expression "flower street." I then asked the script writer what it meant and where he picked up the expression. The reply was: "I just made it up myself." I was subsequently told that the meaning had to do with the decoration of flowers, a decoration movement that was going on at the time. I no longer recall the exact meaning, but there can be no mistake that Japanized "English," such as "happy end" or "flower street," was introduced into the Japanese lexicon by people . . . in a more or less similar fashion.[38]

However, not all inventions gain acceptance; nor is this a practice indulged in by everyone. The educational system in Japan gives all students some inkling of English vocabulary and grammar, perhaps enough to provide a common ground for individual expression and creativity, or to allow for a choice of new linguistic strategies. For example, the young lady who has *Dream Girl* embroidered on her sweater might be making a statement about herself that she would find it difficult to make otherwise, given the prevailing Japanese social and linguistic conventions.

The impact of language on an individual in Japan should not be underestimated. This linguistic pressure is sometimes discussed in the media. In the 1970 award-winning bestseller, *Nihonjin to Yudayajin* (*The Japanese and the Jews*), Ben-Dasan (1970: 186) points out that both the learned discourse of a conservative college professor and the radical arguments shouted over loudspeakers by leftist students employ the same level of courteous language considered appropriate for someone addressing a group of people. In 1980, members of the Japanese National Debate Team told me that such argumentation was almost impossible to conduct in Japanese, especially for women. To their knowledge, all debating societies in Japan conduct their contests in English. These examples imply that the Japanese language places constraints on individual language usage. Perhaps one way to circumvent these inhibitions is through the use of loanwords.

The semantic range of some loanwords varies among different Japanese speakers. This may allow for some ambiguity, with its consequent play on connotations whenever loanwords are used.[39] Such ambiguity and appeal to connotation is not unusual in the Japanese language and its literature. Loanwords may provide another linguistic mechanism involving these devices.[40]

Japanese English and Other Non-Native Englishes

Bamgboṣe (1982) postulates a typology to identify varieties of Nigerian English. He posits four levels (from pidgin English to university speech) and four varieties (from extreme phonological/syntactical imposition of the native language on English, to speech identical to that of a native Standard English speaker). However, few of these observations are helpful in the Japanese case. Japan was never colonized by the British, who elsewhere left a linguistic legacy in the form of civil service requirements, government legislation, or a prestige language. Such factors encouraged people to become fluent in spoken and written English. English was never the language of the Japanese public school system, though there were intellectual incentives to acquire at least a reading knowledge. Most important, Japan has never had the cultural and linguistic pluralism which made English convenient as a lingua franca (at least) or a national language (at most).[41] In short, English in Japan never became institutionalized.

The major difference between Japanized English and most other non-native varieties is the degree to which members of the population are fluent speakers. In numerous other countries, many people can speak a simplified pidgin English and a large number possess varying degrees of fluency. In Japan, while the number of highly fluent speakers may be smaller, all people have some ability to use English linguistic resources. Except in special instances (such as among Hawaiian-Japanese), pidgin English per se is not found because it is not needed. Japanese English mainly emphasizes vocabulary items and phrases (many of which are highly productive), rather than morphology or syntax.[42]

The investigation of language contact between Japanese and English is a subject of great import for both theoretical and applied linguistics. The unique use of English loanwords by Japanese people defies most of the classic typologies proposed by Haugen (1950, 1953), Weinreich (1953), Ferguson (1959), or Vildomec (1963). It also stands outside the bounds of Gumperz's (1964) code-switching, where alternating sentential language changes accompany a change in the speech situation, or Kachru's (1978b) code-mixing, where language changes are found in a single sentence in the same speech situation. Perhaps the most practical theoretical approach for the Japanese case involves internal versus external switching, as described by Oksaar (1976) and Hatch (1976), where internal switching depends on social factors and external switching on the fluency of the speaker, his ability to use various emotive devices to establish tone, and his ability to respond to the interlocutor. Uyekubo (1972) and Ervin-Tripp (1967) have shown how important these factors are for the speech of Japanese bilingual children and adults and for Japanese monolinguals, respectively.[43]

Conclusion

I have presented some factors that affect the use of English loanwords in Japanese, and have suggested some ways in which Japanese speakers use these words as a communicative strategy or rhetorical device. Certain social factors seem to indicate differential loanword usage, but the dynamics of the individual personality, the particular speech situation, and the general social context are of at least equal importance. Loanwords may provide a different set of linguistic symbols which might carry neutral or ambiguous meanings, connotations, or affective content. This unique "English" in Japan affords the individual an expanded range of linguistic means to achieve a variety of social ends—without necessarily becoming completely bilingual.

Research on the use of English in Japanese is continuing. Several popular claims about loanwords (e.g., that referents of English loan-words represent things new and modern; that English loanwords are used to intellectually impress others) need rigorous empirical investi-gation. The semantics of "hybrid innovations" (Kachru 1975)—lexical items which consist of an element from a native language along with a component from English—occur frequently in Japanized English but have not been thoroughly studied. Another area which merits attention involves the linguistic constraints (Pfaff 1979; Kachru 1978b) that operate on English loanwords. Is there a limit to the number of English vocabulary items which the Japanese language can tolerate? Why do some items flourish, while others disappear?[44] Some work has been done on the semantic and cognitive aspects of English loanwords, but only on limited topics (e.g., Hinds 1974; Sanches 1977).[45] Japanese-English bilingualism has begun to be explored among adult learners (Ervin-Tripp 1967), bilingual and monolingual children (Uyekubo 1972; Yoshida 1978), and Japanese-American pidgin speakers in Hawaii (Higa 1975; Nagara 1972), suggesting that these areas might also be profitably pursued by those studying English loanwords in Japanese.

Much work still needs to be done in relating this switching or mixing to other aspects of Japanese communicative behavior, such as kinesics, paralanguage, and nonverbal communication. We cannot yet predict where and when an English loanword will be used, who will use it, and what strategies he intends to implement while doing so. It is also unclear how any of the special subcultures of Japan—the Korean minority, the *burakumin* (Japan's "untouchable" caste), or the *yakuza* (ritualized underworld society)—react to or utilize English loanwords. So far, all that is really understood is that the use of English is widespread and is apparently affected by situational and social factors, and that these variables are terribly conflated.[46]

NOTES

1. This research was based on data collected during the summers of 1979 and 1980 in Japan, supported in part by a summer research grant from the University of Illinois. I thank this committee and its chairman, R. T. Zuidema, for their invaluable assistance. I also thank Joseph B. Casagrande, Janet W. D. Dougherty, Braj B. Kachru, Mariko Kaga, Seiichi Makino, and David W. Plath for their help in discussing topics and problems relating to this study and for reading earlier drafts.

2. This use of the term "acculturation" is somewhat unusual; I beg indulgence from fellow anthropologists. For discussions in English on the general structure of Japanese, see Inoue 1979 and Miller 1967.

3. Ohno 1970: 80 speaks of the influence of Korean borrowings before

the 9th century: "The original stimulus to the cultural development of the *Yayoi* [300 B.C. to approximately A.D. 300] probably came from South Korea." There are many accessible texts in English on the history of Japan, including George Sansom's three-volume *History of Japan, to 1334, 1334–1615, 1615–1867* (Stanford: Stanford University Press, 1958). For the post-contact period, see Edwin Reischauer's *The United States and Japan* (New York: Viking Press, 1965) and W. G. Beasley's *The Modern History of Japan* (New York: Praeger, 1963). For a discussion of the Dutch influence on the Japanese language, see Vos 1963.

4. On whom the novel *Shōgun* is (very loosely) based. See P. Rogers, *The First Englishman in Japan* (London: Harwill, 1956), or any of the half-dozen novels based on the incident, such as R. Blacker's *The Needle Watcher: The Will Adams Story; British Samurai* (Tokyo: Tuttle, 1973).

5. English was well on its way to becoming an influence on the Japanese language long before the post–World War II Occupation.

6. As Fukuzawa (1899: 213) pointed out, English became a popular subject for students, even replacing the traditional Chinese studies, but it never became the official language of instruction.

7. Educated people may be quite competent *readers* of English, however.

8. There are also four daily English-language newspapers readily available. Interestingly, there are more English-language newspapers published in Tokyo than in Chicago.

9. Passin (1980: 48) counted 1,300 separate foreign loans in a random issue of *The Yomiuri* newspaper.

10. The Japanese writing system has four sets of symbols: *kanji* (Chinese-based ideographs) for most common lexemes, a syllabary of 46 basic symbols called *hiragana* used for inflections and other morphemes, an angular version of the *hiragana* called *katakana* used as an italics and to write foreign names, and *romanji*, a phonemic transliteration. Occasionally a foreign name or word will be written in *hiragana*, as in *bai-bai* (bye bye) at the end of a television program.

11. The use of English loanwords on artifacts will be discussed at a later date.

12. Mackey 1979 does caution us against taking the percentage of loanwords as a measure of language influence or dominance in a contact situation. However, even with these reservations, the number of English loanwords is quite large. For other statistics on the extent of English loanword usage (though limited to only frequency counts of items found in dictionaries), see Ozawa 1970; 1976.

13. Some scholars (e.g., Pierce 1971) use the term "Japlish" to refer to parts of the nativization processes discussed in this chapter. However, one should not be misled into thinking that this is a variety of English equivalent to, say, Chicano English or Indian English.

14. For a complete description of Japanese phonology, including some remarks on the phonology of foreign words, see McCawley 1968.

15. The basic Japanese phonemes are *a, i, u, e, o, k, s, t, n, h, m, y, r, w,*

and syllabic *n*. The vowels are "Italian" vowels, and most consonants are pronounced somewhat as in English. Vowel length (indicated by repeating the symbol or using a raised bar) and consonant gemination (indicated by repeating the symbol) are also phonemic. The sounds *k, s, t, n, h, m,* and r can form clusters with the semipalatal *y*. The series *k, s,* and *t* have voiced correspondents *g, z,* and *d,* and *b* and *p,* thought to be derivable from *h,* are also present. As Japanese romanization is basically phonemic, the slashed bar symbols have been omitted. Though the sounds *fa, fi, fo,* and *fe* do not occur in native Japanese words (only *fu* is found naturally in this consonant-vowel series), these sounds are found in English loanwords. They are written in *katakana* using the symbol for *fu* plus a subscripted vowel sign. The Japanese *r*-sound is midway between the English /l/ and /r/ (see Sonoda 1975: 145–46). For a detailed discussion of all the constraints on gemination in English loanwords, see Lovins 1973: 81–98.

16. Strictly speaking, the categories "noun," "verb," etc., as used in English are inadequate for Japanese. See Martin (1975).

17. Words of Chinese origin which have been borrowed into Japanese in the past also take this *na* marker: *kirei-na hana* (pretty flower), *shizuka-na machi* (quiet town). Loanwords may, on occasion, take the *-i* adjective marker, as in *now-i onna* (a "now"/contemporary woman).

18. This compounding process seems to be a common way of taking certain English elements into a host language. For example, Kachru (1978a: 36) gives, among others, these instances from Hindi: *begin karnā* (to begin), *worry karnā* (to worry), *control karnā* (to control). Pandharipande (1981) gives similar examples from Marathi: *aṭek yeṇe* (to get an attack), *šɔk basṇe* (to get a shock). One possible reason why such a process is so productive in these languages is that using these compound verbs may express meanings related to the manner in which the acts are performed, thus allowing this device to be used to express attitudinal meanings (Y. Kachru and Pandharipande 1980: 122).

Apparently, as mentioned by Henderson (1948: 39), case markers in this form are often ignored when applied to English loanwords. For example, *rabu suru* should mean "to love" and *rabu o suru* should mean "to make love." However, both seem to be used interchangeably. Likewise, "to like" should be *raiki suru,* but the peculiar *raiki o suru* is also heard.

19. Sonoda (1975: 177) claims that *yū* (you) can occur as an object, subject, or possessive, as in *yū wa dochira kara kita* (Where do you come from?). I have never heard such an example.

20. Cf. *boku no mai-kā* (my "my-car").

21. This summary does not mean to imply that there are no other grammatical aspects of English word borrowing in Japanese. Much research still needs to be done. For example, Kachru 1978b has shown some of the grammatical constraints operating on the borrowing of English into Hindi, and Warie 1977 has discussed such problems in Thai. Sridhar and Sridhar 1980 have demonstrated similar syntactic constraints on English borrowing

in Kannada and Spanish. For a general theoretical discussion on these topics, see Wentz 1977.

22. Makino (1978) has mentioned that visual effects might also be operating in the use of English loanwords. For example, *tabako* (cigarette) is written in *hiragana*, while most other loanwords are written in *katakana*, perhaps indicating the extent to which *tabako* has become adopted. Yotsukura (1971: 116) points out that "news" was taken in as *nyūsu*, not *nyūzu*, because this word, like most English loanwords, was borrowed by sight rather than by sound.

23. Horiuchi (Passin and Horiuchi 1977: 39–41) discusses more than two dozen compounds involving the English word "love."

24. Garneau (1975) terms these "misleading transfer items" and demonstrates how a similar phenomenon is operating in French.

25. Another fascinating aspect of vocabulary nativization in Japanese is seen in the borrowing of place names in sign language (Peng and Clouse 1976). For example, in the sign for New York City (*nyū yōku* in spoken Japanese) the right-hand configuration is finger-spelled *y* of English, intending the *y* of York. The rest of the sign is in regular Japanese sign language.

26. In some cases English words enter Japanese as verbs, after they have been shortened and the *-ru* verbal suffix has been added (Hinds 1974: 94; Seward 1968: 99; Miura 1979: 39–40), e.g., *taku-ru* (to go by taxi), *nego-ru* (to negotiate), *demo-ru* (to demonstrate). After such modification, the new term may be conjugated as a normal Japanese verb, as in *ima kare to negotte imasu* (I'm negotiating with him now). Such items are not common.

27. Little work on Japan has been done by cognitive anthropologists except in confined areas such as kinship studies (see Wallace and Atkins 1965).

28. Ozawa (1976) has updated Ichikawa's data, though he has used only a dictionary as his source.

29. For women, too, presumably—though this was not studied. The use of loanwords (if any) in traditional Japanese sports like *sumō* (Japanese stylized wrestling) or *kendō* (bamboo-sword fighting) was not investigated, either.

30. As an example Horiuchi (1963: 52) gives the following reply, printed by the *Asahi* newspaper, in response to a question about the number of loanwords used in a previous issue: "As a rule, foreign words are to be printed in *kana*. Words which we feel to be strange to the average reader and words which in our estimate are still unfamiliar to the public are usually withheld; the newspaper should try to reach as wide a range of readers as possible by using a vocabulary easy to grasp. Of late the use of 'foreign' words has grown by leaps and bounds. Sometimes the total will be as many as 60–70 to a page. This is a conspicuous phenomenon in the case of articles with close affiliations with the home, sports, arts, radio and TV, and advertisements. Post-war Japan has met with a deluge of technical terms relating to thought, science, techniques, and merchandise. These have seldom been translated nor have *kanji* been adapted to them, and apparently without a

second thought the Japanese have taken them on as they thought the words to be. To all intents and purposes we appear to be a foreign-word loving people. Anything in *kana* looks sweet and fresh. We bow to it and value it overmuch."

31. *The Yomiuri*, August 16, 1980.

32. Though some Japanese authors do write in English (e.g., Kawasaki's *Alien Rice*) their number hardly rivals the scores of Indian and African authors who write in English.

33. This manifests itself in some very interesting product names, such as a coffee creamer named Creap or a soft drink named Calpis. Seward (1968: 67) mentions some earlier examples: Pecker mechanical pencils, Rony Wrinkle rubber prophylactics, Puddy prepared pudding mix, Violent blue jeans. For a French example of how English loanwords are borrowed in advertising, see Knepler 1976.

Plath also points out that some names for products in Japan involve bilingual punning or word-play. For example, the name of the popular Japanese whiskey *Suntory* might be a pun on Torii, the name of the three brothers who founded the company. (A Japanese word for "three" is *san*.) Plath also notes that almost all cigarette brand names are in English (e.g., Peace, Mild Seven, HiLite, Cabin).

34. Of course, some Japanese loans, such as *sukiyaki, kimono, harakiri,* and *kamakazi,* appear in English. Miura (1979: 173–75) lists about 75–100 examples, ranging from the very common to terms used only by specialists in a Japanese craft or art.

35. Makino 1978 suggests that Japanese people have an empathy hierarchy toward individual vocabulary items. They are thought to be most empathetic to *Yamato* (native Japanese) words, less empathetic to Chinese loanwords, and nonempathetic toward Western loanwords.

36. Makino has mentioned that this might be because of the similarity to the older German clinical term *tēbē*.

37. Kachru (1978a) terms this process in code-mixed situations as "neutralization." It is still not clear whether the mechanisms by which English loanwords are borrowed into Japanese fulfill all the necessary conditions of code-mixing.

38. One other thing the scriptwriter might have had in mind was the term *hana-dori* (flower road), used to refer to the long platform by which *kabuki* players entered the stage from their positions near the audience. Plath also notes that the main thoroughfare running through downtown Kobe was known as *furawā rōdo* for many years.

Kachru 1978a claims that in such mixed situations there is a cline of acceptability of mixed forms, ranging from normal code-mixing to unusual "odd-mixing." These parameters, motivations, and criteria have yet to be clearly isolated for English loanwords in Japan.

39. E.g., the name of the famous Japanese singing duo *pinku redi* (Pink Lady). The color conjures up the same feelings of sensuality as does red or

201

pink in English. But when these two girls give interviews in the popular press, they always present a very wholesome image.

40. In the "folk beliefs" of most Westerners, the Japanese are thought to be the world's great imitators. The popular media indicate that many Japanese now believe this, too. However, no satisfactory definition of imitation has ever been proposed, nor have any tests been suggested on how to find it. It is difficult, then, to claim imitation as a possible reason for the large number of loanwords in Japanese without falling into a circular argument.

41. See Kachru 1981 for a description of the Indian situation.

42. As Horiuchi (1963: 51) said, "English is often so near and yet so far from the grasp of the average Japanese citizen."

43. How children acquire loanwords in Japanese has yet to be investigated. It is not known whether television, school, friends, or other factors are the most crucial in imparting this English vocabulary. See Yoshida 1978; Weitzman 1967.

44. E.g., certain loans like *moga* (from the initial sounds of "modern girl," meaning a 1920s flapper) became fashionable but rapidly faded (Miller 1967: 249–50). Plath suggests that the current *za shitī* (the city, i.e., Tokyo) might be another such instance.

45. Hinds examined differential responses to native color terms and English loanwords for color. Sanches studied, in part, how Japanese numerical classifiers were not extended to cover certain English loans.

46. Other references of interest include Baird 1971, Inui 1958, Kunihiro 1967, Mori 1972, Nagasawa 1957, Nishiwaki 1961, Pae 1967, Yazaki 1964, and Yokoi 1973. Loanword dictionaries in Japanese are Arakawa 1977, Nikaido 1980, Oka 1980, Sanseidō Henshū-bu 1979, Shinsei Shuppankai Hen-shū-bu 1978, Yoshizawa 1979, and Yoshizawa and Ishiwata 1979. Landy and Horiuchi 1978 and Masuda 1974 are also useful. English glossaries of some English loanwords in Japanese can be found in Bailey 1962, Matsumoto 1974, and Miura 1979. A later edition of the *Kokuritsu Kokugo Kenkyūjo* study has been released as *Denkikeisanki ni yoru shimbun no goi chosa [A Computer Study of Contemporary Newspaper Vocabulary]* (Tokyo: Shūei Shuppan, 1970). For further discussion and some recent references, see Morrow 1987.

The transliterations used in this article are based on the *Hyōjunshiki/* Hepburn system (but with long vowels indicated by a raised bar), rather than the less popular *Sin-kunreisiki* or *Nipponsiki* systems. This would be of little interest except to the non-specialist, were it not for the fact that a few names in the bibliography are inconsistent with the text transcriptions and might puzzle readers doing further research. All citations and quotes are given as in the original (e.g., Sibata or Ohno, vs. Shibata or Ōno, which would be consistent with the text).

REFERENCES

Annamalai, E. 1978. The Anglicized Indian languages: a case of code-mixing. *International Journal of Dravidian Linguistics* 7(2): 239–47.

Arakawa, Sōbē. 1977. *Kadokawa gairaigo jiten, dai-ni-han* [Kadokawa loanword dictionary. 2nd ed.] Tokyo: Kadokawa Shoten.

Bailey, Don C. 1962. *A glossary of Japanese neologisms.* Tucson: University of Arizona Press.

Baird, Scott. 1971. Contact: English with Japanese. *The Study of Current English* 25(15): 23–28.

Bamgboṣe, Ayọ. 1982. Standard Nigerian English: issues of identification. In this volume.

Ben-Dasan, Isaiah. 1970. *The Japanese and the Jews.* New York: Weatherhill.

Brown, Penelope, and Stephen Levinson. 1978. Universals in language usage: politeness phenomena. Pp. 56–310 in E. Goody, ed., *Questions and politeness: strategies in social interaction.* Cambridge: Cambridge University Press.

Brown, Roger, and Albert Gilman. 1960. The pronouns of power and solidarity. Pp. 302–35 in *Psycholinguistics: selected papers of Roger Brown.* New York: Free Press.

Bruner, J., J. Goodnow, and G. Austin. 1956. *A study of thinking.* New York: John Wiley.

Doglin, J.; D. Kemnitzer, and D. Schneider, eds. 1977. *Symbolic anthropology.* New York: Columbia University Press.

Dunn, S. W., and A. M. Barban. 1978. *Advertising: its role in modern marketing.* New York: Dryden Press.

Ervin-Tripp, Susan. 1967. An Issei learns English. *Journal of Social Issues* 23: 78–90.

Ferguson, Charles A. 1959. Diglossia. *Word* 15: 325–40.

Fishman, Joshua, ed. 1968. *Readings in the sociology of language.* The Hague: Mouton.

———. 1972. *Advances in the sociology of language, II.* The Hague: Mouton.

Fukao, Tokiko. 1979. *Katakana kotoba* [Words in Katakana]. Tokyo: Saimaru Shuppankai.

Fukuzawa, Yukichi. 1899. *The autobiography of Yukichi Fukuzawa.* New York: Schocken Books, 1972.

Garneau, Jean-Luc. 1975. Anglo-French misleading transfer items: a semantic analysis. Pp. 567–83 in P. Reich, ed., *The second LACUS forum.* Columbia, S.C.: Hornbeam Press.

Gaunlett, O. J. 1966. Phonetic discrepancies in Japanese loanwords. *The Study of Sounds* 12: 308–26.

Gumperz, John. 1964. Linguistic and social interaction in two communities. *American Anthropologist* 66(2): 137–54.

———, and Dell Hymes, eds. 1972. *Directions in sociolinguistics: the ethnography of communication.* New York: Holt, Rinehart and Winston.

Hatch, Evelyn. 1976. Studies in language switching and mixing. Pp. 201–14 in W. McCormack and S. Wurm, *Language and man: anthropological issues.* The Hague: Mouton.

Haugen, Einar. 1950. The analysis of linguistic borrowing. *Language* 26: 210–31.

———. 1953. *The Norwegian language in America: a study in bilingual behavior.* Philadelphia: University of Pennsylvania Press.

Hayes, Curtis. 1979. Language contact in Japan. Pp. 363–76 in Mackey and Ornstein 1979.

Henderson, Harold. 1948. *Handbook of Japanese grammar.* Boston: Houghton Mifflin.

Higa, Masanori. 1973. Sociolinguistic aspects of word borrowing. *Topics in Culture Learning* 1: 75–85. Reprinted in Mackey and Ornstein 1979.

———. 1975. The use of loanwords in Hawaiian Japanese. Pp. 71–90 in Peng 1975.

Hinds, John. 1974. Make mine BURAKKU. *Language Research* 10(2): 92–108.

Hirai, Masao. 1978. *Henna kotoba, tadashī kotoba* [Strange words, correct words]. Tokyo: Kyōiku Shuppan.

Horiuchi, Amy. 1963. Department store ads and Japanized English. *Studies in Descriptive and Applied Linguistics* 2: 49–67. Tokyo: International Christian University.

Hymes, Dell, ed. 1964. *Language in culture and society.* New York: Harper and Row.

Ichikawa, Sanki. 1931. Foreign influences in the Japanese language. Pp. 141–80 in I. Nitobe et al., eds., *Western influences in modern Japan.* Chicago: University of Chicago Press.

Inoue, Kyoko. 1979. Japanese: a story of language and people. Pp. 241–300 in T. Shopen, ed., *Languages and their speakers.* Cambridge, Mass.: Winthrop.

Inui, Ryoichi. 1958. *Kokugo no hyogen ni oyoboshita Eigo no eikyō.* [English impact on expressions in the national language]. Tokyo: Mombushō.

Isshiki, Masako. 1957. A comparative analysis of English and Japanese consonant phonemes. *The Study of Sounds* 8: 391–416.

———. 1965. A contrastive analysis of English and Japanese vowel phonemes. *The Study of Sounds* 11: 193–212.

Japanese Ministry of Education (Mombushō). 1955. *Gairaigo no hyōki* [Representations of loanwords]. Tokyo: Meiji Tosho Shuppan Kabushiki Kaisha.

Japanese National Language Research Institute (Kokuritsu Kokugo Kenkyūjo). 1964. *Gendai zasshi kyūjusshu no yōji yōgo* [Vocabulary and Chinese characters in ninety magazines of today]. Tokyo: Shuei.

Kachru, Braj B. 1966. Indian English: a study in contextualization. Pp. 255–87 in C. Bazell et al., *In Memory of J. R. Firth.* London: Longmans.

———. 1975. Lexical innovations in South Asian English. *International Journal of the Sociology of Language* 4: 55–74.

———. 1978a. Toward structuring code-mixing: an Indian perspective. *International Journal of the Sociology of Language* 16: 27–46.

———. 1978b. Code-mixing as a communicative strategy in India. Pp. 107–24 in J. Alatis, ed., *International dimensions of bilingual education.* Washington: Georgetown University Press.

————. 1981. The pragmatics of non-native varieties of English. In L. Smith, ed., *English for cross-cultural communication.* London: Macmillan.

————. 1982. Models for non-native Englishes. In this volume.

————. 1983. *The Indianization of English: the English language in India.* New Delhi and New York: Oxford University Press.

————, and Randolph Quirk. 1981. Introduction to L. Smith, ed., *English for cross-cultural communication.* London: Macmillan.

Kachru, Yamuna, and Rajeshwari Pandharipande. 1980. Toward a typology of compound verbs in South Asian languages. *Studies in the Linguistic Sciences* 10(1): 113–24.

Kawakami, Shin. 1963. *Gendaigo no hatsuon* [The pronounciation of today's language]. *Koza gendaigo* 1: 184–210.

Knepler, Myrna. 1976. Sold at fine stores everywhere, naturellement: a look at borrowed words in French and American magazine advertising. Pp. 309–18 in R. di Pietro and E. Blansitt, Jr., eds., *The third LACUS forum.* Columbia, S.C.: Hornbeam Press.

Kunihiro, Tetsuya. 1967. *Kōzoteki imiron—nichi ei ryōgo taishō kenkyū* [Structural semantics: a contrastive study of Japanese and English]. Tokyo: Sanseidō.

Landy, Eugene, and Horiuchi, Katsuaki. 1978. *Amerika zokugo jiten* [American underground dictionary], 5th ed. Tokyo: Kenkyūsha.

Lovins, Julie. 1973. Loanwords and the phonological structure of Japanese. Ph.D. dissertation, University of Chicago. Reprinted, Bloomington: Indiana University Linguistics Club, 1975.

McCawley, James. 1968. *The phonological component of a grammar of Japanese.* The Hague: Mouton.

Mackey, William. 1979. Toward an ecology of language contact. Pp. 455–60 in Mackey and Ornstein 1979.

————, and Jacob Ornstein, eds. 1979. *Sociolinguistic studies in language contact.* The Hague: Mouton.

Makino, Seiichi. 1978. *Kotoba to kūkan* [Language and space]. Tokyo: Tōkai Daigaku Shuppankai.

Martin, Samuel. 1975. *Reference grammar of Japanese.* New Haven: Yale University Press.

Masuda, Koh. 1974. *Kenkyusha's new Japanese English dictionary.* 4th ed. Tokyo: Kenkyūsha.

Matsumoto, Toru. 1974. *The random dictionary: a glossary of foreign words in today's spoken Japanese.* Tokyo: Japan Times, Ltd.

Miller, Roy Andrew. 1967. *The Japanese language.* Chicago: University of Chicago Press.

————. 1977. *The Japanese language in contemporary Japan.* Washington: American Enterprise Institute for Public Policy Research.

Miura, Akira. 1979. *English loanwords in Japanese: a selection.* Tokyo: Tuttle.

Mori, Hiroki. 1972. *Nihongo no naka no Eigo* [English in Japanese]. Tokyo: Hyōgensha.

Morrow, Philip R. 1987. The users and uses of English in Japan. *World Englishes* 6(1): 49–62.

Nagara, Susumu. 1972. *Japanese pidgin English in Hawaii: a bilingual description.* Honolulu: University of Hawaii Press.

Nagasawa, Jiro. 1957. A study of English-Japanese cognates. *Language Learning* 8: 53–102.

Neustupný, J. V. 1978. The phonology of loanwords in Japanese. Pp. 74–100 in his *Post-structural approaches to language.* Tokyo: University of Tokyo Press.

Nikaido, Tetsuo. 1980. *Gairaigo jiten: shin gairaigo kenkyūkai hen* [Loanword dictionary]. Tokyo: Nittō Shoin.

Nishiwaki, Hiroshi. 1961. Morphological problems in linguistic borrowing. *Studies in Descriptive and Applied Linguistics* 1: 28–42.

Norman, Arthur. 1955. Bamboo English: the Japanese influence upon American speech in Japan. *American Speech* 30: 44–48.

Ohno, Susumu. 1970. *The origin of the Japanese language.* Tokyo: Kokusai Bunka Shinkokai.

Ohye, Saburo. 1967a. The mora phoneme /q/ in English loanwords in Japanese. *The Study of Sounds* 13: 111–21.

———. 1967b. Some phonological problems in language contact. *The Study of Sounds* 13: 83–90.

Oka, Michio, ed. 1980. *Jōyō gairaigo shin jiten* [New daily use loanword dictionary]. 6th ed. Tokyo: Gotō Shoin.

Oksaar, Els. 1976. Implications for language contact for bilingual language acquisition. Pp. 189–200 in W. McCormack and S. Wurm, eds., *Language and man: anthropological issues.* The Hague: Mouton.

Ozawa, Katsuyoshi. 1970. A study of English loanwords in the Japanese newspaper *The Yomiuri.* M.A. thesis, Louisiana State University.

———. 1976. An investigation of the influence of the English language on the Japanese language through lexical adaptation from 1955–1972. Ph.D. dissertation, Ohio University.

Pae, Yang Seo. 1967. English loanwards in Korean. Ph.D. dissertation, University of Texas.

Pandharipande, R. 1981. Nativization of loanwords: the case of Marathi. Manuscript.

Passin, Herbert. 1980. *Japanese and the Japanese.* Tokyo: Kinseido.

———, and Katsuaki Horiuchi. 1977. *Japanese and the Japanese.* Tokyo: Kinseido.

Peng, Fred C. C., ed. 1975. *Language in Japanese society.* Tokyo: University of Tokyo Press.

———, and Debbie Clouse. 1976. Place names in Japanese sign language. Pp. 295–308 in R. Di Pietro and E. Blansitt, Jr., eds., *The third LACUS forum.* Columbia, S.C.: Hornbeam Press.

Pfaff, Carol. 1979. Constraints on language mixing: intersentential code-switching and borrowing in Spanish/English. *Language* 55: 291–318.

Pierce, Joe. 1971. Culture, diffusion and Japlish. *Linguistics* 76: 45–58.

Quackenbush, Edward. 1974. How Japanese borrows English words. *Linguistics* 131: 59–75.

Reischauer, Edwin. 1977. *The Japanese.* Tokyo: Tuttle.

Sanches, Mary. 1977. Language acquisition and language change: Japanese numeral classifiers. Pp. 51–62 in B. Blount and M. Sanches, eds., *Sociocultural dimensions of language change.* New York: Academic Press.

Sanseidō Hen-shū-bu. 1979. *Konsaisu gairaigo jiten* [Concise loanword dictionary]. 3rd ed. Tokyo: Sanseidō Kabushiki Kaisha.

Scherer, Klaus, and Howard Giles, eds. 1979. *Social markers in speech.* Cambridge: Cambridge University Press.

Seward, Jack. 1968. *Japanese in action.* New York: Weatherhill.

Shinsei Shuppankai Hen-shū-bu. 1978. *Shin gairaigo jiten* [New loanword dictionary]. Tokyo: Shinsei Shuppankai.

Sibata, Takeshi. 1975. On some problems in Japanese sociolinguistics: reflections and prospects. Pp. 159–74 in Peng (1975).

Sonoda, Koji. 1975. A descriptive study of English influence on modern Japanese. Ph.D. dissertation, New York University.

Sridhar, S. N., and Kamal K. Sridhar. 1980. The syntax and psycholinguistics of bilingual code-mixing. *Studies in the Linguistic Sciences* 10(1): 203–15.

Ueno, Kagefuku. 1968. Seiyō gairaigo [Western loanwords]. In *Nihon no Eigaku hyakunen* [One hundred years of English studies in Japan], ed. Nihon no Eigaku Hyakunen Henshūbu, I, 543–73; II, 341–64.

Umegaki, Minoru. 1978. *Nihon gairaigo no kenkyū* [Studies on Japanese loanwords]. 4th ed. Tokyo: Kenkyūsha.

Uyekubo, Aiko. 1972. Language switching of Japanese-English bilinguals. M.A. thesis, University of California at Los Angeles.

Vildomec, Veroj. 1963. *Multilingualism.* Leyden: A. W. Sythoff.

Vogt, Hans. 1954. Contact of language. In A. Martinet and U. Weinreich, *Linguistics today.* New York: Linguistic Circle of New York, Columbia University.

Vos, Frits. 1963. The Dutch influence on the Japanese language. *Lingua* 12: 34–48.

Wallace, Anthony F. C., and John Atkins. 1965. The case of a Japanese informant. Pp. 404–18 in S. Tyler, ed., *Cognitive anthropology.* New York: Holt, Rinehart and Winston.

Warie, Pairat. 1977. Some aspects of code-mixing in Thai. *Studies in the Linguistic Sciences* 7(1): 21–40.

Weinreich, Uriel. 1953. *Languages in contact.* The Hague: Mouton.

Weitzman, Keiko Hirano. 1967. A study of the influence of the Japanese phonemic structure in the English of Japanese Americans. *Studies in Descriptive and Applied Linguistics* 4: 131–41.

Wentz, James. 1977. Some considerations in the development of a syntactic description of code-switching. Ph.D. dissertation, University of Illinois.

Yazaki, Genkurō. 1964. *Nihon no gairaigo* [Japanese loanwords]. Tokyo: Iwanami Shoten.

Yokoi, Tadao. 1973. *Gairaigo to gaikokugo: pazuru ni yoru gogaku nyūmon*

[Loanwords and foreign languages: an introduction to language study through puzzles]. Tokyo: Gendai Jānarizumu Shuppankai.

————. 1978. *Gairaigo no goten* [Dictionary of loanword mistakes]. Tokyo: Jūkoku Minsha.

Yoshida, M. 1978. The acquisition of English vocabulary by a Japanese-speaking child. Pp. 91–100 in E. Hatch, ed., *Second language acquisition.* Rowley, Mass.: Newbury House.

Yoshida, Yasuo, et al. 1973. *Japanese for today.* Tokyo: Gakken.

Yoshizawa, Norio. 1979. *Zukai gairaigo jiten* [Illustrated loanword dictionary]. Tokyo: Kadokawa Shoten.

————, and Toshio Ishiwata. 1979. *Gairaigo no gogen* [Etymology of loanword origins]. Tokyo: Kadokawa Shoten.

Yotsukura, Sayo. 1971. Review of *The Japanese language,* by R. A. Miller. *Linguistics* 76: 103–32.

Zuengler, Jane. 1982. Kenyan English. In *The other tongue: English across cultures,* ed. Braj B. Kachru. Urbana: University of Illinois Press.

PART III

Contact and Change:
Question of a Standard

11

Henry Kahane

American English: From a Colonial Substandard to a Prestige Language

For more than two millennia, there has been a chain of world languages, one after the other. Each of these phases is linked to a certain constellation of cultural features developed in a certain area; and the culture of that area carries the language abroad.

Thus Greek, in the period of Hellenism, carries the culture of intellectualism in science, philosophy, and art, and becomes a must for the educated from Rome to Asia Minor. Latin is resuscitated in the Carolingian period for the necessities of ecclesiastic and mundane administration, and for seven or eight centuries remains the vehicle of written communication in the Western world. The chivalric culture of medieval aristocracy, rising in Provence and France, carries these languages (often not clearly separable) over the Western world and beyond, from England to the Crusader states. Renaissance Italy brings us into the modern world, with the educated courtier who combines the two traditions of the humanist and the knight; Italian is part of his equipment. And French, again in the eighteenth and nineteenth centuries, spreads through the innumerable courts modeled after Versailles, and the language of the courts survives as the language of international diplomacy, sifting down into the bourgeoisie and remaining a distinctive mark of that bourgeoisie far beyond Europe, in Latin America, the Middle East, and Africa.

Ours is the day of American English. As early as 1780, John Adams made a remarkable statement (which, not by chance, is the starting point also for the paper by Shirley Heath in this volume). He proved to be prophetic when he said: "English [i.e., American English] is destined to be in the next and succeeding centuries more generally the language of the world than Latin was in the last, or French is in the present age. The reason is obvious, because the increasing population in America, and their universal connection and correspondence with all nations . . . force their language into general use." What is remarkable in Adams's statement is his percipience at such a pristine stage in the history of the country.

Indeed, in 1780 American English is still the underdog, still a colonial substandard. The colonial regime reaches its end, but the linguistic class system is still vigorous. "A gentleman," says Princeton's President Witherspoon in 1781, "will not imitate a peasant." In this diglossia, British English is the H language, the prestige language. Loyalty to the British tradition means, linguistically, purism. We are reminded of the language question in early modern Greece, around 1800: during the struggle for independence, the upper classes, who often were loyal to the Ottoman overlord, tried to resuscitate their H language, essentially learned Byzantine Greek, as the national standard, while rejecting the vernacular because of its democratic implications. America's H language, in the early period of the Republic, and far beyond, continued the British elitist tradition, building on three models: current standard English, the English classics, and the Greco-Latin strain in Western neo-humanism. To the conservative mind, the winds of change, the forces of linguistic emancipation, spell loss of the linguistic values: loss of the past, loss of norm, loss of standard. Three specific aspects evidence the deviation of the American language from the British standard: the prevalence of the vernacular in the evolving new standard; the growth of unorthodox lexemes and structures labeled innovations; and the openness toward adoption of foreign elements.

The decolonized society of the New World represents a most interesting linguistic experiment. It tries to be a society for Everyman, and its language develops into a language of Everyman. The new norms of life imply acceptance of the vernacular as the foundation of the standard. The social revolution is evident in the democratization, the informalization of its linguistic representation. The story of spoken American English, of the American koiné, is, indeed, one of linguistic democratization. It has been in existence from before 1700, and it survives, in principle, into our days, in the prestige accorded to our relatively integrated American vernacular. Dr. Benjamin Rush, signer of the Declaration of Independence, rejects the British paradigm: "The present is the age of simplicity of writing in America." Noah Webster, to whom language was as national as customs, habits, and government, sensed early, in 1789, a divergence of the "language in North America from the future language of England." Webster was, so to speak, the discoverer of the national language; but who was its speaker? The pioneer has been suggested; the average Ohio boatman of 1810, the plainsman of 1815, the cultural misfit, or simply the colonist. But the real activists in the koiné-forming process are the children who indoctrinate newcomers' children by imposing the norms of the koiné. Linguistic adaptation is achieved in just one generation.

The essential developments of American English, then, consist of a decline in Anglophilia, the standardization of informal speech, the leveling of social dialects, the integration of foreign elements. These developments are, from one standpoint, the symptoms of — or from another standpoint, the stimuli for — the upward mobility of American society. The pioneers of yesteryear have turned into middle-class citizens. In principle, the koiné-forming agents of the past are still at work in our time: pulpit, school, and publishing, vitalized, of course, by that macro-force, the electronic media. Webster's "standard of our vernacular tongue" is today's "Network Standard."

Nowhere, I am tempted to say, is Network Standard as faithfully codified as in that monumental dictionary known as WIII, Webster's Third. WIII appeared in 1961, and it immediately provoked a most interesting debate, essentially concerning the level of the American English inventorized. The controversy unfolds before the background of our own contemporary problems. There evolve three major grounds of objection to WIII: permissiveness, trust in usage, and loss of tradition. Yet, to the defenders of the work, the true promoter is not the teacher but the sociologist. The dictionary is a report on what is, not on what should or should not be, and WIII offers, as has been said, "a full account of the resources of the American language of the 'sixties.'" The preceding WII, in 1934, presented the formal style of the language then current but by now recessive. WIII records the informal style of the 'fifties which is developing into the new standard. The speech patterns of the middle class are replacing the habits of the so-called literary aristocracy; conversational style permeates written communication; the difference between the two forms of expression, written and spoken, which long marked Western civilization, has narrowed down in our age and culture. The inclination toward informality as well as the reduced distinction between the written and spoken levels are correlated with a noticeable position against purism. WIII, as an objective lexicological inventory, is at the same time a document evidencing the change in society. Informality of style, increased exposure to language, and lexical explosion reflect the forces of modern life as they have been evolving in the half-century since World War I: mass education, the growth of democracy, unprecedented movements of populations, the expansion of mass media, social and intellectual movements, urbanization, technological developments, increased magazine and newspaper reading, travel. Transformed into the medium of language, these innovations mean multiplication of technical jargon, gobbledygook, colloquial manufacture of neologisms, slang. In short, the rapid changes of life are mirrored in language, in our American English.

We come to the second phase of our story. With the events of the First World War, and increasingly since the Second, the former Cinderella has turned into the world language of our times. The development follows an old cycle. The internationally dominant position of a culture results in a forceful expansion of its language, with the reverse correlate: the expansion of the language contributes, by its very expansion, to the prestige of the culture behind it. A world language is the most typical case of an *H* language: the language of the upper classes in a diglossic environment. The concept of "world language" implies a two-pronged process of linguistic acquisition and integration.

As to acquisition: at a certain historical moment the prestige language, as the prime carrier of modern developments, social, intellectual, and technical, must be learned by the foreigner wanting or needing to be up-to-date. The forms of second-language acquisition have varied, of course, from culture to culture: the sons of the wealthy Roman families were taught Greek by Greek slaves (obviously the archetype of our profession); Latin for the Byzantine bureaucracy was provided in government schools; the instruction of Latin in the Middle Ages lay in the hands of the Church; French in eighteenth- and nineteenth-century Germany was transmitted by tutors and governesses, and in our century is taught by the government-sponsored schools of the Alliance Française. Today, an unprecedented demand has turned the teaching of American English into an American academic industry labeled ESL or TESL, aiming at maximum efficiency in teacher training, textbooks, and testing.

The second impact, integration, is the linguistic correlate of a cultural model: the prestige language becomes the fountainhead of widespread and large-scale borrowing of, essentially, characteristic lexemes. The sum of these borrowings evidences the sundry linguistic fields which represent the impact emanating from the source culture and involving the man on the street.

The difference between these two kinds of diffusion, acquisition and borrowing, is of sociolinguistic interest. Whereas the acquisition of an international prestige language is widely a classbound process, the borrowings from the same language easily become everyone's possession. The *terminus technicus* of foreign origin has a general appeal. The Latinisms of imperial Rome borrowed by Hellenistic Greek, as evidenced in the Egyptian papyri, survived in the Byzantine demotic; the Gallicisms of the chivalric culture borrowed by German survived in the rustic Middle-Low German dialects; the fashionable Italianisms spreading in the colonial empire of Venice on the Greek coasts and islands became a mark of fishermen and farmers. The lexical democratization of a world language is, perhaps, most evident in the case of the Greek of early Christianity: a large set of technical terms spread and became part and parcel of everyday speech— *angel/ devil/ bishop/ church*. The same happens now with American English.

The diffusion of Americanisms is, by itself, a process characteristic of these times. This unprecedented explosion of Americanisms is the effect of a concatenation of events. With the political preponderance of the United States after World War II, its technological advances, its supremacy in world economics, and the new forms of its way of life exerted their global influence. The visibility and audibility of these influences, supported by the developments of that second industrial revolution, the mass media, internationalized information. The mass media of the target countries—press, film, television, advertising, commercials—are the channels which spread the high prestige of Americanness, and the prestige of Americanness is linguistically transformed into Americanisms. These cover the linguistic fields of mass media/pop art/economics/business/the consumer society/ technology/the lifestyle of the young. The Americanisms abroad, interestingly, circumscribe essentially the same linguistic fields which we considered as the characteristic lexical features of Webster's Third.

One typical issue of the German weekly, *Der Spiegel* (April 29, 1974), contained more than 160 Americanisms, covering primarily American business organization, its cult of efficiency, and its hectic informal style of life, with a stress on both social relations and technology. Characteristic examples of business organization: *Team/ Broker/ Promoter/Service.* Terminology of efficiency: *Know-how/Trend/ Test/Lobby.* Social psychology: *Image/Fan/Stress/Backlash.* Fads: /*Jogger/Jeans/Rock/Afro-look.* Technology: *Hifi/Instant-on/Aftershave Lotion/Bulldozer.* Calques: *Gehirnwäsche* ∼ *brainwashing/ Speerspitze* ∼ *spearhead/Kletterer* ∼ *climber/umwickeln* ∼ *involve*. These borrowings clearly render the European image of America.

And finally, a glimpse of the third phase in the history of a world language—the attitudes displayed by those who are affected by it. This process has been investigated by a young scholar at the University of Illinois, Pierre Trescases. I shall try to outline some of his insights into the very illuminating case of France.

French has twice been a world language itself, in the twelfth century, and again from the seventeenth to the nineteenth; but twice it has also been on the passive end of the process, in the sixteenth century, when the giant of the Renaissance, Italy, covered the West with Italianisms, and now in the twentieth century with the impact of Americanisms. The Italian episode, although different in certain ways from the American, is of considerable interest to us; since it has concluded, it allows us to evaluate from a historical perspective those facets which, in the present-day case of American English, are still in the midst of evolution.

The impact of the Italian Renaissance hurt the French pride. It hurt what Humanistic tradition labeled the *Hercule gaulois,* the Gallic Hercules. In states where citizens feel a political-cultural inferiority, language turns into their foremost symbol of national defense. Defense of the language means defense of the nation; in Yardeni's recent phrasing, linguistic patriots consider borrowing anti-patriotic. Du Bellay, the great sociolinguist of the times, wrote in 1549: "The same natural law which requires everyone to defend his birthplace likewise obliges us to watch over the dignity of our language." Similarly, the foreign language turns into a symbol of the foreigner—since he is disliked, his language is disliked. The Italians are disliked because of their courtly style, displayed, above all, at the court of Henry III (1574–89); they are disliked because of their cultural hegemony, their successful minority in France, their mores. The effeminate Italians (mused a contemporary author, Estienne Pasquier) as represented by the courtiers, have an effeminate language . . . their language is corrupt, since they have dissolute mores. The famous linguist Henri Estienne stated in 1578 that neologisms go hand in hand with the new (that is, bad) mores. The words *charlatan* and *bouffon* are from Italian; but a Frenchman could not be a *charlatan* or a *bouffon,* only an Italian could. The foreignisms turn into a class symbol. The Italianisms are the mark of courtly life, that is, of an aristocratic style; and the bourgeoisie of the time rejected them as characteristic of that upper class.

The attitude of the French toward today's Americanisms presents, *mutatis mutandis,* the same picture. After World War I and increasingly after World War II, the United States, replacing French hegemony, becomes a menace to French pride. Out of the feeling of military-political inferiority grows an intellectual superiority complex, resulting in a cultural-ethical hostility toward the United States. The language becomes the symbol against which the hostility is most strongly in evidence. Americanisms symbolize colonialism; they are America's fifth column; they express submission; they reveal a preference for dollars over francs. The defense of the *génie français* is realized through a defense of the French language, and linguistic nationalism takes on a warlike character. Duhamel said in 1968: "Our first duty is to watch over the purity of our language. Importing vocabulary is a sign of weakness." The enemy is *franglais*. Americanisms are danger/invasion/ cancer. Borrowing is treason. Foreignisms are compared to useless immigrants. Etiemble, the foremost fighter against *franglais*, has written an exposé with the slanted title, *From French Prose to Atlantic Sabir. Atlantic sabir* means Atlantic pidgin; in other words, he interprets American English as the base language of a new lingua franca which replaces French.

Let me phrase the battle of the French intelligentsia against Americanisms succinctly, as a set of conservative political and cultural attitudes. The anti-attitude symbolizes a belief in tradition and norm, in elitism, in the intellectual's skepticism toward technology; it symbolizes an anti-democratic reaction against the women, the young, and mass culture; it symbolizes anti-Americanism and a rejection of multilingualism and multiculturalism. The attitude against Americanisms, in short, reflects the struggle against the cultural and social revolution which marks the decline of the traditional French civilization.

To sum up my observations, by interpreting the example of American English as the prestige language of today's world, I have tried to isolate three facets involved in this process of ascent. First, the evolving of a new style of life, of modernism, of dynamics in the culture behind the source language, makes it dominant at a certain period of history. Second, the spread of the language obeys the principle that "the medium is the message." And third, a complex pattern of acceptance and rejection exists in the target cultures, with the forces of tradition battling the magnetism of change. Only all three phases together—growth, diffusion, and attitudes—tell us the story.[1]

NOTE

1. The specific features indicated here that turned American English into an international language were followed up in Kahane 1986.

REFERENCES

Bellay, Joachim du. 1549. *La deffence et illustration de la langue française*. H. Chamard ed., 1948. Paris: M. Didier.

Dillard, Joey Lee. 1972. *Black English: its history and usage in the United States.* New York: Random House.

———. 1975. *All-American English.* New York: Random House.

Duhamel, Jean. 1968. O.R.T.F. et la langue française. *Revue des Deux Mondes* (April 1): 386–92.

Estienne, Henri. 1578. *Deux dialogues du nouveau langage françois italianizé et autrement desguizé, principalement entre les courtisans de ce temps.* P. Ristelhuber ed., 1885. Paris: Alphonse Lemerre. [The relevant passage is in I, 96.]

Etiemble, René. 1952. De la prose française au sabir atlantique. *Les Temps Modernes* 8: 291–303.

Jung, Marc-René. 1966. Hercule dans la littérature française du XVle siècle: De l'Hercule courtois à l'Hercule baroque. *Travaux d'Humanisme et Renaissance* 79. Genève.

Kahane, Henry, and Renée Kahane. 1976. Abendland und Byzanz: Sprache. *Reallexikon der Byzantinistik,* ed. P. Wirth. Amsterdam: Verlag Adolf M. Hakkert. I, 345–640.

———. 1977. Virtues and vices in the American language: a history of attitudes. *TESOL Quarterly* 11: 185–202.

———. 1979. Decline and survival of Western prestige languages. *Language* 51: 183–98.

———. 1986. A typology of the prestige language. *Language* 62: 495–508.

———, and Roberta Ash. 1979. Linguistic evidence in historical reconstruction. In Rauch and Carr 1979: 67–121.

Mathews, Mitford M., ed. 1931. *The beginnings of American English: essays and comments.* Chicago: University of Chicago Press.

Pasquier, Estienne. ca. 1560. *Choix de lettres sur la littérature, la langue et la traduction.* D. Thickett ed., 1956. Textes Littéraires Français. Genève: E. Droz. [The relevant passage is on p. 88.]

———. 1560–1621. *Oeuvres choisies.* L. Feugère ed., Paris, 1849; reprinted Genève: Slatkine Reprints, 1968. [The relevant passage from the *Recherches de la France,* II, 91–92.]

Rauch, Irmengard, and Gerald E. Carr. 1979. *Linguistic method: essays in honor of Herbert Penzl.* The Hague: Mouton.

Read, Allen Walker. 1936. American projects for an academy to regulate speech. *Publications of the Modern Language Association of America* 51: 1141–79.

Sledd, James, and Wilma R. Ebbitt. 1962. *Dictionaries and that dictionary: a casebook on the aims of lexicographers and the targets of reviewers.* Chicago: Scott, Foresman.

Trescases, Pierre. 1978. Les attitudes françaises envers les grands courants d'emprunt: italianismes et américanismes. Ph.D. dissertation, University of Illinois at Urbana-Champaign.

Webster III. 1961. *Webster's third new international dictionary.* Springfield, Mass.: G. and C. Merriam Co.

Wells, Ronald A. 1973. *Dictionaries and the authoritarian tradition: a study in English usage and lexicography*. The Hague: Mouton.

Yardeni, Myriam. 1971. *La conscience nationale en France pendant les guerres de religion (1559–1598)*. Publications de la Faculté des Lettres et Sciences Humaines de Paris-Sorbonne, sér. "Récherches," 59. Louvain and Paris.

12

Shirley Brice Heath

American English: Quest for a Model

In the late eighteenth century, when successful completion of the American Revolution depended in large part on diplomacy which would insure a substantial loan from the French and the Dutch, there appeared in the mailbags of the Continental Congress a long and curious letter from John Adams. In the midst of his mission to gain money for continuing the Revolution, Adams had written a letter proposing that the United States consider seriously the social and linguistic consequences of spreading English around the world. In this and other letters, Adams proposed an institution to do what the British had never seriously done: to extend English around the world. This challenge, if taken up by the United States, should carry two responsibilities: to determine a model of American English, and to consider political and economic forces critical to the spread of American English (Heath 1976b).

Fifty years later Francis Lieber, a German immigrant to the United States, envisaged a rather different approach to establishing American English as an international language, and as the second language of many U.S. citizens. Lieber, the first editor of the *Encyclopædia Americana* and a prominent political philosopher, corresponded with a great number of academic and political decisionmakers in the United States. In this correspondence he periodically considered ways in which Americans should view their language, and the unique role in language history for which American English was destined. He urged scholars to study English in its non-native contexts, i.e., in those locations outside Great Britain to which English had been transplanted. American scholars, in particular, should focus attention on how varieties of

American English developed within the United States. Numerous scholars of the period set up American English and British English as two subjects of synchronic inquiry. Lieber proposed instead to study American English diachronically, as it became first a variety of British English and then a language form which itself developed varieties.

Attention to English in its American non-native context during the first century of nationhood is marked by two methods of determination, exemplified by the approaches of Adams and Lieber. The first, proposed by Adams, aimed to give a public institution the task of prescribing and promoting a language standard as an ideal for individual speakers for international use, and for the nation as a promoter of English as an international tongue. In this case, the quest for a model depended on the elite's recommending a standard, using it in their own writings and public speech, encouraging its use in American literature, and altering or possibly eliminating societal influences contrary to maintenance of this model (Read 1936; Heath 1976b). The second model, urged by Lieber, was a process for studying language in use and language change; the goal was to define and describe American English in use. This approach was intended not to establish one language form as a model, but to describe the existing structures of American English, to discover patterns of language change, and to report attitudes toward language change. Lieber, a non-native speaker of English, proposed a description of American English as it was used in specific contexts, and a comparison of this description with one of British English in similar contexts. Lieber wished these descriptions to be available over time, so they might indicate patterns of change for the two language varieties. Specifically, these data might enable scholars to draw conclusions regarding the processes of change a language of wider communication might undergo in non-native contexts. In addition, Lieber believed study of the acquisition of English by non-native speakers in America would indicate changes in English introduced by speakers of different mother tongues. Furthermore, such studies involving individual speakers would reveal some of the reasons why English was chosen and maintained as a second language by different groups in the United States. What functions did English serve for citizens who also retained their mother tongue in the United States? In other words, Lieber proposed that Americans did not yet know enough about their language use and changes to establish a single model. If they indeed decided to establish a model, they would need to know much more than they then knew.

Each of these methods of developing a model, that proposed by Adams and that undertaken by Lieber, illustrates specific types of linguistic awareness about American English and its spread to contexts beyond the United States. Each suggests a different attitude toward language, processes of language change and language evaluation, and different uses for knowledge gained from the study of language. Each then becomes a valuable source for the study of the history of linguistics, language change, and the attitudes and behaviors of speakers in the period prior to the development of the public school system, the demise of public oratory, and an increased dependence on printed materials in the United States. Before the mid-nineteenth century, there was a decided focus on studying spoken language and its effect on determining American English. An American literature had not yet developed to the point of worldwide acceptance judged necessary by many intellectuals to insure establishment of language forms used in that literature (see Matthews 1892). Thus oral interactions, including conversations, college debates, public oratory, and lecture series, as well as the political talk of congressional leaders, were the data on which any description of American English had to depend (Heath 1976a). For Francis Lieber, these data were most important for their contribution to understanding processes of language change, and interrelationships between evaluations of language forms by specific groups and changes occurring in the language.

Francis Lieber and Notes on "Americanisms"

Now to examine the views of Francis Lieber on approaches to defining and describing American English, during a period of American history when quests for a model usually took the prescriptive approach. Lieber, for whom the study and recording of language was an avocation, is almost completely unknown among today's linguists.[1] Historians who have examined his writings and interpreted his influence on American culture have either spurned or overlooked his work on language (e.g., Friedel 1947). Yet this German-American political philosopher recognized, recorded, and analyed many aspects of language variation and standardization. Born and raised in Prussia during the time of Frederick William III, Lieber grew up during the Napoleonic era, participated in the Waterloo campaign, and was wounded at the Battle of Namur. Arrested in 1819 for his political views, he was forbidden to study at any university except Jena, where he received his degree in 1820. Disillusioned in efforts to aid in Greece's war of liberation, Lieber went to Italy in 1822, where he found employment as a library assistant for Barthold George Niebuhr. Lieber returned to Germany in 1823 and was given permission to study in Berlin, but was arrested with a group

of young liberals in 1823 and jailed for six months. In 1826 he went
to England, where he taught languages and wrote for German peri-
odicals. Within a year the opportunity to manage a gymnasium and
swimming school in Boston gave him his long-awaited chance to come
to the United States. Shortly after his arrival, however, Lieber became
bored with his job and decided to prepare the *Encyclopædia Americana,*
a translation and remolding of the German encyclopedia *Conversations-
Lexikon.* He published the first edition in thirteen volumes between
1829 and 1833. In 1835 he was elected to the chair of history and
political economy at the University of South Carolina, where he
remained for twenty-one years. There he wrote his *Manual of Political
Ethics and Civil Liberty and Self-Government,* as well as numerous pieces
on language and politics, patriotism, and the nature and origin of
human language. He kept up an active correspondence with others
interested in various aspects of language: William von Humboldt,
Henry Schoolcraft, Joseph Story, Edward Everett, Henry Wadsworth
Longfellow, John Pickering, and Albert Gallatin. In this correspondence
and in his copious notes on language Lieber was not consistently
scientific, detached, and objective; value terms and harsh judgments
of speech and speakers occur throughout his work. With sometimes
extreme inconsistency, he denounced "corruptions" of language one
day and praised dialect diversity and vocabulary expansion the next.
Yet his writings contain the essence of notions such as *register, variation,*
and *pidginization.* He adapted and developed several terms for describing language change processes: *amplification* referred to the adorn-
ments of language or hypercorrections used by insecure speakers (see
below); *holophrastic* referred to languages which were not "analytical,"
but "expressed whole phenomena with condition, mortification, gender,
relation, etc. in one word" (NLI: 33–34). Many of Lieber's explanations,
though couched in the phrases available in his day, have much in
common with today's descriptions of language use in context.

As the Civil War approached, Lieber decided he could not remain
in the South, where his long-standing opposition to slavery had made
him increasingly unpopular. He went to New York, where he was
appointed to the chair of history and political economy at Columbia
College. In 1865 he transferred to the law school, where he devoted
the remainder of his life to archival research and scholarship on
military and international law.

During the 1849–51 period Lieber kept notes on language in the
United States; these are included in ten notebooks he prepared during
this brief period. In these notes he advocated systematic study of
American English which would focus not only on lexicon, but also on

the sound system and grammar of the language. He abhorred what he viewed as the narrow-minded obsession with lexicon which most other scholars of Americanisms followed in this period. Etymological studies of particular words also held little attraction for him. Lieber preferred to focus on what he considered the critical factors of language change: interactions among speakers, interrelationships between written and spoken channels, and the political power accorded the language in the development of political unity and in nationalism as a unifying attitude toward the state.

In the entry for "Americanisms" in an early edition of his *Encyclopædia Americana*, Lieber called attention to what he viewed as the unique situation for linguistic investigations which the development of American English in the United States provided:

> ... England and the United States afford the first instance in history of two great independent and active nations daily developing new and characteristic features, situated at a great distance from each other, and having a common language and literature. These relations must, sooner or later, exert a decisive influence upon the common dialect; for no language is so settled as not to undergo continual changes, if spoken by a nation in the full vigor of social and political life. Authority, in regard to language, will go far, but never can withstand for a long time the energies and wants of a free, industrious and thinking people (1831: 211).

Lieber believed that scholars should consider, as part of the context of language, the sociocultural and political forces which promoted language and its relation to cultural affairs such as literature, art, and science. Of particular interest to language planners today is his analysis of language change in varying political contexts. Lieber believed language developed in accordance with circumstances. The U.S. government's democratic efforts and attempts to establish new political forces led to the creation of new words. A political philosopher, perhaps best known today for his publications on this topic, Lieber claimed that he introduced the words *nationalism, internationalism, individualism, city-state, interdependence, commonwealth of nations,* and *Pan-American* to the vocabulary of American English.

Processes of Change for Language Varieties in Contact

A major assumption behind Lieber's work was the right of linguistic minorities in the United States to retain their own languages while adding English as a second language. Nevertheless, Lieber spoke out strongly for the right of the American political system to choose one language for "nationalization." He recognized that the use of a common language in government and aspects of "national culture" (such as literature, journalism, art, and political philosophy) was necessary. In these spheres an idea, American English, as distinct from British English, would develop. This standard, or variety, drew the greatest attention from lexicographers. However, additional varieties of American English would emerge among various groups and in different regions. It was important to recognize the development of all these varieties; only through collection of data on uses of language in various contexts could such an understanding of these varieties emerge. Knowledge about language structure and use could inform decision-makers who might formulate language policies or programs for others.

Lieber's ten notebooks of observations on language show his irritation with the inadequacies of language data and the narrowness of definitions used by those who attempted to prescribe language use. He charged that individuals failed to define the term *Americanism*; furthermore, in many cases those who collected lexical items for volumes of Americanisms were not familiar enough with British English to know of the existence of these same items outside the United States. Lieber defined American contributions to the lexicon of English as: (1) new words, (2) words with meanings which differed from those used in England, (3) words whose original meanings had been preserved by Americans while British usage had changed, (4) provincialisms preserved in use and meaning in the United States just as they had been upon their introduction to the colonies, and (5) words obsolete in England but still in use in the United States (1831: 210–11).

Beyond careful attention to specific linguistic contexts of lexical items, Lieber focused on the setting, speakers, and contexts of usage in the United States. It was not enough to know that change had taken place; the conditions and results of change were most important. Lieber identified two major processes of change: *simplification* and *amplification*. By *simplification* Lieber referred to changes through which one language variety became simpler than another variety: sentences were shorter, the lexicon smaller, inflections fewer, paraphrases and repetitions more numerous. *Amplification* was a process through which a language variety became more complex: the lexicon was more dependent on Latin, sentences were longer and included greater subordination, and inflections were increased. For Lieber the relative social, political, and economic conditions of speakers were major determinants of these change processes for language varieties in contact.

Lieber identified four conditions or occasions when language became simplified. In the first, a language was being acquired by either a native speaker or a second-language learner. The second occurred when speakers tried to alter their speech for comprehension by listeners of presumed low intelligence. The third took place when two languages came in contact and a pidgin resulted. The fourth was the condition in which one or more languages in contact became more "analytic." In today's terms, these conditions could be termed acquisition, adaptation, pidginization, and analytization. Acquisition was a condition which fascinated Lieber; he studied the process in his own children, in the children of slaves he observed in the Southeast, and in Laura Bridgeman, a child of some notoriety in the early nineteenth century scientific world because she was both blind and deaf. Lieber also noted that simplification, though of different types, took place in both first- and second-language acquisition. Reduplication was the most obvious feature of children's language. Lieber's notebook entry for *Pimmeky-Mimmeky* illustrates his attention to these features: "In England, at least in and about London, used by children and in familiar talk for puny, little with contempt, as a pimmeky-mimmeky boy. This word is harmozophonic and, at the same time has the reduplication, which children, savages etc. so much delight in" (NLI: 58). Lieber also noted that fewer phonological categories, a smaller lexicon, less inflection, and loss of the verb *to be* occurred in the early stages of both first and second language acquisition. Individuals acquiring a second language had a reduced lexicon, shorter sentences, and, in the initial stages of learning, merged the phonological systems of the mother tongue and the second tongue into a single system. Separation of the two systems came at a particular point of fluency. For German and English, Lieber predicted the areas of interference or merging in order of their likelihood of occurrence. He also wrote a "brief and practical German Grammar" in which he attempted to compare the structure and lexicon of German with that of English. He recommended in the preface a contrasting analysis of the two languages and the need for "practical grammars," explaining, "There is no way of teaching . . . so cheering to the scholar as the one I have persued [sic] namely to make of the many points of affinity, starting points of instruction. I have, in addition, strictly adhered to the principle of making my grammar as practical as possible, though I might entirely deviate in doing so, from long established order" (1838). In correspondence with his son, who was away in school in Germany, Lieber frequently provided contrastive grammar lessons in English and German. He was keenly aware of the problems facing German speakers who wanted to learn English for practical uses in the United States.

Adaptation was the second condition for simplification to which

Lieber gave attention. One language variety is made simpler by the speaker for the use of people who are regarded as not fully competent, either linguistically or intellectually. Adapted language is the talk used in addressing young children, foreigners, and those of a lower class or station. Lieber suggested that within every community of speakers there existed individuals who were regarded as unable to understand readily the normal speech of the community. Power groups adapted their language in accordance with predetermined notions of the abilities of those individuals. The result of adaptation was that "everything not absolutely necessary to point out the most material and, generally, physical objects is left out . . . hence all subjunctive, all nicer conditions, relations, all mutual dependence, all delicate discrimination, all continued expression of a condition already once indicated is non existing . . . just as it finds no place in the nursery grammar" (NLVI: 168).

Lieber was particularly disturbed that some commentators on language equated simplicity of grammatical form with simplicity of cognitive development and abilities. While professor of political philosophy at the University of South Carolina, Lieber had collected numerous examples of Negro speech. He sometimes used these to argue for a rational analysis of the language of blacks and other powerless groups. To those who said that blacks and others who used simplified varieties of English were incapable of abstract thought, Lieber pointed out that language input to these individuals often did not include abstractions. The attributes of objects or events were not explained to either children or servants. Furthermore, professionals did not offer these explanations to their clients. Instead, these individuals were given examples or applications of abstract theories or descriptions of attributes. "So difficult is it for the human mind to understand abstract ideas that to make clear to a child, the meaning of any quality, for instance *malicious, mild*, we explain the word and immediately give an instance which latter [*sic*] makes the thing clear. The same with servants, the same with all people, lawyers, students of politics etc. The instance makes clear" (NLI: n.p.). Lieber charged that those who denied that West Indian creole languages or the language of American blacks used abstractions confused effect with cause. Their simplified language would show the effects of the simplification of language initiated by the power figure, the ultimate cause of any simple language used by powerless groups.

Yet another condition of simplification noted by Lieber for the first stages of language contact was pidginization. In cases of pidginization, there were restrictions on the uses for power languages. Lieber collected data from travelers in South America, the Caribbean, and the United States to substantiate his views of pidginization. In particular, his comparisons of Chinook jargon and what little knowledge he could gather of the pidgins and creoles of the Caribbean made him highly suspicious of a single-source theory for the origin of pidgin languages. Lieber noted the tendency toward truncation and monosyllables, retention of the intonation patterns of the first language, and the adoption of lexical items from the language of power. Lieber saw processual similarities shared by all pidgins and creoles, in terms of changes in the original languages of contact.

Lieber's final condition for simplification was that of analytization. He believed that certain language varieties, by the very nature of their grammar and the density of their lexicon, could be seen as representing a specific stage of language contact. Some languages were highly inflected; others, more "analytic," had less inflection. Lieber noted that for some languages which remained in contact over a long period of time, loss of inflection and the redistribution of functions among the remaining elements in the language resulted. Though he realized the history of American English was too brief to draw conclusions of this sort, Lieber could not resist speculating on changes in its lexicon. Lieber regarded English as highly polysemantic with each word carrying numerous meanings. However, there were far more homonyms in American English than in British English, and Americans used periphrastic constructions much more frequently. Lieber expressed this by saying: "The clavichord on which the Englishman plays has a wider keyboard. The American is far more fluent, but the Englishman possesses a richer stock of words" (NLI: 29).

Amplification was the opposite process of change for English in its non-native context; it occurred when individuals acquiring a new language, or style of speaking for particular uses, attempted to over-correct or exaggerate stylistic features used by their language models. Insecurity about language use contributed to many types of amplification. This malady was not restricted to children, blacks, and foreigners; it also afflicted American writers who were insecure about the worth of their productions as measured against British and European standards. For those in the first category (children, blacks, foreigners, or others of lower status) Lieber noted the use of verb phrases instead of single verbs and the incorrect formation of verbs from nouns. For example, he heard a young black girl say, when looking at a picture of a man looking through a telescope, "he is sighting something" (NLI: 24–25). Lieber believed that individuals who dealt with language in workaday communication, such as mariners or others who received directions, tended to form verbs from nouns; for example, *assemblaged* for *assembled, flighted* for *fled, certificated* for *certified, pleasured* for *pleased.*

Lieber observed that, when writing, U.S. citizens used words of Latin origin more frequently than Anglo-Saxon or English words. For formal uses Americans seemed to choose overstatement: politicians were called "great men," "men of great intellect." For this exaggerated language use, Lieber blamed newspapers, often written by journalists who had had, in his view, deficient educations and did not know how to write simple prose.

Other aspects of linguistic insecurity characterized American English. To hold one's place in conversation and to reinforce conversational partners, an American often used *well.* Tag questions and other mechanisms used by the insecure to "hedge" on the certainty of their statements were noted by Lieber. Of the Southern expression "most generally sometimes," Lieber said: "if I am asked what is the meaning, I would answer just what it indicates. It is the expression of an unskilled person asserting and taking away again, as an unskillful draughtsman rubs out half he has drawn. It means more than sometimes, less than most generally, brief it means generally" (NLI: IV, 32; V, 136).

The place of the word *interesting* as a filler in conversation was noted by Lieber as used by "many lightly educated persons who nevertheless largely mingle in society... It is a word used when want of command does not suggest the proper and specific word." Lieber judged that women and ministers were especially fond of it (NLI I, 46–47).

Conclusion

In considering language in non-native contexts, Lieber proposed processes of change and stipulated specific conditions which would restrict or encourage them. In particular, he observed that English or any language being introduced as an international or national tongue would assume specific functions because of its particular uses in the public sphere. He urged non-native speakers of English not to attempt to maintain their own language for literature, but to accept the predominance of English-language literature, law, science, and art. Language shift in certain functions was, however, specifically not recommended by Lieber; these functions were in-group associations with family and friends. The existence of what are today recognized as registers and domains of usage was noted by Lieber in his analysis of code-switching. He himself used English and German in much of his personal correspondence; he wrote poetry in German, political philosophy in both English and German, and official letters in English. He suggested that the order in which English should be learned was (1) politeness formulae, (2) "common intercourse" for public occasions, and (3) for the special purposes of business and specific occupations. The question of other domains was much more difficult; in these, non-native speakers would "feel the leaden weight of a foreign language weighing heavily on their tongue," and when they spoke of those things "dearest to their hearts," they would choose their mother tongue (1835: 202). However, they would also shift from language to language according to topic, setting, and audience.

Linguists and sociolinguists must today judge Lieber as a man ahead of his time. He was concerned with processes of language change and language in social contexts. He collected and commented on the development of pidgins and creoles, language varieties within English, and the language of the powerful and the powerless. He attempted to describe and name processes of change which occurred as a result of dialect convergence and the interrelationships of specific registers of individuals in social or professional contexts. He noted that when two speech communities which share a minimum of linguistic competence and common cultural understanding come together, each must adopt special strategies for communication. These strategies in turn lead to processes of language change, either simplification (occurring in acquisition, adaptation, pidginization, or analytization) or amplification which lead to shifts in syntax and lexicon.

As linguists eager for a view of language and language use in past social contexts, we can only regret that Lieber's wide-ranging interests and his increasing distraction by the Civil War and the abolitionist movement kept him from devoting himself entirely to recording language attitudes, speech events, and social and psychological forces of language change. His writings represent one way of approaching the question of a model of American English. As an immigrant to the United States during a period of intense nationalistic development, Lieber reacted to problems of national and individual language choice. He recommended a policy promoting a national language and tolerating other languages for use in education. He advocated cooperation of philologists, missionaries, and government personnel in formulating language decisions. He practiced and promoted careful observation and recording of language in use. He formulated theories of language change based on his understanding of register and channel, constraints in communication between individuals of different class and educational backgrounds, and his view of simplification and amplification processes for languages in contact and interpersonal communication.

The type of linguistic relativism recommended and practiced by Lieber decreased markedly after the mid-nineteenth century. By the 1890s those who were trying to provide a model of American English turned again to the prescriptivism Adams had recommended. Reformers seeking a model of American English wished to place the responsibility for language choice and change on public institutions—namely, public schools and literary societies. Grammars for those learning English as a second language during this period prescribe grammatical rules, proscribe other languages, and recommend specific behaviors for rapid assimilation (Heath 1980).

Historical research, often invoked to show "how we got where we are," can also provide a perspective from which to compare current interpretations of behavior with interpretations of past societies. In addition, a historically informed sociolinguistics may help keep us from reinventing the wheel when we write our programmatic statements or observe specific communities. Lieber said: "A living language does not only mean a language spoken by a living people, but also a living thing itself with all the capacities, rights and necessities of life, that is, of *change, expansion,* and *elimination.* " He further recommended study not only of languages themselves, but also of their ideologies: "The ideology of languages is yet in its infancy, and waits the hand of genius to methodize and elucidate it. If, however, it shall continue to advance, as it has done within the last thirty years, there is no doubt but that it will, in time, throw considerable light on the history of man" (NL: n.p.). Lieber's study of English in non-native contexts offers a challenge—an assessment of where we have traveled in the hundred and fifty years since his quest for a model, and a suggestion of attention to the ideology behind that model.[2]

NOTE

1. Research for this paper was supported by a grant from the National Endowment for the Humanities in 1975 and from Winthrop College. Lieber was first introduced to an audience of linguists in "Standard English in the United States: An Early National View from an Inside Outsider," a paper given by this author at a University of Chicago conference on Language Variety and Its Implications for American Cultural Pluralism in 1977. Special acknowledgment is here given to Martha Holder of Winthrop College for her work as research assistant on this project. The manuscripts upon which this chapter is based are in the Lieber collections of the Library of Congress, Caroliniana Library (University of South Carolina), and the Henry E. Hun-

tington Library (San Marino, California). Citations from the ten volumes of Lieber's Notes on Language at the Huntington Library appear as NL, plus volume number, and are used here with permission of the Huntington Library.

2. For further discussion of the issues related to this topic and references to other sources, see Ferguson and Heath, eds. 1981.

REFERENCES

Ferguson, Charles A., and Shirley B. Heath, eds. 1981. *Language in the USA.* London: Cambridge University Press.

Friedel, Frank. 1947. *Francis Lieber: nineteenth-century liberal.* Baton Rouge: Louisiana State University Press.

Heath, Shirley Brice. 1976a. Early American attitudes toward variation in speech: a view from social history and sociolinguistics. Forum lecture, LSA Institute.

———. 1976b. A national language academy? Debate in the new nation. *International Journal of the Sociology of Language* 11: 9–43.

———. 1980. Standard English: biography of a symbol. Pp. 3–32 in *Standards and dialects in English,* ed. T. Shopen and J. M. Williams. Cambridge: Winthrop.

Lieber, Francis. 1831. Americanism. Pp. 210–11 in *Encyclopædia Americana,* I. Philadelphia: Carey and Lea.

———. 1835. *The stranger in America.* Philadelphia: Carey, Lea and Blanchard.

———. 1838. A brief and practical German grammar on a new plan with particular reference to the grammatical affinities between the German and English idioms.

Matthews, Brander. 1892. *Americanisms and Briticisms.* New York: Harper and Brothers.

Read, Allen Walker. 1936. American projects for an academy to regulate speech. *PMLA* 51: 1141–79.

13

Rodney F. Moag

The Life Cycle of Non-Native Englishes: A Case Study

The non-native varieties of English furnish fertile, and relatively untapped, ground for study of the processes of sociolinguistic change. These varieties have grown up in recent times as second languages in multilingual former colonies of Great Britain; hence the alternative terms "new Englishes" and "Third World Englishes." The three terms, as used by Kachru (1977) and others, are synonymous, save in the case of Caribbean English (where "non-native" does not apply, since the vernacular variety, Creole, is also English [LePage 1968: 440]).

The last areas to come under colonization, whether as British colonies or as protectorates of Australia or New Zealand, were the South Pacific Islands. Tonga, Samoa, Nauru, Fiji, Papua New Guinea, Tuvalu (Ellice Islands), the Gilberts, and the Solomon Islands were colonized in the late nineteenth and early twentieth centuries; all are independent now, while the Cook Islands, American Samoa, Niue, and the Tokelaus are not yet free. English plays a part as either a foreign language (FL) or a second language (SL) in all of the above. Since the emerging variety here has not been reported in the linguistically oriented literature, the first goal here will be to set South Pacific English in its rightful place alongside the other recognized non-native varieties of English. The second goal will be to set forth a tentative "life cycle of non-native Englishes" following the model of Hall's (1962) "Life Cycle of Pidgin Languages," including the constituent processes by which the variety begins as a FL, becomes a SL, and reverts to FL status again. I shall draw primarily on the case of Fiji, owing to my three years' research and university teaching in that country; but I shall also draw secondarily on data from other islands in the region, and from beyond.

Constituent Processes of the Life Cycle

Four processes are posited as significant constituents of the life cycle: transportation, indigenization, expansion in use and function, and institutionalization. A fifth, restriction of use and function, does not apply in all cases.

Figure 1. The Life Cycle of Non-Native Englishes

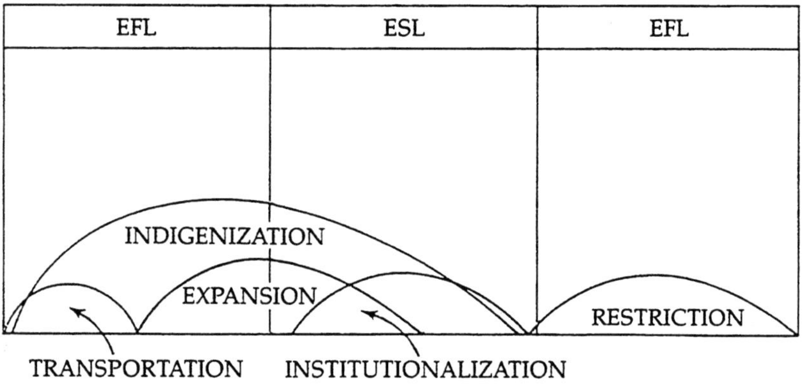

It is not possible to regard these as stages in the strict sense, since they are not fully consecutive. Each process begins in the order stated, but once under way, it overlaps with succeeding processes. Indigenization, for example, precedes, but runs concurrently with, expansion of use and function, and well into institutionalization. (See Ch. 7 in this volume; also Kachru 1983.)

Transportation

Little need be said about this first process, save that it involves bringing English into a new environment for purposes of a more or less permanent nature, such as colonial administration. Contact between English-speaking aliens and some segment of the local population, usually a very limited one, will be frequent and recurrent enough, and the dominance of the visitors will be clear enough, to require that the locals learn English. The most common case is that of a class of clerks trained and retained to assist a colonial administration, but other relationships are also possible. The first ESL group in the Belgian Congo consisted of house servants of English-speaking missionaries.

Indigenization

Indigenization, a term used in Moag and Moag (1977: 3), is a process of language change by which the new variety of English becomes distinct from the parent imported variety, and from other indigenized varieties elsewhere. Kachru (1977) has used "nativization" in much the same sense. The first step occurs when English-speaking newcomers come into contact with items of the local material and nonmaterial culture for which there are no equivalents in their home environment or language. In Fijian English, there can be no other word for *daruka* (a local vegetable) or for *vesi* (a local hardwood), since they are not known or named elsewhere. Similarly, institutions such as *kerekere* (a system of gaining things by begging for them from members of one's own group—a recognized system in Fijian society [Capell 1973: 95]) and *mataqali* ("the primary social division in Fiji" [Capell 1973: 142]) have no precise or succinct English translations. Hence, only local terms for them will serve.

A multilingual, multicultural setting such as Fiji's leads to multiple borrowing. *Bhājī* (a class of greens), *dāl* (a class of lentils), *pūjā* (a Hindu devotional ceremony), and *divālī* (the Hindu festival of lights) are items and concepts drawn from Hindi.

Weinreich's (1951: 85) hierarchy of the likelihood of borrowing lists "sentence words without syntactic function," such as interjections, as having "very great" likelihood of borrowing, whereas "free morphemes with syntactic functions," such as nouns and verbs, have only "considerable" likelihood. Samples of indigenized varieties of English from around the world would seem to call for free lexical items being in first (rather than second) position, in terms of either degree of borrowing or order of occurrence.

Bright (1973: 213) identifies two types of initial contact between colonials and natives in the New World, one focusing on the indigenous culture, the second focusing on the conqueror's or invader's culture; both resulted in the borrowing of such free morphemes. Bright does not rank these chronologically or in any other way, but the former seems typical of situations relating to exploration or trading, while the latter would be typical of established conquest and colonization. In the South Pacific, an extended period of sandalwood trading, whaling, exploration, and later mission activity preceded actual colonial rule, but these all involved the use of the vernaculars (see Geraghty 1978 and Schütz 1972: 29–35).

At least some early linguists recognized that language contact situations could result in structural as well as lexical borrowing (Boas 1929: 6). This later led to the recognition of linguistic areas in South Asia (Emeneau 1956), the Balkans, and with Indian languages in California (Gumperz 1968: 466). More recently the transfer of discourse features, including communicative norms (Richards 1982), have been noted. In this initial phase of the indigenization process, however, there are conditions which effectively block borrowing above the lexical level from native languages into English, and probably vice versa. Local learners of English are subjected to an extremely high degree of exposure to native speaker models, whether in the classroom or on the job, and they use English primarily for communication with native-speaking aliens. Under these conditions there is full reinforcement of native-like features of the language. Non-native features which second-language speakers might introduce would not only find no reinforcement, but would be very likely to receive explicit correction. The situation is completely reversed later, but at this point the sociolinguistic climate will tolerate only the importation of specific items for which there is no direct equivalent in the imported native-speaker model of English.

The second phase of the indigenization process comes when members of the local colonial elite (and/or the cadre of menial servants) begin to use English for communication among themselves. This happens in two distinct though not necessarily disconnected ways. First, English may begin to be used as a lingua franca, in addition to or instead of local link languages, enabling those of different language backgrounds who may work or live together, due to the new colonial system, to communicate with each other in a more intensive way than was customary in the pre-colonial situation.

Second, English often tends to become the preferred medium for discussing topics associated with the alien, but now in most senses dominant, culture. Both of these tendencies can occur, and will reinforce each other, in a multilingual setting where they are the harbingers of the more generalized expansion of use and function to come. The topical conditioning of the use of English can operate in a monolingual setting as well, when the new items and institutions brought by the new rulers are alien and have no ready equivalents in local language or culture. This phase sees the transfer of more native features into English, as locals bring familiar items and conventions in their own languages and cultures into play in the new situation. These include additional lexemes, grammatical features through direct transfer or overgeneralization, and communicative norms. (See Chs. 16, 17, 18 in this volume; also Smith, ed. 1987.)

This particular phase tends to have considerable longevity, persisting as long as English education remains an elitist phenomenon. In Fiji, the government assumed responsibility for education in 1916; it began promoting English by insisting that schools teach it in order to receive government grants-in-aid, and by requiring that only certified teachers teach it. A full generation later, in an anthropological study of the second most important island, Quain wrote that "all but the highest education is accomplished in the language of Bau (Standard Fijian). I did not see more than half a dozen Fijians on Vanua Levu with a working knowledge of English, and most of these had been imported from more sophisticated regions to perform official duties" (1948: 68). Through the colonial period three separate commissions urged giving greater prominence to English, but not until the 1960s were enough school-agers actually enrolled in secondary schools to make this possible (Fiji *Report* 1970). The New Hebrides are still in this stage, with the government having taken over education from the churches (who used the vernaculars) in the late 1950s.

Subsequent phases of the indigenization process run concurrently with later processes in the life cycle. They will, therefore, be subsumed under the following two sections.

Expansion in Use and Function
This process begins with the extension of English (or the degree of its use) to new domains, particularly education, the media, and government services. English may have been used in these domains previously, but only by an elite group of locals; witness the quote from Quain, cited above.

Obviously, expansion must first take place in the domain of education, since the requisite skills of literacy and aural comprehension must be acquired before the populace can use English for paperwork and face-to-face contact with clerks and government officials. That English-medium education is a necessary but not a sufficient condition for the diffusion of the language through the society is exemplified in the South Pacific by the island kingdom of Tonga. This monolingual nation has English-medium education from the upper primary grades onward, but English is still a foreign (not a second) language in the society. A Tongan can do everything he needs to do, save complete his high school matriculation, in his own language. Radio broadcasting is almost exclusively in Tongan, the weekly newspaper is bilingual, and all government communications are either bilingual or, at the lower level, solely in Tongan. The English versions are principally for the benefit of the expatriates who work at higher administrative levels in the government, or as secondary school teachers. This example indicates that the concept "home-school bilingualism" (Kloss 1966: 10; Christopherson 1973: 74) is inadequate, since it does not tell us anything about the role of the home language and the school language in other domains of societal activity.

The expansion process, if fully run, sees the role of English shift from that of a foreign to a second language. This process seems to be blocked in monolingual societies, whatever the stage of development of the local vernacular. In a number of multilingual settings it is clearly influenced, and even potentially precluded, by the presence of a contending local "mid language" (Abdulaziz 1972) already operating as a lingua franca, such as Swahili in East Africa and pidgin in three Pacific nations. The degree of expansion possible for English will be governed by several factors, including the prestige of the mid language, its degree of "language modernization" (Kloss 1966: 15) or "state of development" (Ferguson 1977: 44), and its functions and degree of use within the critical domains.

In the New Hebrides, for example, a condominium government is jointly administered by Great Britain and France; some children attend English-medium schools, and others French-medium schools. Pidgin, locally called Bichelamar (Guy 1964), is the only language which can unite all the people. It is already used widely by all the churches, in the bilingual newsletters published by both governments (one English and Bichelamar, the other French and Bichelamar), and in the speeches and tracts of major political parties; furthermore, it has more radio air time than either colonial language. English seems destined to play a fairly limited role in the New Hebrides, particularly if Pidgin should undergo two final steps in its growing legitimatization, i.e., becoming the medium of instruction in primary school, and being made the official language of government (as now seems likely).

Pidgin is also expanding in use and function in Papua New Guinea (Wurm 1977: 334). Its official promotion for use in education and as the official language of the country has been thwarted as much by the presence of a competing local lingua franca, Hiri Motu, as by the expansion of English. Both local languages enjoy sufficient use in both formal and informal domains to limit the advance of English. This is less true in the Solomon Islands. There, though pidgin is the sole national lingua franca, it is still basically an oral language occupying only domains of informal social contact, oral political activity, and more indigenous types of radio programs. English, for the time being at least, has full sway in written domains, though this could change quite rapidly if the current efforts to standardize pidgin orthography are successful. (For Papua New Guinea English, see Smith 1986.)

Multilingual nations such as Fiji, which lack a contending national lingua franca, give English a clearer path to second-language status. The neutral role of English in such situations has been acknowledged by several writers, including Kloss (1966: 8) and Pride (1978). This neutrality is political in character, i.e., giving no group the advantage of having its own language singled out for official status. Also important is the social neutrality of English which functions as follows within monolingual societies or groups. Many vernaculars have special registers, or systems of address, for persons of distinct social standing. Fijian has a chiefly subcode; Tongan has distinct forms for addressing commoners, nobility, and royalty; a septimodal system exists in Samoa (Malia 1976). Under the impact of modernization, young people growing up in these societies today do not gain active control over these special subcodes. Tongans and Fijians have told me that they find English the only safe medium in which to address those of higher status (Moag 1978c: 74). English not only hides their inability in the specialized vernacular registers, but also allows them to meet traditional superiors on a more or less equal footing. This is aided by the fact that English in the second-language context has a more limited repertoire of social variants.

The birth of an informal variety. On the one hand, lack of internal variation makes the non-native variety of English a social as well as political leveler. On the other hand, a major feature of the indigenization and expansion processes is an increase in internal variation through the creation of a separate stylistic variant used for informal purposes. Such varieties are well reported for West Africa, India, Singapore and Malaysia, and the Philippines. Because of the special situation in the Caribbean, the informal variety came first and became mother tongue for imported plantation workers. The catalytic agent for these informal varieties is often the "all-English rule" in government or mission-operated schools. Teachers and administrators institute the rules as a means of providing maximal practice in the target language. The pupils, showing far more sociolinguistic awareness than their pedagogues, immediately realize that the English they have been taught in the classroom is entirely inappropriate to their activities on the playground. In the absence of any precise model, they are forced to draw upon their own resources—with the result that this variety shows a much higher proportion of local and interlanguage (Selinker 1972) features. Two investigators have documented the influence of local languages in Fiji, though using different names for the new variety of English: " 'the dialect' seems to share certain grammatical features with Fijian" (Kelley 1975: 36–37). "Fiji Pidgin seems to have an identical vowel system and shared politeness markers and gestures to Fijian" (Geraghty 1977: 4–5).

The first name employed for the informal variety of English in Fiji was "playground English." I have elsewhere coined the term "Colloquial Fiji English (CFE)" (Moag and Moag 1977: 3) and have cited a few characteristic borrowed lexical items. *Paisa* (money), *choro* (to steal), and *paidar* (on foot) are taken from Fiji Hindi. Fijian examples such as *kasou* (drunk), *lamu* (afraid), and *talasi* (to steal) are in this category. None of these items would be found in Standard Fiji English.

The results of languages in contact are, of course, two-way, involving mutual borrowing. This does not mean, however, that the degree of borrowing will be equal in each direction. At the most superficial level (that of lexemes) the number of items borrowed into local languages from English, which serves as "a global carrier wave for news, information, entertainment, and administration and as the language in which has taken place the genesis of the second industrial and scientific revolution" (Strevens 1977: 115), will be far higher than that which even the most indigenized variety of local English takes on from the vernaculars. Moag (1979) mentions the extensive English borrowings in Fiji Hindi and Fijian, and lists of English loans in Fijian appear in a phonological treatment by Schütz (1978b). Mutual borrowing has been documented in all other major ESL areas as well. The following extreme (but not an atypical) example was overheard from a young female Fiji Indian sales clerk: "*Shīlā* account book use *karā*, I think." ("Shila used the account book, I think.") The italics show that the female name, Shīlā, and the verb *karā*, needed to make the borrowed verb "use" syntactically acceptable, are the only native items in the sentence. The order of major constituents (subject-object-verb) in the kernel sentence clearly marks it as Hindi, not English.

In a language contact situation such as in Fiji, on the discourse level, casual observations seem to indicate that more features are borrowed into English from vernaculars than vice versa. The balance of borrowing tips in the opposite direction on the semantic-syntactic level. This suggests two complementary clines of borrowing which, together, illustrate an approximate representation of the effects of long-term contact. It is given here in the hope of sparking the detailed studies needed to test its validity. (See Subramani 1980 and Ch. 16 in this volume.)

Institutionalization of the New Varieties

This is a gradual process, and it is not easy to pinpoint precisely when it begins. Several factors play an important role in the process, however; these are dealt with in turn below.

The role of local creative writers. The publication in Australia of the Papuan Vincent Eri's novel, *The Crocodile*, in 1970 and the publication in New Zealand of *Sons for the Return Home* by the Samoan Albert Wendt in 1973 were hallmarks in the evolution of the newly emerging South Pacific literature. These were, however, directed as much at audiences in native English-speaking countries as at island audiences. Though no novels have yet been published by writers in Fiji, their poems and short stories are clearly directed mainly to a home audience. The founding of the South Pacific Creative Arts Society and the publication of the *Mana Annuals*, beginning in 1973, expressly "to influence islanders to write, and . . . to submit what they write," and the appearance of *Mana Review* since 1976, containing literary criticism as well as creative writing, are symptomatic of both the regional character and the ongoing nature of South Pacific literature. The motivation for these writers was aptly expressed by one of their number, Subramani: "At the moment there is a great deal of interest in creative writing in Fiji, and it is clear from recent developments that local writers will employ English to examine themselves and communicate their identities to the rest of the world" (1978: 142). There is, to date, a certain amount of literary activity in the vernaculars in Fiji (Moag 1978a: 135–37), and writers from the New Hebrides sometimes translate their works into Pidgin.

The first generation of creative writers in the region have, for the most part, received their secondary or tertiary training abroad, in native English-speaking countries. The crop of younger writers now coming up are largely students at the University of the South Pacific in Fiji; they have received all of their education in an ESL environment. A distinctly regional character is found in the works of both groups, in terms of both themes and linguistic norms. Hindi words and phrases are liberally sprinkled throughout the works of Nandan, Pillai, and Subramani; Fijian terms appear in the writing of Seru and others. Nacola's plays liberally employ Colloquial Fiji English (1976).

Local literary activity becomes institutionalized when it becomes regenerative. Works from all of the above-mentioned authors play a large part in the English curriculum of the University of the South Pacific, and are now finding their way into the secondary school curricula. This new literature serves dual functions, motivating students to take up the pen themselves, and providing a model for accepted

241

norms when they do so. The local importance of English writers in India, West Africa, and the Caribbean is well reported elsewhere in the literature. (See Chs. 14, 15 in this volume.)

The role of localization of teachers. LePage (1968: 439–40) provides a very clear description of the linguistic consequences of the extension of secondary education to the general populace, and of the subsequent localization of the teaching staff in the Caribbean. In the colonial period a local elite, taught and trained by expatriate English-speaking teachers, usually finished their educations abroad, in native English-speaking countries such as the United States, Canada, or Britain. The bulk of the population acquired no meaningful competence in standard English during their few years of primary education. Nowadays more secondary schools have been built, and teacher-training institutions are opened locally; a generation of students arises which has been taught completely by West Indian teachers, and which has received all of its training in the home country. I would agree with LePage that this produces "speakers of a more divergent dialect" (1968: 439), but not with his proposed remedial program to correct the steadily widening gap between "what is supposed to be happening in the schools and what is actually happening" (1968: 440). Increasing divergence from the imported native model during the institutionalization period is as inevitable as it is abhorrent to most expatriate (and even local elite) observers and educators (see Kachru 1977: 33 and Ch. 3 in this volume).

The opening of the University of the South Pacific in 1968 meant that, by 1972, locally trained diploma- and degree-holders were being supplied to the education systems of the eleven South Pacific nations which that institution serves. In Fiji, secondary teachers, and all tertiary ones save at the university itself, are localized. A growing proportion of them are locally trained, largely by ESL speakers. Secondary schools in the other South Pacific nations are still predominantly staffed by expatriate teachers, but localization is under way and should be complete within the foreseeable future.

The end result of localization of teachers is a stable situation in which the young people of the society learn the formal variety of English from second-language-speaking locals, who also learned it from second-language speakers. There is negligible input from native-speaker models, particularly aural ones.

The role of the media. The press and radio also play a part in the legitimization of the new non-native English. In terms of a spoken model, all locally originated programs in Fiji, both scripted and ad-libbed, are now handled by local personnel. As was the case with secondary education, the Fiji Broadcasting Commission was staffed and run by expatriates up to the 1970s in all its English-medium activities. English-language staffs are still expatriate in the New Hebrides and in American Samoa, but are fully localized elsewhere, though the amount of English versus vernacular programming varies markedly along at least two dimensions throughout the South Pacific. The multilingual (ESL) countries have a substantial amount of English-language programming, while the independent monolingual (EFL) nations, Tonga and Samoa, have little save the international news relayed from Radio Australia. Colonial versus independent status is also a significant dimension, as evidenced by the higher proportion of English programming in the monolingual Cook Islands and American Samoa. Local English program personnel have generally not received their language training overseas. Native models still comprise a small part of the radio service, however, both through relayed news broadcasts and through a few transcribed programs furnished from the BBC and the Voice of America. There is no television in the region outside the French territories, save in American Samoa, which airs both locally originated educational programs and commercial programs from the United States on film.

The print media in Fiji and the rest of the South Pacific are at a less advanced stage of localization. Most writers and subeditors for Fiji's two daily English newspapers are locals, but the chief editor and one or two writers on each are still expatriates. Conditions vary from country to country, according to language situation and political status. The New Hebrides has no commercial press. The English text for the biweekly newsletter put out by the colonial government is, not surprisingly, written by expatriates. The bilingual weekly papers in Tonga and Samoa have already been mentioned above.

Even with full localization of the media, there will inevitably be a higher proportion of native-speaker-model material in the written domain than in the aural one. Papers use numerous items from the international news services, and popular books and magazines abound in the bookstores. The English-language movies are all imported from native-speaking countries, but their clear lack of relevance to the local context, and their only occasional attendance (compared to daily newspaper reading) give them less influence as a model. It seems clear that local news items will be read or listened to with greatest attention and that the local themes, cultural assumptions, and language style will have the greatest real impact. Several observers, including LePage (1968: 441), have pointed out that speakers of the "new Englishes" often believe themselves to be speaking one of the older, more accepted, models, usually British English. The distinction between idealized and real behavior is all important here. If the kind of conditioned switching between different varieties within the new English outlined by Kachru (1977: 32) exists, then we must conclude that, on the subconscious level at least, speakers are aware of the differences that distinguish their own indigenized English from that of other native-speaking and second-language-speaking countries, and that they can select, albeit intuitively, a model to follow. Within this context the localization of media staff becomes clearly significant, both as a creative force and as a reinforcing one. Movies, broadcasts, and printed matter produced outside the region become peripheral. The role of the media has been little acknowledged (hence their situation has not been reported) in treatments of the other new Englishes. Observations during travel and casual reports by others seem to substantiate a similar pattern of the change from expatriate to local staff, and performance model, in the English media of most Third World countries.

   The role of vernacular use and policy. The place of the vernacular languages in the overall language use pattern has a direct bearing on the role which English can assume. A brief "sketch of language use patterns in Fiji" appears in Moag and Moag (1977: 9–10), and a more detailed "sociolinguistic sketch of Fiji" can be found in Moag (1978c: 69–77). Basically, Fiji society is moving away from the linguistic diversity which Gumperz (1968: 469–70) cites as typical of "inter-mediate" societies, though this is happening at different rates in different communities. For the Indians, the first stage involved the disappearance of the regional Indian languages and the adoption of Fiji Hindi as home language by all of the present generation (Moag 1977, 1979). Fijian dialects are still spoken in their home regions, but are increasingly influenced by the standard dialect (Schütz 1972: 107). Geraghty's (1977) research shows instances of whole villages adopting standard dialect.

   The second stage involves the decreasing participation in religious and other cultural rituals where formal or ritual varieties of Hindi or Fijian are used. Rituals which are retained are altered to curtail the use of these varieties. The very different Indian and Fijian firewalking ceremonies are now run mainly as fund-raising events for temples, or as attractions at tourist hotels, respectively; English is used, in deference to the new type of audience. The third stage involves enlarging the functions of the new informal variety of English, Colloquial Fiji English (CFE), with two results. First, more specialized local lingua francas are forced out—Pidgin Fijian and Pidgin Hindi are still used, but less so. Second, use of the inter-communal contact code is extended into contexts involving only members of one community. Geraghty (1977: 4) reports the use of CFE between Fijians, and attributes this to the carryover of English's high prestige even to the homegrown informal variety.

As urbanization and development proceed, more and more locals aspire to white-collar jobs, and to the English competence needed to obtain them. Two studies of Indian parents in Fiji in the 1950s showed a clear preference for English rather than vernaculars in the schools (Adam 1958). A fourth stage in the ascendancy of English involves the modification of official policies so as to advance English and downgrade vernaculars. Through the 1950s, secondary school pupils prepared for and took the Hindi and Fijian language exams in both the junior and senior Cambridge examinations, thereby achieving enough proficiency in the standard formal variety to be able to read and take part in cultural events, etc. Now that vernaculars are optional, nonexaminable subjects, they receive little attention, if indeed they are taught at all (Moag 1978a: 135). Thus the educational system has passed from a biliterate to a transitional one (Fishman 1978: 409), where the vernaculars are used as media of instruction, with accompanying ESL classes, only for the first three years, and solely for the purpose of preparing pupils to function in the succeeding seven or more years of English medium ahead. The products of this system exhibit what I have termed "skewed bilingualism" (Moag 1978b: 3). Students have functional competence in only one formal language variety, Standard Fiji English. Whenever they wish to participate in formal activities, then, whether inter- or intra-communal, people will naturally use English. Siegel (1973: 2) found a shift from Standard Hindi to English in formal domains. Moag (1979) reports most Fiji Indians having only passive aural competence in Standard Hindi. Fijian is in a somewhat better situation than Hindi, owing both to the use of the same alphabet as English and to the slower pace of modernization within that community (Moag 1978a: 136), but Geraghty (1977) does report that urban Fijians tend to avoid traditional activities in which formal Fijian is used. The relative position of vernaculars versus English in other South Pacific countries has already been mentioned.

Restriction of the Use and Function of English

This final stage in the life cycle is not evident in any South Pacific nation. It does appear imminent in the Philippines, and is clearly under way in other multilingual nations of Asia and Africa. It involves the displacement of English by a local official language, usually through the processes of language planning as described by Rubin and Jernudd

(1971) and others, in those very domains of government activities, education, and the media which had permitted English to rise to a position of dominance during the pre-independence period. Fishman has rightly pointed out that a society cannot tolerate the luxury of two languages occupying the same functional territory (1978: 411). Thus when newly independent governments of the Philippines, Malaysia, and India (among others) mount vigorous campaigns promoting the national language, English is bound, in time, to revert to the status of a foreign language studied and used by a small elite—the status which it held much earlier in the life cycle. In Malaysia, for instance, Malay has become the language of instruction not only through secondary schooling, but in many university subjects as well. Anyone obtaining a government job must know it, whatever his mother tongue.

This new EFL stage contrasts with the EFL stage at the beginning of the life cycle, in that use of English is more limited. The elites in the new independent nations use English only in technical and scientific subjects at the university level, and for some professional activities, whereas formerly the local colonial elite used the language in all activities relating to school and work.

The concept of life cycle implies that there is both a beginning and an end to the process and organism under study. Once the local national language is firmly established, the creative writing, media activities, and other support mechanisms in English will fade. There could then be a reorientation away from the indigenized non-native model and toward an external native model of English. This potential death of the new English variety has not yet happened in any country, but may be in the cards for Malaysia, the Philippines, and perhaps even India.

Some Implications of the Proposed Life Cycle

The above life cycle for non-native varieties of English is tentative at this point. It is presented here as a theoretical construct, but one formulated after considerable research and observation in ESL societies in the South Pacific and elsewhere. Detailed studies of English-using societies around the world could further test its validity. The remainder of this article will briefly cover some questions arising from the life-cycle construct, and from the linguistic results of English becoming an institutionalized second language.

Salient Questions Arising from the Life Cycle
Does the language situation truly stabilize after institutionalization of the indigenized variety? One basic tenet of linguistics is that language

is always changing. Is it possible that language situations, too, are forever in a state of flux? The East Indians, who form roughly half the population of Guyana, have recently lost their native Hindi; the present generation has Creole (English) as its native tongue (Bickerton 1977). However, the remainder of the populace has had Creole as L_1 since the country was settled, and there are no significant indigenous languages. In Fiji, an ESL society, the present generation of Chinese have already switched to English (Yee 1974: 16). A similar trend may be under way in Singapore (Platt 1977: 364). Is it possible that the tendency to use Colloquial Fijian English with communal mates could eventually cause the larger vernaculars to succumb? Might second-language status for English prove to be only a passing phase, with English inexorably becoming a native language in some societies and a foreign language in others? This would not be inconsonant with "the spread of English" as described by Fishman et al. 1977 and Kachru 1986.

What becomes of the informal variety when English reverts to FL status? The most informal and indigenized varieties are the code-mixed ones found in the Philippines and India (Kachru 1977: 33). Will Mixmix in the Philippines (Sibayan 1977), colloquial Malaysian English (Tongue 1974; Paauw 1977), and others gradually fade from use under the ascendancy of Tagalog, Malay, etc.? If so, what will take their place? Will they, on the other hand, undergo further change, probably in the form of relexification from the national language, thereby becoming an informal variety of the vernacular? These varieties will bear careful watching in the next decade or two.

Is restriction of use and function the final stage in the process? Or will further changes be in store? It seems difficult to imagine Third World nations becoming so isolated from the currents of world events that they would revert to sole use of the vernaculars. It even seems improbable today that another language might displace English as the international language of science and technology. The one certainty in studying anything, however, is that the currently prevailing innovations will seem grossly outmoded to the next generation.

The Linguistic Effects of ESL Status

Skewed bilingualism. For English to be a second language, its use must not be restricted to a small elite, but must be fairly generalized in the society. It is difficult to set a minimum percentage, but in a modernizing society Kloss's suggestions of "all literate adults" and "all secondary school graduates" (1966: 15) seem to adequately define the segment of the population which will be bilingual. It is important to recognize that monolingual EFL groups will persist in outlying geographic areas and in lower social classes.

Localized performance model. The inevitable localization of the performance model of English was discussed earlier. Bickerton (1977: 55) refers to the absence of a native model in the English of Fiji, stating that this places it "intermediate between Pidgin and 'good foreigner version.' " The indigenized model is both conditioned and supported by the internal function of the new variety cited next.

Internal function of English. In the ESL society, English is used primarily for internal purposes. A small elite continues to use it for external (international) purposes, but it is not a linguistically significant group in the society.

A more native-like language acquisition. With a foreign language, only the formal variety is acquired; learning takes place largely through formal study, mainly in adolescence or adulthood. During the colonial period, the study of English may well begin in the earliest primary classes, and a good deal of informal learning goes on when other subjects are taught in the English medium. With English occupying a broad range of domains in the ESL, post-colonial society, many children acquire some active competence in the informal variety of English before entering school. Further learning of this variety continues in school, through playground activities, and in informal socialization, shopping, and other activities outside of school.

Informal learning here also plays a larger role in the acquisition of the formal variety. Besides English-medium classes—where formal correction of errors may still go on—less formal learning takes place when one attends public functions, reads newspapers, notices, and the like, or listens to the radio. Strevens (1977: 115) states the new functional role of the formal variety thus: "There came a demand in the wake of independence . . . for English to be taught for practical communicative use. The assumption was that English would continue as part of a general education for citizenship, but would be separated from the literary, social, and cultural values of Britain or the United States." According to Kachru (1977: 32), English (a second language) "imbedded in the native sociocultural matrix of the area" comes to have a pattern of acquisition much like that of native languages.

Vernaculars endangered. Expansion of the use and function of English brings about a corresponding decrease in use and function of the vernaculars. I have already raised the question of whether the vernaculars can long survive in this limited role. Informal English is already making inroads into their remaining domains. The experience with Gaelic in Ireland teaches that a vernacular cannot be reclaimed, even by a massive program, once it has been abandoned by the vast majority (97%) of the population.

In ESL nations like Fiji it is still not too late. Governments must engage in language planning to determine the balance of roles for English and the vernaculars which is in keeping with the long-term goals of the society; then they must devise and implement plans to bring them into being. All potential plans must, of course, be cost effective, but the initial research need not be prohibitively expensive. In 1973 the Maori Education Unit of the New Zealand Council for Educational Research launched a five-year study of language use and attitudes in areas of Maori settlement, at a cost of $70,000 (Benton 1975: 3). The resulting plans will serve only 8 percent of New Zealand's population. Other countries are engaged in even more ambitious programs to benefit small linguistic minorities. Since the total population is involved in issues of language choice and policy in ESL societies, the highest priority should be given to conserving and effectively using the nation's language resources, including its vernaculars.[1]

NOTE

1. For recent surveys of English in the South Pacific, and updated bibliographies on the varieties, see Watson-Gegeo, ed. 1986 and Subramani 1980.

REFERENCES

Abdulaziz, M. H. 1972. Triglossia and Swahili-English bilingualism in Tanzania. *Language in Society* 1: 197–213.

Adam, R. S. 1958. Social factors in second language learning. Ph.D. dissertation, University of London.

Benton, Richard A. 1975. Sociolinguistic survey of Maori language use. *Language Planning Newsletter,* East-West Culture Learning Institute 1(2): 3–4.

Bickerton, Derek. 1977. Pidginization and creolization: language acquisition and language universals. Pp. 49–69 in Valdman, ed. (1977).

Boas, F. 1929. Classification of American Indian languages. *Language* 5: 6.

Bright, William. 1973. North American Indian language contact. Pp. 210–27 in Dil, ed. 1976. Also in Sebeok 1973.

Capell, A. 1973. *A new Fijian dictionary.* 4th ed. Suva: Government Printer.

Christopherson, Paul. 1973. *Second language learning: myth and reality.* Harmondsworth: Penguin.

Dil, Anwar, ed. 1976. *Variation and change in language: essays by William Bright.* Stanford University Press.

249

Emeneau, M. B. 1956. India as a linguistic area. *Language* 32: 3–16.

Eri, Vincent. 1970. *The Crocodile*. Ringwood, Victoria, Australia: Penguin.

Ferguson, Charles A. 1977. Linguistic theory. In *Bilingual education: current perspectives. Vol. II: Linguistics.* Washington, D.C.: Center for Applied Linguistics.

Fiji. 1970. *Report for the Year, 1970.* London: Her Majesty's Stationery Office.

Fishman, Joshua A., et al. 1977. *The spread of English.* Rowley, Mass.: Newbury House.

———. 1978. Bilingual education: what and why? In Lourie and Conklin, eds. 1978.

Geraghty, Paul. 1977. Fiji Pidgin and bilingual education. *Fiji English Teachers' Journal* 12: 2–8.

———. 1978. Fijian dialect diversity and foreigner talk: the evidence of premissionary manuscript. Pp. 51–67 in Schütz, ed. 1978b.

Gumperz, John J. 1968. Types of linguistic communities. In Joshua Fishman, ed., *Readings in the sociology of language.* The Hague: Mouton.

Guy, J. B. M. 1964. *Handbook of Bichelamar.* Canberra: Australian National University. Pacific Linguistics, series C, no. 34.

Hall, Robert A., Jr. 1962. The life cycle of Pidgin languages. *Lingua* 11: 151–56.

Kachru, Braj B. 1977. The new Englishes and old models. *English Teaching Forum* 15(3): 29–35.

———. 1983. *The Indianization of English: The English language in India.* New Delhi: Oxford University Press.

———. 1986. *The alchemy of English.* Oxford: Pergamon Press. Reprinted 1990, Urbana: University of Illinois Press.

Kelley, Sister Francis. 1975. The English spoken colloquially by a group of adolescents in Suva. *Fiji English Teachers' Journal* 11: 19–43.

Kloss, Heinz. 1966. Types of multilingual communities: a discussion of ten variables. Pp. 7–17 in Lieberson, ed. 1966.

LePage, Robert B. 1968. Problems to be faced in the use of English as the medium of education in four West Indian territories. Pp. 431–42 in Joshua Fishman et al., *Language problems of developing nations.* London: John Wiley and Sons.

Lieberson, Stanley, ed. 1966. *Explorations in sociolinguistics.* Bloomington: Indiana University Press.

Lourie, Margaret A., and Nancy Faires Conklin, eds. 1978. *A pluralistic nation: the language issue in the United States.* Rowley, Mass.: Newbury House.

Malia, Sister Mulipoya-Lui. 1976. Review of *Pidgin and Creole languages* by Robert A. Hall, Jr. *Journal of African Languages* 6: 83–86.

Mana Annual of Creative Writing. 1973. Suva, Fiji: South Pacific Creative Arts Society.

Mishra, Vijay, ed. 1979. *Rama's banishment: a centenary volume of the Fiji Indians.* Auckland: Heinemann.

Moag, Rodney F. 1977. *Fiji Hindi: a basic course and reference grammar.* Canberra: Australian National University Press.

———. 1978a. Vernacular education in Fiji. *South Pacific Journal of Teacher Education* 6(2): 134–40.

———. 1978b. Bilingualism-biculturalism: where is it going in the Pacific? *Directions* 1: 3–7.

———. 1978c. Standardization in Pidgin Fijian: implications for the theory of Pidginization. Pp. 68–90 in Schütz, ed. 1978b.

———. 1979. The linguistic adaptions of the Fiji Indians. Pp. 112–38 in Mishra, ed. 1979.

———, and Louisa B. Moag. 1977. English in Fiji: some perspective and the need for language planning. *Fiji English Teachers' Journal* 13: 2–26.

Nacola, J. 1976. *I native no more*. Suva, Fiji: Mana Publications.

Nandan, Satendra. 1974. My father's son. Pp. 12–16 in Wendt 1974.

Paauw, Scott H. 1977. Malaysian English: a descriptive study. Unpublished research paper, Universiti Sains Malaysia.

Pillai, Raymond. 1975. Preliminary inspection. *Mana Annual of Creative Writing 1974*. Suva, Fiji: South Pacific Creative Arts Society.

Platt, John. 1977. A model for polyglossia and multilingualism (with special reference to Singapore and Malaysia). *Language in Society* 6: 361–78.

Pride, John. 1978. Communicative needs in the learning and use of English. Paper presented at the East-West Center Conference on English as an International Auxiliary Language. Honolulu, Hawaii, April 1–15, 1978.

Quain, Buell Halvor. 1948. *Fijian village*. Chicago: University of Chicago Press.

Richards, Jack. 1972. *Error analysis: perspectives on second language acquisition*. London: Longmans.

———. 1982. Singapore English: rhetorical and communicative styles. In *The other tongue: English across cultures*. Ed. Braj B. Kachru. Urbana: University of Illinois Press.

Rubin, Joan, and Jernudd, Bjorn H., eds. 1971. *Can language be planned?* Honolulu: University Press of Hawaii.

Schütz, Albert J. 1972. *The languages of Fiji*. Oxford: Clarendon Press.

———. 1978a. English loanwords in Fijian. In Schütz, ed. 1978b.

———, ed. 1978b. *Fijian language studies: borrowing and pidginization. Bulletin of the Fiji Museum*.

Sebeok, Thomas A., ed. 1973 *Current trends in linguistics*. Vol. 10: *Linguistics in North America*. The Hague: Mouton.

Selinker, L. 1972. Interlanguage. *International Review of Applied Linguistics* 10(3): 209–31.

Seri. 1974. Fiji. Pp. 4–6 in Wendt, ed. 1974.

Sibayan, B. P. 1977. Language and identity. Paper presented at SEAMEO Regional Language Centre, Twelfth Regional Seminar, Singapore.

Siegel, Jeff. 1973. A survey of language use in the Indian speech community in Fiji. Unpublished field study for the Culture Learning Institute, East-West Center, Honolulu.

Smith, Anne-Marie. 1986. Papua New Guinea English. Ph.D. dissertation, University of Papua New Guinea.

Strevens, Peter. 1977. English for special purposes: an analysis and survey. *Studies in Language Learning* 2(1): 111–35.

Subramani. 1975. Sautu. *Mana Annual of Creative Writing 1974.* Suva, Fiji: South Pacific Creative Arts Society.

———. 1977. Tell me where the train goes. *Third Mana Annual of Creative Writing.* Suva, Fiji: South Pacific Creative Arts Society.

———. 1978. English for Fiji? *South Pacific Journal of Teacher Education* 6(2): 140–43.

———. 1980. From myth to fabulation: emerging South Pacific literature. Ph.D. dissertation, University of the South Pacific, Suva.

Tongue, R. 1974. *The English of Singapore and Malaysia.* Singapore: Eastern Universities Press.

Valdman, Albert, ed. 1977. *Pidgin and creole linguistics.* Bloomington: Indiana University Press.

Vatoko, Kali, and Albert Leomala. 1975. "Nomo Stap Long Taon" and "Mi Stap Sori Nomo." *Mana Annual of Creative Writing 1974.* Suva, Fiji: South Pacific Creative Arts Society.

Watson-Gegeo, Karen, ed. 1989. English in the South Pacific. Special issue of *World Englishes* 8(1).

Weinreich, Uriel. 1951. Research problems in bilingualism, with special reference to Switzerland. Ph.D. dissertation, Columbia University.

Wendt, Albert. 1973. *Sons for the return home.* Auckland, New Zealand: Longman Paul.

———. 1974. *Some modern poetry from Fiji.* Suva, Fiji: South Pacific Creative Arts Society.

Wurm, Stephen A. 1977. Pidgins, Creoles, lingue franche, and national development. Pp. 333–57 in Valdman, ed. (1977).

Yee, Sin Joan. 1974. *The Chinese in the Pacific.* Suva, Fiji: South Pacific Social Sciences Association.

PART IV

Literary Creativity in the Other Tongue

14

Edwin Thumboo

The Literary Dimension of the Spread of English

My approach to the topic may initially seem unduly removed from essentials. The reason derives from the general thrust marking discussions of the literatures that developed upon the spread of English. Such discussions have tended to short circuit the critical process by applying without reconsideration of the theories, assumptions, and practices formed within and for mother-tongue bases, as if new literatures were fully part of the same literary continuum. There are grounds—presently adduced—to question seriously the appropriateness of this assumption.

But first a caveat. Many current terms are rendered unsatisfactory by the rapid, extensive, complicated, and still continuing spread of English, which has outstripped the perspectives, concepts, and terminology that sought to describe and assess it. A substantive question concerns orientation. While positions differ and theories/hypotheses compete, the body of scholarly work on language is now steadily augmented by research findings about and from "non-native" varieties and bases. Similar developments are occurring in the study of the literatures. Criticism still assumes a one-language, one-literature equation: varieties of a language lead to varieties of a literature. That is definitely not the case with English. There is obvious concession in the label "new literatures in English," a label predictably interim. When did American literature emerge as such? We have Australian literature (and a dictionary of Australian English) and New Zealand literature defined by criticism, fueled chiefly from within, alert to elements—linguistic, attitudinal—that nourish an ethos. Moreover, "new literatures" itself seems a misnomer when applied to India, where the creativity predates Macaulay's Minute of 1835. Nor is "second tongue" accurate, as a majority of the writers wield English as their first language. Nor is "contact literature" a firmly suitable alternative. The literature in English only *starts* as contact literature because, after it acquires body, momentum, and contemporary preoccupation, its "contact" character becomes historical, part of origins. Nonetheless, such terms continue to be useful. To replace them would call for acts of definition and elaborate exception-making not for this occasion.

Phases of Spread

The English language and its literature moved toward multiplicity in three broad sweeps, to (1) Scotland, Wales, and Ireland; (2) North America, Australia, New Zealand, and South Africa; (3) Asia, Africa, the West Indies, the Pacific, and other geographical pockets. Important for my present purpose, in this rough chronology of some five hundred years, are the generalized factors distinguishing each movement. In the first, the language spread by arms, politics, and culture, as part of an assimilative process, through rearranged fiefdoms, principalities, and kingdoms, of Anglo-Saxon–Norman hegemonies over Celts. The Irish, for instance, have hardly had difficulty with the English language—only with the English regime. And lest we forget, at the setting of the sun, the greatest English wits have been Irish. Moreover, the differences were part of a symbiotic relationship arising from a large measure of shared culture, if not shared politics.

In the second movement, language and culture spread as English speakers spread. Major institutions of identity were transferred, at times replicated, and grew. Strong, constant contact with England, at times paradoxical, maintained bonds that survived such varied and chronologically separate happenings as the American War of Independence, the Boer War, the reaction in Australia and New Zealand when Britain joined the EEC, and South Africa's expulsion from the Commonwealth. I do not propose that the historical and contemporary relationships among these nations are simple. John Steed, Rambo, and Crocodile Dundee reflect three unique masculine discourses beneath whose gesture and dress lie complex psychosociolinguistic variables and distillations; they are interesting, but in no way threatening to the deep structures held in common by the Anglo cultural combine.

It is the third movement that provides my subject. British expansion overseas had its origins chiefly in trade—new markets for manufacture and fresh sources of cheap raw material. Responding to internal political, economic, and industrial hungers and to competition among European powers, trade gradually mutated into a sustained colonialism. Britain, with the largest muster of dominions and colonies, proved the most successful; English, introduced to facilitate administration and commerce, became transplanted in every colony. Without exception, it remained to flourish variously as national language, official language, or auxiliary language for technology, science, regional and international finance, and education. English links communities, ethnic groups, national regions, and nations within regions such as ASEAN (the Association of Southeast Asian Nations), the West Indies, and the Pacific Islands. It is at the heart of programs to modernize and performs a mixture of roles supported by governments and ambitious parents.

This third movement harbors a second spread: the horizontal and vertical embedding of English within a nation. Linguists are generally aware of this phenomenon, but literary scholars and critics often overlook it. Some are born into a language, others have it thrust upon them; succeeding generations achieve it, and those succeeding them are then born into it. A cycle starts, gathers momentum, and cumulatively affects the shape of English and the other languages involved. The case of India apart, such linguistic multiplicity derived from colonial boundaries drawn under a power principle that ignored the logic of tribes and subtribes, nations, etc. Unintentionally, those boundaries laid the foundation for English as a link language and for those problems and vulnerabilities connected with tribal-ethnic rivalry.

New Literatures and Old Traditions

The complex background of the new literatures is manifest in the following divisions of the third movement. First, there are nations that claim long and elaborate written and oral literary traditions; e.g., India, Sri Lanka, and Malaysia. Second are those that possess powerful, sophisticated oral traditions; e.g., Nigeria, Ghana, Kenya, Papua New Guinea, and Samoa. Third, there are areas created by colonial needs, such as Singapore, with a population drawn substantially from the surrounding Malay sultanates, South China, South India, Jaffna in Sri Lanka, and Hadramant; and the West Indies, mainly populated by Africans with East Indians and a smaller number of Chinese, with the Indians as bilinguals and a variety of English as the sole language for the others. There is also a fourth category—and perhaps a fifth, if we were to separate out Black North America—areas where the Anglo

257

culture and/or power dominates indigenous peoples; e.g., the Maoris in New Zealand and the Zulus in Africa.

In matters of culture and environment some predictability is ensured by *saty negeri, satu bangsa, satu ugama.*[1] I have taken from the Malay because *ugama* has an apt comprehensiveness not easily translatable. It also anticipates a point to come: how to put Tamil or Ijo or Teochew (that is, "bilingual") life into English. In the singularity of a relatively firm political, cultural unity, virtually all aspects of social life become common through slow evolution. Cause and effect lie within narrow parameters; there is resilience. Drastic changes occur, but they test rather than exhaust the capacity to understand and to cope with them.

In the already complex instance of monocultures—as broadly defined by one language, one people, and one religion—structures overlap, extend, at times contradict and compete to create specific and general tensions. Each component culture has its distinctive semiotic systems; each occupies the same space-time continuum; each is gripped by the forces of national development; each is exposed to interpenetration through the formal and informal political, economic, social, and educational context that often pushes a policy of bilingualism. Among the chief conduits are the processes of modernization and the increasing adoption of English and the international culture that directly or indirectly comes with it. Social engineering on this scale makes for rapid change.

Language—and literature—have a special place. As Halliday (1978: 2) points out:

> There are two fundamental aspects to the social reality that is encoded in language: to paraphrase Lévi-Strauss, it is both "good to think" and "good to eat." Language expresses and symbolizes this dual aspect in its semantic system, which is organized around the twin motifs of reflection and action—language as a means of reflecting on things, and language as a means of acting on things. The former is the "ideational" component of meaning; the latter is the "interpersonal"—one can act *symbolically* only on persons, not on objects.
>
> A social reality (or a "culture") is itself an edifice of meanings—a semiotic construct. In this perspective, language is one of the semiotic systems that constitute a culture; one that is distinctive in that it also serves as an encoding system for many (though not all) of the others.
>
> This in summary terms is what is intended by the formulation "language as social semiotic." It means interpreting language within a sociocultural context, in which the culture itself is interpreted in semiotic terms—as an information system, if that terminology is preferred.

258

That participants are able to "predict" with advantage assumes a language in common, extensively embedded in the personal and social realities through its role in "reflection and action." A sufficient history of usage is implied, one overlapping other semiotic systems and subsystems such as religion, philosophy, science, the study of language itself, and literature. Language is both instrument and re-pository. All of this would ordinarily apply to "indigenous" languages of third movement nations, each with its time-sanctioned place within the relevant social reality. Peranakan Malay and Hokkien in Singapore and Malaysia are examples that have made interesting and instructive adjustments in their respective semiotic systems.

The arrival of English and its conversion from imperial, foreign language to one increasingly "nativized" is fascinatingly important. So, too, are questions of what English to teach, the choice of texts and methods and the frame for bilingualism, and research priorities. But the concern here is with literature, the making of which is bracketed by other interests, individual rather than public, reflecting creative options rather than policy. The writer—dramatist and novelist more than poet—must create a suitable English-language semiotic system in a non-English social reality. Powerful elements of culture and attitude come with the language. Present as part of the colonial inheritance, they are maintained, even strengthened, by the formal study of English and the international culture of the mass media, especially television. In order to explore and carry a new social reality, English has to be uncluttered, freed from certain habitual associations; it must develop a new verbal playfulness, new rhythms, additions to its metaphorical and symbolic reach to explain and amplify feelings and ideas about literature and life and cater to the claims of the imagination.

A great deal of the literary practice of the English-language semiotic system is retained in a third movement setting. It is connected to a great, vital, subtle literature in a language whose flexibility makes it adaptable. It has been reorchestrated and augmented with strategies and concepts from the indigenous languages and literatures. The innovations can be as broad, declared, and sustained as Gabriel Okara's *The Voice* (see Thumboo 1985 for a discussion) or as subtle as Raja Rao's short story *The Cow of the Barricades* or Okot p'Bitek's *Song of Lawino*. The need to innovate is inevitable because it is connected to reorienting the language to express a set of perceptions, a vision faithful to the collective but varied experience and aspirations of a people.

Similar complexities are to be discovered under other heads. Comprehending the dynamics of how attributes are transmitted from one generation to another is an exercise that takes us beneath the generalizations into the details, the byways of a culture. How is education achieved, formally and informally? Do particular colors have special significance? Is the week a four-day or seven-day event? Is pregnancy before marriage a social and/or religious disaster or necessary proof of fertility? There are large and small questions. We cannot trace their import to the *n*th degree, but the more we attempt, the better our recognition of significances, flexibilities.

Much of the recent and contemporary experience of colonies and ex-colonies is similar. An example is the basic reaction to colonialism itself, though even here the final push toward independence ranged from the relatively quiet Sri Lankan experience to the Mau Mau blood sacrifice that forms a major theme in Ngũgĩ wa Thiong'o's fiction and essays.

Contexts of New Literatures

The new literatures in the second tongue are by and large associated with nations hard in search of a commonality. These nations did not exist in their present politico-geographical incarnations; with few exceptions, they brought together diverse groups, in some instances formed by tribes sharing a great deal, in others by ethnic groups originally sharing little. Whatever the mix, they lacked the opportunity for gradually paced evolution into a single people. This achieving of a single identity was linked to the compulsion to modernize, to achieve integrated social, political, and economic infrastructures. Political stability was required as a base for economic development, followed by education and physical well-being. These primary requirements were imposed by the historical moment, by the state of society. And culture was and is a major essential instrument in this growth of a people, one in which writers have a role. As Chinweizu (1983: 21) and others have pointed out:

> They are acutely aware of literature's capacity to prepare for life, and even on occasion to move them to action. After all, the nationalist novels of Rizal had sparked the Filipino revolution against Spanish colonialism in 1896; and Al-Hakim's *The Return of the Soul* had moved Nasser to the role he played in Egyptian and Arab history. Most of these writers recognize that it is not given to many works to intervene so directly in history. Like Achebe, they would agree with Garcia Marquez that "literature is a long-term weapon." They therefore concentrate on examining, through literature, fundamental questions of national history, national identity, national purpose, and national morality and outlook.

Seen against this background, the challenge to individual creativity is broadly twofold. First, the writer must grasp and then make
sense of his complicated milieu. Second, the writer must handle
language and genre.

More than for the writer who inhabits one language, one culture,
and one literary tradition, the writer's situation in the new literatures
is open to compulsions revealed by the array of forces at work in a
multilingual, multicultural, multiliterary society. As implied earlier,
where the language goes, the criticism and its key assumptions tend
to follow. Richard Hoggart (1982), for instance, discussing "Culture
and Its Ministers," does not approve of "culture as state-formation"
(195) and has reservations about the "idea of culture as a national
identity" (189). He believes in "the notion of an artist as both inside
and outside his society" (188). According to Hoggart, "the authentic
marks of literature" require a combination of "radicalism and honesty"
(192). His analysis is comprehensive and sensitive; because he cannot
break free from his basic ideological position, his analysis tends to be
prescriptive, to impute positions not always sustained by realities. In
referring to new nations, Hoggart claims that

> the spreading of culture is less a matter of individual self-fulfillment as
> an immersion in, a dyeing in the vat of one's traditional culture. There
> is no suggestion of a movement towards an independent culture and
> independent critical self-awareness (or towards the free play of informed
> opinion which the existence of such individuals can set off). It is rather
> as though people were expected, separately or—preferably—in known
> groups (family, village, sub-tribe, etc.), to become linked umbilically to
> the one great mother. [183]

Traditional vs. Modern

The notion of "traditional culture" was created chiefly by colonialism,
cultural confrontation, and the impulse to modernize: the Thais,
Chinese, and Japanese are not prone to see their culture as either
traditional or modern. In any case, Hoggart's central assumptions are
that traditional cultures are not sufficiently independent to support
"independent critical self-awareness." This is patently odd. Traditional
cultures whose members see them as continuities that maintain a sense
of self, of orientation in the flux of contemporary cultural fashion, are
elaborate. They were not magically received whole. That they are
commonly conservative should not blind us to the fact that they
evolved, absorbing and discarding elements, occasionally reoriented
radically in one sector, with gradual ramifications elsewhere. Examples

would include the entry of Islam into India; of Hinduism, Buddhism, and Islam into Southeast Asia; of Buddhism into China, Burma, Thailand, and Japan; and of Tang culture into Japan and Korea. Nor was the capacity to invent absent. (Sufism is but one of many instances.) Moreover, "individual self-fulfillment" and "critical self-awareness" are notions or ideals whose degrees of realization are largely themselves supported by a culture, whether "traditional" or "modern." However much we might like to think so, they are hardly absolutes in a cultural context. Questions of degree are involved, and they are being missed. More than a billion people are consequently swept into and dyed by confident generalizations. The confidence and the stance—and margins of actions they generate—all rest on a history of Britain's continual internal and external achievement. Napoleon did much for the British sense of self; it paid off a hundred years later in the Kitchener recruitment poster. The accumulating political, social, intellectual, scientific, and economic capital from the late eighteenth century made for a powerful Englishness whose depth and comprehensiveness comprise an unspoken constant, even today. It ensures a set of useful reflexes, a sense of oneness that many envy.

> Society needs artists to translate the people's feelings, the aspirations, the beliefs, the values into art forms, into dances, dramas, music, paintings, literature, etc., so that these experiences can be accumulated and portrayed effectively and transmitted continuously for the benefit of present and future generations. The subsequent generations of people will then be able to understand their roots better, will then know what binds them together as a people and as a nation.
>
> Of course, not all artistic works are inspiring and effective in reflecting the past and present. The key is in excellence. An artistic work can only evoke a response from the viewer or reader if he can relate to it; and if the work is executed to a high degree of artistry. [Wong 1987: 2]

These "official" sentiments are shared by many writers; they are implicit in much contact literature, especially in the early phases of growth. They are inevitable in a multiracial society where sectional interests become less aggressive and more inclined toward a national ethos based on an enlarging consensus.

The most cursory acquaintance with the growth of nations from tribe to complex social, political, and economic entity reveals how constructive energies were preoccupied with correlations between political and cultural boundaries. There is an unremitting attempt to preserve and then engender and extend homogeneity in a spirit most sharply manifest in the clan, which is the largest unit within which the individual finds himself fully at home. In conditions of geographical and cultural stability, the dynamics of the group are marked by a constant sharing through integration. Over time, emblems of order are taken as natural. The ambience of national history, of common destiny, is reinforced by myth, legend, religions, and much else; a collective imagination emerges and in turn nourishes and is nourished.

Within such a stability, language plays a binding function. Words acquire denotative and connotative power. Students of English language and literature should have little difficulty recalling that before England became part of Great Britain, national spirit marked the literary imagination. Chaucer's *Canterbury Tales* describes emergent types: Prioress, Franklin, Knight. Consider Shakespeare. While his poetry and his psychology build up powerful images of the universal in man, in society, this should not blind us to the fact that he was perhaps the most political and historically aware writer of his age.

As a semiotic system, language has a special place through its dual role "organized around the twin motifs of reflection and action." Literature has its special place through straddling the system associated with language and the very range of materials it incorporates, materials ranging from striking individual obsessions to reworkings of earlier works. Consider Anouilh's *Antigone* from Sophocles (*Oedipus the King, Oedipus at Colonus,* and *Antigone*) and Aeschylus (*Seven against Thebes*) or Jean Rhys's *The Wide Sargasso Sea* in relation to *Jane Eyre,* or Michel Tournier's *Friday,* a retelling of Robinson Crusoe's story, or J. M. Coetzee's *Foe,* which purports to be built upon the world of *Robinson Crusoe.*

A writer living in a country that is seeking to unify and to defuse ethnic tensions—often complicated by class conflict—would naturally respond to issues associated with nation building. Almost every Third World writer rewrites and expands upon the originality of the indigenous, uncovering and giving perspective. Life that was peripheral, an anthropological footnote under a colonial dispensation, is given center stage. This process occurs not merely in Third World countries where English is used; that sense of nationalism—and its practical side—can also be found in Hungarian, Czech, and Polish literatures, again at appropriate times in their history.

Impulses behind the New English Writing

Unless we identify and connect these and other preoccupations, it would be difficult to see in perspective the impulses behind the emergence of the new literatures in English. First are the reasons for writing. These include explaining society to itself, reconstructing the

263

past, exploring the binding of diverse peoples and cultures with the idea of commonality, and giving imaginative expression to the array of forces fashioning society. Other attendant themes include the effect of political and moral corruption—catastrophes played out in the lives of ordinary men and women—or the ambiguous changes wrought by modernization. In a very real sense, themes have often chosen writers, a phenomenon neatly summed up by Nadine Gordimer (1973: 11): "Black writers choose their plots, characters and literary styles; their themes choose them. By this I mean that themes are statements or questions arising from the nature of the society in which the writer finds himself immersed, and the quality of the life around him. In this sense the writer is the voice of the people beyond any glib political connotations of the phrase." Gordimer's remarks pertain to South Africa, where apartheid has perpetuated the worst features of a colonial regime hardened by the fact that the colonizers are themselves white natives. The blacks there live under an unremitting oppression so extensive that black poets cannot help but feel its tragic intensity, as revealed in Stanley Motjuwadi's *White Lies* (Royston 1973: 12). Motjuwadi's passion, in less intense form, can be found in the earlier phase of most new literatures, in variations of themes from those touching on racism, political suppression, and economic exploitation to those about snobbery and intellectual inequality.

In these literatures there is an attempt to restore dignity, to reestablish the self, and to compensate for deprivation and depersonalization. The Australian aboriginal novelist and poet Colin Johnson says, "Creative writers like myself can re-decipher and reinterpret mythology, legends and stories, to a certain extent modernise it or give it relevance and have that tradition going from the 'dreaming' of the beginning to 1983 and onwards. That is where we will link up again with what has been lost somewhat by relying on alien forms of literature" (Breitinger and Sander 1985: 2). Such connections between writer and society, almost compelled by a reading of contemporary events, are often sanctioned by tradition. It is not unusual for the artist to see himself as a medium, a shaping conduit. Kofi Awoonor, whose poem-novel *This Earth My Brother* remains among the most profound explorations of individual psyche and society, describes a role that Hoggart and others, bred by a different intellectual, aesthetic climate, would possibly find strange. The artist lives in a society where "forms and motifs already exist in an assimilated time and world construct, and so he serves only as the instrument of transforming these into an artistic whole based on his own imaginative and cognitive world, a world which exists and has meaning only within the larger world. He is not a visionary artist, per se, like the European artist who projects into space and time structures which simply were not there before. There is no otherness locked in the private psyche of his vision" (Awoonor 1976: 166). Although the artist, his function especially, was not always this tightly circumscribed, firm conventions generally governed the choice and treatment of subjects. Nonetheless, it provides for a sharp contrast to Hoggart's writer—partly of and partly out of society, and of a culture not "formally organised." In third movement paradigms, the writer is moved by a sense of the contemporary that converts into powerful injunctions.

Nor is the dissimilarity confined to conceptions of the artist's role. Perceptions of the world as physical construct likewise differ. While making it clear that she is generalizing, Kamala Markandaya (1973: 22) states that for the West "the earth was created for man: an assumption that seems to be used, consciously or unconsciously, to justify almost any kind of assault upon the animal kingdom and upon the systems of the earth itself." I have had occasion to suggest that prior to the mid-nineteenth century—later, if we exclude Japan—there was a broad contrast between European and Asian attitudes to scientific discoveries. Asia did not fully exploit their practical value, while Europe did, mainly because Asia went more fully into metaphysics while Europe delved predominantly into physics. I find it intriguing to speculate on whether the fact that Europe was dominated for so long by one religion which, despite schisms, allowed a fairly stable view of man and his universe, of man and God, of the separation of the sacred from the secular, encouraged a concomitant scientific spirit and method. Did such earlier centers of scientific inquiry as Egypt and Greece lose the capacity because new religions and fundamentally disruptive new worldviews broke their continuities?

Physics and metaphysics: Markandaya's own background urges that "everything exists in its own right" (22). She goes on to say that while she does not import that perception directly into her work, nonetheless it seeps in. The sacredness of the Earth—in a Blakean sense, interestingly enough—and the conviction that it is the source of life are to be found in almost all her novels. The conviction generates a kind of fortitude embodied, for instance, in Rukmini in *Nectar in a Sieve*, as well as in *The Coffer Dams*, where the Europeans find "tropical" nature discomforting although the "natives" are fully at home. Without an understanding of the vision behind notions of the luminous, the cosmic, the nature of human beings and their place in the universe, our perceptions would be impoverished.

265

The Genetics of Culture

The genetics of culture, the reference to semiotic systems, and the three-stage paradigm proposed are necessary preludes to a grasp of the precolonial and colonial pasts and their impact on present-day events and expectations. I do not want to dwell overmuch on colonial occupation, but it seems worthwhile to realize how extensive and deep deracination went. Albert Wendt (1982: 203–4), whose views are invariably temperate, had this to say: "Over the last two centuries or so, that most fearful chill, institutionalised in colonialism, was our perpetual cross in Oceania." He sees that chill continuing with the raising of national flags, the first hurrahs on the stroke of midnight. There are the tasks of deconstruction, reconstruction, and construction. The global system still projects looming inequalities between the First and the Third Worlds, inequalities that exert powerful influence on cultures and fledgling economies.

Deracination, distortion, and gradual dismantling of indigenous cultural institutions and practices undermined the quality of life, made for a defensive sense of self and sense of community. For instance, traditional performing arts—including dance drama that implied magic such as the *mahyong,* which uniquely fulfilled spiritual needs through an aesthetic event—were either neglected or suppressed as superstitious, pagan, barbaric. In Southeast Asia and elsewhere, similar architectonic disturbances were and are still felt. Muhammad Haji Salleh (1977: vi) sees that the "Malay-Indonesian civilisation is in the state of drift, after a forcible uprooting of its culture by the Dutch and British colonialists, and the bombardment of popular culture originating in the west."

The sense of cumulative loss, assessed in some instances as beyond restoration, was exacerbated by distorted images of indigenous people. They hardened into clichés and stereotypes which supported a mental wall far more stubborn than anything actual. The effect is devastating in fact, in fiction, in memoirs, in travelers' tales; examples occur in the colonizers' utterances in E. M. Forster's *A Passage to India.* What is said of interracial contact often derives from and in turn nourishes racist myths. There are countermythologies about the white man, some equally cruel and misguided. But these had no influence on policies governing schools, hospitals, sports, social intercourse, the maintenance of law and order, clubs, tertiary education, jobs, leave regulations, etc. A native "put in his place" at times felt *he* was guilty of a misdemeanor.

I do not want to give the impression that before colonialism, life was perfect. It was not. One index in Southeast Asia was the heavy emigration, from India and China principally. Life was hard in their southern regions, in China especially, where warlords and Kuomintang-Communist rivalries were miseries for the peasants. But as Nkosi points out in reference to South Africa, "The adjustment made by Africans defeated by other Africans produced minimum psychological damage. On the other hand European colonialism represented something wholly different: its transforming power was enormous; its challenge to African values total and inexorable; its exclusiveness was the final blow to even that need which the conquered feel to identify with the victorious" (1983: 31).

For many writers the establishment of a refurbished, complete self and society, with history and a sense of recovered dignity, was a primary function. Elechi Amadi's *The Concubines*, Ngugi's *The River Between*, and Achebe's *Things Fall Apart* have for their themes the imaginative reconstruction of life in traditional society either before or at the time when the force of the white man was felt. *The Concubines* and *Things Fall Apart* are essential to a sense of continuity through the values embodied in the past and for images of the complex humanity that marked traditional life before the coming of the white man. As Albert Wendt put it, "The imagination must explore with love, honesty, wisdom, compassion; writers must write with *aroha/ aloha/alofa/loloma*, respecting the people they are writing about, people who may view the void differently and who, like all other human beings, live through the pores of their flesh and mind and bone, who suffer, laugh, cry, copulate and die" (1982: 123).

The Writer and the Milieu

The writer has interests, values, and a vision of life constructed out of satisfactions and dissatisfactions with his immediate situation and its larger milieu. The milieu—whose possible complexity is limited only by the semiotic systems referred to earlier as defining the total content of society—provides an inheritance that is simultaneously a constraint and a challenge. On the one hand are the forces of conformity, which are powerfully conservative; on the other are the impulses of an international culture, strongly "western" and riding upon the global jet-stream of American English. To maintain tradition and to modernize are seen either as a dilemma or a challenge whose dialects impinge upon and revise the notions of life and its contexts. Reorientations and retrievals apart, modernization means, among other things, the creation of new intellectual reflexes, the enlargement of

267

freedoms, the creation of a new order for the betterment of both individual and society. The emergence from colonization involves at least four freedoms. The political is in some ways the most clear cut, though the routes to it have been various. Brunei was granted independence without a fuss; Kenya had to fight a bloody war. Next comes economic freedom, a difficult task, but one to be accomplished in some measure if a nation is to have stability. It requires planning, sustained effort, and noncorrupt governments, all of which are not always in sufficient evidence. The third freedom requires internal all-round strength—political, economic, social, and cultural—to maintain independence, to be able to withstand the more ambiguous pressures exerted by power blocs. Finally, there is psychological independence, which is perhaps the hardest to achieve.

Given the forces at work in his situation, the writer's interest, expectations, and response to the riddles and enigmas of this society translate into essential notions about life and contacts. As Gordimer has noted, the writer's themes have chosen them. These themes are connected with what I have elsewhere described (1984: 24) as a series of grammars the chief of which comprise "interests" and "motives."

> The sets of interests which accrue constitute what may be described as a grammar for living, one governing action, thought, the way we view events and experiences.
> Like anyone else, the writer is subject to the same process but with two notable differences. The first is that the grammar of his interests nourishes a deeper, more personalised grammar of motives—to borrow Kenneth Burke's phrase—generated by and connected to the demands of his vocation. The grammar links life and art and is partly inherited, partly made, augmented and modified by him. When we identify cardinal influences, primal vision, key themes or structural, metaphorical and imagistic traits or sources of iconography and the assemblage of their elements that give singularity to a writer's work, we are in fact mapping this narrower, specialised grammar. These features have to do with technique and substance. Technique derives from and returns to sources in his basic or adopted literary tradition or traditions. The second concerns contacts between the writer as individual and the total environment of which he is a part. But as both individual and environment alter, so does the grammar whose pattern is forged, after all, by the organic interplay between self and society.

I consider these grammars essential to an appropriate orientation for the study of new literatures in English, for it is precisely the absence of such orientation (and not a lack of intelligence) that leads to confident but misleading criticism and discussion. The grammars alter, in response to changes in society and in the individual, in writer and reader. The writer's dilemma is whether to maintain a consistency or to run the risk of apparent contradictions. Faint hearts do not found literatures or new varieties of languages. Such grammar formation is not new to English. American, Australian, and New Zealand literature share a great deal with English literature and with each other; they are linked by deep-rooted religions and by philosophical, scientific, intellectual, and other traditions. The new literatures are seldom, if ever, linked to the same extent. They share the language, the major genres, certain creative strategies—such as those deriving from oral narrative—and critical practices. Their literary ecology, if inclusive, is shaped by the literary traditions of their other languages. The literature in English in India, in Nigeria, in Singapore, is part of Indian, Nigerian, and Singaporean literature. The writer is formed by two worlds, at times belonging to richly complicated multiliterary ecosystems (see Thumboo 1983). He has twin perspectives, one established by English, the language of his creativity, the other by his mother tongue and its associated literature or literatures. It is worth remembering that the literary system of Europe that T. S. Eliot outlined in "Tradition and the Individual Talent"—especially the specific lines of descent from Homer, through Virgil and Dante, down to the national literatures— has counterparts in other literary ecosystems. In India, for instance, there are Sanskrit texts and the great epics.

Moreover, historical parallels arise in the writer's reshaping of English and his material, subject, and themes. There is the case of Anglo-Irish literature, one of whose dominant figures, W. B. Yeats, I see as a Third World poet of a special kind. Familiarity with the growth of American English and American literature, or with specific topics such as sociopolitical themes, in say, recent Arabic and Israeli literature or the frame of nationalism in French Canadian fiction, would certainly create a fuller sense of the issues taken up in the new literatures. One must look at them from within, on their own terms, through a paradigm that is flexible yet structured enough to power reorientations.

Each language harbors its own logic, its own system of latent and manifest content. English is no exception. Its prestige originally made it attractive to the indigenous ruling/upper class; they were the first bilinguals who knew a foreign language. Siblings and children benefited through an earlier start and the higher status enjoyed by their families. English became a second language and, in some cases, a first language. Here is Lewis Nkosi's experience: "I was reading an incredible amount, reading always badly without discipline; reading sometimes for the sheer beauty of the language. I walked about the streets of the bustling noisy city with new English words clicking like coins in the pockets of my mind; I tried them out on each passing scene, relishing their power to describe and apprehend experience" (quoted in Alvarez-Pereyre 1984: 5–6).

One feels the excitement in discovering the ability to name things and experiences, and to apply words to give some order, thus setting up a personal semiotic system. That modifying ability engages what Markandaya has called the cortex—that part of the mind, mysterious and not fully known, that enables the person to become a writer, broadly similar to the capacity that Coleridge described as the primary imagination. While Markandaya sees culture, ethos, and roots as being powerful, fundamental, and self-sustaining, what really matters is the "extraordinary cortex that exists in all of us, a cortex that, as it were, governs morality and the sensibility of creation, and like anything else can be cultivated or neglected" (1973: 15–16).

Such a cortex, revealed through the power of its metaphors and images, is essential both to the writer's development and to the reshaping of English in new environments. It is behind the creation of idiolect. It helps the writer negotiate between the demands of two traditions, one inherited, the other brought by English and its great literature. Its new users feel impelled to adapt, to orchestrate a thrust reflecting everyday realities as well as the nuances of its new home. Yet that undertaking cannot always be embarked upon easily. There are those who, like Parthasarathy, feel comfortable in English and (in his case) less so in Tamil, a fact that set up "painful but nevertheless fruitful tension with regard to poetry" (1973: 27).

This challenge confronts almost every bi- or multilingual writer. His bilingualism is one of three broad types—proficient, powerful, or limited; his position in this cline is not static, because quite often one language gains dominance. A bilingual person has at least two language universes, and each language works with its own linguistic circuits. How the two associate depends on whether the languages as neighbors inhabit the same space and time and can bend to serve creative purposes.

Multilingual Context and Linguistic Innovations

Language in a sense determines not only consciousness but also one's perception of reality. This suggests a kind of linguistic determinism close to that proposed by Whorf's *Mirror of Language,* from which it follows that speakers or users of different languages possess different patterns of thought. The Whorfian hypothesis has taken hard or soft forms. The soft form is useful especially in its suggestions that there is a tendency for the individual to think along avenues that have been defined by the whole of language. Scope for initiative and variation allows the proficient bilingual to bring into his creative language (in this case, English) some of the strategies and other resources of his native language and its literature. It also provides for the possibility that the proficient bilingual has a sharper perception of reality because he is bifocal.

Be that as it may, the search for idiom and idiolect is ongoing. What F. W. Bateson (1934; quoted in Wellek and Warren 1955: 177) said about the changing language of poetry would apply to the language of literature as a whole: "the age's imprint in a poem is not to be traced to the poet but to the language. The real history of poetry is, I believe, the history of the changes in the kind of language in which successive poems have been written. And it is these changes of language only that are due to the pressures of social and intellectual tendencies."

There is one notable difference between these changes in a monolingual situation and in a bilingual or multilingual situation. When we talk about the spread of English, we usually have in mind its spread *to* countries. What is more important at the micro level is its spread *within* so-called second-language areas. The learning of English is at a premium, both as a foreign language and as a second language. In Singapore, for instance, it is the medium of instruction throughout the educational system. The model adopted seeks to reflect an International Standard English close to British English. But the writer's innovations in order to create an ideolect quite often do not follow the general drift of the language as it is promoted educationally. This generalization must be modified to take into account the genre in which the writer works. As a rule, poetry is acrolectal, although there are instances where basilect is used. In drama the characters speak or ruminate in the lect appropriate to their intellectual and social background. Fiction claims a larger number of registers. Even with the first-person narrative we can assume that if the narrator is an acrolectal speaker, it would be possible for him to narrate across the lectal range of the world depicted. Many writers are concurrently atempting to evolve their own ideolect.

Within a basically monolingual situation, such as that which obtains in England, we can see this evolution over the years. In the case of poetry, we have the Metaphysical period, during which the use of conceits dominated; then we have the eighteenth century, with its fiction and theory of kinds; and next the Romantic period, where

271

there is a loosening, as it were, of the idiom and therefore a greater variation in styles.

The second-language situation is quite different. The writer is faced by unusual possibilities and therefore unusual challenges. The work of Kamala Das is exemplary. English is not Das's mother tongue, yet the poetry she writes in it is powerful at its best. On the other hand, her short stories are in Malayalam. What is striking here is the confident and powerful claim to two languages. (See also Chs. 16, 17, 18.)

The case for the use of English has been argued back and forth in almost all the new literatures. An early and in some ways still telling statement regarding the problem is provided by Raja Rao in his foreword to his novel *Kanthapura*. Here the tensions, the auguries of opportunity, are delicately defined: a language that is not one's own is balanced against a spirit that is one's own. English is said to be "alien," yet it is recognized as not being really alien. It serves intellectual, not emotional purposes. There is the interesting claim that we are all instinctively bilingual; there is the contention that you cannot write like the English, nor is it possible to write only as Indians. There is the conviction that the use of English in India will prove to be as distinctive as that which has emerged in Ireland and America. Raja Rao's stress on the necessity to reorient, to adjust, and to adapt the language is something that others in India have recognized.

Whatever their stance, their choice of genre, their choice of material, writers portray individuals and the warp and woof of society. At times their writing consists chiefly of their own reactions to and seekings about life, in a language that is simultaneously a private and a public possession. Language is the chief medium of consciousness, the instrument through which the external world is received, analyzed, and internalized; it is the instrument of creativity, of reaching out. It mediates upon the flow between the writer and his social reality. Creativity pushes him beyond mere description—meaning as it is— to assemble new meanings that capture the temper, the quintessential flavor of the times, linking generations and roving among decades. He takes his substance from the unique, the perennial, and the temporary, the buoyant and the ordinary—which may prove unexpectedly unique to others. He examines the surface and deep structures of his material and themes, exploring in a single moment the vocabulary of under-standing and expression, inventing in order to extend the depth and power of both. English for the writer is a language that gives and a language that receives.

The study of language is conducted through three main related branches: historical linguistics, descriptive linguistics, and comparative linguistics. These rest in varying degrees (depending on purpose, availability of data, and similar factors) on the study of phonetics and phonology, grammar (morphology and syntax), the lexicon and semantics. The upsurge of linguistics in third-movement situations, especially as a science, as an important area to be taught and researched, has tended to concentrate on English. Other languages, whether indigenous or brought through immigration, have yet to receive proportionate attention. Pragmatics apart, reasons for the spare attention include a shortage of linguists with the required background; the limitations of conceptions and terminologies; and insufficient coordination to pull together previous and current work. But the most crucial factor is the fact that English is the language in common. Scholarship on the language depends a great deal on how it is used by writers in Asia, Africa, the Pacific, and elsewhere. Linguists tap and add to the study of the language and literature of the mother-tongue bases. The scale is international and backed by a certain historical depth. On the other hand, the influence of, say, Ijaw, Yoruba, Ibo, Iwe, Kikuyu, Acholi, Illocano, and Jamaican Creole, or of Mandarin, Tamil, Hindi, Urdu, and Malay, is local or regional in context and import.

Yet the work has to be done if we are to increase our understanding of the back-, middle-, and foreground to the new literatures in English. Although they may write in English, virtually all writers of these literatures are bilingual, bicultural, and (for those in multicultural societies) touched by more than two semiotic systems. The result of that search for an idiolect is a verbal edifice that is under constant enlargement and modification, responding to shifts in the grammars of motives and interests. The edifice has two main doors: one to the world of English, dominated by its linguistic and literary systems; the other to the systems (linguistic, literary, social, philosophical) of the social reality or realities the writer inhabits.

New Contexts for English

The English language and its literary tradition are used for creating a literature whose impulse and inspiration derive from a social reality distinct from that on which the language and literature previously rested. In these circumstances, traditional assumptions about the function of the artist and the legitimate concerns of literature cannot apply in toto. English is writing into a new experience, requiring fresh gesture, a different reach. Part of the strength and capacity of English to absorb modifications and extensions lies in its wealth of synonyms, alluring shades of meaning to be controlled, giving generous room for that movement from the denotative to the connotative, from the latent to the manifest. The new flow of meaning is in some sense a personal creation. If powerful and made accessible through context, the newly invented can work its way into general usage. The more radical the innovation, the less likely its adoption; Okara's *The Voice* or Tutuola's *The Palmwine Drinkard* are extreme examples, the former based on a concerted attempt to impose Ijaw structure upon English, the latter a consistent but personal variety of English. Each establishes its own semiotic system, and each succeeds to a degree through its links with the larger system of English as an international language and the varieties of native-based and new literatures. They constitute a network for both writer and reader, a network offering entry into the system despite the fact that some of their linguistic and literary elements, strategies, concepts, and assumptions differ, at times starkly.

Questions about language dominate part of the social reality. The place of English, especially as a bridge between ethnic groups, as modernizing, as a creative instrument, forms a set of concerns inevitably reflected in the new literatures. Colonial and postcolonial politics are involved, as are ethnic rivalries and suspicions; the implications of caste and class, of being "educated" and "less educated." Life is always firmly behind language and literature. Each character, whether partially or fully developed, is a pool of consciousness, of understanding and ignorance, of darkness and light, of enlightenment and prejudice. The difficulty is not merely one of an appropriate lect. It extends to forming a lectal range that can reflect a multilingual or bilingual situation. The following passage from Achebe's *Arrow of God* is exemplary. The Igbo Unachukwa uses fractured English when speaking to an Englishman; yet when he speaks to a fellow Igbo, the English must improve, as we are to assume that his Igbo is at least good:

"Dat man wan axe master queshon."
"No questions."
"Yassah." He turned to Nweke. "The white man says he did not leave his house this morning to come and answer your questions."

In order to sustain the impression of the shift from English to Igbo, *queshon* becomes *questions*.

While we are concerned here with creativity in English, it should be noted that the problems are equally present for those who use "indigenous" languages such as Tagalog, Bengali, and Malay, or other migrant languages, of which Tamil and Mandarin in Singapore and Malaysia would be instances. The human situation is complicated by bi- and trilingual, polydialectal factors, not so much for the individual participants as for those who wish to grasp the whole. The writer is concerned to articulate his interest, his vision, and the themes ensuing therefrom. When he reads contemporaries and predecessors, whether in the original or in translation, his motives differ from those of a critic; it is part instruction, part nourishment. If he essays criticism, the practice is informed by writerly insights. The frame of reference for the critic is significantly broader, for while he may be engaged with a particular text or writer, his very role implies a concern with a literature or literatures. He is concerned, in varying degrees, with periods, with movements, with judging writers, preferring one to another and providing grounds for his preferences. His view combines a sense of the contemporary and a sense of the past, the writer with the production of the literature. The writer installs his vision in his work; the critic considers this vision as well as that of other writers. In the context of African literatures in English, it means no less than finding a frame for discussing and evaluating the works of, say, Kofi Awoonor, Chinua Achebe, Gabriel Okara, Elechi Amadi, Ngũgĩ Wa Thiong'o, Oko p'Bitek. Extend the list to include the Anglophone writers in Heinemann's African Writers series—then Indian, West Indian, Southeast Asian, and South Pacific literatures in English, not to mention their links with "indigenous" literary traditions—and you have a fair conception of the critical tasks. For each writer there is perception and performance, active and passive stance ranging from a feel for the larger political and social realities to the specifics of individual thought and feeling.

Criticism is simultaneously a generalizing and a specifying activity. There is the tempting assumption that a work is to some degree characteristic, that its distinctiveness can be accounted for within the prevailing semiotic systems. Moreover, a work that demonstrably cuts against the grain, however powerfully disturbing (Joyce's *Ulysses* is an obvious example), can be accommodated; it does not bring in the context of another linguistic-literary semiotic system. The literature and its language continue to change through revolution and evolution. Donne, Dryden, Fielding, Wordsworth, Eliot, Joyce, and Yeats were innovators, major figures who opened up new possibilities of language and structure that influenced their contemporaries. Thus the revolution settles down to an evolution, establishing a mode, a period. It makes for a degree of acceptable generalization in which the discussion of text or issue has force beyond the specific occasion. Instances are the metaphysical conceit or the theory and practice of Augustan poetic diction. Continuities of literary history encourage the emergence of a critical tradition vigilant of the literature in the language.

The situation is radically dissimilar within the new literatures. They have variety best understood in terms of origins, antecedents, and contemporaneity, attempting to retain much that is traditional in various spheres of life and yet wishing to incorporate change. For the writer, every attempt is a new beginning whose relevance is best judged retrospectively, as the means for judgment are themselves being formed. Innovations are not calculated to alter or refurbish a creative tradition; rather, the tradition, in some instances barely discernible, is emerging. Robust as well as lesser talents are equally in search of creative means, of shaping vision. The overall frame within which specific as well as more general studies can profitably proceed will incorporate a number of foci to sharpen our response. The first focus is for linguistic and literary studies to link up wherever possible, and so avoid what Quirk (1974: 65), referring to the study of Old, Middle, and contemporary English literature, described as "a dichotomy between the relatively modern writings that can be 'appreciated' (these are called 'literature') and the relatively early writings that cannot be (and these are called 'language')." The danger would arise from the divergence in the varieties of English that have resulted from the formal and informal adoption of English within a polity where writers have quite different mother tongues, to the greater divergence between the clines of English in, say, the West Indies, the Philippines, and India. Literature draws upon the full stretch of language. While the standard educated varieties are mutually intelligible in a substantial way, the pidgins and creoles have a local habitation and a name.

Models for the Spread of English

The two most recent models for the spread of English are proposed by Kachru and Quirk. They raise important issues whose full implications for nations in the third movement will emerge increasingly from theoretical and applied research. But comprehensive, sustained language surveys require substantial funds and specialists. Language is power.[2] Given limited resources and unlimited needs, governments of third-movement nations are forced into pragmatism, a formula of priorities. The concentration on language in education stresses its practical value, which is quite rightly paramount. Fortunately, scholarly enterprise, however modest in isolation, has a cumulative effect. The study of language and the application of linguistic concepts and methods have contributed to the greater definition of our understanding. An increasing number of texts have attracted stylistic/linguistic analysis. Emmanuel Njara, for instance, has done very useful work on a selection of African novels. And Winfred Lehmann's treatment, sensitive, discriminating, and precise, of Raja Rao's short story "The Cow of the Barricades" both enriches and structures our understanding, linking the linguistic and literary interest. Lehmann's

> presentation proposes within a model of communication three strata; a phonological, a grammatical, and a semiological. Assuming these strata, a text linguist interprets the linguistic material relating the physical phenomena or articulatory and auditory mechanisms using sound waves with the communication situation, including the referential realm, the culture, the language, the social setting and the participation of communicator and audience. These distinctions already make up a rich area for analysis by the text linguist and literary critic. But the three strata provide grounds for added richness. In each of these linguistic strata there are sub-strata with their own elements; the elements are interrelated by means of the formulae known in linguistic study as rules. For illustration I list the seven sub-strata in the grammatical stratum. Beginning with the largest entity these sub-strata are: discourse, paragraph, sentence, clause, phrase, word and the smallest segment of grammatical form, the morpheme. Exploring the treatment of these substrata and of their characteristic elements by a poet might well occupy any literary critic. Phrased differently, the exploration of such well-identified arrays corresponds to the literary critic's task: making explicit the characteristics of their critical procedures in "der Kunst des Lesens— the art of reading." [n.d.: 20–21]

Such analysis via strata and substrata will, as Lehmann suggests, make "explicit the characteristics of critical procedures." The other point apposite to the general thrust of what I have been saying is that while the procedures have been applied to native-based English literatures, they have yet to be systematically employed in the study of new literatures. Starts have been made, but they do not always take into account "the referential realm, the culture, the language, the social setting and the participation of communicator and audience"; i.e., the social reality *and* the constituting genetic/semiotic systems. And where they do, there remain problems of balance between the emphases on each realm.

The network of issues connected with criticism of and creation in the new literatures is endless. It metamorphoses as life and language move. But two further suggestions may provide a useful concluding note. The first concerns the formation of an idiolect; the second, critical approaches. Quarrying into English—or any language—to secure an inwardness sufficient to manage irony, pun, paradox, specific rhythms, striking metaphor, intricate patterns of images, and shades of meaning is never easy. Moreover, the process of formulation is not always conscious. The writer judges as his own critic, but what he judges is both consciously and unconsciously formulated. The mind has its secret thesaurus in which words long unused emerge aptly. The general process includes using language to explore and define an idea, a feeling; the contrary state is an idea, a feeling in search of words. For the writer in the third movement the challenge is complicated by a bilingual, bicultural inheritance. Concepts, the link between custom, behavior, the cosmos, and language as posited by the mother tongue often cannot move across into English. Achebe did not see this as representing a serious problem, but others have. Perhaps it depends on one's experience with English, with the conception of creativity's demands in a polydialectal situation. Writers as geographically dispersed as Edith Tiempo (Philippines), Derek Walcott (Jamaica), and Gabriel Okara (Nigeria) have thought it necessary to bend English to achieve satis-factory statement (see Thumboo 1986: 253–54). Acts of translation and transcreation mark their creativity, though in this case critical judgments do not possess an original text as benchmark. Nonetheless, the methods of translation, especially those used in English and indigenous languages and covering work in both directions, are useful, if we keep in mind the essential spirit of freedom noted as far back as John Dryden's introduction to Ovid's *Epistles* (1680):

> All translation, I suppose, may be reduced to these three heads. First, that of metaphrase, or turning an author word by word, and line by line, from one language into another. The second way is that of paraphrase, or translation with latitude, where the author is kept in view by the translator, so as never to be lost, but his words are not so strictly followed as his sense, and that too is admitted to be amplified, but not altered. The third way is that of imitation, where the translator (if now he has not lost that name) assumes the liberty not only to vary from the words and sense, but to forsake them both as he sees occasion; and taking only some general hints from the original, to run division on the ground-work, as he pleases.

That new literatures are at least bicultural formations—in which English and its literary inheritance are common—has not been suffi-ciently realized, except by those who belong to the social reality or one that is comparable. This has led, among other things, to the feeling in certain quarters that criticism from the outside, the mother-tongue bases especially, remains metropolitan centered and, at times, imperial. The sense of distance, of minimal sympathy was never a widespread sentiment in the Anglo diaspora. The coming of age of their literatures was not traumatic: their social realities were offshoots, grafts. The new literatures, which belong to ex-colonies, are a different case altogether.

Nor have critics belonging to the third movement been innocent of misinterpreting works that rest on their own or other social realities. But greater difficulties are faced by those from outside these realities. Some have worked through these; their work shows that without that grasp, inappropriate assumptions or questionable points of departure may misdirect attention. The most potent sin is the tacit assumption that as they use English, or a variety of it, the new literatures are an extension of English literature, and that its critical practice ought to cope with these fledglings comfortably. This is hardly the case when put to the test. Where the criticism has been illuminating, we find reorientations that take into account the contexts of the work.

Identities of New Literatures

We ought to treat the new literatures as separate in certain essential aspects despite their sharing of English. Moreover, they are—with the exception of West Indian English writing—but one of two, three, or more literatures within the social reality. The focus on English should be balanced by the realization that the literature in it is part of a national literary system upon which its survival and growth depend. Such are the complexities to be unraveled that the methods of comparative literature may be adopted with profit. The justification strengthens as we move into each literature and discover its distinctiveness, its unique place in a possible whole. Provided that the comparative spirit is sensitively attentive and exploratory, its methods will take us further toward understanding and judging new literatures, individually and as a group, how they relate to each other and to mother-tongue-based literatures, and whether we can ultimately attempt an overview of all literatures in English.

Comparative literature as a discipline reflects Euro-American interests. (The implications of recent developments for the study of new literatures are considered in Thumboo 1987.) The basic comparative frame is set by taking literatures in two or more languages, the general assumption being "one language, one literature." A relatively recent development (see Grimm 1986) is the study of the literature in one language (in this case, German) written by minorities and in different geographical localities. Grimm discusses whether these literatures are extensions or "second literatures" and makes the point that a more "differentiated terminology and approach" will have to be adopted. Because the writers he refers to share, in addition to language, a relatively homogeneous culture, the phenomenon of spread is akin to the spread in the first and second movements I outlined. In coping with the new literatures, the comparative approach would be dealing with enormously more varied social realities and therefore would require the working out of appropriate concepts, terminologies, and approaches. The challenge ought to prove fruitful in the meeting. Comparative literature works by way of disciplined inquisitiveness, considers background, and looks at literatures in the context of cultural and other manifestations. It considers literatures in translation, either on the page or in the mind of the bilingual reader, and is more likely to consider creative adjustments to English in response to new social realities. While it generalizes about the strengths and resources of particular languages for this or that purpose and ranks texts from them, it is not inclined to rank languages. Moreover, its approaches include those by way of genre and theme, both unfashionable as major foci in the criticism of English literature, but useful in discussing the new literatures. These potential advantages apart, it is less likely to have a hidden agenda.

I have sought to suggest what historical and contemporary forces lie behind the emergence and shaping of the new literatures in English, and possible ways of looking at them. The preoccupation with theme, with linguistic and literary resources within and in response to main and subordinate social realities, is by no means exhaustive. This chapter is a plea for constructive understanding as a prelude to literary judgment. There are no conclusions, only beginnings. The urging of more sharply focused and informed criticism of the individual literatures must resist irredentist impulses. Collectively, such criticism should form part of a common enterprise that will, over the long term and especially if it combines literary and linguistic studies, bring about a clear, richer sense of how English has not only spread but also brought forth new literatures upon which the sun will never set.

NOTES

1. When translated from the original Malay into English, this slogan becomes "One land, one people, one religion."
2. See *World Englishes* 5:2-3 (1986), which is devoted to papers given at a 1986 conference on "The Power of English: Cross-Cultural Dimensions in Literature and Media," East-West Center, Honolulu.

REFERENCES

Achebe, Chinua. 1964. *Arrow of God*. London: Heinemann.
————. 1969. *A man of the people*. London: Heinemann.

Alvarez-Pereyre, Jacques. 1984. *The poetry of commitment in South Africa.* London: Heinemann.

Amirthanayagam, Guy, ed. 1982. *Writers in East-West encounter: new cultural bearings.* London: Macmillan.

Awoonor, Kofi. 1976. Tradition and continuity in African literature. Pp. 166–72 in Smith 1976.

Bateson, F. W. 1961. *English poetry and the English language.* 2nd ed. New York: Russell. (3rd ed., Oxford: Clarendon, 1973.)

Breitinger, Eckhard, and Reinhard Sander, eds. 1985. *Studies in Commonwealth literature.* Tübingen: Gunter Narr Verlag.

Chinweizu. 1983. Decolonising the wind. *South* (January): 19–21.

Das, Kamala. 1973. *The old playhouse and other poems.* New Delhi: Orient Longman.

Dembo, L. S., ed. 1968. *Criticism: speculative and analytical essays.* Madison: University of Wisconsin Press.

Ee Tiang Hong. 1976. *Myths for a wilderness.* Singapore: Heinemann.

Egejuru, Phanuel Akubueze. 1978. *Black writers/white audience: a critical approach to African literature.* New York: Exposition Press.

Ezekiel, Nissim. 1976. *Hymns in darkness.* New Delhi: Oxford University Press.

Feinberg, Barry, ed. 1974. *Poets to the people.* London: Allen Unwin. (2nd ed., London: Heinemann, 1980.)

Forster, E. M. 1924. *A passage to India.* Abinger edition, London: Arnold, 1978.

Gordimer, Nadine. 1973. *The black interpreters: notes on African writing.* Johannesburg: SPROCAS/RAVAN.

Grimm, Reinhold. 1986. Identity and difference: on comparative studies within a single language. Pp. 28–29 in *Profession 1986.* New York: Modern Language Association of America.

Halliday, M. A. K. 1978. *Language as social semiotic: the social interpretation of language and meaning.* London: Arnold.

Hoggart, Richard. 1982. *An English temper: essays on education, culture and communication.* London: Chatto.

Huxley, Elspeth. 1957. *The red rock wilderness.* London: Chatto.

———. 1962. *On the edge of the rift.* New York: Morrow.

———. 1968. *White man's country.* 2 vols. London: Chatto.

Johnson, Colin. 1985. Interview with Colin Johnson. Pp. 11–14 in Breitinger and Sander 1985.

Kachru, Braj B. 1985. Standards, codification and sociolinguistic realism: the English language in the Outer Circle. Pp. 11–30 in Quirk and Widdowson 1985.

Kavanagh, Robert Mshengu. 1985. *Theatre and cultural struggle in South Africa.* London: Zed Books.

Lehmann, Winfred. Literature and linguistics: text linguistics. Pp. 18–29 in Narasimhaiah and Srinath n.d.

Markandaya, Kamala. 1973. One pair of eyes: some random reflections. *The Literary Criterion* 11.1: 14–25.

Narasimhaiah, C. D., and C. N. Srinath, eds. N.d. *English, its complementary role in India.* Mysore: Dhvanyaloka.

Njara, Emmanuel. 1982. *Stylistic criticism and the African novel.* London: Heinemann.

Nkosi, Lewis. 1981. *Tasks and masks: themes and styles of African literature.* Harlow: Longman.

———. 1983. *Home and exile and other selections.* Harlow: Longman.

Parthasarathy, R. 1973. The Indian writer's problems: poet in search of a language. *The Literary Criterion* 11.1: 126–29.

———. 1977. *Rough passage.* Delhi: Oxford University Press.

Quirk, Randolph. 1974. *The linguist and the English language.* London: Arnold.

———, and H. G. Widdowson, eds. 1985. *English in the world: teaching and learning the language and literatures.* Cambridge: Cambridge University Press.

Rao, Raja. 1971. *Kanthapura.* Delhi: Orient Paperbacks.

Royston, Robert, ed. 1973. *Black poets in South Africa.* London: Heinemann.

Salleh, Muhammad Haji. 1977. *Tradition and change in contemporary Malay-Indonesian poetry.* Kuala Lumpur: Penerbit Universiti Kebangsaan Malaysia.

Smith, Rowland, ed. 1976. *Exile and tradition: studies in African and Caribbean literature.* Dalhousie: Dalhousie University Press.

Soyinka, Wole. 1965. *The interpreters.* London: Andre Deutsch.

Thumboo, Edwin. 1984. The writer and society: some Third World reminders. *Solidarity* 99: 24–32.

———. 1985. Twin perspectives and multi-ecosystems: tradition for a Commonwealth writer. *World Englishes* 4.2: 213–21.

———. 1986. Language as power: Gabriel Okara's *The Voice* as a paradigm. *World Englishes* 5.2-3: 249–64.

———. 1987. New literatures in English: imperative for a comparative approach. Paper delivered at Conference on Literature in English: New Perspectives, Graz, Austria, Apr. 21–24.

Wellek, René, and Austin Warren. 1955. *Theory of literature.* London: Jonathan Cape.

Wendt, Albert. 1982. Towards a New Oceania. Pp. 202–15 in Amirthanayagam 1982.

Wong Kan Seng. Minister of Community Development, Republic of Singapore. Speech, Annual Cultural Awards Presentation. Singapore, Feb. 10, 1987.

15

Ann Lowry

Style Range in New English Literatures

The new English literatures are essentially a linguistic legacy of the British colonial period. The body of scholarship discussing the development of such literatures in various genres and specific regions (see, e.g., Aggarwal 1981; King 1979; Narasimhaiah 1976) or providing an overview of such literatures in a world context (see Jones 1965 and King 1980) has been slowly increasing in recent years. Students of English or comparative literature have traditionally studied the uses, changes, and stylistic innovations in English within the confines of its native areas.

Research on new English literatures remains on the periphery of the traditional boundaries of English studies. During the last two decades, however, scholars of literature and linguistics have recognized—and partly described—this new dimension of English literature and its linguistic, cultural, and literary implications. Here I shall focus on selected aspects of stylistic devices used in two such new English literatures, Indian English and Caribbean English, with special reference to fiction by R. K. Narayan, Mulk Raj Anand, and V. S. Naipaul.

The Novel in New Contexts

The novel, after developing in Europe, later became a significant literary genre in areas of colonial influence. The United States was one of the first and most significant places where a new literary tradition developed, based on European (primarily British) models. Mark Twain's *Huckleberry Finn* (1885) has been cited as "a major turning point in American writing, the point at which American style came into its own as distinct from British style." Telling his story in the words of the young, uneducated Huck, Twain used nonstandard English "not for local color, but for character" (Traugott and Pratt 1980: 338). Since then, American writers of widely varying backgrounds have made their protagonists tell their own stories in language just as authentic as it may be nonstandard. The novels of Jewish writers such as Saul Bellow and Philip Roth, southern writers including William Faulkner and Eudora Welty, and black writers, among them Zora Neale Hurston and Ralph Ellison, indicate the kaleidoscope of voices rising from the pages of twentieth-century American fiction.

The English language and the novel as a genre were transplanted to other colonial regions as well. As significant numbers of Indians, Africans, and others became educated in English, a few were attracted to the novel, the sonnet, and other non-indigenous literary forms. The changes in English vocabulary and syntax were more rapid and obvious among these writers and speakers than among those for whom standard English is the sole or primary tongue. A dazzling and highly unusual Indian writer, G. V. Desani, has described his own stylistic experimentation as follows: "I have chosen the craft of writing. And my entire linguistic creed . . . is simply to find a suitable medium. I find the English language is that kind of medium. It needs to be modified to suit my purpose" (Narasimhaiah 1978: 406).

Though Indian, African, and Caribbean literatures in English are small and new when compared to their British or American counterparts, they have, after some hesitation on the part of both local and international critical establishments, been received into the family of world literatures in English. Third World writers in English must tread a fine line between the perils of incomprehensibility on one hand and nondescriptness on the other. Their works must appeal to large and potentially lucrative American and British markets; yet each novel must contain "exotic elements" of character, theme, and setting, as well as language, if it is to succeed financially. A contemporary American writer can earn a living by writing books which characterize (or caricature) one of the nation's numerous ethnic groups (e.g., John Updike on American WASPs); whether his books appeal to readers in London or Lagos or Lahore makes no difference. Not so for the Indian, African, or Caribbean writer.

The Indian and Caribbean Situations

Indians have been writing English-language fiction for the last half-century. Of the first generation, three writers are generally viewed as outstanding: Mulk Raj Anand, R. K. Narayan, and Raja Rao. All three published their first fictional works in the 1930s; while Raja Rao has since divided his intellectual efforts between fiction and philosophy (or combined them, as in his novel *The Serpent and the Rope*), Anand and Narayan have continued to devote themselves to fiction, occasionally writing essays and autobiographical works as well. Though born only a year apart, the two are in most other respects quite unalike. Mulk Raj Anand, born in 1905, spent his early years in the Punjab; he traveled to Britain for his higher education and became involved with leftist political thinkers during the 1930s. His progressive political orientation combined with his Indian background to result in *Untouchable* (1935), his first published novel and still his most famous work. During the subsequent decades Anand has continued to wield his literary pen in the interests of sociopolitical causes.

R. K. Narayan was born in 1906, at the opposite end of the subcontinent. He speaks Tamil as well as English, and knows some Kannada; his life has been spent mainly in Madras and Mysore, and he has traveled abroad only in his later adulthood. Whereas Anand is known for his political commitment, Narayan is equally noted for his philosophical detachment and irony. His first novel, *Swami and Friends*, was published (as was Anand's) in 1935. Among the score of novels, stories, and essay collections to appear since that time, *The Financial Expert* (1952) is one of his most praised works; the protagonist, Margayya, has been hailed as "probably Narayan's greatest single comic creation" (Walsh 1971: 19).

Whereas English is a second language in India, it is the primary language in much of the Caribbean. As the literary scholar Kenneth Ramchand (1970: 82) has noted, for the Caribbean writer there is "no possibility of choice between English and another language"—one writes in English if one writes at all. The indigenous Carib population was erased long ago, and was replaced by African, European, and East Indian immigrants, all with different languages. While the British were able to assert the supremacy of English in the administrative and educational systems, this did not entail the demise of African and Indian languages and speech patterns in the Caribbean.

White authors have been publishing their fictional works since the early years of this century, but novels by non-white Caribbean authors are a more recent development. Whereas Indian English fiction was developing in the 1930s, non-white Caribbean authors did not begin receiving widespread notice until the 1950s. The independence of the former British West Indies is likewise more recent than India's. One wonders whether political independence must be in the offing for literary figures of a different race to be "taken seriously" by the

Western/white critical establishment. No doubt those who have studied African literatures in English have asked themselves this same question.

Among Caribbean writers there are several important black novelists, including George Lamming and Wilson Harris. V. S. Naipaul is at least their equal. Most critics agree that Naipaul's longest novel, *A House for Mr. Biswas* (1961), is one of the very best Caribbean English novels to date. He is a generation younger than Anand and Narayan; at about the time when the two elder authors were born, Naipaul's grandfather moved from Uttar Pradesh to Trinidad. The grandson lived on that island from his birth in 1932 until leaving for Oxford in 1950. He has remained in Britain since that time, although taking numerous trips abroad, including journeys to India and back to Trinidad, and he has married a British woman. His first published novel, *The Mystic Masseur,* appeared in 1957.

Naipaul himself has written (1973: 12) of the predicament of the Indian (or Indian-descent) writer in English: "It is an odd, suspicious situation: an Indian writer writing in English for an English audience about non-English characters who talk their own sort of English. . . . I cannot help feeling that it might have been more profitable for me to appear in translation." The Indian critic Meenakshi Mukherjee (1971: 23) has also alluded to this situation in her discussion of the problems of trying to establish a distinct literature in a language in which a great literature (in this case, British) already exists. Much has been written on the use of English by Indian novelists; critics have analyzed sentence structures, the uses (or avoidance) of Indian words, and other elements. Two important second-language problems mentioned by Ramchand (1970: 78) with regard to Caribbean authors also have application in the Indian context. First, "there may be difficulties of expression arising from an inadequate grasp of basic features of the language"; second, "an author who thinks in one language instinctively and writes in another is liable to modify the adopted language," perhaps even unconsciously. These adaptations and variations from British Standard English have been noted, often in tones ranging from lament to ridicule, by Western scholars and critics.

New Styles in New Settings

Rather than looking at the language of the narrator, or the themes and structure, or exotic elements of plot and setting—as most critics of Indian English and Caribbean English fiction have done so far—I shall here focus on the language of the fictional characters themselves, and the methods and contexts in which that language is conveyed.

Dialogue is of primary importance; I shall examine the spoken language of the characters, rather than the written language of the authors. All three authors considered here are quite capable of writing and speaking standard English, but this is not true of their fictional creations, Bakha, Margayya, Ganesh, and Mr. Biswas. Indeed, the difference between the style of the narrative and the voice of the fictional character can be developed with the intent of heightening incongruity (Ramchand 1970: 102). While such incongruity is often emphasized for its comic effect, Ramchand asserts that "dialect is [now] used in so many different human contexts by West Indian writers that it has been freed of the stereotype" of the comic Negro or other minority figure (1970: 88). Of the many possible ways to use English in dialogue of non-native speakers (or simply non-speakers) of English, the novels of Anand, Narayan, and Naipaul demonstrate some of the most creative and diverse options. Following a discussion of the three authors' techniques, I shall briefly assess their similarities, differences, and implications for future work by these and other authors.

R. K. Narayan: *The Financial Expert*

The Financial Expert, like Narayan's other novels, contains few Indian words, and those that do appear are carefully italicized: *ghee, dhoti, puja, karma,* and *sanyasi,* for example. The goddess Saraswathi, mentioned in passing at one point, is carefully described in a footnote for the reader unfamiliar with Hindu mythology. Despite the care he obviously feels obliged to take to insure that a Western reader will understand his work, Narayan apparently feels that the advantages of English outweigh the disadvantages. In an interview he once observed: "Until you mentioned another tongue I never had any idea that I was writing in another tongue. My whole education has been in English. . . . I am particularly fond of the language . . . it is . . . very adaptable . . . and it's so transparent it can take on the tint of any country" (Walsh 1971: 7). The word "transparent" is interesting in this context—implying a sort of clarity on one hand, but reminding us of a barrier, something that must be looked through, on the other.

All of the characters in *The Financial Expert* speak grammatically correct English, sometimes surprisingly so. Margayya, the financier of the title, is the main speaker, but subordinate figures also provide examples of proper—verging on ornate—dialogue. A peasant observes, "We should not talk about others unnecessarily" (Narayan 1953: 13); a police inspector announces that Margayya "has come after his son, Balu, about whom a card has emanated from here" (p. 138).

The correct uses of "unnecessarily," "emanated," "about whom," and a passive verb construction in these sentences are typical of Narayan but unlike the dialogue of most other non-native English novelists. One is led to consider two possibilities: either the people in the small South Indian village of Malgudi speak grammatically, albeit not in English, and Narayan is simply conveying their speech patterns to an English-speaking readership; or else he is concerned with portraying the foibles of his characters through means other than grammar or accent. The former prospect, of universal correct speech, seems less likely when one looks at an early episode involving Margayya's son, Balu, while he is still a small boy: " 'Don't say so,' screamed the boy in his own childish slang. 'I'm hurt. I want a peppermint' " (p. 10). If this is "his own childish slang," it is difficult to see how an adult could have conveyed the message much differently.

Only on one occasion does Narayan mention that his characters are actually speaking a language other than English. When Margayya goes to see a priest, hoping for advice on how to win the Goddess of Wealth to his cause, the priest "recited a short verse and commanded Margayya to copy it down in Sanskrit, and side by side take down its meaning in Tamil" (p. 45). The obvious implication is that Margayya is a native speaker of Tamil. Indeed, there is no occasion on which he or other Malgudi residents would need to speak a language other than Tamil, for theirs is an out-of-the-way spot, visited rarely by people from other parts of India, and even less often by those from other parts of the world. Narayan's main fictional intent seems to be to portray—some might say, expose—universal human dreams and foibles such as greed, pride, humility, and compassion by dealing with everyday people in an unimportant village. Though the reader is constantly aware that *The Financial Expert* is set in India, one is not so likely to think about the characters' speech patterns. In Narayan's case, the style of the narrator is not substantially different from the styles of the speakers.

Mulk Raj Anand: *Untouchable*

What a contrast when one examines Mulk Raj Anand's *Untouchable!* While Narayan's English may be "transparent," Anand's is spattered with so many Hindustani words that the Western reader may feel he is looking through frosted glass. Sentence structure remains nondeviant in both narration and dialogue, but within a sentence it is not unusual to find one or more non-English words. What is the average Western reader to make of dialogue such as this: " 'So proud of his izzat! He just goes about getting salaams from everybody' " (Anand 1935/6: 13). The Westerner might be familiar with *salaam*, but it is less likely that he will know the meaning of *izzat* (honor)—a word which is, in itself, somewhat difficult to define, since it has deep cultural and often caste connotations. The problem is further heightened by a failure to italicize Hindustani words when there is an English word that would be written the same way: "Angrez log" (English people) may look like a kind of firewood to one who is not aware of the proper pronunciation, much less the accurate meaning of the term. The Western reader can understand statements such as "He walked like a Laften Gornor!" (p. 53) and "The santry inspector that day abused my father" (p. 56), but he will probably assume that these are merely mispronunciations of English words, rather than terms which have been borrowed from English and which now have been nativized with their own roles in other Indian languages.

A wide range of styles can be found in this one small book. Bakha, the eighteen-year-old illiterate sweeper who is the title character, often seems quite childlike in thought as well as speech. However, occasionally the reader encounters dialogue such as this: " 'My father is ill,' replied Bakha, 'so I am going to sweep the roads in town and the temple courtyard in his stead' " (p. 39). Here the uses of "ill" and "in his stead" seem a bit odd. And while the reader is expected to know the meanings of words like *izzat* (honor), *bania* (merchant caste), *gulabjamun* (Indian sweet), *vilayat* (England, abroad), and *swadeshi* (native, indigenous) from a context which is sometimes nonexistent, one is occasionally provided with a bit of overinformation. For example: "Bakha felt weak. He realized that an Untouchable going into a temple polluted it past purification" (p. 64).

The most contextually significant phrases in *Untouchable* are not the untranslated non-English words, but the phrases which have been translated from Hindustani into English. These consist primarily of swear words, "Ohe, lover of your mother" (p. 10), "you illegally begotten" (p. 15), "cock-eyed son of a bowlegged scorpion" (p. 51), and many others. All of these terms appear only in dialogue, of course, whereas the direct borrowings described above occur in both dialogue and narrative. These epithets, so numerous and so literally translated, can affect the reader in either of two ways: they can seem jarring, or they can soon come to be viewed as routine and meaningless. With Anand, it is important to remember that style is not insignificant, but it remains always the handmaiden of the ideological message. In *Untouchable*, which perhaps seems best when read as it was written— that is, at a whirlwind pace—Anand intends to show the unjustifiable and seemingly eternal oppression of the sweeper. Bakha cleans latrines and gutters; he eats food which others fling from their second-story windows, even though it may first land in the street; he can't even brush past a brahmin, whereas a man from the same high caste has license to molest Bakha's sister, who should be equally untouchable. Though several solutions to the problem of untouchability are presented near the end of the novel—involving Christ, Gandhi, and the prospective arrival of the flush toilet—Anand stresses not the solution, but the shocking and depressing problem itself. With that intent in mind, his frequent use of abusive dialogue is both appropriate and meaningful, and therefore stylistically important.

Untouchable is unusual in that one of its characters is a British missionary who speaks Hindustani. We know that none of the Indian characters speaks his language (i.e., our language), and we are constantly reminded of that fact when we hear utterances such as *are; hai, hai; han; nahin,* and so on. But Colonel Hutchinson, a Salvation Army man, must be able to deal with these people on their own terms if he is to spread the Gospel among them, and thus he must speak (or try to speak) Hindustani. Anand notes that, although the Colonel's "tongue was like a pair of scissors which cut the pattern of Hindustani into smithereens," Bakha nevertheless "felt honored that the sahib had deigned to talk Hindustani to him, even though it was broken Hindustani" (p. 135). The author then elaborates on swear words, the only Hindustani phrases known by most sahibs, giving both the originals and the English translations. The Colonel's wife is not happy to see the sweeper boy approaching her house: "Bakha had not known the exact reasons for her frowns, but when he heard the words bhangi and chamar, he at once associated her anger with the sight of himself" (p. 145). It is abundantly clear that while Bakha's speech appears in English on the printed page, the author has translated that speech from another language.

V. S. Naipaul: *The Mystic Masseur* and *A House for Mr. Biswas*

In *The Mystic Masseur* and *A House for Mr. Biswas,* all of V. S. Naipaul's important characters are of Indian descent. In the former, Ganesh, the mystic masseur, and his wife, Leela, are able to speak Hindi, though they do not do so as a matter of course. This short novel focuses primarily on them; on Leela's father, Ramlogan; and on a couple of other adults. The narrative covers a number of years, but since Ganesh and Leela have no children the characters and their linguistic abilities remain much the same throughout.

A House for Mr. Biswas covers the entire life span of Mr. Biswas, from the day of his birth to his death forty-six years later. Mr. Biswas (like his creator, V. S. Naipaul) is a third-generation East Indian in the West Indies. He speaks Hindi in his youth, and his mother, Bipti, never learns any other language, even though she lives all her life on an island where only one-third of the population is of Indian descent and fewer still know Hindi. Mr. Biswas first uses English dialect to talk with his friend Alec, a schoolboy of Portuguese descent who does not know Hindi. Later, after Mr. Biswas has married Shama and moved in with the Tulsi family (his in-laws), the narrator notes that "there was as yet little friendliness between them [Shama and Mr. Biswas] . They spoke in English" (Naipaul 1961: 104). This lack of friendliness is likewise manifest in Mr. Biswas's relations with other residents of the Tulsi compound: "Mr. Biswas nearly always spoke English at Hanuman House; it had become one of his principles" (pp. 118–19). Later, after all four of his children have been born and the older ones are attending school, Mr. Biswas's elderly mother comes to live with them for a time; by then, "though the children understood Hindi they could no longer speak it, and this limited communication between them and Bipti" (p. 426). Thus Mr. Biswas's initial lack of "friendliness" with his bride will result, a generation later, in adult offspring who speak only one language (English), just as Mr. Biswas's mother spoke only one language (Hindi).

One can trace the ascent of English dialect throughout the novel, even though the whole work is written in English. Naipaul uses a three-part system: (1) standard (educated) English dialogue stands for Hindi speech, unless otherwise noted; (2) English dialect is conveyed as spoken; (3) in a few rare cases English dialogue is spoken by one of the characters, but the hesitation and care with which he/she speaks is always noted by the narrator. Until the time of his marriage, Mr. Biswas and his own family speak Hindi (i.e., standard English); then he and his wife speak English dialect, but she and her relatives speak Hindi. When the couple move out of the Tulsi house, they and their children speak only English dialect, except on a few occasions where "Hindi" speech is again used.

Naipaul's use of standard English for Hindi dialogue may seem odd at first glance, but his method is "surprisingly effective" (White 1975: 39). The characters are native speakers of Hindi, and hence would be acquainted with Hindi grammar and vocabulary through daily use, if not through schooling. Pronouns, verb forms, and articles — some of the most noticeable "problems" in dialect—are all used correctly in the "Hindi" dialogue. One brief example may serve to note this shift. Here his older daughter begins by accusing Mr. Biswas:

> "Ma said you beat her," Savi said.
> Mr. Biswas laughed. "She was only joking," he said in English.
> "She upstairs, rubbing down Myna," Savi said, in English as well. [p. 194]

The first sentence, " 'Ma said you beat her,' " is in Hindi because of the proper verb form, the past tense "said." Naipaul says the father is answering in English, because the correct sentence structure ("She *was* only joking," *not* "She only joking") would otherwise have implied Hindi. And Savi's final statement, "She upstairs," could stand without the narrator's explanation that it is in English — for it to have been in Hindi, the girl would have had to say, "She *is* upstairs." Perhaps Naipaul notes the use of English because Savi's last previous statement was in Hindi. As soon as her father speaks English, however, she replies in kind. Here we see an example of "a tendency in West Indian dialects . . . to dispense with tense markers in the verb where context or where another grammatical feature is adequate" (Ramchand 1970: 95).

Linguists have noted various features in the English speech of Indians, and in Indian English fiction. One such feature is the reduplicated item, "used for emphasis and to indicate continuation of a process" (Kachru 1976). While Kachru has observed such items in the novels of Anand and Raja Rao, they also occur in Naipaul's work. With regard to Ganesh, the mystic masseur, people "said, 'He full with worries, but still he thinking thinking all the time' " (p. 32); Ramlogan, Ganesh's prospective father-in-law, later queries, " 'Ain't you was learning learning all all the time at the town college?' " (p. 35). A second such feature mentioned by Kachru is "the formation of an interrogative construct in which Indian English speakers do not necessarily change the position of the subject and the auxiliary items." Leela's first question for Ganesh, her husband-to-be, is " 'You could write too, sahib?' " (p. 45). Often the tag "not so?" at the end of a statement also gives interrogative force. Finally, some word forms which appear in Hindi have been portrayed in the "Hindi" (i.e., standard English) speech of Mr. Biswas's relatives. When he is a small child, his mother once "cried, 'Stop this bickering-ickering and let us go to look for the boy' " (p. 28). Also appearing are "paddling-addling," "apologize-ologize," and his sister-in-law's impatient disparagement of Mr. Biswas's reading tastes in her reference to "Marcus Aurelius

Aurelius." These constructs do not normally appear in the English dialect speech of the characters, but the potential for generating new word forms in English dialect seems to lie in this type of reduplication. (See also Kachru 1981 and 1983.) Several kinds of situations best lend themselves to the use of the vernacular language—bargaining, joking, lying, swearing (Fishman 1982)—and the non-native speaker usually avoids English in such situations. Naipaul points out the uniqueness of the following episode:

> "This insuranburning," Mr. Biswas said, and his tone
> was light, "who going to see about it? Me?" He was put-
> ting himself back in the role of the licensed buffoon. . . .
>   Mrs. Tulsi began to splutter. "He want," she said in
> English, choking with laughter, "to jump—from—the
> fryingpan—into—into"
>   They all roared.
>   "—into—the fire!"
>   The witty mood spread. [p. 204]

Much later in this dialogue, the narrator notes that Mrs. Tulsi is "still chuckling over her own joke, the first she had managed in English."

While many other features of English dialect could be mentioned, with examples from the speech of Naipaul's characters, it is more profitable to move now to an analysis of the uses of Hindi in Trinidad. Naipaul makes observations on several such uses, either in his own narrative or through the mouths of his fictional characters. When Ganesh's father takes the youngster to a school in town for the first time, their appearance and dress are noted by the local residents:

> "Let them laugh," the old man replied in Hindi. . . .
> "Jackasses bray at anything."
>   "Jackass" was his favorite word of abuse; perhaps be-
> cause the Hindi word was so rich and expressive: *gaddaha*.
> [p. 20]

Here it is not only the sound of the Hindi word, but the fact that he doesn't want the bystanders to understand his comment, that causes the father to choose Hindi.

Ganesh, as a masseur, later uses Hindi as part of his "mystical process" when dealing with those who come to him for treatment. Leela acts as his translator when he deals with his black clientele. When she says she wants to end her involvement in translating, Ganesh acquiesces, saying, " 'I only wanted to make sure this time. It make them feel good, you know, hearing me talk a language they can't understand. But it not really necessary' " (p. 136). In *A House for Mr. Biswas,* Shama fails to give a black customer in the Tulsi shop the treatment the woman feels she deserves; the woman demands to see the manager. Then "Mrs. Tulsi spoke some abuse to Shama in Hindi, the obscenity of which startled Mr. Biswas. The woman looked pacified" (p. 85). Here it is not the *content* of the speech, but the mere *existence* of it, that has mollified the non-Hindi-speaking customer. On another occasion, however, a black man who wants to prepare a "buth suttificate" for Shama's children is said to have "disliked the way Indian women had of using Hindi as a secret language in public places" (p. 43).

Lest it be thought that the Hindi-speaking population of Trinidad is linguistically omniscient, Naipaul satirizes the Indians' own fascination with words they do not know or understand. When the Tulsis set Mr. Biswas up in business, his shop is named "Bonne Esperance." And when Ramlogan and Ganesh have agreed that the latter should marry Leela, the following discussion of the wedding invitations occurs. Ganesh protests at first:

> "But you can't have nice wording on a thing like a
> invitation."
> "You is the educated man, sahib. You could think
> of some."
> "R.S.V.P.?"
> "What that mean?"
> "It don't mean nothing, but it nice to have it."
> "Let we have it then sahib! You is a modern man,
> and too besides, it sound as pretty wordings." [p. 49]

"Modernity," especially with regard to marriage customs, is also treated in *A House for Mr. Biswas* (pp. 99–100), with a similar satirical intent.

From the quotations of Naipaul's characters, it should now be clear that the author attempts to convey a certain type of West Indian speech almost solely by modifying English syntax. Naipaul does not change spellings or anything of that nature; as a result, his dialogue is extremely readable but also very Caribbean. As one critic put it, "The main features of the native language he preserves are the simplified grammar, limited vocabulary (very few completely foreign words of African and Indian origin), and slightly unique but plain syntactical structures, with normal spelling." His dialogue is "not far removed" from West Indian Standard English (Hamner 1973: 77). In Naipaul's novels, even those without much education know how to spell when they write; Leela is a bit flamboyant with her punctuation, but otherwise her two early written statements are quite clear:

NOTICE, IS. HEREBY; PROVIDED: THAT, SEATS!
ARE, PROVIDED. FOR; FEMALE: SHOP, ASSISTANTS!
[p. 44]

I, cannot; live: here. and, put; up. with. the, insult, of:
my. Family! [p. 89]

Later, when Ganesh is on his way to wealth and fame, Leela modifies her spoken English. ("She used a private accent which softened all harsh vowel sounds; her grammar owed nothing to anybody, and included a highly personal conjugation of the verb to be" [p. 155].) She becomes involved in social welfare work and writes a report for a newspaper. By now her punctuation has dwindled to an acceptable level.

Leela writes only one article, but Mr. Biswas is a full-time journalist for a number of years, and Naipaul's Ganesh and Narayan's Margayya both publish books. Those books are on quite different subjects, but the fictional creations of both authors show almost a greater fascination with printing than with language itself. When Mr. Biswas seeks his first job as a reporter, he is "thrilled to see the proof of an article, headlined and displayed. It was a glimpse of a secret" (p. 320). When Ganesh shows his published book to a neighbor, they marvel over the status the words have assumed on the printed page— " 'They look so powerful,' Beharry said" (p. 97). Both Ganesh and Margayya have encounters with printers, and both try to avoid betraying their ignorance. First, Naipaul's masseur:

> "Look, how much you know about this thing?". . . .
> Ganesh smiled. "I study it a little bit."
> "What point you want it to be in?"
> Ganesh didn't know what to say. "Eight, ten, eleven, twelve, or what?" Basdeo sounded impatient.
> Ganesh was thinking rapidly about the cost. He said firmly, "Eight go do me."
> Basdeo shook his head and hummed. . . . [p. 96]

And then Narayan's Margayya:

> Lal asked: "Shall we print in demy or octavo?"
> . . . Margayya frankly blinked. . . . He said grandly:
> "Each has its own advantage; it's for you to decide. . . ."
>
> . . . .
>
> But Lal turned up with a new poser for him: "Shall we use ordinary ten-point Roman or another series which I use only for special works? It's also ten-point but on an eleven-point body."

Body? Points? Ten and eleven? What was it all about?
Margayya said: "Ah, that is interesting. . . . I should like
to see your eleven-point body." He had a grotesque vision
of a torso being brought in by four men on a stretcher.
[pp. 83–85]

There is one great difference between Naipaul's character and Naray-an's, however. Whereas Ganesh, the mystic masseur, is interested in writing as a creative process, Margayya, the financial expert, is publishing a book written by someone else, purely in hopes of making money in the bargain. His motive is not self-expression, but self-advancement.

Conclusion

Enough of the fictional characters; let us return now to the authors themselves for a final assessment. Narayan, who writes both narrative and dialogue in standard English, is an author directly concerned with South India, though his works have universal human implications and themes. Anand, whose dialogue constantly reminds us that the characters are *not* speaking English, is the writer of India at large; whether set in a Punjab village or an Assam tea plantation, a peasant hut or a rajah's palace, his works have a pervasive (some might say, overwhelming) ideological intent. Naipaul is largely a man without a country. Unlike some black Caribbean writers who have sought to return to their African roots, he has repudiated both the India of his ancestry and the Trinidad of his youth.

Coulthard has asserted that the expatriate experience may have important effects on Caribbean writers, delivering them "from temptations of local color [and] general folksiness" while also making them aware of "greater complexities of human relationships in the world outside the West Indies" (Coulthard 1962: 71ff.). Though our Caribbean writer, Naipaul, is the only expatriate of the three, Narayan and Anand have also demonstrated their abilities to avoid the pitfalls of folksiness and provincialism. Were this not so, their novels would appeal only to linguists interested in non-native Englishes. But, fortunately, these three writers have also captured the attention of literary scholars, as well as captivating the general reading public. Their positions in world English literature are assured. Furthermore, they have helped to establish the legitimacy of Indian English and Caribbean English literatures, thus paving the way for other writers in these areas.

REFERENCES

Aggarwal, Narindar K. 1981. *English in South Asia: a bibliographical survey of resources.* Gurgaon and New Delhi: Indian Documentation Service.

Anand, Mulk Raj. 1935/6. *Untouchable.* Delhi: Orient, 1970.

Bailey, Beryl. 1966. *Jamaican creole syntax.* Cambridge: Cambridge University Press.

Coulthard, G. R. 1962. *Race and colour in Caribbean literature.* London: Oxford University Press.

Fishman, Joshua A. 1982. Sociology of English as an additional language. In this volume.

Hamner, Robert D. 1973. *V. S. Naipaul.* New York: Twayne.

Jones, Joseph. 1965. *Terranglia: the case for English as world literature.* New York: Twayne.

Kachru, Braj B. 1976. Indian English: a sociolinguistic profile of a transplanted language. In *Dimensions of bilingualism,* special issue of *Studies in Language Learning* (Unit for Foreign Language Study, University of Illinois).

———. 1981. The pragmatics of non-native varieties of English. In L. Smith, ed., *English for cross-cultural communication.* London: Macmillan.

———. 1983. *The Indianization of English: the English language in India.* New Delhi: Oxford University Press.

King, Bruce. 1979. *West Indian literature.* London: Macmillan.

———. 1980. *The new English literatures: cultural nationalism in a changing world.* New York: St. Martin's Press.

Mukherjee, Meenakshi. 1971. *The twice-born fiction: themes and techniques of the Indian novel in English.* New Delhi: Arnold-Heineman.

Naipaul, V. S. 1957. *The mystic masseur.* Harmondsworth: Penguin, 1964.

———. 1961. *A house for Mr. Biswas.* Harmondsworth: Penguin, 1969.

———. 1973. *The overcrowded barracoon.* New York: Alfred A. Knopf.

Narasimhaiah, C. D. 1976. *Commonwealth literature: a handbook of selected reading lists.* Delhi: Oxford University Press.

———. 1978. *Awakened conscience: studies in commonwealth literature.* New Delhi: Sterling.

Narayan, R. K. 1952. *The financial expert.* New York: Farrar, Straus and Giroux/ Noonday Press, 1959.

Ramchand, Kenneth. 1970. *The West Indian novel and its background.* New York: Barnes and Noble.

Theroux, Paul. 1972. *V. S. Naipaul: an introduction to his work.* New York: Africana Publishing.

Thorpe, Michael. 1976. *V. S. Naipaul.* Writers and Their Work #242. London: Published for the British Council by Longman Group.

Traugott, Elizabeth Closs, and Mary Louise Pratt. 1980. *Linguistics for students of literature.* New York: Harcourt Brace Jovanovich.

Walsh, William. 1970. *A manifold voice: studies in commonwealth literature.* London: Chatto and Windus.

———. 1971. *R. K. Narayan.* Writers and Their Work #224. London: Published for the British Council by Longman Group.

———. 1973. *V. S. Naipaul.* Edinburgh: Oliver and Boyd.

White, Landeg. 1975. *V. S. Naipaul: a critical introduction.* New York: Barnes and Noble.

PART V

Discoursal Strategies:
Text in Context

16

Braj B. Kachru

Meaning in Deviation: Toward Understanding Non-Native English Texts

In order to avoid explanatory digressions, I shall assume that we agree on some basic concepts and terms.[1] First, in describing the non-native varieties of English worldwide (whose users constitute roughly 30–40 percent of English speakers), a distinction has to be made between the institutionalized and the performance varieties (see, e.g., Smith 1981). Second, in terms of language use in such non-native contexts, we must separate what we have labeled as a "deviation" from a "mistake." As explained in the chapter on "Models for Non-Native Englishes," a deviation can be contextualized in the new "unEnglish" sociolinguistic context in which English actually functions; its "meaning" must, therefore, be derived with reference to the *use* and *usage* appropriate to that cultural context. Such use results in a number of productive processes which are variety specific and context specific. Because such innovations have gone through various processes of nativization, both linguistically and culturally, a description of such formations must consider the context of the situation (Kachru 1980b) as relevant for the analysis. A mistake, on the other hand, does not necessarily have an underlying sociolinguistic explanation: it may be essentially a marker of acquisitional inadequacy, or it may indicate a stage in language acquisition. A discerning native or non-native speaker will not consider a mistake to be within the linguistic code of English. Through such an approach we will gain better understanding of the functional identity of these varieties of English, varieties which are used in an entirely different network of personal interactions, media needs, and register ranges as compared to their native counterparts. The fast-increasing body of the non-native English literature (a subject to which I will return later) thus acquires a defining context, as we have seen in the preceding chapters by Thumboo and Lowry. If that context is not appropriately understood, the significance of this literature is diminished.

Two Perspectives: Theoretical and Applied

I shall first provide both a theoretical and an applied context within which to discuss the topic. In recent years, two central issues have been brought to the forefront. One is what I consider the applied concern: in applied linguistics, for example, Kaplan (1966 [1980]; see also Clyne 1981) has raised a set of questions concerning the "cultural thought patterns" in intercultural education.[2] Kaplan's concerns are essentially pedagogical and are specifically related to the teaching of English as L_2. He claims that "the English language and its related thought patterns have evolved out of the Anglo-European cultural pattern. The expected sequence of thought in English is essentially a Platonic-Aristotelian sequence, descended from the philosophers of ancient Greece and shaped subsequently by Roman, Medieval European, and later Western thinkers" (400–401). He continues, "learning of a particular language is the mastering of its logical system" (409). In keeping with his pedagogical focus, Kaplan argues that "the foreign student is out of focus because the foreign student is employing a rhetoric and sequence of thought which violates the expectations of the native reader" (401). The teacher's reaction, therefore, is likely to be that the student's paper "lacks cohesion, organization or focus."

Kaplan also makes two other points. One is that "applied linguistics teaches the student to deal with the sentence, but it is necessary to bring the student beyond that to the comprehension of the whole context" (410). Second, "it is necessary to recognize that a paragraph is an artificial thought unit employed in the written language to suggest a cohesion which commonly may not exist in oral language" (411). Fourteen years later, in a 1980 addendum, Kaplan confesses that "the kind of discourse study recommended in this paper has never caught on" (416). He then identifies points on which he has changed his view during the intervening fourteen years. However, one point which still remains valid is the culturally or linguistically determined "preferred order in discourse bloc" (416).

Now let us turn from the pedagogical concern to the theoretical issue. Ferguson (1978, 1982) raises an important question which directly relates to research on any aspect of multilingualism. Referring to not-so-uncommon language situations of "diglossia, standard language with dialects, decreolization continuum, and so on. . . . Most linguists are getting reconciled to the fact that they must include an account of variation in writing the grammar of a language" (1978: 99). Recognizing such situations, linguists must ask, "What goes on in a speech community that uses let us say four languages?" (1978: 101). That situation is typical of, for example, parts of Africa or South Asia. Such questions cannot be of merely marginal interest to linguists—for the fact is that monolingualism, a linguist's dream for descriptive convenience, is not the general rule, but the exception in language situations.

Ferguson is correct in observing that theoretical generalizations and "universal explanatory principles" (Ferguson 1982) cannot be formulated without accounting for such situations. He recognizes the "natural status" of "the notion 'a language,' " but at the same time he believes that "such an assumption does not exclude the study of partial, restricted and marginal language behavior" (1978: 98). The criteria for determining the unit for such a description are *autonomy, stability,* and *functional range* (1978: 98). Clearly, Ferguson is here thinking of a special type of linguistic behavior, while at the same time he is raising a more general issue: "if variation turns out to include varieties so different that we would want to call them different languages, we might still have to put them in grammar." Taking the linguistic bull by its horns, he asserts: "I am saying multilingualism may be a legitimate object of linguistic description" (1978: 104).

Any investigation of non-native Englishes is a study in bi- or multilingualism, and it warrants a fresh theoretical and descriptive perspective. In presenting the above views of Kaplan and Ferguson, I do not claim that their positions have not been espoused by others before or since. I am merely using their claims as typical of two positions, and as a convenient point of departure.

How, then, has linguistic research proceeded toward understanding and describing the non-native Englishes? The insights gained through earlier research on such varieties parallel those which linguists gained at various stages in the development of linguistic theory. There is a parallel between the dominant linguistic paradigms and the attitudes, descriptive techniques, and methods used to describe these varieties.

Such research had roughly three phases. The first emphasized the acquisitional characteristics within the framework of specific language acquisitional models. Almost identical models and hypotheses were applied to language learning situations in, for example, Africa, South Asia, and Japan. These situations clearly differ in terms of motivations for learning, traditions of teaching, and the functional uses of English (see, e.g., Kachru 1980a; Smith 1981; Strevens 1980). However, since it was claimed that "integrative" motivation is better than "instrumental" motivation, that dictum was applied to all L_2 situations. One earlier exception to such studies, though not a pedagogically oriented one, is Schuchardt's (1891 [1980]) paper on "Indo-English." Schuchardt could serve as a model for many who followed him, but unfortunately this paper was not available in English until Gilbert translated and published it in 1980. The field essentially remained with prescriptivists, who isolated language study from language use, whether in acquisitional or in functional terms.

The structural approach to language dominated until the early 1960s. The inadequacies of this phase for the study of non-native Englishes were essentially four. (1) There was no recognition of the *functional displacement* of language and its implications for linguistic innovations. (2) Emphasis fell on L_2 acquisition with "native-like" control, with no distinction between institutional and performance varieties. (3) "Interference" came to be viewed as a "violation" of the code of L_1. (4) Units of language were segmented for easy taxonomic classification, with the sentence being the highest unit of description. As far as I know, the concept of "interference varieties" as legitimate varieties of English did not emerge from the side of the native speakers of English until Quirk et al. (1972) recognized such varieties among the varieties of contemporary English in their monumental grammar.

The structuralist paradigm, as we already know (and I will not beat the dead horse), was inadequate not only to account for language description, but also to account for the underlying differences in the institutionalized varieties of English. This point, in another context, has been discussed for almost two decades by, among others, Firth, Halliday, Labov, and Pike.

In American linguistics it was not until what has been called the "Chomskyan revolution" that new insights were gained in language description, especially about the interrelationship of sentences. Such analyses were a natural step toward our understanding of the cohesion and interrelation of syntactic networks. But again, the paradigm was not related to the functional aspects of non-native Englishes. Then came an era of acute cynicism in the 1970s, with new explorations in various branches of linguistics and essentially a rethinking of the goals of the discipline. A vital contribution of this period is the analysis and descriptions of units larger than the sentence, and understanding concerning the choices which users of a language make as members of a society. As a result of such theoretical concerns, the empirical focus has rapidly come to rest on several "socially realistic" paradigms of linguistic research.[3] In the 1970s some paradigms were more influential than others, but only a few affected the research on and understanding of the complex phenomenon of second-language study: for instance, Labov's work, and that of Halliday (especially 1973 and later), Hymes (1962 and later; see also Saville-Troike 1982), Gumperz (1964 and later), and Ervin-Tripp (for a discussion see, e.g., 1978).[4] The concept of "contrastive discourse" or "contrastive stylistics" never gained any serious adherents, though some studies have been attempted in this direction using various models (e.g., Dehghanpisheh 1972; Larsen-Freeman 1980; Maftoon-Semnani 1979; Sajavaara and Lehtoneh, 1980; Trimble et al. 1978; see also, for references, Houghton 1980). On the whole, very little insightful research has been done on multilinguals' linguistic behavior, especially in traditionally multilingual societies. Perhaps the earlier attitude toward multilingualism in the West is partly responsible for this situation.[5]

Nativized Englishes: Directions in Research

The nativized Englishes have still not been given the attention they deserve in variational or literary studies, or in work on contrastive discourse or language acculturation. This is unfortunate, since the history of non-native Englishes is a long one, going back almost two hundred years in some parts of the world, and covering such culturally and linguistically dissimilar contexts as Africa, South Asia, the Far East, the Philippines, and the West Indies. With such a deep-rooted tradition in linguistically and culturally pluralistic societies, we have a priceless repository of material for research on the study of language acquisition, acculturation, and change.

In terms of acculturation, two processes seem to be at work. One results in the *deculturation* of English, and another in its *acculturation* in the new context. The latter gives it an appropriate identity in its newly acquired functions. The Indians have captured the two-faceted process by using the typical Sanskrit compound *dvija* ("twice-born") for Indian English. (The term was originally used for the Brahmins who, after their natural birth, are considered reborn at the time of caste initiation.) Firth (1968: 96) therefore is correct in saying that "an Englishman must de-Anglicize himself"; as must, one could add, an American "de-Americanize" himself, in their attitudes toward such varieties, and for a proper appreciation of such acculturation of Englishes (see Kachru 1983).

This initiation of English into new culturally and linguistically dependent communicative norms forces a redefinition of our linguistic and contextual parameters for understanding the new language types and discourse types. Those who are outside these cultures must go through a *variety shift* in order to understand both the written and the spoken modes of such varieties. One cannot, realistically speaking, apply the norms of one variety to another variety. I am not using the term "norm" to refer only to formal deviations (see Kachru 1980a); rather, I intend to refer to the underlying universe of discourse which makes linguistic interaction a pleasure and provides it with "meaning." It is the whole process of, as Halliday says, learning "how to *mean*" (1974). It is a very culture-bound concept. To understand a bilingual's mind and use of language, one would have, ideally, to be ambilingual and ambicultural. One would have to share responses to events, and cultural norms, and interpret the use of L_2 within that context. One would have to see how the context of culture is manifest in linguistic form, in the new style range, and in the assumptions one makes about the speech acts in which L_2 is used. A tall order, indeed! (See Y. Kachru 1991.)

This redefined cultural identity of the non-native varieties has not usually been taken into consideration.[6] There have been primarily three types of studies in this area. The first type forms the main body—understandably so, since these are devoted to pedagogical concerns. In such studies, any deviation has been interpreted as violating a prescriptive norm, and thus resulting in a "mistake." The urge for prescriptivism has been so strong that any innovation which is not according to the native speaker's linguistic code is considered a linguistic aberration. If one makes too many such "mistakes," it is treated as an indication of a language user's linguistic deprivation or deficiency. Second, some linguistic studies focus on formal characteristics without attempting to relate them to function, or to delve into the contextual needs for such innovations. This separation between *use* and *usage* has masked several sociolinguistically important factors about these varieties. The third group of studies deals with the "contact literature" in English, perhaps used on the analogy of "contact languages." Such literature is a product of multicultural and multilingual speech communities, and it extends the scope of English literature to "literatures in English." Most such studies are concerned with the themes, rather than with style. (For further discussion, see, e.g., Chs. 14, 15.)

Strategies, Styles, and Domains

In relating the strategies, styles, and domains of language use, a configuration of factors must be considered, the most important being the underlying cultural assumptions. The verbal strategies and culturally determined innovations are, therefore, not necessarily "linguistic flights" (Whitworth 1907: 5) to be avoided, since these are not part of *native* speakers' linguistic repertoires. These strategies and devices are meaningful to the "insider" who actually uses the variety of English, though in an "outsider's" judgment such innovations might "jar upon the ear of the native Englishman" (Whitworth 1907: 5).[7] The question then is: Who is to judge? This point has been demonstrated with reference to black English by Labov (1969), and with reference to the non-native Englishes by, among others, Bokamba (1982), Chishimba (1980a and 1980b), Kachru (1965 and later), Kandiah (1981), Llamzon (1969), Platt and Weber (1980), Richards (1982), and Stanlaw (1982).[8]

The concept of *cohesion* has both formal and functional prerequisites which ideally must be seen from an "insider's" point of view. In culturally and linguistically pluralistic contexts, language *shift* and *mix* may be part of the repertoire. (For a detailed discussion and bibliography, see Kachru, 1983.) In many situations where the *domain* seems to be identical between varieties, we might find that the language type which is considered *appropriate* is not necessarily identical. Even in the varieties of English, there is a mutual expectancy between the culturally determined domain and the appropriate language for it. It is not merely a question of finding a one-to-one relationship between the domains and language types in different varieties. In addition to style range, one must consider the more complex, and to some extent more elusive, proficiency range within each variety.

Cohesion and Coherence in Text

Considerable confusion is involved in the use of terms such as *text*, *discourse*, and *narrative* (see Rauch and Carr 1980). Following Halliday (1978: 108–9), I will use *text* to refer to "the instances of linguistic interaction in which people actually engage: whatever is said, or written, in an operational context, as distinct from a citational context like that of words listed in a dictionary. . . . In other words, a text is a semantic unit; it is the basic unit of the semantic process." Functionally, "text can be defined as actualized meaning potential." (See also Halliday and Hasan 1976.)

There is no paucity of anthropological, sociological, and linguistic frameworks available for such analysis.[9] My concern is neither to evaluate such studies nor to select any particular one for its methodology. I will simply mention two concepts used by Widdowson which have methodological bearings on "the area of enquiry that goes under the general name of discourse analysis" (1979: 61). Widdowson is particularly appropriate here because he has had an impact on general studies and pedagogical materials related to "communicative competence," especially in English as L_2. In his 1979 study, he proposes the concepts of *rules of usage* and *rules of use*. Rules of usage "represent the language user's knowledge of the formal system of his language" (64). This is, as he says, language competence in the Chomskyan sense. Rules of use "account for the language user's knowledge of speech acts . . . and constitute the basic communicative source of reference." The first type is termed *cohesion procedure,* and the second type, *coherence procedure.* If put in an alternate framework, the first refers to the *formal* appropriateness, and the second to *functional* appropriateness. (See also Kachru 1983 and earlier.) Widdowson agrees that both are "subject to variation." He is also aware that problems arise when we attempt to transfer rules of use from one universe of discourse to another. The question for us then is, What *norms* apply to the institutional varieties with reference to *cohesion* and *coherence* procedures? The appropriateness of these procedures is with reference to what may be termed the communicative unit (Sinclair and Coulthard 1975), the contextual unit (Kachru 1965 and later, esp. 1980c), or the context of situation (Firth 1957). These units essentially constitute participants in "interactive acts" (Widdowson 1979: 68), and are determined by the "context of culture" and "context of situation." What is "contextual deviation" from the native speaker's point of view is appropriate in terms of "procedures," outlined by Widdowson, for the non-native contexts.[10]

A *variety shift* may, then, entail knowledge about the "procedures" specific to a *localized* variety of English. It seems, furthermore, to be very significant for understanding the "contact literatures" in English. (See Smith, ed. 1987.)

Contextualizing Text Types

I shall consider a number of text types, ranging from newspaper headlines to a number of sentences, in order to bring out the variety-specific "meaning" in deviation. First, let me illustrate my point by using selected examples from English-language newspapers in Asia, essentially from South Asia. These newspapers have the largest reading public and are the primary link across the region. English is the only language in which practically every state and region in (for example) India has a newspaper. The long journalistic tradition and continuing intranational needs for communication have gradually fostered the development of specific South Asian newspaper language types in headlines, announcements, advertising, etc. Below I shall consider, among others, some headlines, reviews, and announcements of events such as marriages and deaths.

A native speaker of English, not familiar with the cultural and linguistic pluralism in South Asia, considers these language types lexically, collocationally, and semantically deviant. Such a reaction is understandable. Nevertheless, in South Asian or African English, it is through such formal deviation—including that of mixing—that language acquires contextual appropriateness. True, native speakers' cohesive and coherence procedures have been "violated." But how else can a "transplanted" language acquire functional appropriateness? A language pays a linguistic price for acculturation—for not remaining just a "guest or friend," but, to use Raja Rao's words (1978: 421), for becoming "one of our own, of our own caste, our creed, our sect and of our tradition." This family identity cannot be given to a guest without initiating him into the tradition. The price for acquiring such membership is nativization. It is with reference to such nativization that the following examples should be understood.

Panchayat system upholds ideals of human rights[11]
(*The Rising Nepal*, Kathmandu, December 17, 1978;
  one column)

More subsidy for gobar gas plants
(*The Hindustan Times*, New Delhi, May 7, 1977; one column)

Krishibank branch needed
(*The Bangladesh Observer*, Dacca, June 21, 1979; one column)

Shariat courts for attack
(*Dawn*, Lahore, December 3, 1979; one column)

Indian Muslims are bumiputras
(*The Sunday Times*, Singapore, April 26, 1981; one column)

JNU karamcharis begin dharna
(*The Statesman*, New Delhi, May 12, 1981; one column)

Marathwada band over pandal fire
(*The Indian Express*, New Delhi, May 9, 1981; one column)

DESU workers gherao staff
(*The Indian Express*, New Delhi, May 9, 1981; one column)

Paan masala "causes rare disease"
(*The Hindustan Times*, New Delhi, May 5, 1981; one column)

"Lakhpati" swindler held
(*The Hindustan Times*, New Delhi, May 9, 1981; three columns)

> 55 Jhuggis gutted
> (*The Hindustan Times,* New Delhi, May 3, 1981; one column)
> "Shaleenta" drive ends
> (*The Statesman,* May 3, 1981; one column)

This type of mixing is not restricted to headlines. Consider the following randomly selected reports:

> Urad and moong fell sharply in the grain market here today on stockists offerings. Rice, jowar and arhar also followed suit, but barely forged ahead. [*The Times of India,* New Delhi, July 23, 1977]

> Fish stalls in many small markets have nothing for sale. Rohu costs Rs 16 a Kg. while bekti, parshe and tangra are priced between.... Hilsa, which is the most popular among the Bengalis in the rainy season.... [*The Statesman,* Calcutta, May 12, 1979]

This type of nativized lexicalization raises several points. For instance, when an appropriate English lexical item is available, why do papers like *The Times of India* or *The Statesman* prefer a native item, for example, *jowar* (sorghum), *arhar* (pigeon peas), or the various types of fish?

Reviews

It is difficult to say whether the following review of a performance by the well-known classical musician M. S. Subbulakshmi could have been presented without profuse lexicalization from register-specific items from Sanskrit:

> "Chandrasekhara" (Dr. V. Raghavan's composition) was rendered with a clear intonation as to set off the structural beauty. Together with the alapana it was a grand essay of Kirvani.... Dharmavati was chosen for Ragam, Tanam and Pallavi. Singing with an abandon, M. S. set off the distinct character of the mode and followed with a methodically improvised Pallavi. The swaraprastara was full of tightly knit figures. [*Deccan Herald,* Hyderabad, July 26, 1977]

The same is true of the following illustration:

> The note dhaivat, komal and suddha seemed to be eluding the singer at times. The other thing which Gaekwad would have done well was to avoid billing ragas in succession with most notes in common. (The first three ragas had gandhar, madhyam, dhaivat, and nishadh, all suddha.) [*The Statesman,* New Delhi, May 8, 1981]

There is no attempt in such writing to explain the terms or concepts. Bilingual and bicultural competence is taken for granted.

The native speaker of English, if unfamiliar with such contextually appropriate mixing, is naturally marked an "outsider." In a sense, such illustrations represent development of a typical register of music, for example, in Indian English which may be unintelligible even to an uninitiated Indian English speaker.

Matrimonial Advertisements

The matrimonial advertisements listed below are from prestigious national English newspapers. All involve mixing, mainly with borrowed Sanskrit lexical items. Mixing of the type illustrated here is restricted to the Hindu community, and to what are called the "caste Hindus." The advertisements (from *The Hindu*, Madras, July 1, 1979) are obviously from educated families who have traditional views on social stratification and color consciousness, and who place complete reliance on the horoscope for finalizing the alliance.

> Wanted well-settled bridegroom for a Kerala fair graduate Baradwaja gotram, Astasastram girl . . . subset no bar. Send horoscope and details.

> Correspondence invited, preferably for mutual alliance, by Smartha family of Karnataka. Write with full family details.

> Non-Koundanya well qualified prospective bridegroom below 30 for graduate Iyangar girl, daughter of engineer. Mirugaservsham. No dosham. Average complexion. Reply with horoscope.

The term *mutual alliance* in the second example is a culturally significant collocation; it refers to an arrangement by which X's daughter marries Y's son and Y's daughter marries X's son. Whatever the other advantages of such an alliance, one obvious advantage is that it restricts the giving or receiving of the dowry.

In Asian varieties of English we notice mixing or lexical innovations of other types, too. Consider the following:

> Tanku Abdul Rahman blessed newly-weds . . . with "tepung tawar". . . . The "akad nikah" took place last Thursday. [*New Straits Times*, Kuala Lumpur, April 27, 1981]

> Matrimonial correspondence invited from respected Punjabi families for my son . . . clean shaven. [Times of India, New Delhi, May 10, 1981]

In the above Malaysian example, the mixing is determined by the religion. In the second case, *clean shaven* has a serious religious connotation: it is indicative of non-conformism with traditional Sikhism in India.

In the matrimonial context another collocation, *minor wife*, common in Thai English, is worth mentioning here. It refers to a "mistress"[12] who is socially accepted as next to (major) wife, e.g.,

> Police said yesterday they could find no motive for the killing but said that Mr. Prapruet had a minor wife who lived in the same soi as his family. [*Bangkok Post*, April 29, 1981]

Obituaries

The non-native users of English have their own way of dealing with death, just as with getting married. The announcement about death, the metaphor of death, and the outward manifestations at funerals are very culture and religion specific. If the medium in which one is to talk of death or to write about it is a non-native language, it certainly must first be acculturated. In South Asia, for example, a person leaves "for heavenly abode" (*The Hindustan Times*, New Delhi, May 8, 1981) due to "the sad demise." In North India, among Hindus and Sikhs, there will be "kirtan and ardasa for the peace of the departed soul" (*The Hindustan Times*, June 30, 1979). An alternate form of announcement is that "the untimely tragic death . . . of . . . happened . . . on . . . uthaoni ceremony will take place on . . ." or the "chautha-uthala" will be performed. In Pakistan, an announcement may state that a person's "soyam Fateha will be solemnized on" and "all the friends and relatives are requested to attend the Fateha ceremony" (*Dawn*, March 14, 1979). The ethnic plurality of, for example, Singapore reflects in the mixing such as "karumakiriye puniathanam pooja will be held on . . ." (*New Straits Times*, Singapore, April 29, 1981). In many of these announcements the underlying metaphor is of the native language. Once it is re-created into English (even if it is "deviant" from a native speaker's point of view), it immediately establishes a cultural and emotional bond with the local reader. For such a reader it is neither sentimental nor over-ornamented; it is contextually proper, and any other way of expressing it would be culturally inappropriate.

Invitations

Wedding invitations, for example, reveal another cultural aspect. The unit of interaction is the family, not the individual. The invitation is written in such a way that a native speaker of English finds it impersonal and vague. A typical printed invitation in North India might read:

> You will be glad to know that the marriage ceremony of dear ———— will be celebrated at ————. Mehndirat and devgoan will be performed on ————. You are requested to make it convenient to reach here with

family well in time to participate in all the connected ceremonies. In case you would like me to invite anyone else from your side, kindly intimate the name and address.

Why is English chosen for such personal, culture-specific contexts? That brings in the question of language attitudes, which I will not address here.

Letters

Letters, either personal, or not so personal, are an excellent medium through which to study the transferred cultural norms in personal interactions. Such correspondence is essentially treated as a mere change of the mode of communication, from spoken to written. What one would say normally in L₁ in face-to-face interaction is expressed in written English. In English the written mode, even in personal interaction, has several rhetorical prerequisites; these include directness in presenting the point, very little stylistic ornamentation, and emphasis on the information content. On the other hand, a typical letter from South Asia, the Far East, or Africa will have the following characteristics: an extremely deferential lexical spread based on the politeness hierarchy of the L₁, and abundant use of blessings in the opening and concluding paragraphs. If the writer is senior in age, the use of blessings seems excessive to a person who is not part of the culture. One might find mentioned names of gods who will bless the receiver of the letter. Perhaps this characteristic of Indian letters made Goffin (1934) remark that Indian English has a moralistic tone, and the Indians cannot keep God out of their English. Consider, for example, the following:

> I always send my love and prayers to you all everyday: unseen unheard. May Lord Shiva always protect you all and look after you.
>
> I am quite well here hoping the same for you by the virtue of mighty god. I always pray to god for your good health, wealth and prosperity. [*The Tribune*, Chandigarh, November 22, 1978]

Consider also the following from Africa (quoted in Chishimba 1980b):

> I have exhorted you then to exorcise the spectre which has been hovering over us like the sword of Damocles.
>
> Your deportment of late has been so unruly that you are now deemed a misfit in this academic institution. With effect from the issue of this letter of admonishment, I expect you to shrink your tentacles within the boundaries of learning.

The two pieces are written by a headmaster, the first in the school magazine, and the second as a letter of warning to a student.

Excessive ornamentation in construction of sentences may result from more than one underlying cause: for instance, deferential style used for one's teacher, register-mixing, culturally different notions of what is "grand" style, or a different concept of what it means to sound learned. Consider the excerpts from a letter received by my colleague Charles Osgood:

> I beg to invite your kind attention to the insatiable thirst for knowledge of an obscure bibliophil [*sic*] that compels him to be a suppliant for your munificence. To get down to brass tacks, I have a good mind to be enlightened by your [all the volumes], but my chronic financial stringency obfuscates the lofty idea. I am on my uppers. In my frowzy den I can only sigh and weep for your latest work (book or research paper).
>
> Would you mind enlightening the thirsty palmer languishing in the icy quagmire of despondency on the names and addresses of the professors adorning the Department of Linguistic Science, University of Illinois?

Acknowledgments

The ornateness and transfer of the deferential style from L_1 to L_2 can be illustrated from another source of educated non-native English, namely, acknowledgments in published books. What might appear unnecessarily docile or servile to a Western reader is again dependent on how an Asian or an African views a teacher or a superior in his culture, and on how the L_1 provides formal choices to structure such a cultural attitude. In English, these factors must be presented in a complex way, and native speakers are left to draw their own conclusions.

> For me, this work has been a labour of love, without any financial and secretarial assistance whatsoever. My great Guru passed away before the work could be completed. I can now only console myself by dedicating it to his revered memory. [J. Singh, *Siva Sūtras*; Delhi, 1979]
>
> The author takes this opportunity to express his indebtedness to . . . for his stately kindness, expansive sympathy and charitable guidance without which the work would not have taken the shape. [S. P. Singh, *English in India*; Patna, 1978]
>
> I owe a deep debt of gratitude to our beloved . . . who corrected me when I was wrong, encouraged me when I was right; supported me when I was in need and shared my responsibilities in the fulfilment of the tasks before me. I must thank, further though in an un-Indian

manner, my own younger brother. [K. P. S. Choudhary, *Modern Indian Mysticism;* Delhi, 1981]

That such a style is important for cultural identity can be shown from an interesting example. When an acculturated (nativized) native speaker of English wants to acquire an Indian identity, and claims the prerogative of being a *śiṣya* ("disciple"), he or she will use the same Indianized English style. In his introduction to the *Vaiṣṇava Āchāryas,* Chuck,[13] who became Acyutānanda Svāmī and "is preaching in India" (ix), adopted the same style for expressing gratitude to his guru.[14]

> I offer my prostrate obeisances first unto all the devotees that have surrendered unto his divine lotus feet and next unto the devotees who will in the future take shelter of his lotus feet, and I then offer my humble obeisances unto his lotus feet again and again. May he bless this first translation attempt so that it may be accepted by the Lord Sri Kṛṣṇa, and may he engage me in the service of the six Govāmiś of Vṛndāvana, Lord Caitanya, and Rādhārāṇī. [*Songs of the Vaiṣṇava Ācāryas;* Los Angeles, 1974: xviii]

Let me now provide an example of a different text type from West Asia (Israel and Iraq). Israeli and Iraqi statements on a raid on a nuclear plant appeared in "unofficial translations" issued by the two governments, as given in *The New York Times* (June 9, 1981). The first paragraphs of the Israeli text read:

> The Israeli Air Force yesterday attacked and destroyed completely the Osirak nuclear reactor, which is near Baghdad. All our planes returned home safely.
> The Government finds itself obligated to explain to enlighten public opinion why it decided on this special operation.

The last sentence says, "We shall defend the citizens of Israel in good time and with all the means at our disposal." Let us contrast this with the Iraqi statement:

> In the name of God, the merciful, the compassionate.
> Great Iraqi people, sons of the glorious Arab nation, it has been known to us from the beginning that many parties local and international, were and still are behind the eagerness of the backward and suspect Iranian regime to stir up the dispute with, conduct aggression against and begin the war against Iraq.

After almost five short paragraphs, the statement then adds, "Compatriots, today we declare that the Zionist enemy planes yesterday carried out an air raid on Baghdad." The concluding paragraphs say,

> The road Iraq has taken in its victorious revolution—the road of

315

freedom, independence and progress, the road of cohesion between the leadership and the masses—will not be abandoned. This road will remain wide open.

God willing, victory to our heroic people and glory to our Arab nation.

It is evident that the rhetorical devices used in these two statements are distinctly different. One might ask: Does this variation provide clues for "cultural variation" which manifests itself in certain types of discourse, and which reveals a "preferred order in discourse blocs" (Kaplan: 1966 [1980]: 416)?

What do the other examples from various text types given above show? Several theoretically and pedagogically important points may be made here. We see at work a number of formal devices used to create the "deference hierarchy" or the "politeness phenomenon" which is an essential part of being a member of these speech communities. This politeness hierarchy is thus formally created in the communicative repertoire of L$_2$. By this device a text that is, for example, deviant at the collocational level acquires appropriateness at the "communicative level." It is therefore not mere lexical (or collocational) interference, but transfer (or re-creation) of a "communicative act" or "interactive act."[15] In order to capture the "meaning" of such texts, the native speaker has to see the other (non-native) varieties of English as an integral part of the other culture, and he must view such texts as a crucial part of culturally determined interaction.

"Contact Literature" in English: Another Look

Let me now return to a substantial body of non-native writing in English, termed "contact literature." The critic Narasimhaiah (1978) has made a plea for broadening the appeal of English studies from that of "English literature" to "literature in English." The concept of "contact literature," as stated earlier, is an extension of "contact language." A language in contact is two-faced; it has its own face, and the face it acquires from the language with which it has contact. The degree of contact varies from lexical borrowing to intensive mixing of units. Contact literatures (for example, non-native English literatures of India, Nigeria, or Ghana, or the francophone literatures, or the Indian Persian) have certain formal and thematic characteristics which make this use of the term "contact" appropriate.

Using a *non-native* language in native contexts to portray new themes, characters, and situations is like redefining the semantic and semiotic potential of a language, making language mean something which is not part of its traditional "meaning." It is an attempt to give a new African or Asian identity, and thus an extra dimension of meaning. A part of that dimension perhaps remains obscure or mysterious to the Western reader. In purely linguistic terms, it entails developing a meaning system appropriate to the new situations and contexts. One has to make various choices to make the linguistic resources of L_2 function in situations where formal equivalence is not always possible.

In understanding the texts, one therefore must remember several points. First, in such literature all the characters use English; the same is not true in real life, since English is only one code in a multi-coded society. Second, English is used in all the situations for all interactions — which, again, is not how English actually functions. Third, each character is assigned a style or a style range appropriate to his or her function. The writer Mulk Raj Anand, for example, is forced to make difficult choices in *Coolie* and *Untouchable*: no real-life coolie speaks English, and no untouchable uses English for interaction within the family. If we use Bernstein's terms, in real life, most of these characters will be using a "restricted code" of their regional language. In a number of areas such codes may even be stigmatized, since they will have speech markers to identify each subgroup on the caste hierarchy. How does one re-create all this relevant linguistic and cultural information in another language? Whatever the device a writer chooses, it is a *deviation* for an outsider.

This predicament of a non-native creative writer in English, for example in India, began as early as 1874, when a Bengali, Lal Behari Day,[16] "translated Indian terms instead of their pure English equivalents to maintain the Indian local colour as well as to add a distinct Indian flavour" (Sarma 1978: 329). Day was Indianizing English for stylistic effect, consciously attempting to re-create a style repertoire in L_2 which would be contextually appropriate to India. The following excerpt is stylistically perhaps one of the first attempts toward nativizing English in "contact literature" in India. Later, in the works of Mulk Raj Anand, Khushwant Singh, Raja Rao, and others, such devices became a characteristic of an Indian identity of English.

> "Come in," said Badan, and jumped out of the verandah towards the door. "Come in, Acharya Mahasaya; this is an auspicious day when the door of my house has been blessed with the dust of your honour's feet. Gayaram fetch an *asan* [a small carpet] for the Acharya Mahasaya to sit on." [Day 1874: 48; quoted in Sarma 1978: 330]

Note that Day is conscious of making his Bengali peasant speak "better English than most uneducated English peasants." He apologetically explains to his "Gentle reader":

> Gentle reader, allow me here to make one remark. You perceive that Badan and Alanga speak better English than most uneducated English peasants; they speak almost like educated ladies and gentlemen, without any provincialisms. But how could I have avoided this defect in my history? If I had translated their talk into the Somerset or the Yorkshire dialect, I should have turned them into English, and not Bengali peasants. You will, therefore, please overlook this grave though unavoidable fault in this authentic narrative. [Day 1874: 61]

The technique and motivation for such stylistic effect have not changed since Day wrote these words. And the need for innovating such stylistic devices has not changed since Day articulated non-native creative writers' concerns (in 1874), and Schuchardt (1891 [1980]) analyzed such innovations from a linguistic point of view.

In contact literature, then, we see that deviation acquires a meaning at each level and reveals itself like a spectrum. The lexical deviation acquires meaning at the sentential level, and a deviant sentence is meaningful in relation to other sentences. But the appropriate functional meaning is part of the text type, within the context of situation. I have provided a number of such illustrations at various levels in other studies. (For further references, see, e.g., Aggarwal 1981, Kachru 1965 and later, and Chishimba 1980a, b and Smith, ed. 1987.)

Implications

The perspective presented here may confuse a prescriptive, norm-oriented English specialist. I am not making particular pedagogical claims. My concern is to point out that, as an object of serious linguistic and literary research, the non-native Englishes have many facets. A number of these are still untouched, and several others have been underresearched. I shall enumerate some of them here.

First, the bilingual's discourse—both "mixed" and "unmixed"—is itself an object of study for what Ferguson terms "bilingual's grammar" (1978). Through such studies we might gain deeper understanding about the communicative strategies of multilingual societies. Second, our understanding of variational study is still restricted to bidialectalism and some code-mixing. We have only begun research in stable multilingual societies in terms of areal features (e.g., Emeneau 1956; Masica 1976).

Third, English is unique in its distribution over culturally and linguistically distinct situations. On the basis of the types of nativization, it might be possible to develop universals of bilinguals' behavior. English provides one constant linguistic variable which can be used for such generalizations.

Fourth, contrastive studies seem to have stopped where they should actually have begun. In the long tradition of such studies, no attempt has been made to arrive at a serious understanding of contrastive discourse, and to analyze the cultural and linguistic transfers which change cohesive and other characteristics of texts. The "interference" phenomenon which received so much attention at the phonological and lexical levels, and some attention at the grammatical level, has yet to be fully explored in its all manifestations, especially in discourse.

Fifth—and here I return to contact literatures in English—the thematic studies of non-native English literatures have yet to study how culture-bound styles are "transcreated" in L_2 with close approximation to the style range available to a writer in his L_1. The "transcreated" style undoubtedly has an underlying model, be it from the native oral tradition, the L_1 style range, or the concept of style based on Sanskritic or Perso-Arabic traditions (in South Asia). *Kanthapura* of Raja Rao is a case in point.

Sixth, research during the last decade has provided many insights into the structure and function of code-switching and code-mixing. The implications of these phenomena on language change are significant. At first the change may be gradual or register-specific, but slowly it spreads—as happened, for example, in several Indian and African languages. (For a detailed discussion and references, see Kachru 1978, 1980c, 1981, Paradis 1978, and Bhatia and Ritchie 1989.)

All these aspects are interrelated. If we are to understand the workings of the bilingual's code repertoire and the use of such repertoires, it is essential that we understand all of them, in order to understand the ecology of language function.

Conclusion

There is now clearly a need for an attitudinal change toward the institutionalized non-native Englishes. Equally important, there is a need to redefine research areas and priorities, both in theoretical terms and for applied research. It may also be useful to consider whether the generalizations made for the formal and functional characteristics of non-native Englishes apply to other institutionalized non-native languages across cultures and language areas; for example, French, Arabic, Persian, or Sanskrit.

Are there any universals of nativization or linguistic acculturation? If so, what implication do they have for language acquisition, for language use, and for our understanding of the mystique of bilingualism or multilingualism?

In applied linguistics, too, we need new perspectives for research on communicative competence, and specifically on English for cross-cultural communication. It is through such research that we can gain insight about the pragmatics of English in non-native contexts. And, finally, given the status and spread of English around the world and its variation, we might agree with Ferguson (1982: vii) that "the whole mystique of native speaker and mother tongue should probably be quietly dropped from the linguists' set of professional myths about language."

NOTES

1. An earlier version of this chapter was presented as an invited paper at the Seminar on Varieties of English, SEAMEO Regional Language Center, Singapore, April 20–24, 1981.

2. For a discussion and references to later publications of Kaplan and others on this topic, see Clyne 1981, and particularly Houghton 1980.

3. See, e.g., Labov 1970, 1972a, b; for the Firthian contribution and other relevant references, see Kachru 1980b; for a historical perspective, see, e.g., Newmeyer 1980.

4. Other theoretical and applied studies are: Alston 1980, Christensen 1965; Cicourel 1969; Cole 1978; Dressler 1977; Gray 1977; Grimes 1975; Lakoff 1972; Monaghan 1979; Morgan 1977; Myers 1979; Posner 1980; Rauch and Carr 1980; Sankoff 1980; and Van Dijk 1977.

5. For relevant references see, e.g., Kachru 1981 and Paradis 1978.

6. By and large, the insights of such models and research have not been applied to non-native Englishes. An exception is the application of the Firthian framework of contextualization to some South Asian English texts. (See Kachru 1965 and later; see also Kandiah 1981, which raises several interesting questions.)

7. I cannot resist the temptation of quoting below the complete paragraph of Whitworth so that these words are not interpreted out of context: "I hope no one will take up this little book expecting to find an amusing collection of those linguistic flights to which imaginative Indians occasionally commit themselves. I am myself too painfully conscious of the immense superiority of Indians to Englishmen in the way of acquiring foreign languages, for the preparation of any such work to be a congenial task to me. No; my purpose is entirely different, and is perfectly serious. For many years past,

both in hearing arguments from the Bar and in reading Indian books and newspapers, I have been struck with the wonderful command which Indians—and not only those who have been to England—have obtained over the English language for all practical purposes. At the same time, I have often felt what a pity it is that men exhibiting this splendid facility should now and then mar their compositions by little errors of idiom which jar upon the ear of the native Englishman. Considering, in conjunction with this great natural ability, that the Indians are the inheritors of the most elaborate language that the world has known, and that their forefathers regarded grammar (vyakaran) as a vedanga or limb of their sacred veda, it seems well worth while to try and render them a small service by showing them how their admirable knowledge of our language may be made still more complete" (Whitworth 1907: 5–6).

8. See also, e.g., studies in Bailey and Görlach, in press; Kachru 1981; Smith 1981.

9. For references to some such selected works see note 4, above.

10. For discussion on the need for *local* (non-native) contextual parameters for description of non-native Englishes, among others, see Bokamba 1982; Chishimba 1980a, b; Kachru 1965 and later, particularly 1983.

11. The glosses of native words used in these examples are as follows: *panchayat*, council of five, village council; *gobar*, cow dung; *krishi*, agriculture; *shariat*, canon law of Islam; *bumiputra*, native son—in India the expression *son of the soil* is used in this context; *karamchari*, employee; *dharna*, sit in; *band*, stoppage of work, strike; *pandal*, podium, marquee; *gherao*, surrounding and detaining a person to extract a concession; *paan masala*, a mixture of areca nut, lime, tobacco, etc., used for chewing with a betel leaf; *lakhpati*, a millionnaire—*lakh* is one hundred thousand (usually of rupees); *jhuggi*, an improvised hovel in a slum colony; *shaleenta*, courtesy. Note that all the native lexical items have more or less appropriate equivalents in English, but the native words are preferred for their contextual appropriateness.

12. "Minor wife" seems to be the translation of Thai *mia noi* "little wife"; *soi* refers to "a lane." I am grateful to Lyle F. Bachman for providing these equivalents.

13. Only the first name is given in the text.

14. The style used here is typical of acknowledgments in South Asian languages and is clearly indicative of a culturally determined hierarchy of politeness which is transferred to English. Consider, for example, the following English "rendering" of a passage from a book in Hindi (Krishna Kumar Goswami, *Shaikshik vyākaraṇ aur vyāvhārik hindī*; Delhi: Ālekh Prakāshan, 1981): "The main inspiration for writing this book came from respected teacher Professor Ravindranath Srivastava. He not only inspired me but also read the manuscript carefully and suggested many corrections which enabled the book to come in its present form. I can never repay him for his guidance [teacher's debt], therefore without any formality, I bow my head to him with respect and dedicate this book to his lotus feet" (pp. viv-vv).

15. For an excellent cross-cultural and cross-linguistic study, see "Uni-

versals in Language Usage: Politeness Phenomena," in Brown and Levinson 1978.

16. Perhaps before Day there were other Indian creative writers. For example, as Sarma (1978: 329–30) says, Sochee Chunder Dutt had also "used Indian words liberally," but "the credit for practising Indian English as a distinct form goes to Lal Behari Day. He made use of the devices of Sochee Chunder Dutt with better discrimination and a more serious purpose."

REFERENCES

Aggarwal, Narindar K. 1981. *English in South Asia: a bibliographical survey of resources.* Gurgaon and New Delhi: Indian Documentation Service.

Alston, William P. 1980. The bridge between semantics and pragmatics. Pp. 123–34 in Rauch and Carr 1980.

Bailey, Richard W., and Manfred Görlach, eds. In press. *English as a world language.* Ann Arbor: University of Michigan Press.

Bhatia, Tej K., and William C. Ritchie, eds. 1989. Code-mixing: English across languages. Special issue of *World Englishes* 8(3).

Bokamba, Eyamba G. 1982. The Africanization of English. In this volume.

Brown, P., and S. Lavinston. 1978. Universals in language usage: politeness phenomena. In Goody 1978.

Chishimba, Maurice M. 1980a. The English language in the sociolinguistic profile of Zambia: the educational aspects. Manuscript.

———. 1980b. Some bilingual and bicultural aspects of African creative writing. Manuscript.

Christensen, F. 1965. A generative rhetoric of the paragraph. *College Composition and Communication* 16: 144–56.

Cicourel, A. V. 1969. Generative semantics and the structure of social interaction. *International Days of Sociolinguistics.* Rome.

Clyne, Michael. 1979. Communicative competences in contact. *ITL* 43: 17–37.

———. 1981. Culture and discourse structure. *Journal of Pragmatics* 5(1): 61–66.

Cole, Peter. 1978. *Syntax and semantics: pragmatics* Vol. 9. New York: Academic Press.

Day, Lal Behari. 1874. *Govinda Samanta or history of a Bengal raiyat.* London: Macmillan. 2 vols. Reprinted 1878 under the title *Bengal peasant life.*

Dehghanpisheh, E. 1972. Contrastive analysis of the rhetoric of Persian and English paragraphs. In *Proceedings of the second annual seminar of the Association of Professors of English in Iran.* Tehran: Department of University Relations and Cooperation/Association of University Professors of Iran.

Dressler, Wolfgang U. 1977. *Current trends in text linguistics.* New York: Walter de Gruyter.

Emeneau, Murray B. 1956. India as a linguistic area. *Language* 32: 3–16.

Ervin-Tripp, Susan. 1978. Whatever happened to communicative competence? Pp. 237–58 in Kachru, ed. 1978.

Ferguson, Charles A. 1978. Multilingualism as object of linguistic description. Pp. 97–105 in Kachru, ed. 1978.

———. 1982. Foreword. In this volume.

Firth, J. R. 1957. *Papers in linguistics: 1934–1951*. London: Oxford University Press.

———. 1968. Descriptive linguistics and the study of English. In F. R. Palmer, ed., *Selected papers of J. R. Firth 1952–59*. Bloomington: Indiana University Press.

Goffin, R. C. 1934. *Some notes on Indian English*. S.P.E. Tract no. 41. Oxford: Clarendon Press.

Goody, E. N., ed. 1978. *Questions and politeness: strategies in social interaction*. Cambridge: Cambridge University Press.

Gray, B. 1977. *The grammatical foundations of rhetoric: discourse analysis*. The Hague: Mouton.

Grimes, J. E. 1975. *The thread of discourse*. The Hague: Mouton.

Gumperz, John J. 1964. Linguistic and social interaction in two communities. In Gumperz and Hymes, eds., *The ethnography of communication*, special issue of *American Anthropologist* 66(6), part 2.

Halliday, M. A. K. 1973. *Explorations in the functions of language*. London: Edward Arnold.

———. 1974. *Learning how to mean: explorations in the development of language*. London: Edward Arnold.

———. 1978. *Language as social semiotic: the social interpretation of language and meaning*. Baltimore: University Park Press.

———, and R. Hasan. 1976. *Cohesion in English*. London: Longman.

Hartmann, R. In press. *Contrastive textology*. Heidelberg: Gross.

Houghton, Diane. 1980. Contrastive rhetoric. *English Language Research Journal* 1: 79–91. Birmingham, England: Department of English, University of Birmingham.

Hymes, Dell. 1962. The ethnography of speaking. Pp. 13–53 in T. Gladwin and W. Sturtevant, eds., *Anthropology and human behavior*. Washington, D.C.: Anthropological Society of Washington.

Kachru, Braj B. 1965. The *Indianness* in Indian English. *Word* 21: 291–410.

———, ed. 1978. *Linguistics in the seventies: directions and prospects*. Forum Lectures presented at the 1978 Linguistic Institute of the Linguistic Society of America. Special issue of *Studies in the Linguistic Sciences* 8(2).

———. 1978. *Code-mixing as a verbal strategy in India*. In James Alatis, ed., *International dimensions of bilingual education*. GURT. Washington, D.C.: Georgetown University Press.

———. 1980a. Models for new Englishes. *TESL Studies* 3: 117–50. Division of English as a Second Language, University of Illinois. Also in this volume.

———. 1980b. "Socially realistic linguistics": the Firthian tradition. *Studies in* the *Linguistic Sciences* 10(1): 85–111. Also in *International Journal of the Sociology of Language* 31: 65–89.

———. 1980c. The bilingual's linguistic repertoire. In B. Hartford and A. Valdman, eds., *Issues in international bilingual education: the role of the vernacular.* New York: Plenum.

———. 1981. Bilingualism. Pp. 2–18 in *Annual review of applied linguistics: 1980.* Rowley, Mass.: Newbury House.

———. 1982. *The other tongue: English across cultures.* Urbana: University of Illinois Press.

———. 1983. *The Indianization of English: the English language in India.* New Delhi: Oxford University Press.

Kachru, Yamuna, ed. 1991. Symposium on speech acts in World Englishes. *World Englishes* 10(3).

Kandiah, Thiru. 1981. Lankan English schizoglossia. *English World-Wide: A Journal of Varieties of English* 2(1): 63–81.

Kaplan, Robert B. 1966. Cultural thought patterns in inter-cultural education. *Language Learning* 16: 1–20. Also in K. Croft, ed., *Readings on English as a second language: for teachers and teacher trainees.* 2nd ed. Cambridge: Winthrop 1980.

Labov, William. 1969. The logic of nonstandard English. *Georgetown Monographs in Languages and Linguistics* 22. Also in Labov 1972b.

———. 1970. The study of language in its social context. *Studium Generale* 23(1): 30–87. Also in Labov 1972b.

———. 1972a. *Sociolinguistic patterns.* Philadelphia: University of Pennsylvania Press.

———. 1972b. *Language in the inner city: studies in the black English vernacular.* Philadelphia: University of Pennsylvania Press.

Lakoff, R. 1972. Language in context. *Language* 48(4): 907–38.

Larsen-Freeman, Diane, ed. 1980. *Discourse analysis in second language research.* Rowley, Mass.: Newbury House.

Llamzon, Teodoro A. 1969. *Standard Filipino English.* Manila: Ateno University Press.

Lowry, Ann. 1982. Style range in new English literatures. In this volume.

Maftoon-Semnani, P. 1979. A contrastive study of the rhetorical organization of American-English and Persian expository paragraphs. Ph.D. dissertation, New York University.

Masica, Colin P. 1976. *Defining a linguistic area: South Asia.* Chicago: University of Chicago Press.

Monaghan, J. 1979. *The neo-Firthian tradition and its contribution to general linguistics.* Linguistiche Arbeitern, 73. Tübingen: Niemeyer.

Morgan, J. L. 1977. Linguistics: the relation of pragmatics to semantics and syntax. Pp. 57–67 in *Annual Review of Anthropology.* Palo Alto, Calif.: Annual Reviews.

Myers, Terry, ed. 1979. *The development of conversation and discourse.* Edinburgh: Edinburgh University Press.

Narasimhaiah, C. D., ed. 1978. *Awakened conscience: studies in commonwealth literature.* New Delhi: Sterling.

Newmeyer, Frederick J. 1980. *Linguistic theory in America: the first quartercentury of transformational generative grammar.* New York: Academic Press.

Paradis, Michel. 1978. *Aspects of bilingualism.* Columbia, N.C.: Hornbeam Press.

Platt, John, and H. Weber. 1980. *English in Singapore and Malaysia: status, features, functions.* Kuala Lumpur: Oxford University Press.

Posner, Roland. 1980. Semantics and pragmatics of sentence connectives in natural language. Pp. 87–122 in Rauch and Carr 1980.

Quirk, Randolph, S. Greenbaum, G. Leech, and J. Svartvik. 1972. *A grammar of contemporary English.* London: Longman.

Rao, Raja. 1978. The caste of English. Pp. 420–22 in Narasimhaiah 1978.

Rauch, Irmengard, and Gerald F. Carr. 1980. *The signifying animal: the grammar of language and experience.* Bloomington: Indiana University Press.

Richards, Jack C. 1982. Singapore English: rhetorical and communicative styles. In Kachru 1982.

Sajavaara, K, and J. Lehtoneh, eds. 1980. *Jyvaskyla contrastive studies 5: papers in contrastive discourse analysis.* Jyvaskyla: University of Jyvaskyla.

Sankoff, Gillian. 1980. *The social life of language.* Philadelphia: University of Pennsylvania Press.

Sarma, Gobinda Prasad. 1978. *Nationalism in Indo-Anglian fiction.* New Delhi: Sterling.

Saville-Troike, Muriel. 1982. *The ethnography of communication: an introduction.* Oxford: Basil Blackwell.

Schuchardt, Hugo. 1891. Das Indo-Englische. *Englische Studien* 15: 286–305. [English translation in *Pidgin and creole languages: selected essays by Hugo Schuchardt,* ed. and trans. Glenn G. Gilbert. 1980. London and New York: Cambridge University Press.]

Sinclair, J. M., and Coulthard, R. M. 1975. *Towards an analysis of discourse.* London: Oxford University Press.

Smith, Larry E., ed. 1981. *English for cross-cultural communication.* London: Macmillan.

Sridhar, S. N. 1982. Non-native English literatures: context and relevance. In Kachru 1982.

———. 1987. *Discourse across cultures: strategies in World Englishes.* London: Prentice-Hall.

Stanlaw, J. 1982. English in Japanese communicative strategies. In this volume.

Strevens, Peter. 1980. *Teaching English as an international language.* Oxford: Pergamon Press.

Sugimoto, E. 1978. Contrastive analysis of English and Japanese technical rhetoric. Pp. 177–97 in Trimble et al. 1978.

Trimble, M. T., L. Trimble, and K. Drobnic 1978. *English for specific purposes: science and technology.* English Language Institute, Oregon State University.

325

Van Dijk, T. A. 1977. *Text and context: explorations in the semantics and pragmatics of discourse.* London: Longman.

Whitworth, George C. 1907. *Indian English: an examination of the errors of idioms made by Indians in writing English.* Letchworth, Herts: Garden City Press. (Later edition, 1932, Lahore.)

Widdowson, Henry. 1979. Rules and procedures in discourse analysis. Pp. 61–71 in Myers, ed. 1979.

17

Cecil L. Nelson

My Language, Your Culture: Whose Communicative Competence?

When approaching a language transplanted to a new cultural and linguistic context — as, for example, English in India — one is brought to various realizations about the notion of *language* and the *varieties* that a language may develop.[1] Communicative competence, the ability to put a language to use in appropriate ways in culturally defined contexts, may become a problematic notion when applied in the situation of such a transplanted language, because the cultural contexts that defined "appropriateness" in the parent situation are not necessarily the same in the new situation.

One must note that very different problems arise depending on the observer's native culture. For one from the "donor" language community, questions are mostly variations on "What has happened to our language?" For one from the adopting culture, the questions are more varied, including "Why is this language here? Why do I/we need it? What will it do to my/our sense of ourselves as Indians/Africans/Nigerians?"

The notion of *varieties* of a language and the corollary notion of *non-native varieties* are now commonplace. However, an attitude disallowing the legitimacy of the notion of a "non-native" variety of English undeniably exists. In two studies (B. Kachru 1976, 1990) Indian graduate students in India were asked to label their English as Indian, British, American, or other: only about half (56 percent) identified themselves as Indian English users. When asked to identify their preference of a model of English to be adhered to in formal instruction, about 67 percent of both faculty and graduate students responded "British English"; only 23 percent of the graduate students and 27 percent of the faculty admitted to a preference for Indian English. Bamgboşe (1982) has written, "One noticeable effect of the refusal to accept the existence of a Nigerian English is the perpetuation of the myth that the English taught in Nigerian schools is just the same as, say, British English; a corollary myth is that teachers of English, even at the primary school level, are capable of teaching this model effectively. In our teaching and examinations we concentrate on drilling and testing out of existence forms of speech that even the teachers will use freely when they do not have their textbooks open before them." The notion that there is no "English" but the Queen's English seems relatively widespread in extensive quarters of the English-using world. Clifford Prator (1968) wrote about what he called "The British Heresy in TESL," namely the liberal attitude exhibited in *not* insisting on a native (British) model to be presented to and elicited from nonnative learners of English. (See B. Kachru 1976 for detailed discussion.) And we "native" English teachers, by and large, teach—and correct—our ESL students according to our native models. We probably consider this "natural." There is an inescapable implication in much of what we say and write: namely, that certain segments of the academic/TESL world community have a vested interest in keeping English as "ours," and giving (or selling) it to "them."

While all language use is creative enough that it may be difficult to pin down the features that constitute "American" as different from "Australian" English, there is no doubt that users can identify others by their linguistic performances. The structures that we produce can be broadly identified as representative of one or another variety of a language. There is relatively little doubt, for example, that this article is written in "English." We refer to it as "Standard" English largely because it contains no regionalisms—no features, that is, that would mark it as belonging to one or another area of the country to the exclusion of another (see Strevens 1982). We refer to it as "American" because it has features that we could all agree "look like" American English, as opposed to, say, Australian or British, although we might be hard put to it to describe and define those features comprehensively. This is sometimes a good deal harder to discern in written than in spoken language: see Strevens (1982) on the difference between "grammar" and "accent."

We agree that there are differences, but we insist on a broader sameness—we all speak "English." Or do we? It is not difficult to come up with noteworthy, if not really troublesome, differences between American and British English. So we agree that there are *varieties* of native Englishes. Various considerations of historical happenstance and imposition must be kept in the back of one's mind when using that prejudicial word *native*, but by and large we agree that a "native" language is one spoken as the primary language (to use Strevens's term) of the community in question; that is, learned first in childhood, used exclusively or at least preferentially in all dealings public and private, and supported—again, probably exclusively—in statute and education.

What about English where it is *not* the first language of its users but is still a very important language in the communiity? Such a situation exists in large areas of the former colonial territories, including much of Africa and Asia. In these areas English has acquired features that make it recognizable as typical of a continent, country, or even smaller division, depending on the experience of the recognizer, just as the speech of an American, Briton, or Australian can be identified. When English came to new continents, it changed in various ways. Some were normal diachronic changes that are to be expected of any speech community separated from its "parent" community. Some were in direct response to the new environment: the names of new peoples, plants, animals, and geographical features. But what we today call *non-native English* is being used in response to new cultural and linguistic settings as well. B. Kachru (1977: 32) has written about the parallelism between *speech event* and *social event*; the culture in which English is used determines its applicability and its innovations at all linguistic levels.

Some of the English so produced can be decoded by the same means that one appeals to in dealing with the creative aspect of language on a day-to-day basis; and some of the texts of non-native English literatures can be dealt with in the same way that would be used to make sense of any stylistically "unusual" author. Some elements of non-native English, however, are outside the native speaker's frame of social, cultural, religious, and grammatical reference. The reader or hearer may have to make new efforts when he encounters such text; he may have to extend his linguistic, literary, historical, cultural awareness to meet the new demands. The native speaker has long been on the inside looking out, and wary of admitting outsiders to the "fellowship" of legitimate users of the language. As the non-native varieties of English grow in importance and productivity, the native-variety user may now find himself to be the outsider, the one who must resort to looking unfamiliar items up in the glossary provided by a thoughtful author, such as those found in "the American edition" of Raja Rao's *Kanthapura*, or in Chinua Achebe's *Things Fall Apart*.

The "non-natives" have, of course, been adopting and adapting

English for a long time—and not only, as some might think, in dealing with "us." As a *link language,* English is playing increasingly important *intranational* roles in its new multilinguistic settings. (See Ch. 16.)

In India, between 36 and 40 million people find English a necessary part of their lives. In 1979, about 7,000 books were produced in English in India, about 38 percent of the total. Hindi was in second place, with just under 3,000, or only about 16 percent of the total (of 18,500 books). Newspapers in English in India are in second place after those in Hindi: over 9,000, about 22 percent, are produced in English, as compared to 24 percent in Hindi (1978 figures). English and Hindi are the only pan-Indian broadcast languages on All-India Radio: of 21 hours of daily broadcast time, Hindi was first, with about 17 percent, and English second, with almost 10 percent (1981 figures from B. Kachru 1983: 219–20).

Of course, one feature of the modern non-native varieties is that they are, generally speaking, second languages in their respective countries. With a second language imposed upon a first, one typically finds that learners speak "with an accent" attributable to features of their first language. Some features of this accent can be quite subtle. (See Nelson 1982 for discussion.)

Writers also write "with an accent," as it were. As one reads non-native variety text, it becomes immediately clear that some devices and elements that are acceptable to the non-native variety author are not the same as those in native-variety texts. From the level of lexical redefinition to that of style features and discourse arrangement, the text is "marked" as non-native. These features establish the context of the text and allow the native-variety reader a glimpse of cultures and situations very different from those he is used to.

Some features are more or less "purely" linguistically classifiable. For example, one set of elements in the Indian English novel *Kanthapura* (1938/1963), by the well-known author Raja Rao, consists (from the point of view of the native-variety reader) archaisms, such as *four and twenty* instead of *twenty-four.* It is very unlikely, in view of the variety of styles evident not only among texts by the same author, but also within the one text, that such features are the result of weaknesses of second-language learning; rather, they must be intentional attributes of the discourse of certain characters in the work (cf. Nelson 1988).

The first problem one encounters in casting any aspersions on non-native writing is that *native* writing is far from error free. It is becoming increasingly difficult to maintain a distinction between native and non-native variety writing on the basis that one (the former) is generally "better" than the other. One should make reasoned criticisms, without failing to take note of the linguistic facts of creativity and diachronic processes. It may be fair—at least it is usual—to say that some deviations found in non-native writing are troublesome in ways that examples that one might note in native writing are not: they are held to be *consistently inconsistent,* in some respects—trouble with articles, verb tenses, reference agreement. But, if one looks at, say, editions of introductory textbooks in various fields, it is likely that one will encounter numerous readily apparent errors, especially embarrassing in language-teaching materials.[2]

Kanthapura, for example, displays many deviations (as opposed to mistakes) from standard native English models. Some of these deviations are marginally acceptable to native readers:

(1) The Tiger, his words were law (*Kanth.* 6)
(2) he goes, Moorthy, from house to house (9)
(3) there were other stories he told us, Jayaramachar (12)

The context of the complete text makes it clear that each is a resumptive reference. In Example 1, *his* refers to *The Tiger,* and similarly in the other two. I routinely correct such sentence structures in the writing of my students with reference to "good style," but I would hesitate to call them "wrong" in the real world, since many native speakers regularly use such constructions, as *He's really grown, Joshua,* and *How is she liking school now, Jessica?* The expectations of the participants and the communicative effectiveness of speech events determine our evaluations of "communicative competence."

Another type of deviation in the English of *Kanthapura* involves the use of verb tenses:

(4) After that he [Bhatta] *would take* his coconut and money offerings and hurry down to Pandit Venkateshia's house. . . . Bhatta *is* the First Brahmin. He *would be* there before it *is* hardly eleven . . . , he *would begin* to make the obsequial grass-rings. . . . (*Kanth.* 21)

The tense information is necessary to the flow of the narrative, and there is no obvious compelling reason to mix tenses. But Y. Kachru (1984) has pointed out that such deviations from native English tense sequencing may reflect first-language discourse rules. In terms of the native English tense usages expected here, the mixture of past and present time references is confusing to the native reader, but it reflects linguistic culture. For discussions of world English discoursal features see Smith (1987), Y. Kachru (1990), and Valentine (1988).

Example 5 is from *The Serpent and the Rope* (1960), by the same author, Raja Rao. In this passage the reportage sequences are just what one would expect (the father has not yet died):

> (5) That evening Madeleine *was* like my own mother. She said *had* my mother still *been* alive she *would have flown* with me to be beside her in her pain. Death and birth mean different things to different peoples of the earth; to me Madeleine's presence *would have meant* the daughter-in-law coming home . . . ; truly it *would have been* "the crossing of the threshold." I almost felt if she *came* Father *could* not *die,* he *would* not *die.* How, when the first daughter-in-law *came* home, *could* the father *die?* (54)

It is apparent that the author controls a wide range of English usage; therefore the reader must assume that he acts for a purpose. One can argue about that—style, literaary merit, or whatever—but not on the basis of weak control of language.

Intuitively, one may rank creative writers, such as Raja Rao, at the upper end of a *cline of bilingualism,* a very useful notion developed by B. Kachru (1977) in which second-language users are viewed as ranged along a scale from zero speaker to full bilingual. The writing of journalists ranks in the middle of the cline, and the writing of students somewhat lower. Journalism and other workaday writing provide a greater number and variety of examples of deviation from native models and internal inconsistency of usage and structure. But, again, English-as-first-language productions are not totally fail safe models:

> (6) Atlanta deaths rise; killer wants caught? (*Terre Haute Tribune* headline, 2/14/81)

Example 6 reflects regional usage: in west-central Indiana, one may use the perfect participle after *want* and *need,* as in *my tires need rotated.* Hence, while non-standard, this deviation does reflect a recognizable form of "native" English. Compare the tense-sequencing in example 4 above, also recognizable to users of that variety.

Examination of almost any page of non-native English journalism will provide similar examples which, however, one may criticize in different terms from those used above:

> (7) They are promising a *clean good life* for us. (*Times of India* 12/9/84: 1)

> (8) The US has already supplied to Pakistan *an* TPS-43 high power *radars* . . . which are now being used in their . . . control system. (*TI* 10/7/84: 1)

(9) US move to give highly offensive arms to Pakistan (headline, *TI* 10/7/84: 1)

(10) The E-2C will give tremendous tactical advantage to the Pakistan air force and help it monitor *all-Indian* Air Force aircraft right from the time they *switched* on their *energies* at their airfields. (*TI* 10/7/84: 1)

(11) More than *one lakh people had been affected* by the holocaust. (*TI* 12/9/84: 1)

(12) The Indian Army last fortnight inflicted heavy casualties on Pakistan forces as *they* repulsed strong attacks to dislodge *them* (Indian troops) from *key position* in the Nubra Valley in the Ladakh region. . . . (*Hindustan Times* 7/7/84: 1)

(13) This correspondent *who* was the only foreign journalist to be in Jaffna since November 30, when the government imposed military administration and severely restricted the movement of the people within the district as well as to and from Jaffna. (*TI* 12/9/84: 1)

Item 7 violates adjective order restrictions, codified in reference grammars as "adjectives of general description (such as *good*) precede those of condition (such as *clean*)": *a good clean life*. There is no loss of meaning here; it just "sounds funny."

Item 8 shows a wrong use of the article on two counts: first, it should not appear with its plural head noun (agreement in the following relative clause indicates the plural is intended); second, it is in the wrong form preceding "T." Many students—native and non-native—produce such errors; in those afflicted, the condition seems inexplicably resistant to correction.

Item 9 is an interesting case of a change in sense forced by modification of the adjective, since "offensive arms" (or better, "weapons") means what it is supposed to, but "highly offensive" does not.

Item 10 offers simply a substitution of a wrong word for a similar-looking word, *energies* for *engines*—again, a not atypical student error. Other apparent errors in this sentence are the inappropriate use of the past tense (*switched on*), and use of a hyphen to join *all-Indian* into a unit, as in "All-India Radio."

Item 11 is actually appropriate, since *lakh* is a number (100,000), but the monolingual English reader does not recognize it as such. The Indian English reader would not find it disturbing, of course. Also present in this sentence is a past perfect *had been affected* rather than *were affected* or perhaps *have been affected*.

Item 12 is more strikingly hard to read: the references are confused and confusing. Note the writer's recognition of this, as evidenced by his attempt to save the sentence with a parenthetical reference clarification. This is a favored ploy among many more literal-minded students. An additional item of interest is the missing article or plural in the phrase *from key position*.

Item 13, an incomplete sentence, could be saved simply by deleting *who*. Student writers often lose themselves in such needless complexity.

Student writing, referred to in asides in much of the above, generally provides similar examples. Again, U.S. students may not be notably better writers, on average, than their international classmates:

(14) Things *are always not* what they seem to be. For instance, I *had gotten* a ride home from one of my high school teachers. *Nevertheless,* someone *seem* me getting into his car and the *worse was being thought. Nonetheless* I was *confronted* for taking a ride home with my teacher and *the worse was thought.* As I say again, "Things are *always not* what they seem to be." (U.S. student essay)

(15) People are *basicly* the same, *that* they tend to do something, just because everyone else is doing it and not because they *fill* that *its* right. I *fill its* the way people *things* that is so funny. Take me for instance I usually go bowling with my friends, not because I always want to but just because I want to be with *my friends.* . . . Our world is *base* on *thing* such as that. . . . (U.S. student essay)

The number of obvious language errors in these examples leads one to wonder how students communicate well enough to get anything done.

ESL student writing shows us many of the same sorts of errors:

(16) The children do not pack out even on many occasions, when they are married, in case of men, they still reside in their families or fathers apartments but what dictate for them is the time they would be raising children in the Nigerian family. (Nigerian student essay)

(17) Women managers *working hand in hand* with men (Singaporean student essay)

(18) Some students like to *go outstation* on weekends. (Malaysian student essay)

(19) lackadacious (for an appropriate use of "lackadaisical"; South African student essay)

Occasionally there is an instance of real gibberish, such as in example 16. Note that even this example is not too bad for the first two or three lines: if you move the *even* to follow *not,* and put a period after *married* to begin a new sentence at *in case of,* it starts out making sense. More common, though, are recognizable distortions of grammar or sense, and sometimes delightful malapropisms, as in 17. Item 18 shows an instance of standard varietal usage meaning "into the country" (see Lowenberg 1986); and the coinage in 19, by a South African student (Zulu speaker), is not too jarring.

The reader's attitude must play a major role in assigning status to a particular text. The hierarchy of how seriously the reader expects to take a text is determined more by the information (known or assumed) that he brings to the reading than by factors within the text itself. (See B. Kachru 1986, 1988 for discussion of attitudinal factors in accepting texts and users across varieties of English, especially with regard to the relevance of the native speaker in world Englishes generally; cf. Quirk 1988, 1989.) The reader expects to work at reading "creative writing"; he looks for nuances, subtleties, "turns of phrase," coinages—in short, "creativity" on the part of the author. When he reads a newspaper, on the other hand, he dislikes extraneous surprises. When he reads student writing, red pen in hand, he is set to pounce on whatever he cannot readily interpret—or, if his *threshold of intelligibility,* to use Catford's (1950) phrase, has been lowered by years of training and exposure to non-native Englishes, he pounces on whatever he imagines would not be readily familiar to a less experienced monolingual reader. There may be some justification for this. One knows (or assumes) that the native user, at least at the upper end of the cline of facility, could draw upon his competence to correct errors of structure and usage if they were brought to his attention. Among users of non-native varieties, and especially among those who are learners of English without the background of a variety in the process of nativization, the likelihood of displaying consistency in revision diminishes. In any event, it is clear that my knowing the source of a text has much to do with my interpretation of, response to, and identification with it. The power and persuasiveness of a text is, to at least some extent, determined before the actual reading has even begun.

Non-native Englishes exist as realities in the world, and native-variety users, particularly those in language teaching, may find themselves having to do something about that fact, practically and attitudinally. While we may recognize the uses of, for example, Indian English, and may even praise the works of Indian English literature that strike our fancy, we continue to call them "non-something," therefore "not-quite-right something." If we recognize that there are differences between British and American English, yet we can avoid saying that one is "right" and the other "wrong," what allows us to continue to distinguish a native ("right") variety of English from a non-native ("wrong") variety? Will there come a time, for example, when my university will admit Nigerian students without making them take the English Placement Test, just as Canadian students are admitted now? After all, as we have seen, the native speaker *is* the outsider looking in when he approaches Indian and African text.

The dividing factor might be identified, if somewhat simplistically, with reference to *confidence* and *consistency*. For Indian English to assume an ascendant place in the world, the attitudinal allegiance of the users of Indian English must be such that they can say to themselves and to the world, "I am a speaker of Indian English. I do not aspire to be indistinguishable from a British or American speaker. English as I know it and use it serves my needs, fulfills its functions as a communicative system for me." (See K. Sridhar 1989 for discussions of English as a coexisting communicative system in India.) Furthermore, the English of the Indian or other users must be consistent, at least as internally coherent and thus intra-varietally communicative as any of the current "native varieties." (Such parity should not be hard to achieve, if the native-variety examples cited above indicate the state of literacy in the native-English-using world.) If this means, for example, that Indian rhetorical conventions will allow the use of the present tense in reported speech (as in example 4), then so be it. After all, many American speakers use this "mixture" today in reference to still or always true contexts ("He *asked* me where the Union Building *is*").

As long as we continue to *compare*, say, Indian and American English, we will of course see "differences," and almost inevitably construe these as *mistakes* on the part of the new variety. We could do the same thing to British and American English, but we don't. Historical and cultural factors cement "us" and separate "them." One must have second thoughts about the communicative competence of native speakers as demonstrated by performance examples such as those given above, and about the comparisons of native to non-native competence. Non-native creativity, and indeed, diachronic changes of all sorts, are constantly judged in comparison to native models. In such a comparison, the standard always wins. If the expanding use of English worldwide continues (see Crystal 1985), we will be brought more and more to recognize English *as a world language*. This is not to say that one will be free to say whatever one likes and call it "English." Rather, the community of speakers will by sheer numbers and geographical distribution require active accommodation from all participants to retain a high degree of intelligibility across varieties. (See Smith 1988 for discussion of intelligibility issues.) For one body to claim "ownership" of English on some basis of historical antecedence is pragmatically unsound thinking. As Smith (1976: 1) puts it, "English belongs to any country which uses it, and may have as wide or as limited a use (either as an international or auxiliary language) as is felt desirable." Recognition of this fact will pay in some measure for the plethora of linguistically colonialist attitudinal sins of the past.

Communicative competence will always remain a relative term and concept. Some people will write faster, more fluently, and more clearly—often depending on the situation and the reader. What is clear (or acceptable) at first reading to you may not be to me, because creating the text comes from our experiences and contexts, as it does from the writer's. An accident of birth does not necessarily make one user more communicatively "competent" than another who may have a wider range of experience, larger vocabulary, and better "feel" for language use. Each English user must now say, "It is my language," and then adapt it variously to appropriate contexts, in "my" culture or another's.[3]

NOTES

1. This is a revised and updated version of an article that first appeared in *World Englishes*. 4.2 (1985): 243–50.

2. Examples such as i and ii below would probably be instantly labeled "typos," a more "excusable" form of mistake—in linguistic terms, *"performance errors"*:

(i) She could not *breath* by herself, so a respirator pumped air. . . . (*NY Times* 12/16/84: 1)

(ii) Many VCR owners . . . will sneak a *peak* at X-rated tapes. . . . (*Time* 12/24/84: 47)

An example such as iii is a bit harder to justify, since it involves sense, not so easily ascribable to mere "typing error":

(iii) A cruel joker . . . *falsely spread the rumor that*. . . . (*Time* 12/24/84: 55)

3. See also Y. Kachru, ed., Symposium on speech acts in World Englishes, *World Englishes* 10(3) (1991).

REFERENCES

Bamgboṣe, Ayọ. 1982. Standard Nigerian English: issues of identification. In this volume.

Catford, John. 1950. Intelligibility. *English Language Teaching* 1: 7–15.

Crystal, David. 1985. How many millions? The statistics of English today. *English Today* 1: 7–9.

Kachru, Braj B. 1976. Models of English for the third world: white man's linguistic burden or language pragmatics? *TESOL Quarterly* 10: 221–39.

———. 1977. The new Englishes and old models. *English Teaching Forum* 15: 29–35.

———. 1983. The pragmatics of non-native Englishes. Pp. 211–40 in Braj B. Kachru, *The Indianization of English: the English language in India*. New Delhi: Oxford University Press.

———. 1986. *The alchemy of English: The spread, functions and models of non-native Englishes*. Oxford: Pergamon Press.

———. 1988. The spread of English and sacred linguistic cows. Pp. 207–28 in Lowenberg, ed. 1988.

———. 1990. Models for non-native Englishes. In this volume.

Kachru, Yamuna. 1984. Discourse analysis and second language acquisition research: issues and directions. Paper presented at AAAL, Baltimore, 28 December.

———. 1990. Culture, style and discourse: expanding noetics of English. In this volume.

Lowenberg, Peter H. 1986. Sociolinguistic context and second-language acquisition: acculturation and creativity in Malaysian English. *World Englishes* 5(1): 71–83.

———, ed. 1988. Language spread and language policy: issues, implications, and case studies. Georgetown University Round Table on Languages and Linguistics 1987. Washington, D.C.: Georgetown University Press.

Nelson, Cecil L. 1982. Intelligibility and non-native varieties of English. Pp. 58–73 in *The other tongue: English across cultures*, ed. Braj B. Kachru. Urbana: University of Illinois Press.

———. 1988. The pragmatic dimension of creativity in the other tongue. *World Englishes* 7(2): 173–81.

Prator, Clifford H. 1968. The British heresy in TESL. Pp. 459–76 in Joshua Fishman, Charles A. Ferguson, and J. Das Gupta, eds., *Language problems of developing nations*. New York: John Wiley and Sons.

Quirk, Randolph. 1988. The question of standards in the international use of English. Pp. 229–41 in Lowenberg, ed. 1988.

———. 1989. Language varieties and standard language. *JALT Journal* 11(1): 14–25.

Rao, Raja. 1960. *The serpent and the rope*. New York: Pantheon.

———. 1983. *Kanthapura*. New York: New Directions. (First published, London: George Allen & Unwin, 1938.)

Smith, Larry E. 1976. English as an international auxiliary language. *RELC Journal* 7(2). Reprinted in Smith, ed. 1983: 1–5.

————, ed. 1983. *Readings in English as an international language.* New York: Pergamon Press.

————. 1987. *Discourse across cultures: strategies in world Englishes.* London: Prentice-Hall International.

————. 1988. Spread of English and issues of intelligibility. In this volume.

Sridhar, K. K. 1986. Sociolinguistic theory and non-native varieties of English. *Lingua* 68(1): 39–58.

————. 1989. *English in Indian bilingualism.* Delhi: Manohar.

Strevens, Peter. 1982. World English and the world's Englishes; or, whose language is it, anyway? *Journal of the Royal Society of Arts* (June): 418–31.

Valentine, Tamara M. 1988. Developing discourse types in non-native English: strategies of gender in Hindi and Indian English. *World Englishes* 7(2): 143–58.

18

Yamuna Kachru

Culture, Style, and Discourse: Expanding Noetics of English

This chapter focuses on the role of style in conveying cultural meaning *in addition to* defining text types in terms of configurations of linguistic features. The term *style* refers to those configurations of formal linguistic features of the text that not only define the manner of expression but also indicate speakers' and writers' attitudes and belief systems.[1]

In recent research in discourse analysis, two major concerns have been text type research (Biber 1984, 1986; Biber and Finnegan 1988; Grabe 1984, 1987) and sociocultural/ethnographic factors in text structure (Choi 1988a, 1988b; Clyne 1983, 1987; Hayashi 1987, 1988; Hinds 1980, 1983, 1987; Y. Kachru 1983, 1987, 1988; Tannen 1982, 1984, among others). The second concern is related to the wider issue of cognition and culture (Holland and Quinn 1987) on the one hand and ethnic styles of socialization (Heath 1983, Ochs 1982, among others) on the other. This chapter is largely motivated by the second concern, that of sociocultural factors in text, but utilizes the methodology of the first, i.e., text type research.

I would first like to make explicit what I mean by *culture* and *style,* the two central notions in the title. Next I will present the relevant background information on Indian English (hereafter, IE) and describe the corpus used for this study. Finally, I will present the analysis of the corpus and demonstrate that formal configurations of style features do convey cultural meaning.

Culture and Meaning

Culture can be defined as shared knowledge, i.e., what people "must know in order to act as they do, make the things they make, and interpret their experience in the distinctive way they do" (Holland and Quinn 1987). The first part in this definition ("act as they do") refers to behavior in general, including verbal behavior; the second ("make the things they make") refers to artifacts; and the third ("interpret their experience") refers to the structure of knowledge. Both the first and the third parts are relevant to my purposes here, since linguistic structure necessarily reflects the structure of knowledge. This relationship between linguistic structure and structure of knowledge is one of the major interests in the study of verbal behavior. Consequently, a great deal of research related to verbal behavior (e.g., structure of narrative, memory and recall of texts, structure of expository and argumentative writing, interpretation of texts) has found it necessary to refer to investigations in ways of structuring knowledge, or cognitive structure (see, e.g., Abelson 1976, Bartlett 1932, Bobrow and Collins 1975, Johnson-Laird 1981, Kintsch 1974, Minsky 1975, Rumelhart 1975, Sanford and Garrod 1981, Schank and Abelson 1977, Tannen 1979, Thorndyke 1977, among others).[2]

It is a well-established fact that one acquires a social identity, and within the framework of social identity a personal or individual identity, along with the acquisition of a first language (Halliday 1975). The nature of the relationship between language acquisition and/or linguistic competence and socialization on the one hand, and grammar of language and "grammar of culture" on the other has been of great interest to sociolinguists (see, e.g., Bright 1968, D'souza 1988).[3] As suggested by D'souza (1988), it is justifiable to claim that notions of appropriateness that regulate linguistic behavior are derived from the grammar of culture.

Cultural meaning is expressed in the cognitive structures as well as norms of behavior people utilize when using language, which is of interest to sociolinguists. On the other hand, the role of language in shaping, storage, retrieval, and communication of knowledge has also been recognized in the notion of noetics (Becker 1982). My aim is to discuss both the linguistics and the noetics of IE.

Defining Style

Both linguistic and literary studies have traditions of characterizing text types in terms of form, content, and function. Notions such as genre, register, and style have generally been utilized to do so. Genre is usually defined in terms of rhetorical form; register, in terms of *field* (topic or subject matter of discourse), *tenor* (interpersonal relationship between or among participants), and *mode* (spoken vs. written).[4] Style has been used in many senses by literary critics and linguists, but may be defined in terms of choice of linguistic form in speech/writing to indicate manner of expression, rather than ideas expressed.

"Style of stance," on the other hand, has been defined in terms of linguistic form indicative of the speaker/writer's attitudes toward and belief with regard to the content and source of information conveyed (Biber and Finnegan 1988). In grammars of English, certain linguistic items have been identified as markers of attitude and belief.[5] Chafe (1986) discusses speaker/writer-oriented items under the label "evidentials" and distinguishes several types of markers. The central notion is that of *knowledge*, "the basic information whose status is qualified one way or another by markers of evidentiality" (262). The markers are those of reliability of knowledge, modes of knowing (i.e., belief, induction, hearsay, and deduction), and source of knowledge (e.g., evidence for induction, language for hearsay, and hypothesis for deduction; for belief, the source is said to be problematic). Knowledge can be matched against verbal resources or categories and also against expectations.

A few examples may make the above clearer. Expressions such as *certainly, definitely, surely* are markers of more reliable information, whereas *normally, generally, primarily* are markers of statistical reliability, and *may be, perhaps, probably* are markers of less reliable information. *Must* (in sentences such as *He must be here*) signals induction with a high degree of reliability; *seem,* on the other hand, indicates less certainty on the part of the speaker/writer. *See, hear, feel* (in sentences such as *I see that you are very tired*) convey the sensory basis of induction, whereas *supposed to be, apparently* signal hearsay evidence. Jackendoff (1972) earlier discussed the adverbs cited above as "speaker-oriented" adverbs (56ff.). Brown and Levinson (1978) discussed some of these items under "hedges," an aspect of the proposed category of "negative politeness," i.e., the speakers' presumptions about the relevance or interest of what is communicated to the audience.

Obviously, "style of stance" is a subset of "style." The latter notion can be broadened further by including the forms that signal a high involvement of the speaker/writer with the topic; e.g., use of a first-person pronoun, choice of nouns and verbs with emotive content, exclamatory sentences, expressions of personal hopes and wishes.[6] All these provide clues to the speaker's or writer's attitudes. Style, in this sense, can be defined as the configuration of the entire range of linguistic features that indicates (a) manner of expression, (b) the speaker/writer's attitudes or beliefs toward the content and source of information conveyed, and (c) the presumption of relevance to the hearer(s)/reader(s) of that information.

Indian English: A Brief Overview

English is the "associate" Official Language of the Republic of India, Hindi in Devanagari script being the Official Language of the Union. Though English was introduced into the subcontinent by the British as an instrument of colonial rule, the language took root and is now considered an equal of the indigenous languages. For example, for its annual award the Sahitya Akademi (the literary academy of India) evaluates creative literature in IE as it does in all the other national languages. A number of linguistic studies of IE have already demonstrated how the language has been nativized and made a suitable medium for expressing values of Indian culture and civilization (e.g., B. Kachru 1983, 1986; Y. Kachru 1983, 1987, 1988). These studies discuss not only the nativization of the phonology, lexicon, and grammar of English (B. Kachru 1983, 1986) but also the utilization of native conventions of speech and writing in English (e.g., Y. Kachru 1983, 1987, 1988; Valentine 1988) and the impact of the bi-/multi-lingual context of India on creativity in English (B. Kachru 1986: ch. 10; Nelson 1985). These studies clearly demonstrate that English is no longer a foreign language in the sense in which this term is normally understood in literature; nor is it exclusively an exponent of the British culture. What dictates the norms of use of English in India is an Indian "grammar of culture." It is against this background that I am examining style in IE.

Data and Methodology

The data consist of fifty essays written by college students (under-graduates) from several small and medium-sized towns and a large metropolitan city in India, and a body of texts randomly selected from a news magazine, *India Today* (Delhi), for a project on rhetorical structure in IE writing. The essays were all written extemporaneously within a forty-five-minute class period as an expository writing task and were, on average, 450 words long. The texts selected from the magazine are 6 editorial comments and 12 articles on various topics including politics, fashion, a human interest story, and religion. The texts vary in length from 600 to 2000 words. Thus the total corpus is about 40,000 words.

The data were computerized and a computer program was written to identify the key word in context, listing all adverbs that could be used as stance markers. In addition, all sentences with first-person subjects and all passages with a high involvement style were isolated. Although the corpus is not large or comprehensive in terms of genres, registers, and modes, the distribution of selected features in IE writing is notable. I will discuss the occurrence of stance-marking adverbials in the total corpus, the conclusions in the essays written by the college students expressing personal hopes and wishes or using modals of obligation and propriety, and occurrence of evidentials (Chafe 1986). Other features must await a more comprehensive study; these include occurrences of exclamatory sentences in the essays, and occurrence of attitudinally marked nouns (e.g., "The whole ceremony of the marriage has become *a farce* . . . [essay 7]), verbs (e.g., " . . . marriage is a sacred bond which should not be *contaminated* with evils like the dowry system" [essay 7]), and adjectives (e.g., "Like a *diabolic* adder it [the dowry system] stings the life of many innocent people . . ." [essay 9]).[7] The features identified here show a 'high involvement' style, which seems to set IE academic and journalistic writing apart from the varieties discussed by Chafe (1986) and Biber and Finnegan (1988).[8]

Results

Before discussing the results of the analysis, a few words as to how stance-marking adverbial expressions were counted may be helpful. In addition to counting occurrences of adverbials listed in Biber and Finnegan (1988), adverbials such as *miserably, pessimistically, normally, usually, roughly,* and *genuinely* were counted and assigned to the appropriate categories. For instance, the first two from the above list belong to category F; the last belongs to category D, and the rest belong to category B of Biber and Finnegan (1988). Expressions such as the following were also counted, since they seem to be performing the same function: *in fact, it is obvious that,* and *of course*. All categories identified in Chafe (1986) were also counted and the figures for academic writing compared.

The distribution of stance-marking expressions in the corpus is as follows. The figures represent percentage of occurrence of different classes out of the total number of adverbial expressions.[9]

In Biber and Finnegan (1988), 71 percent of the Press (here, Article) category is characterized by a "faceless" style, i.e., by very few stance-marking adverbials. In contrast, in the Indian data, there was no difference in the occurrence of stance-marking adverbials between the articles and the essays: the ratio of such expressions to

Table 1. Percentage of Stance-Marking Adverbials (Classes A-F)

Classes of Adverbials	Essays	Articles	Whole Corpus
Honestly	4	5	5
Generally	28	13	20
Surely	15	25	20
Actually	13	8	10
May be	20	18	18
Amazingly	20	31	27

the total number of words was almost even in both categories. This indicates that the IE Press is far from being "faceless." The same is true of academic writing, as is clear from the sample essay reproduced in Appendix B.[10] A complete list of stance-marking adverbials that occur in the corpus appears in Appendix A.

A few examples of editorial comments with stance-marking adverbials are as follows:

(1) His mandate was for change, but, *sadly,* too little has changed. (*IT,* Jan. 15, 1987: 9)
(2) Far from not having a constituency, the Opposition has a large body of supporters whom it has *abjectly* failed to give voice to. (*IT,* Apr. 30, 1988: 5)
(3) These, *ironically,* were *precisely* the grounds on which the representative Barnala government was dismissed and President's Rule declared. (*IT,* Dec. 15, 1988: 7)

According to Chafe (1986), in American English academic writing, markers of degrees of reliability had 4.18 occurrences per thousand words. Expression such as *I think, I guess, I suppose,* which indicate knowledge arrived at through belief, had only 0.6 occurrences per thousand words. Although inductive inference markers (e.g., *seem, obvious, evidently*) occurred more frequently, the figure was still low: 2.4 per thousand words. Sensory evidence markers (e.g., *feel, look, like*) as well as hearsay evidence markers (e.g., *have been said, supposed to be, apparently*) occurred rarely in conversation and almost never in academic writing. (In academic writing there were, of course, many examples of citations that are usually not considered markers of hearsay evidence.) Deduction markers had an occurrence of 4.4 per thousand words in academic writing, as compared to 2.9 in conversation. Hedges (e.g., *sort of, kind of*) rarely occur in academic writing, with only 0.4 per thousand words as compared to 3.6 occurrences in conversation. By far the most common evidentials to occur in academic writing and in conversations are markers of expectation (e.g., *of course, oddly enough, in fact, at least, even, only, but, however, nevertheless*): 13.9 per thousand words in writing, 17 in conversation.

The occurrences of these categories in the essays in the corpus under investigation, as compared to their occurrences in the AE academic writing, are shown in Table 2.[11]

Table 2. Occurrences of Evidentials in AE and IE Academic Writing
        (per thousand words)

Evidentials	AE	IE
1. Degree of reliability	4.18	2.2
2. Belief	.6	.64
3. Induction	2.4	.24
4. Sensory evidence	—	.84
5. Hearsay evidence	—	1.76
6. Deduction	4.4	4.76
7. Hedges	.4	—
8. Expectations	13.9	5.68

Table 2 does show differences between AE and IE academic writing. Note that the IE essay writers did not use markers of reliability very often; that is, most statements were bald assertions. Although IE writers do not use markers of induction, they do use markers of sensory and hearsay evidence more readily. In the use of markers of deduction and hedges, the two varieties seem comparable. However, IE academic writers do not use expectation markers to the same extent as the AE academic writers.

A majority of the essays end on a personal note:

(4) To wipe out this [dowry system] will be like a rise from the stagnant, putrid pool to the greatest height of perfection. Living will be a bliss! (essay 9)

(5) But the solution to this social evil is yet to be found. Try, till you succeed should be our motto for a good and healthy society. Dowry has to be eradicated and Brides saved! (essay 32)

(6) It is a responsibility of the girls of today to have a fixed stand and oppose this undesirable system. And we all hope we will succeed. (essay 41)

Most essays end either with a "should" statement or a "wish"/ "hope" statement (66%):

(7) It is an evil which *should* be removed completely and then only will there be happiness. (essay 1)

(8) The Government *should* also be very strict in making people compelled to obey the law, made for it [the dowry]. (essay 3)

(9) They [the people caught breaking the law with regard to dowry] as well as the youths of India *should* stand united to oppose this cruel practice which is a black spot on our democratic system. (essay 5)

(10) They [the boys and girls] *should* realise that marriage is a sacred bond which should not be contaminated with evils like the dowry system. (essay 7)

Conclusion

IE rhetorical style is characterized by high involvement as compared to the AE rhetorical style. This style is characterized by a higher frequency of occurrence of stance-marking adverbials in journalistic writing, and a difference in the use of evidentials and frequent use of personal hopes and wishes in academic writing. This is not surprising, in view of the fact that Indian languages such as Hindi employ the same style in expository writing.[12] The tradition of writing in Indian languages basically derives from the Sanskritic tradition. Since several features of the Sanskritic tradition have been discussed elsewhere in some detail (e.g., in Y. Kachru 1988), here I will mention just one relevant feature. As Table 2 shows, whereas markers of sensory and hearsay evidence do not occur in AE academic writing, they do in IE academic writing. This feature can be traced back to the Sanskritic tradition in that sensory as well as verbal evidence is recognized as a valid means of acquiring *pramā* or certain knowledge. All major systems of Indian philosophy and logic (e.g., *vedānta, sāṃkhya, nyāya*) list both sensory perception or that which is experienced directly (*pratyakṣa*) and that what has been pronounced by authority (*śabda* or *āpta vacana*) among valid evidence (*pramāṇa*). In turn, *āpta vacana* includes not only the Vedas (the scriptures) but also other spoken and written testimony of various kinds.[13] The rhetorical style of IE thus reflects an attempt to create the Sanskritic noetics in English: it expresses the same cultural meaning that the Indian languages do. In this sense, English in India has truly become an Indian language.[14] Of course, a more detailed study based on a larger and more comprehensive corpus is needed to see if the findings of this study can be further corroborated.

APPENDIX A

Adverbials

abjectly, absolutely, actually, adequately, awfully, allegedly, barely, basically,

347

blatantly, boldly, certainly, clearly, commonly, completely, consistently, definitely, directly, (no) doubt, effectively, easily, especially, exquisitely, extremely, (in) fact, fatally, feverishly, forcefully, frankly, (in) general, generally, genuinely, gradually, greatly, hopefully, increasingly, indeed, intensely, ironically, legally, literally, luckily, mainly, manifestly, may be, mercilessly, miserably, mostly, naturally, necessarily, normally, obviously, of course, optimistically, perhaps, personally, pessimistically, possibly, potentially, presumably, probably, purely, rarely, really, reasonably, repeatedly, reportedly, rightly, rigidly, roughly, rudely, ruthlessly, sadly, severely, simply, specially, stealthily, strictly, (be) supposed to, supposedly, surely, surprisingly, suspiciously, (in) theory, totally, tragically, truly, (it is) true that, ultimately, unanimously, undoubtedly, unequivocally, unfortunately, uniquely, usually, viciously, virtually, willingly.

APPENDIX B

Essay 34

Dowry System

Dowry system is one of the major social as well as cultural problem, which acts as a hindrance in the progress of India. This is one of the ancient systems which was genuinely done in good faith. "Daan" or "sacrifice" was given to a daughter by her father at the time of her marriage. It was supposed to be a good deed.

But, with the passage of time, evil conquered this good deed. A system of dowry started in which the bridegroom and his family demanded from the bride's family. This dowry now involves all material things, including cash, jewelry and daily domestic appliances.

Not only this, today "bride-killing" due to the non-fulfillment of the items demanded has also become prevalent. They either poison the brides or burn them to death with some fuel-oils. Torture is a normal and common phenomenon.

This system has produced so much chaos and confusion that no girl and her family is certain of a secured future. Everyone is guided by their fate and destiny.

But all this does not mean that there is no solution to the problem. After all, it is man-made. If man can create a problem, he will definitely find a solution to it. But the thousand million dollar question is: at what cost? Is it at the cost of hundreds of innocent girls who marry for their security?

The Government of India is trying its level best for the solution of this problem. There are many laws regarding to this. The Dowry Act also involves this problem. The major problem facing this is that both literates or illiterates and rich or poor, are victims of this evil system. The punishment of this leads to the life-imprisonment, but still it is true that this dowry system is prevailing.

Personally, I do not know how to conclude. Pessimistically, I may say that this will continue, regardless of any law. Optimistically, I may say that nature will help when man fails, but with the lurking fear that this is a man-made crisis. So, man has to find the solution and definitely as fast as possible.

NOTES

1. This definition is expanded further and discussed in greater detail later.

2. The knowledge we possess as users of language is a special case of the knowledge we have about what is going on in the world around us. The question that needs to be answered in case of production and comprehension of discourse is the following: How do we organize the knowledge of the world and activate only a small but relevant part of it when needed? A number of proposals have been put forward to account for the organization, storage, retrieval, and use of knowledge structures in discourse production and comprehension. Examples are notions such as *frame* and *script* of artificial intelligence (Minsky 1975, Schank and Abelson 1977), and *scenario* (Sanford and Garrod 1981), *schema* (Bartlett 1932, Rumelhart 1975), and *mental model* (Johnson-Laird 1981) of psychology. For a concise description of these notions, see Brown and Yule 1983: 236–55.

3. For the relationship between socialization and linguistic competence, see Bernstein 1971, 1973; for the notion "grammar of culture," see Bright 1968; for the relationship between grammar of language and "grammar of culture," see the discussion in D'souza 1988.

4. See Halliday and Hasan 1976 for a detailed discussion of the term *register.*

5. See the discussion of adverbials in Quirk et al. 1985, especially the categories of "courtesy subjuncts" (569ff.), "emphasizers" (583ff.), and "style and content disjuncts" (615ff.).

6. A noun such as *blunder* carries more of an attitudinal load than a *mistake*; the same is true of a verb such as *smirk* as compared to *smile*, and an adjective such as *putrid* as compared to *foul smelling*. See also the examples from the IE texts in the section on Data and Methodology.

7. In the above and the following examples, I have added the items in [ ] to make the intended referents of the pronominals clear.

8. No attempt has yet been made to subject the data to the statistical procedures of cluster analysis (Biber and Finnegan 1988). Once a larger corpus has been collected and analyzed, it would be worthwhile to carry out such analyses to define styles in Indian English; at this point, it seems premature. I am only interested in identifying lines along which further investigation may be fruitful.

9. The classes of adverbial expressions utilized here as categories are the same as in Biber and Finnegan 1988.

10. No article from *IT* is reproduced here; an instance of an editorial comment with a number of stance-marking adverbials is article 11 in the corpus entitled "Demoralising Drift," *IT*, Dec. 15, 1988, p. 7.

11. The categories of evidentials are the same as in Chafe 1986.

12. See Y. Kachru 1988 for a discussion of conventions of writing in Hindi.

13. See Monier-Williams 1899 for a definition of the Sanskrit terms; see Matilal 1986 and Potter 1977, 1981 for a discussion of the nature of evidence in Indian philosophical and logical systems.

14. A further justification for this claim may be found in recent research on speech acts in Indian English as reported in *World Englishes* 10:3 (1991).

REFERENCES

Abelson, R. P. 1976. Script processing in attitude formation and decision-making. Pp. 33–45 in J. S. Carroll and J. W. Payne, eds., *Cognition and social behavior*. Hillsdale, N.J.: Lawrence Erlbaum.

Adams, M. J., and A. Collins. 1979. A schema-theoretic view of reading. Pp. 1–22 in R. O. Freedle, ed., *New directions in discourse processing*. Norwood, N.J.: Ablex.

Bartlett, F. C. 1932. *Remembering*. Cambridge: Cambridge University Press.

Becker, A. 1982. The poetics and noetics of a Javanese poem. Pp. 217–38 in Tannen 1982.

Bernstein, B., ed. 1971. *Class, codes and control: theoretical studies towards a sociology of language*. Vol. 1. (Primary socialization, language and education). London: Routledge and Kegan Paul.

———. 1973. *Class, codes and control: applied studies towards a sociology of language*. Vol. 2. (Primary socialization, language and education). London: Routledge and Kegan Paul.

Biber, D. 1984. A model of textual relations within the written and spoken modes. Ph.D. dissertation, University of Southern California.

———. 1986. Spoken and written textual dimensions in English: resolving the contradictory findings. *Language* 62: 384–414.

———, and E. Finnegan. 1988. Adverbial stance types in English. *Discourse Processes* 11(1): 1–34.

Bobrow, D., and A. Collins, eds. 1975. *Representation and understanding: studies in cognitive science*. New York: Academic Press.

Bright, W. 1968. Toward a cultural grammar. *Indian Linguistics* 29: 20–29.

Brown, G., and G. Yule. 1983. *Discourse analysis*. Cambridge: Cambridge University Press.

Brown, P., and S. C. Levinson. 1978. Universals of language usage: politeness phenomena. Pp. 56–311 in Esther M. Goody, ed., *Questions and politeness: strategies in social interaction*. Cambridge: Cambridge University Press.

Chafe, W. 1986. Evidentiality in English conversation and academic writing. Pp. 261–72 in W. Chafe and J. Nichols, eds., *Evidentiality: the linguistic coding of epistemology*. Norwood, N.J.: Ablex.

Choi, Y.-H. 1988a. Text structure of Korean students' argumentative essays in English. *World Englishes* 7: 129–42.

———. 1988b. Textual coherence in English and Korean: an analysis of argumentative writing by American and Korean students. Ph.D. dissertation, University of Illinois.

Clyne, M. 1981. Culture and discourse structure. *Journal of Pragmatics* 5: 61–66.

———. 1983. Linguistics and written discourse in particular languages: contrastive studies: English and German. *Annual Review of Applied Linguistics* 3: 38–49.

———. 1987. Discourse structure and discourse expectations: implications for Anglo-German academic communication. Pp. 73–83 in L. E. Smith, ed., *Discourse across cultures: strategies in World Englishes.* New York: Prentice-Hall.

D'souza, J. 1988. Interactional strategies in South Asian languages: their implications for teaching English internationally. *World Englishes* 7(2): 159–72.

Grabe, W. 1984. Written discourse analysis. *Annual Review of Applied Linguistics* 5: 101–23.

———. 1987. Contrastive rhetoric and text type research. Pp. 115–37 in U. Connor and R. Kaplan, eds., *Writing across languages: analysis of L₂ text.* Reading, Mass.: Addison-Wesley.

Halliday, M. A. K. 1975. *Learning how to mean: explorations in the development of language.* (Explorations in Language Study.) London: Edward Arnold.

———, and R. Hasan. 1976. *Cohesion in English.* London: Longman.

Hayashi, R. 1987. A study of floor management of English and Japanese conversation. Ph.D. dissertation, University of Illinois.

———. 1988. Simultaneous talk from the perspective of floor management of English and Japanese speakers. *World Englishes* 7(3): 269–88.

Heath, S. 1983. *Ways with words: language, life, and work in communities and classrooms.* Cambridge: Cambridge University Press.

Hinds, J. 1980. Japanese expository prose. *Papers in Linguistics* 13(1): 117–58.

———. 1983. Contrastive rhetoric: Japanese and English. *Text* 3(2): 183–95.

———. 1987. Reader vs. writer responsibility: a new typology. Pp. 141–52 in U. Connor and R. Kaplan, eds., *Writing across languages: analysis of L₂ text.* Reading, Mass.: Addison-Wesley.

Holland, D., and N. Quinn. 1987. *Cultural models in language and thought.* Cambridge: Cambridge University Press.

Jackendoff, R. 1972. *Semantic interpretation in generative grammar* (Semantic Interpretation). Cambridge, Mass.: MIT Press.

Johnson-Laird, P. N. 1981. Mental models of meaning. Pp. 106–26 in A. K. Joshi, B. L. Webber, and I. A. Sag, eds., *Elements of discourse understanding.* Cambridge: Cambridge University Press.

Kachru, B. 1983. *The Indianization of English: the English language in India.* New Delhi: Oxford University Press.

———. 1986. *The alchemy of English: the spread, functions and models of nonnative Englishes.* Oxford: Pergamon Press. Reprinted 1990, Urbana: University of Illinois Press.

Kachru, Y. 1983. Linguistics and written discourse in particular languages: contrastive studies: English and Hindi. *Annual Review of Applied Linguistics* 3: 50–77.

———. 1987. Cross-cultural texts, discourse strategies and discourse interpretation. Pp. 87–100 in L. Smith, ed., *Discourse across cultures: strategies in World Englishes*. Englewood Cliffs, N.J.: Prentice-Hall.

———. 1988. Writers in Hindi and English. Pp. 109–37 in A. Purves, ed., *Writing across languages and cultures: issues in contrastive rhetoric.* (Written Communication Annual: An International Survey of Research and Theory). Newbury Park, Calif.: Sage.

Kintsch, W. 1974. *The representation of meaning in memory.* Hillsdale, N.J.: Lawrence Erlbaum.

Matilal, B. K. 1986. *Perception: an essay on classical Indian theories of knowledge.* Oxford: Clarendon Press.

Minsky, M. 1975. A framework for representing knowledge. Pp. 217–77 in P. H. Winston, ed., *The psychology of computer vision.* New York: McGraw-Hill.

Monier-Williams, M. 1899. *Sanskrit-English Dictionary.* Reprinted 1976, Delhi: Motilal Banarsidass.

Nelson, C. 1985. My language, your culture: whose communicative competence? *World Englishes* 4(2): 243–50. Revised version in this volume.

Ochs, E. 1982. Talking to children in Western Samoa. *Language in Society* 11: 77–104.

Potter, K. ed. 1977. *The encyclopedia of Indian philosophy.* Vol. 2. Delhi: Motilal Banarsidass.

———. 1981. *The encyclopedia of Indian philosophy.* Vol. 3. Princeton, N.J.: Princeton University Press.

Quirk, R., S. Greenbaum, G. Leech, and J. Svartvik. 1985. *A comprehensive grammar of the English language.* London: Longman.

Rumelhart, D. 1975. Notes on a schema for stories. Pp. 211–36 in Bobrow and Collins 1975.

Sanford, A. J., and S. C. Garrod. 1981. *Understanding written language.* Chichester: Wiley.

Schank, R., and R. Abelson. 1977. *Scripts, plans, goals and understanding.* Hillsdale, N.J.: Lawrence Erlbaum.

Tannen, D. 1979. What's in a frame? surface evidence for underlying expectations. Pp. 137–82 in R. O. Freedle, ed., *New directions in discourse processing.* Norwood, N.J.: Ablex.

———, ed. 1982. *Spoken and written language: exploring orality and literacy.* Norwood, N.J.: Ablex.

———. 1984. *Conversational style: analyzing talk among friends.* Norwood, N.J.: Ablex.

Thorndyke, P. W. 1977. Cognitive structures in comprehension and memory of narrative discourse. *Cognitive Psychology* 9: 77–110.

Valentine, T. 1988. Developing discourse types in non-native English: strategies of gender in Hindi and Indian English. *World Englishes* 7(2): 143–58.

PART VI

World Englishes in the Classroom: Rationale and Resources

19

Braj B. Kachru

Teaching World Englishes

The present international status of English is rightly justified on the basis of the numerical strength of its non-native speakers; the cross-cultural and localized functional range the language has developed in various domains; the excellence of its literary traditions; and the dominance of the language in trade, commerce, banking, tourism, technology, and scientific research. But this is not the whole story about the diffusion of English.

What draws an increasing number of people in the remote parts of the world to the study of English is the social attitude toward the language. It is, therefore, understandable why the most fundamentalist and anti-Western governments (e.g., Libya and Iran) consider it advantageous to use English in their rhetoric for presenting their points of view before the world. And it is not surprising that most anti-English movements in Asia and Africa use English as the medium to whip up anti-English feelings. Even those who are prominent in anti-English movements are pragmatically very sensible parents: they see to it that their children receive excellent education in English-medium schools. After all, English has power, and they want their children to be equipped with this powerful linguistic tool (Kachru 1986a).

However, this cross-cultural functional range of English is very rarely used to demonstrate the *internationalization* of the language: its acculturation in contexts that have resulted in new contours of the language and literature, in linguistic innovations, in literary creativity, and in the expansion of the cultural identities of the language. The implications of the internationalization of English have yet to be reflected in the curricula of teacher training programs, in the methodology of teaching, in understanding the sociolinguistic profile of the language, and in cross-cultural awareness.

The current sociolinguistic profile of English may be viewed in terms of three concentric circles. These circles represent the types of spread, the patterns of acquisition, and the functional allocation of English in diverse cultural contexts.[1] The Inner Circle refers to the traditional cultural and linguistic bases of English. The Outer Circle represents the institutionalized non-native varieties (ESL) in the regions that have passed through extended periods of colonization. Even if only 10 percent of the population in the Outer Circle uses English, it adds up to about 110 million. The Expanding Circle includes the

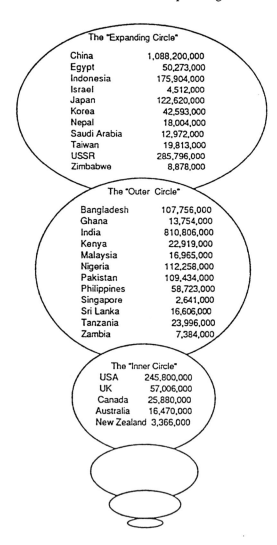

The "Expanding Circle"

China	1,088,200,000
Egypt	50,273,000
Indonesia	175,904,000
Israel	4,512,000
Japan	122,620,000
Korea	42,593,000
Nepal	18,004,000
Saudi Arabia	12,972,000
Taiwan	19,813,000
USSR	285,796,000
Zimbabwe	8,878,000

The "Outer Circle"

Bangladesh	107,756,000
Ghana	13,754,000
India	810,806,000
Kenya	22,919,000
Malaysia	16,965,000
Nigeria	112,258,000
Pakistan	109,434,000
Philippines	58,723,000
Singapore	2,641,000
Sri Lanka	16,606,000
Tanzania	23,996,000
Zambia	7,384,000

The "Inner Circle"

USA	245,800,000
UK	57,006,000
Canada	25,880,000
Australia	16,470,000
New Zealand	3,366,000

regions where the *performance* varieties of the language are used essentially in EFL contexts (i.e., varieties that lack official status and are typically restricted in their uses; for a detailed discussion, see Kachru 1985).

The numerical profile is impressive indeed. Even if we use a conservative estimate of the users of English (i.e., 800 million), about 57 percent are non-native users (Strevens 1982). The optimistic figure of 2 billion users, of course, increases this percentage significantly (Crystal 1985). However, the term "users" is rather tricky, particularly in the non-native context. The vagueness of its use is somewhat reduced by restricting it to "educated speakers," though by the use of that term too we are opening a can of worms. The result of this spread is that, formally and functionally, English now has multicultural identities. The term "English" does not capture this sociolinguistic reality; the term "Englishes" does. (See Kachru 1992.)

Why, then, are the implications of this sociolinguistic reality not recognized? The answer to this question is rather complex. It involves issues of attitude, of power and politics, and of history and economics. These attitudes are nurtured by numerous fallacies about the users and uses of English across cultures.

Six Fallacies about the Users and Uses of English

The fallacies are of several types; some based on unverified hypotheses, some based on partially valid hypotheses, and some due to ignorance of facts.

Fallacy 1: That in the Outer and Expanding Circles, English is essentially learned to interact with native speakers of the language. This, of course, is only partially true (e.g., Smith, ed. 1983; Kachru 1988a, 1988b). The reality is that in its localized varieties, English has become the main vehicle for interaction among its non-native users, with distinct linguistic and cultural backgrounds—Indians interacting with Nigerians, Japanese with Sri Lankans, Germans with Singaporeans, and so on. In such interactions, the *English* English, or *American* English conventions of language use are not only irrelevant; these may even be considered inappropriate by the interlocutors. The culture-bound localized strategies of, for example, politeness, persuasion, and phatic communion "transcreated" in English are more effective and culturally significant (Kachru 1981 and Y. Kachru, ed. 1991).

Fallacy 2: That English is necessarily learned as a tool to understand and teach American or British cultural values, or what is generally termed the Judeo-Christian traditions. This is again true only in a very restricted sense. In the pluralistic regions of the Outer Circle, English is used as an important tool to impart *local* traditions and cultural values. A significant number of linguistic innovations in English reflect such local culture and sociopolitical contexts (for references see Kachru 1986b).

Why is English used for such local integrative roles? Several reasons come to mind; e.g., the neutrality of English in relation to competing local and national languages and the pan-national uses of English in multilingual contexts. In many regions of the Outer Circle, English is the only language that cuts across languages and national boundaries. And in its localized variety, English is the language of higher education, pan-regional administration, national and international business, a link language for the defense network, the media, and a language for literary creativity.

Fallacy 3: That the goal of learning and teaching English is to adopt the native models of English (e.g., the Received Pronunciation, or General American; see, e.g., Quirk 1988). This claim has no empirical validity. The Inner Circle is a "model provider" in a very marginal sense. In the Outer Circle, the local model has been institutionalized, and the educated varieties of such models have always been used in the classroom, in various interactional contexts by the administrators, politicians, educators, and by the legal experts. True, there is schizophrenia about the perceived model and actual linguistic behavior, but this is an issue of linguistic attitude. The concept "native speaker" is not always a valid yardstick for the global uses of English (Christopherson 1988 and Kachru 1988a, 1988b; see also Ch. 3 in this volume).

Fallacy 4: That the international non-native varieties of English are essentially "interlanguages" striving to achieve "native-like" character. This hypothesis has several limitations, as has been shown, for example, by Sridhar and Sridhar and Nelson (Chs. 5, 17 in this volume). Whatever the validity of this hypothesis in second-language acquisition in general, its application to the institutionalized varieties of English in the Outer Circle needs reevaluation.

Fallacy 5: That the native speakers of English as teachers, academic administrators, and material developers provide a serious input in the global teaching of English, in policy formation, and in determining the channels for the spread of the language. In reality, the native speakers have an insignificant role in the global spread and teaching of English.

Fallacy 6: That the diversity and variation in English is necessarily an indicator of linguistic decay; that restricting the decay is the responsibility of the native scholars of English and ESL programs. This fallacy has resulted in the position that "deviation" at any level from the native norm is an "error." This view ignores the functional appropriateness of languages in sociolinguistic contexts distinctly different from the Inner Circle.

The list does not end here. These six fallacies are merely illustrative. For further discussion on theoretical, methodological, formal, functional, and attitudinal fallacies, see Kachru (1987).

English in the Real World

In the Outer Circle the varieties of English have their own local histories, literary traditions, pragmatic contexts, and communicative norms. Functionally, these varieties are first *African, South Asian,* and *Southeast Asian;* only in a secondary sense are they international. In their international functions these varieties are used only by a small segment of the total English-using populations.

The multiple identities of English have given a new direction to the English language and literature. This has happened in many important and lasting ways—for example, in the expansion of the canon. The reference points and underlying cultural and literary assumptions are no longer exclusively Judeo-Christian; there is a larger set of reference points, historical, cultural, mythological, and literary. These come from diverse cultures of, for example, South Asia, Southeast Asia, and West Africa. It is in this interesting sense that English is an *international* language. These assimilative and creative aspects of English have yet to be fully recognized. In fact, English has become an international language in a much more serious sense than the conventional use of the term "international language" implies (see Kachru 1987, 1992).

What way of life does English represent? I do not believe the profession has in a serious sense attempted to answer this question. It is evident that English does not represent one or two ways of life; therein lies its strength. The evidence of this is in the way English is used in the "new literatures," in English newspapers, and in function-specific varieties of English (ESPs) developed in India, Nigeria, Singapore, and the Philippines, to give just four examples (see Kachru 1986c and Part V in this volume).

Why Teach World Englishes?

The reasons for teaching world Englishes are abundant. The changing sociolinguistic profile of English has been responsible for slaughtering many sacred linguistic cows (see Kachru 1988a, 1988b). The processes of the slaughter and its implications deserve the serious attention of scholars, particularly in ESL-related fields.

But there is more to it. The global uses of English in linguistically, culturally, and economically diverse contexts have provided refreshing new data and new insights in several interdisciplinary areas of research, including the following: *language acquisition* (e.g., Sridhar and Sridhar 1986); *cross-cultural discourse* (e.g., Smith, ed. 1981, 1987; Kachru 1981, 1986b; Y. Kachru 1985, 1987); *bilingual's creativity* (Kachru 1983a); *language contact and convergence* (for references see Kachru 1986b); *language attitudes* (e.g., Smith, ed. 1983); and *lexicography* (e.g., Kachru 1983b).

We need to look the facts squarely in the face. One must address questions which will contribute toward understanding the sociolinguistic and other factors in a global context, questions such as the following: What are the underlying dynamic forces that characterize the spread of English? What are the functional domains assigned to English in various multilingual and multicultural societies, and their implications for the language? What are the processes and implications of the nativization of English, and Englishization of local languages? What are the contexts in which English is taught, and what type of personnel are staffing ESL/EFL programs? What are the attitudes of learners, teachers, and users of English toward their own and other varieties and subvarieties (e.g., Nigerian Pidgin, basilect, mixed varieties)? What role does the Inner Circle play in the present spread of English and in its codification? How can the non-native literatures in English (e.g., African, Asian) be used as a resource for cross-cultural awareness and for understanding linguistic creativity and innovations (Kachru 1986d, 1992, Smith 1987, Thumboo 1988)?

World Englishes in the Classroom

How can a teacher initiate a paradigm shift—attitudinally and methodologically—in the classroom? There is, of course, no unique answer to the question; much depends on the level of the class and the specific goals for teaching. The following points deserve attention, particularly for training professionals and for teaching advanced students.

1. *Sociolinguistic profile:* an overview of English in its world context with discussion of selected major varieties, their users and uses. A clear distinction to be made between the use of English in a monolingual society, as opposed to a multilingual society; and its implications (e.g., mixing, switching).

2. *Variety exposure:* an exposition of the repertoire of major varieties of English, native and non-native: their uses and users, specific texts related to various interactional contexts, shared and non-shared features at different linguistic levels.
3. *Attitudinal neutrality:* for teaching purposes, one might focus on one specific variety and at the same time emphasize *awareness* and *functional validity* of other varieties.
4. *Range of uses:* the functional appropriateness of the lectal range of varieties within a specific variety (e.g., from educated varieties to the pidgins and basilects).
5. *Contrastive pragmatics:* the relationships of discoursal and stylistic innovations and their relationships to the local conventions of culture (e.g., strategies used for persuasion, phatic communion, apologies, condolences, and regrets).
6. *Multidimensionality of functions:* the linguistic implications of the functional range, as in, for example, the media, in literary creativity, in administration, in the legal system.

Resources for Teaching World Englishes

There still are limited resources for teaching world Englishes. I have given below a partial list of materials for background reading.

1. *Bibliographies:* Viereck, Schneider, and Görlach 1984.
2. *General surveys:* Bailey and Görlach, eds. 1982; Cheshire, ed. 1991; Fishman et al. 1977; Greenbaum, ed. 1985; Kachru, ed. 1982, 1986a; Lowenberg, ed. 1988; McCrum et al. 1987; Noss, ed. 1983; Platt et al. 1984; Pride, ed. 1982; Quirk and Widdowson, eds. 1985; Smith, ed. 1981, 1983.
3. *Issue-Oriented Studies:* (a) *World Englishes and applied linguistics/language and politics:* Kachru 1986a, 1990; Kachru and Smith, eds., 1986; (b) *Intelligibility:* Kachru, ed. 1982 (ch. 4); see also Smith and Nelson 1985; Smith, ed. 1981; (c) *Sociolinguistic issues:* Kachru 1986b, 1988a; K. Sridhar 1986.
4. *English literatures:* Kachru, ed. 1982 (chs. 18, 19, and 20 for references), 1986d; King 1979; Narasimhaiah, ed. 1978; Taiwo 1976; Thumboo 1988.
5. *Discourse strategies and nativization:* Smith, ed. 1981, 1987; Kachru 1983a; see also relevant chapters in *Annual Review of Applied Linguistics* 1982; Y. Kachru, ed. 1991; Bhatia and Ritchie, eds. 1989.

6. *Standards and norms:* Kachru 1986b, esp. chs. 5, 6, and 7, and 1991; Quirk 1988, 1990; Tickoo, ed. 1991.
7. *Journals:* There are now several journals specifically devoted to English in the world contexts: *English World-Wide: A Journal of Varieties of English* (1980–; Amsterdam and Philadelphia: John Benjamins Publishing Company); *World Englishes: Journal of English as an International and Intranational Language* (1985–; Oxford: Pergamon Press); and *English Today* (1985–; Cambridge: Cambridge University Press).

Conclusion

The teaching of world Englishes not only is academically challenging, but also opens refreshing new avenues for cross-cultural theoretical and applied research. What is needed is a shift of two types: a paradigm shift in research and teaching, and an understanding of the sociolinguistic reality of the uses and users of English. We must also cease to view English within the framework appropriate for monolingual societies. We must recognize the linguistic, cultural, and pragmatic implications of various types of pluralism; that pluralism has now become an integral part of the English language and the literatures written in English in various parts of the non-Western world. The traditional presuppositions and ethnocentric approaches need reevaluation. In the international contexts, English represents a repertoire of cultures, not a monolithic culture. The changed sociolinguistic profile of English is difficult to recognize, for good reason. The traditional paradigm based on the fallacies discussed above, however undesirable, continues to have a grip on the profession. What makes matters more complex is the fact that active interest groups want to maintain the status quo. Let us hope that such attitudes cannot continue for too long, and that the sociolinguistic reality and pragmatism will eventually prevail.

NOTE

1. Countries such as South Africa and Jamaica are difficult to place within the concentric circles. In terms of the English-using populations and the functions of English, their situations are rather complex.

REFERENCES

Bailey, Richard, and M. Görlach, eds. 1982. *English as a world language.* Ann Arbor: University of Michigan Press.

Bhatia, Tej K., and William C. Ritchie, eds. 1989. Code-mixing: English across languages. Special issue of *World Englishes* 8(3).

Cheshire, Jenny, ed. 1991. *English around the world: sociolinguistic perspectives.* Cambridge: Cambridge University Press.

Christophersen, Paul. 1988. "Native speakers" and World English. *English Today* 4.3: 15–18.

Crystal, David. 1985. How many millions? The statistics of English today. *English Today* 1 (January): 7–9.

Fishman, Joshua, et al. 1977. *The spread of English: the sociology of English as an additional language.* Rowley, Mass.: Newbury House.

Greenbaum, Sidney, ed. 1985. *The English language today.* Oxford: Pergamon.

Kachru, Braj B. 1981. The pragmatics of non-native varieties of English. In Smith, ed. 1981; also in Kachru 1983.

———, ed. 1982. *The other tongue: English across cultures.* Urbana: University of Illinois Press.

———. 1983a. The bilingual's creativity: discoursal and stylistic strategies in contact literatures in English. *Studies in the Linguistic Sciences* 13.2 (Fall): 37–55; also in Kachru 1986.

———. 1983b. Toward a dictionary. In B. Kachru, *The Indianization of English.* New Delhi: Oxford University Press.

———. 1985. Standards, codification and sociolinguistic realism: the English language in the Outer Circle. In Quirk and Widdowson, eds. 1985.

———. 1986a. The power and politics of English. *World Englishes* 5.2–3: 121–40.

———. 1986b. *The alchemy of English: the spread, functions and models of non-native Englishes.* Oxford: Pergamon Press. Reprinted, Urbana: University of Illinois Press, 1990.

———. 1986c. ESP and non-native varieties of English: toward a shift in paradigm. *Studies in the Linguistic Sciences* 16.1: 13–34.

———. 1986d. Non-native literatures in English as a resource for language teaching. In C. J. Brumfit and R. A. Carter, eds., *Literature and language teaching.* Oxford: Oxford University Press.

———. 1987. The past and prejudice: toward demythologizing the English canon. In R. Steele and T. Treadgold, eds. *Language topics: essays in honour of Michael Halliday.* Amsterdam and Philadelphia: John Benjamins.

———. 1988a. The spread of English and sacred linguistic cows. Pp. 207–28 in Lowenberg, ed. 1988.

———. 1988b. The sacred cows of English. *English Today* 4.4.

———. 1990. World Englishes and applied linguistics. *World Englishes* 9.1: 3–20.

———. 1991. Liberation linguistics and the Quirk concern. *English Today,* 25 January, 3–13.

———. 1992. The second diaspora of English. In Tim W. McMahon and Charles T. Scott, eds., *English in its social contexts.* New York: Oxford University Press.

————, and Larry E. Smith, eds. 1986. The power of English: cross-cultural dimensions in literature and media. Special issue of *World Englishes* 5.2–3.

Kachru, Yamuna. 1985. Discourse analysis, non-native Englishes and second language acquisition research. *World Englishes* 4.2: 223–32.

————. 1987. Cross-cultural texts, discourse strategies and discourse interpretation. In Smith, ed. 1987.

————, ed. 1991. Symposium on speech acts in World Englishes. *World Englishes* 10(3).

King, Bruce. 1979. *The new English literatures: cultural nationalism in a changing world*. New York: St. Martin's Press.

Lowenberg, Peter, ed. 1988. *Language spread and language policy: issues, implications and case studies*. Washington, D.C.: Georgetown University Press.

McCrum, Robert, et al. 1987. *The story of English*. New York: Viking.

Narashimhaiah, C. D., ed. 1978. *Awakened conscience: studies in commonwealth literature*. New Delhi: Sterling.

Nelson, Cecil. 1985. My language, your culture: whose communicative competence? *World Englishes* 4.2: 243–50; also in this volume.

————. 1988. Why NEs are not LIPOAs ("interlanguages"). Paper presented at the colloquium on World Englishes: Issues and Challenges of the 1980s, TESOL 1988.

Noss, R. B., ed. 1983. *Varieties of English in Southeast Asia*. Singapore: Regional Language Center.

Platt, John, H. Weber, and H. M. Lian. 1984. *The new Englishes*. London: Routledge.

Pride, John, ed. 1982. *New Englishes*. Rowley, Mass.: Newbury House.

Quirk, Randolph. 1988. The question of standards in the international use of English. Pp. 229–41 in Lowenberg, ed. 1988.

————. 1990. Language varieties and standard language. *English Today*, 21 January, 3–10.

————, and Henry Widdowson, eds. 1985. *English in the world*. Cambridge: Cambridge University Press.

Smith, Larry E., ed. 1981. *English for cross-cultural communication*. London: Macmillan.

————. 1983. *Readings in English as an international language*. London: Pergamon.

————. 1987. *Discourse across cultures: strategies in World Englishes*. London: Prentice-Hall International.

————, and Cecil Nelson. 1985. International intelligibility of English: directions and resources. *World Englishes* 4.3: 333–42.

Sridhar, Kamal K. 1986. Sociolinguistic theory and non-native varieties of English. *Lingua* 68.1: 39–58.

Sridhar, S. N., and Kamal K. Sridhar. 1986. Bridging the paradigm gap: second-language acquisition theory and indigenized varieties of English. *World Englishes* 5.1: 3–14; also in this volume.

Strevens, Peter. 1980. *Teaching English as an international language.* Oxford: Pergamon.

———. 1982. World English and the world's Englishes; or, whose language is it, anyway? *Journal of the Royal Society of Arts* 120, 5311: 418–31.

Taiwo, Oladele. 1976. *Culture and the Nigerian novel.* New York: St. Martin's Press.

Thumboo, Edwin. 1988. The literary dimensions of the spread of English: creativity in a second tongue. In Lowenberg, ed. 1988; revised version in this volume.

Tickoo, Makhan L., ed. 1991. *Language and standards: issues, attitudes, case studies.* Singapore: SEAMEO Regional Language Centre.

Viereck, Wolfgang, E. W. Schneider, and M. Görlach. 1984. *A bibliography of writings on varieties of English, 1965–1983.* Amsterdam: John Benjamins.

Notes on Contributors

AYO BAMGBOSE is professor of linguistics in the Department of Linguistics and African Languages, University of Ibadan, Nigeria.

EYAMBA G. BOKAMBA is professor of linguistics and African studies and director of the Division of English as an International Language, University of Illinois at Urbana-Champaign.

CHIN-CHUAN CHENG is Jubilee Professor of Liberal Arts and Sciences, professor of linguistics and Chinese, and director of the Language Learning Laboratory, University of Illinois at Urbana-Champaign.

CHARLES A. FERGUSON is emeritus professor of linguistics, Stanford University.

JOSHUA A. FISHMAN is Distinguished University Research Professor in Social Sciences, emeritus, Ferkauf Graduate School of Psychology, Yeshiva University.

SHIRLEY BRICE HEATH is professor of linguistics and English, Stanford University.

BRAJ B. KACHRU is professor of linguistics, comparative literature, education, and English as an International Language, University of Illinois at Urbana-Champaign.

YAMUNA KACHRU is professor of linguistics and English as an International Language, University of Illinois at Urbana-Champaign.

HENRY KAHANE is Emeritus Center for Advanced Study Professor of Linguistics, University of Illinois at Urbana-Champaign.

PETER H. LOWENBERG is associate professor of linguistics in the Department of Linguistics and Language Development, San Jose State University.

ANN LOWRY is senior editor at the University of Illinois Press.

RODNEY F. MOAG is associate professor and acting chair in the Department of Oriental Languages and Literatures, University of Texas at Austin.

CECIL L. NELSON is associate professor of English, Indiana State University, Terre Haute.

LARRY E. SMITH is interim director of the Institute of Culture and Communication, East-West Center, Honolulu.

KAMAL K. SRIDHAR is associate professor of linguistics, State University of New York at Stony Brook.

S. N. SRIDHAR is associate professor of linguistics, State University of New York at Stony Brook.

JAMES STANLAW is assistant professor of anthropology at Illinois State University.

PETER STREVENS was visiting professor in the Division of English as an International Language, University of Illinois at Urbana-Champaign, at the time of his death in 1989.

EDWIN THUMBOO is professor of English at the National University of Singapore.

Index

Index

Trinidad, 286, 296
Trudgill, Peter, 109, 116, 144n
Tutuola, Amos, 153, 159n, 273
Tuvalu (Ellice Islands), 233
Twinned accent, 40

Ubahakwe, E., 93
Uganda, 108
Ulysses, 275
Umegake, Minoru, 179, 184
Un-English, 58, 59, 62, 163, 301
United Kingdom, xvi, xvii, xxiii, 28, 29,
    32, 38, 43, 49, 51, 53, 60, 65, 69n,
    76, 77, 80, 82, 85, 108, 118n, 140,
    144n, 150, 165, 167, 211, 212, 224,
    233, 238, 242, 248, 256, 263, 285
United Nations, 30, 39
United States, xxi, xxiii, 2, 8, 28, 30, 31,
    38, 43, 51, 65, 76, 77, 82, 84, 86, 88,
    95, 108, 115, 118n, 119n, 162, 165,
    167, 193, 215, 216, 220, 221, 223,
    225, 226, 228, 230, 242, 248, 283
Universal language: *see* International
    Language
Untouchable, 285, 288–90, 317
Urdu, 273
Ury, W., 125
Usage: domain of, 229–30; local norms
    of English, 109; rules, 308
Uttar Pradesh, 286
Uyekubo, Aiko, 196, 197

Valentine, Tamara M., 331, 343
Vanua Levu, 237
Variation, 223; models of, xv
Variety: exposure, 362; shift, 306, 308; of
    English, form and function, 55–56
Vaz, Fleur, 114
Verbal behavior, 341
Verbal repertoire, 101
Vernacular languages: and role of En-
    glish, 244–45
Viereck, Wolfgang, 12n, 361
Vildomec, Veroj, 196
Vocabulary, *see* Lexis
Voegelin, C., 65, 125
Voegelin, F. M., 125
Vogt, Hans, 188
The Voice, 141, 259, 274
Voice of America, 243

Volapük, 2
von Humbolt, William, 223

Wade-Giles system, 168
Walcott, Derek, 278
Wales, 256
Walwadkar, R., 92
Wang Li, 165, 166
Ward, I. C., 50, 51, 65
Weber, Heidi, 93, 100, 110, 118n
Webster, Noah, 30, 53, 212
Webster's Third, 213, 215, 222
Wei, Yuanshu, 174
Weinreich, Uriel, 101, 102, 188, 196, 235
"Well" (word), as conversational tool,
    229
Wendt, Albert, 241, 266, 267
West Africa, 20, 29, 37, 54, 93, 158, 239,
    242
West African English, 28, 34, 95, 103,
    132, 136, 158n, 159n; literature, 67,
    69n
West African languages, 126–28
West Indian Creole, 227
West Indies, xxiii, 48, 69n, 251, 256, 257,
    276, 305
Western Borneo, 110
Western Samoa, 108
Whinnom, Keith, 164
Whitaker, F., 50
White Lies, 264
Whiteley, W. H., 125, 142
Whitten, W., 50
Widdowson, Henry, 10, 38, 75, 307, 308,
    361
The Wide Sargasso Sea, 263
Wolfram, W., 49
Wong, I. E., 92
Wong, I. F. H., 54
World Englishes, xix, 27, 280n, 337n; in
    the classroom, 10; three Concentric
    Circles of, 38; pragmatic context, 7;
    teaching, 357–64; resources for, 361–
    62
World Englishes, xx, 28, 362
World language, 214
World writing in English, 67
Wurm, Stephen A., 238

Xiong, Delan, 173

UNIVERSITY OF ILLINOIS PRESS
1325 SOUTH OAK STREET
CHAMPAIGN, ILLINOIS 61820-6903
WWW.PRESS.UILLINOIS.EDU